Jonathan Prentiss Dolliver

JONATHAN PRENTISS DOLLIVER

A Study in Political Integrity and Independence

By THOMAS RICHARD ROSS

STATE HISTORICAL SOCIETY OF IOWA

IOWA CITY 1958

PRINTED IN THE UNITED STATES OF AMERICA BY
THE ECONOMY ADVERTISING CO., IOWA CITY, IOWA

To The Memory Of
FRANK FULLERTON ROSS
WILLIAM ROSS PERINE
JOHN E McCORKLE

Editor's Foreword

DURING the past eleven decades twenty-seven Iowans have served the Hawkeye State in the United States Senate. Five of these men—Augustus Caesar Dodge, George Wallace Jones, James Harlan, Samuel Jordan Kirkwood, and William Boyd Allison—have been the subject of full-length discussion in the Iowa Biographical Series published by the State Historical Society of Iowa. Jonathan Prentiss Dolliver, the subject of the present volume, is the sixth United States Senator from Iowa to have his career delineated in the Iowa Biographical Series—which now numbers nineteen volumes.

In his study of Jonathan P. Dolliver, Professor Thomas R. Ross presents a vivid yet scholarly picture of one of the most colorful of our United States Senators. It is the story of a man whose high ideals, rare courage, and brilliant oratorical genius won for him national recognition. No greater tribute could have been paid to this outstanding Iowan than to have been chosen with William Jennings Bryan as speaker at the centennial of the birth of Abraham Lincoln at Springfield, Illinois. This book, in turn, appears most opportunely, on the occasion of the centennial of the birth of Jonathan P. Dolliver.

The Society is extremely fortunate in having the career of one of Iowa's most illustrious sons depicted graphically, yet dispassionately, against the backdrop of a period marked by political tumult and the emergence of the United States as a world power.

WILLIAM J. PETERSEN

Office of the Superintendent
State Historical Society of Iowa
Iowa City, Iowa

Acknowledgements

MANY PEOPLE in various walks of life have assisted in the preparation of this book. In appropriate places in the footnotes I have attempted to give recognition and thanks to each for specific contributions.

I am especially indebted to my wife, Jean McCorkle Ross, not only for enduring the inconveniences which are the usual lot of the wife of a professor writing, but also because it was she who first suggested to me the need for a biography of Jonathan P. Dolliver and who through the years constantly encouraged and helped me in the research for and writing of this one.

Professor Arthur Schlesinger, Jr., of Harvard University read the entire first draft of the manuscript. His penetrating criticism and his helpful suggestions saved me from many slips of phrasing and errors in interpretation. Likewise of indispensable aid was the work of Dr. Mildred Throne, associate editor of the State Historical Society of Iowa and specialist in Iowa history and biography, who carefully scrutinized each page of the typescript. She contributed of her scholarly store of historical knowledge to the improvement of this book, prepared the index, and with skill, patience, and never-failing good humor managed the innumerable details of seeing the copy through the press.

Special thanks are also due to Miss Frances P. Dolliver of the faculty of the Warren Harding school in Des Moines who, through interviews and numerous letters, generously provided information concerning her father and made available family papers and photographs not otherwise obtainable.

Curators of manuscript collections and librarians have invariably extended me every courtesy. Dr. William J. Petersen, dynamic superintendent of the State Historical Society of Iowa, not only gave me unrestricted access to the various collections in his keeping but provided me with office and library facilities for many weeks and showed me much kindness and consideration whenever I visited Iowa City. Claude R. Cook and Emory H. English of the Iowa State Department of History and Archives in Des Moines were also helpful to me in numerous ways, as were officials at the Library of Congress and librarians at Harvard University, West Virginia University, the State University of Iowa, and Davis and Elkins College.

I wish to acknowledge my obligations to Ralph M. Sayre, dean of the College of Idaho, for permitting me to read his notes on the life of Albert B. Cummins and for sharing with me his ideas on the Dolliver-Cummins relationship. Equally great is my debt to Professor Gordon F. Hostettler, chairman of the department of speech and dramatic arts at Temple University, who allowed me to quote from his unpublished doctoral thesis on Dolliver's oratorical career and graciously made available for my use letters in his possession concerning Dolliver.

Others whose assistance was helpful were Professor Arthur M. Schlesinger, Sr., Professor James M. Callahan, Mr. J. M. Guy Brown, the Reverend Robert Dolliver, Congressman James I. Dolliver, Senator Alben W. Barkley, Professor Leland L. Sage, Professor Richard G. Long, Professor S. Benton Talbot, Professor Knox Wilson, Dr. George S. May, Dr. Robert Rutland, Tommy Ross, Mrs. Adelaide Seemuth, Mrs. Ann Harshbarger, Mary Willis, Margaret Isner, and Joan Montgomery.

Finally, I am profoundly grateful to the Danforth Foundation of Saint Louis for a generous Teacher Study Grant in 1955-1956. That grant, in addition to a leave of absence arranged for me by President David K. Allen and Dean S. Wilds DuBose of Davis and Elkins College, greatly facilitated the completion of this work.

THOMAS RICHARD ROSS

Davis and Elkins College,
Elkins, West Virginia.

Contents

Illustrations

Cartoons

-I-

In The Beginning

Character is not made overnight. When it appears in transcendent degree it is usually the product of generations of disciplined ancestry, or a stern environment, or both.

Allan Nevins, *Grover Cleveland*

ON SATURDAY, February 6, 1858, the day that Jonathan Prentiss Dolliver was born in Preston County, Virginia, there were bitter words and fist fights in the House of Representatives in Washington. About two A. M., in the midst of a prolonged debate over the proposed admission of Kansas to the Union, Laurence Keitt of South Carolina seized Galusha Grow of Pennsylvania, called him a "damned Black Republican puppy," and tried to choke him. A general melee ensued during which Henry Clay's son, James, staggered drunkenly up on one of the oak desks and bawled at the members to stop fighting. On this same date, *Harper's Weekly*, in an article describing the "profuse and gaudy decorations" of the new chamber of the House of Representatives, sighed for "something more in keeping with the gravity of the interests to be adjusted in that room, and the sober air which ought to pervade the debates of an American Congress." [1]

Unfortunately, the "interests" which desperately needed to be "adjusted" were growing fast apart in February, 1858. Within a month a Southern Senator, attempting to justify slavery, set forth his "mudsill" theory of society. A few weeks thereafter Abraham Lincoln, in Illinois, stated the issue clearly: " 'A house divided against itself cannot stand.' . . . This Government cannot endure permanently, half slave and half free." [2] The nation was approaching, if she had not already passed, the point of no return on the road to civil war.

Among Virginians, especially those in the western section of the state, there was great uneasiness. The members of the Assembly of 1857-1858 seemed to believe that dismemberment of the Union was inevitable, and the long standing rift between the western and eastern parts of the state widened as rumors of the possibility of secession increased. [3] The citizens of Preston County were deeply disturbed by such talk. Regarding secession as ruinous, these loyal

1

highlanders maintained that "safety could only be found beneath the Stars and Stripes of the undivided Union of States."[4] The *Preston Register*, a Democratic weekly established at Kingwood in the year of Dolliver's birth, expressed the nationalist sentiment of the area by adopting as its masthead motto the old Jacksonian toast, "The Union must and shall be preserved!"[5]

Into this nation on the verge of civil strife, into the "Old Dominion" on the brink of her political disruption, Jonathan Prentiss Dolliver, second son of James J. and Eliza Brown Dolliver, was born, among the people of Kingwood, Preston County, in what would soon become the new state of West Virginia. The exact hour that "Prent," as his family called him, first filled his lungs and gave notice of his arrival is not recorded. That he was vocal cannot be doubted — he was ever that. The earliest surviving comment about him concerns the noise he made. When his two-year-old brother, Robert, unacquainted with babies, heard the new-born Jonathan crying, he inquired whether there was a chicken in the bedroom.[6]

Dolliver's ability to express himself was to bring him national fame and election to the House of Representatives within three decades of his birth. His oratory aided his career as a Republican nationalist in Congress in an era when the political climate was only slightly less turbulent than that which prevailed in the Hall of Representatives on the night of his birth. He came into the world at a dramatic moment, with men clashing in deadly earnest over the destiny of the nation, a great political party splitting asunder over vital issues, and the voices of moderation smothered amid the shrilling of extremists. In many respects the day of Dolliver's birth was to be symbolic of his career and portentous of the year of his death.

Jonathan Dolliver's forebears were excellent people. On his father's side they were among the early settlers in the Cape Ann section of Massachusetts Bay Colony. The name was originally spelled Dalyber and is said to have derived from a valley in North Junterice, Wales.[7] So far as can be determined, the first of the family to migrate to North America, probably some time in the 1640's, was Samuel Doliber (c. 1608-1684), a native of Stoke Abbot, Dorsetshire, England, the third son of a well-to-do yeoman, Robert Dalyber.

By 1648 Samuel Doliber was one of the selectmen of Marblehead, Massachusetts. He bought fifty acres of land "situate in Fresh Water Cove, in Gloster" in 1652 and settled there. Two years later, his first wife having died, he married Mary Elwell, daughter of Robert Elwell of Gloucester, and in August, 1656, their son William was born. Of William little is known other than that he married Ann, the daughter of the Reverend John Higginson, owned a house and a half acre of land in Salem, and was the father of Peter, Paul, and Sarah Dolliver.[8]

Peter Dolliver, a cooper by trade, inherited his parents' half acre and added an acre to it prior to his marriage to Abigail Sanders in 1722. His wife was the daughter of Captain Thomas Sanders, commander of the sloop *Merry Meeting*, who served colonial Massachusetts in King George's War and took part in the Louisburg expedition.[9]

The second son of Peter and Abigail Sanders Dolliver was also named Peter. Born in Gloucester, May 3, 1726, he married as his second wife a woman whose father was a distinguished colonial officer, Colonel Thomas Goldthwaite. Colonel Goldthwaite, Jonathan Dolliver's great-great-grandfather, was the most interesting and notable of his paternal ancestors. He was a Boston merchant who served several terms in the General Court of Massachusetts and as a judge. He was commandant of Fort Pownall from 1763 to 1775 and colonel of the 2nd Lincoln County Regiment. A close friend of Sir Francis Bernard and Governor Thomas Hutchinson, Colonel Goldthwaite remained loyal to the crown at the time of the American Revolution. When the British evacuated Boston, he departed with them and eventually went to England, where he died in 1799.[10]

Goldthwaite's daughter, Esther, and her second husband, Peter Dolliver, made their home in Gloucester, where Peter, a merchant and shipmaster, was known as "Captain" Dolliver. A patriot sympathizer during the Revolution, he was appointed a constable to help collect war taxes in Gloucester in 1775 and is thought to have been engaged in privateering against British shipping in New England waters.[11]

Henry Dolliver, the second son of Peter and Esther, went to sea in 1784 at the age of ten as a cabin boy on one of his father's ships and by the beginning of the nineteenth century was master of his own vessel.[12] In 1807, having abandoned New England permanently and the sea temporarily, he married Maria Voorhees of Saratoga County, New York, and settled near Fishkill, where he restlessly awaited the end of President Jefferson's embargo experiment.

The father of Jonathan Prentiss Dolliver, James Jones Dolliver, was born on November 28, 1816, the third son of Henry and Maria Dolliver. Shortly thereafter the family moved from Saratoga County, New York, to Bound Brook, New Jersey, where James J. was reared in a little house not far from the Raritan River.

Captain Henry continued to follow the sea as long as he lived, sometimes having a successful voyage "which gave him plenty of money"; more often though "he would come home poor."[13] The Panic of 1837 further increased the poverty of the Dolliver household, and the burden of helping support the family fell most directly upon James J., the only son still unmarried at that time.[14]

James J. remembered that his mother had "made garments" to pay for his schooling. It would appear from his surviving manuscripts and sermons that he mastered writing, spelling, rhetoric, and acquired some acquaintance with the classical writers. He so impressed the neighbors with his learning that he was eventually invited to teach their children. "I said I wasn't qualified," he recorded, "but I went to teaching school."[15] Being village schoolmaster was not financially rewarding, and when his former teacher, one Van Ostrich, invited him to work in his general store at Flagtown, James accepted. For two years he "drove to New York with butter and eggs" and "clerked" for Van Ostrich, but such a life was too drab and dull for a son of the old sea captain. The wanderlust that had drawn Captain Henry Dolliver from Gloucester to Fishkill and thence to Bound Brook, and which had been satisfied only when he could sail the oceans, was in part shared by his son James.

Like many another poor but ambitious young man, James determined to go west. His sister, Maria, had married David Van Fleet, a farmer, and had moved to Ohio in 1838. Thus, when a Major Latterat offered to take James west in the spring of 1839, young Dolliver was delighted. He drove a wagon team to pay his passage, and after twenty-one days of hard travel in April mud, he arrived in Groveport, some ten miles south of Columbus, Ohio, and not far from the Van Fleet farm. James remained in Groveport for nearly five years, eventually becoming the proprietor of a country store. He prospered as a storekeeper, being genial and gregarious, and his circle of friends and patrons seems steadily to have increased. But he was restless. As the months passed, he found that his life as a small-town merchant was not bringing him contentment or self-satisfaction. "I had to be a preacher," he said, "I knew it from the time I was a little boy."[16]

He yielded to his destiny in 1843 after experiencing what he called a spiritual conversion. He joined the Methodist Episcopal Church and in a short time was admitted "on trial in the traveling ministry" by the Ohio Conference. Immediately thereafter, he sold his business, bought a "horse and saddle bags," and set out to preach. He saw life in a new light, and new purposes possessed him. In 1845, having been assigned a circuit in what was to become the state of West Virginia, the young preacher "crossed the Ohio River" to begin his career as a circuit rider. James Dolliver believed that his "call" had come from God, and he often said that his "conversion was as thrilling as that of St. Paul." Had it not been, he thought, he could never have "forsaken the promises and allurements of a successful business career for those of the Gospel."[17]

As a circuit rider, Dolliver traveled extensively over the mountain trails and into the most remote counties and hamlets of western Virginia. He once estimated that he averaged 10,000 miles a year on horseback in the thirty-five years that he served his church among the mountaineers. Strong of frame, erect, athletic, and with a voice that was rich and inspiring, James Dolliver was a magnetic and persuasive pulpit orator, and he gained lasting fame as one of the great preachers of the area.[18]

The Reverend James Dolliver sought to be identified with the people of his adopted state, and he lost no opportunity to reprove the abuses of slavery. For James J. Dolliver, Northern Methodist, born in New York of old New England stock and grown to maturity in New Jersey and Ohio, slavery was an unmixed evil, a curse upon the face of the land he loved. Although he was sometimes assailed by those who were angered at his antislavery utterances and was occasionally threatened with mob violence, he rode through the stormy fifties, preaching death to slavery. On the whole, his antislavery sentiments won him the friendship and approval of those to whom he ministered. This was especially true in the Morgantown District which was made a part of the Western Virginia Conference in 1848 and in which Dolliver was assigned a circuit.[19]

Not content merely to rail against slavery as a moral evil, James Dolliver was an ardent nationalist and a "staunch Union man from the first moments of the secession agitation."[20] He was one of those Methodist circuit riders who "penetrated the remotest recesses of Northwestern Virginia to preach the gospel and to rally the people to fight for the Union." The influence of such preachers and of the tracts which they distributed may well have been of paramount importance in keeping in the Union that part of Virginia which became West Virginia. For many years it was said that "the Methodists made West Virginia." Twentieth century historians assert that the "movement resulting in the formation of West Virginia was closely related to the evangelical Christianity of the Methodist Episcopal variety."[21] It is reasonable to conclude that had it not been for the adherence of the Methodists of western Virginia to the Northern Church in 1844-1848, and the consequent leavening of the people by the preachers and literature in the liberty-loving sentiment of the North, the story of the state from 1861 to 1865 might have been vastly different.[22]

Inspired with the ardor of youth and the fervor of his intense beliefs, James Dolliver made a profound impression upon the people to whom he ministered. There are still traditions in West Virginia of vast audiences at camp meetings under the sway of his eloquence, and those who knew him in his old age remember "his earnest piety, his simplicity, his transparent sincerity" as well as his optimism, his love of mankind, his faith in God, and his fixed conviction that this is a good world.[23]

During his early years in Virginia, Dolliver made many friends, one of the most notable of whom was Francis H. Pierpont at whose "hospitable place" the itinerant minister spent many a night in the years before Pierpont became Governor. Pierpont was known as one of the ablest and most indefatigable Unionists in the state, and his influence upon the political thinking of James Dolliver was undeniably important.[24]

Undoubtedly the most significant of James Dolliver's Virginia friendships were those he established in the early 1850's with the family of Eliza Brown of

Kingwood, the young woman who was to become his wife. Eliza's father, Robert Brown, was one of the leading citizens of Preston County. His brother, William G. Brown of Morgantown, had already represented their Virginia district in Congress as a Democrat for two terms (1845-1849) and was again to be sent to the national House in 1861 as a Virginia Unionist. He later became the first man to represent his section of West Virginia in Congress after that state was admitted to the Union.[25]

The Browns were originally from Scotland. Their grandfather, John Brown (1738-1770), was born and reared near Edinburgh and educated at the University of Edinburgh. Immediately after his marriage, John took his bride, Ann Morrow, to Londonderry, Ireland, where he managed the estates of Lord Montgomery. This couple had seven children, the last of whom, James Brown, was born in 1761 near Londonderry. "Jamie," as his family called him, grew up in the age of the American Revolution. While in college at Edinburgh he developed a great sympathy for the colonists in their struggle for independence, and nurtured the hope that the success of the Americans would be the example for a movement to liberate Ireland.[26]

In 1785 James married Rachel Hawthorne, sister of John Hawthorne, a sea captain who had served in the Pennsylvania artillery for a time early in the American Revolution and later as a privateer preying upon English shipping. Hawthorne had returned to his native Londonderry after the American war in the hope of assisting in an Irish rebellion, but in due time both Hawthorne and his brother-in-law, James Brown, gave up hope of doing anything for the Irish. Captain Hawthorne then moved permanently to Philadelphia, where he married Mary Calvery and became master of the schooner *Commerce* engaged in Atlantic shipping. He urged his relatives to come to America, and in the autumn of 1789 James and Rachel Brown with others of her family did so. For James it was a means of escape from a difficult situation. He had been "such an enthusiast on the subject of American independence and so outspoken in his sympathy" for Irish liberation that he had "displeased the loyal party in England and Ireland, and it was thought advisable" for him to leave the kingdom.[27]

James and Rachel spent their first winter in America at her brother's home in Philadelphia. In the spring of 1790 they rode south and west into the rich uplands of what was then still a part of Monongalia County, Virginia. There, near the site of the future town of Kingwood, James bought land in Dunkard's Bottom on Green's Run and established a new seat for his branch of the Browns of Edinburgh and Londonderry.

In due time there was a town — Kingwood, unincorporated, established January 23, 1811, the first town in what was to become Preston County — and James Brown was one of the founders and first trustees.[28] Meanwhile there were acres to clear, plant, and harvest; a hewed log house to build; and children to bear and rear.

The first of the family born in Virginia was Robert. He grew up to love the soil, and he spent his life on the farm where he was born, a farm which was carved originally from the vast domain surveyed by George Washington for Lord Fairfax. Robert is said to have been "the counterpart and reproduction of his father, Jamie," a Virginia gentleman who was "calm, courteous, hospitable, broad and liberal in his views." His brother, Congressman William G. Brown, depended much on the "cool and well poised judgment of Robert." In 1821 Robert married his cousin, Ann Hawthorne, "one of the loveliest and saintliest of women." Ann was the daughter of Captain John Hawthorne and Mary Calvery Hawthorne. Her mother had died of yellow fever in Philadelphia in 1793, and the captain had been drowned in an accident in 1796. Little Ann, orphaned at the age of seven, was taken to Kingwood to be reared by Rachel and James Brown.[29]

Three children, Rebecca, John James, and Eliza Jane, were born to Ann and Robert Brown in the house where Robert had been born and where they both had been reared. The only son, John James, was carefully educated at Monongalia Academy and at Washington College in Pennsylvania from which he was graduated in 1845. He then returned to Virginia to begin the study of law in the offices of his uncle, the Congressman.[30] The youngest of the three, Eliza Jane, was born May 9, 1827. She grew into a "small, delicate, quiet" woman, very devout, but with a fine sense of humor.[31]

Eliza was the first of the Brown family to become acquainted with the Reverend James Jones Dolliver. He had ridden eastward from Wetzel County in the winter of 1853-1854 and was invited to fill the pulpit of the brick church in Kingwood during the absence of the minister assigned to that circuit.[32] During the sermon James Dolliver's attention was attracted by a young woman "dressed very plainly and sweetly, no artificials," as he later described Eliza Brown. After the benediction, as the congregation began to file out, Eliza paused at the door in consternation. The church was overheated, and as the cold air from the open doors came into contact with the warm air inside, so much "steam" was created that the young woman feared that the building was afire. The preacher reassured her and learned her name. The next day the two met on the street and were formally introduced by the Reverend William Smith with whom Dolliver was walking. A few weeks later Smith wrote to Dolliver that the Brown family were making inquiries about him and that Eliza, who was "in every respect admirable," had been greatly impressed with him and that it might be well for Dolliver to begin corresponding with her.[33]

After exchanging letters for a little more than a year, during which time they met only once, James J. Dolliver and Eliza J. Brown were married in Kingwood, May 29, 1855. By then the young itinerant minister had become a Presiding

Elder. However, because Robert and Ann Brown did not want their daughter to leave them in their old age, Dolliver resigned that assignment to accept an appointment as a circuit rider in the Kingwood district in order that he and Eliza might make their home with her parents. Eliza said many times during the remainder of her life that she had known the first Sunday she had seen him that James J. Dolliver was the only man in the world for her.[34]

His marriage and the establishment of his home with his wife's family brought James Dolliver into immediate contact not only with Eliza's able father, Robert Brown, and her uncle, the Congressman, but also with her brother, John James Brown. These brothers-in-law became fast friends. Young Brown, a Kingwood attorney, was a devout Methodist layman and an active Democrat. Possessed of a "matchless gift of oratory," he was, like James J. Dolliver, an "intense and steadfast Union man," vigorously opposed to all talk of secession.[35] It was he who in the late fifties became the tireless political leader of the pro-Union forces in Preston County. Without doubt the influence, political and religious, of J. J. Brown and J. J. Dolliver was of great significance in securing in that county a vote of 2,256 to 63 against ratification of the Virginia Ordinance of Secession. Shortly after that triumph, Brown, as a member of the second Wheeling convention, helped pass the motion providing for the division of Virginia into two states. Subsequently, as a delegate to the constitutional convention, he helped frame the first constitution of West Virginia.[36]

The strong antislavery sentiment of his son and son-in-law may have been the deciding factor in Robert Brown's decision to liberate the few slaves that he had inherited — he had never bought or sold one. At any rate, he freed his slaves before the Civil War began, and "all of them immediately settled down around him and proceeded to live off of him for the remainder of his days."[37] He could not have owned many slaves, for in 1860 there were but 45 free Negroes and 67 slaves in the whole of Preston County, an area which had contained only 87 slaves a decade earlier.[38]

Liberty, not slavery, was characteristic of the highlanders of western Virginia. *Montani semper liberi* was the motto of the new state which the Browns, the Pierponts, and many others like them and like the humble Methodist circuit rider, James J. Dolliver, helped bring into being. Love of freedom, devotion to the nation, a strong sense of civic responsibility, deep-seated personal integrity, and sincere religious convictions were qualities that cropped out in generation after generation of Dollivers, Goldthwaites, Hawthornes, and Browns, whether in England or Scotland, New England or Virginia.

From such a heredity, into such an environment came the children of James and Eliza Dolliver, children born in the age of Abraham Lincoln, the third generation to draw their first breath in the old house that James and Rachel Brown had built in the days of George Washington's presidency.

-II-

Boyhood and Education

The nation got Jonathan P. Dolliver, as it has gotten many other great men of the past, from a family of high moral and religious principles.
James Wilson, Secretary of Agriculture, 1897-1913.

THE CHILDREN of James and Eliza Dolliver were, in the order of their births, Robert Henry, born April 1, 1856; Jonathan Prentiss, born February 6, 1858; Mary Ann Hawthorne, born July 21, 1859; Victor Brown, born March 18, 1861; and Margaret Gay, born May 19, 1864. They were a close-knit, happy family. Each child had at least one nickname — "R. H." or "Bob," "J. P." or "Prent," "Mollie," "Vic," and "Gay." The second son was named for Jonathan Prentiss, the husband of Grandmother Brown's aunt, Margaret Hawthorne.[1]

Jonathan Dolliver was a healthy, attractive infant. He had large brown eyes, in shape and color like those of Ann Brown, his grandmother. His Aunt Rebecca described him as he was when she first saw him "in his little willow cradle as beautiful as he could be, his head a mat of curls, 6 months old."[2]

The first years of his life were spent in carefree happiness in the old Brown home near Kingwood. His parents were poor, his grandparents aged, his country beset with the economic and social upheaval of the Civil War. But a small boy wants affection and adventure more than money, and, if Jonathan had none of the latter, he had the former in great abundance. When Confederate raiders came into the vicinity, he helped hide the hams and other foodstuffs and watched his father tether the horses in a secluded laurel thicket. Upon the arrival of the treasurer of Preston County, bringing thousands of dollars in gold coins to be hidden on the Brown farm, Jonathan and Robert were instructed to climb upon the roof of the barn to watch for rebels. Should any be sighted, Grandfather Brown told the boys to cheer lustily for Jefferson Davis, thus to distract and delay any "boys in gray" who might approach.

Sugar, ever a luxury to the poor, was scarce in the Dolliver household in wartime. Jonathan remembered that sugar was "so high in my youth that my good mother went around carrying the key to the under-the-stairs closet on her

9

arm, and I was caught with my head in the barrel under circumstances that prevented my getting out before the exercises began."[3]

Eliza Dolliver churned butter for the family table. Jonathan often watched her from the cellar doorway "in the shadow of climbing roses, with a spring of living water at hand, colder than ice and clearer than crystal," and sometimes she allowed him to take a turn at "counting the strokes which at length brought forth the yellow luxury."[4] He liked to spread great quantities of homemade butter on freshly baked bread, "right out of the oven," and while thus feasting between meals to drink the cream "when any was left over." It is little wonder that he would weigh 220 pounds on his wedding day, or that he was to write to his mother after he had left the old homestead forever, "I have never found a pleasanter spot; our food was not the daintiest and yet I have never enjoyed any so well."[5]

Jonathan's favorite sport, boy and man, was fishing. He spent many joyous hours of boyhood on the banks of mountain streams waiting for unwary trout, bass, or perch to bite. He was also an excellent swimmer, and he loved to roam in the forests. "I was of a meditative frame of mind, given to long walks in the woods rather than to manual labor," he wrote of his boyhood. "There was always something about a shade tree that seemed to fit into the grooves of my moral nature." With the former slaves still at hand, the Dolliver boys seem to have been burdened with few tasks. Not many men who have spent their early years on a farm can think of those hours of the early morning and late evening, known as chore-time, and say as did Jonathan Dolliver: "I remember well the red sunset — how the woods flamed with the departing glory of the day. I don't remember the red-sunrise so well."[6]

At the age of six he wanted to be a farmer, and throughout his life he was interested in agriculture and looked forward to the time when he could retire from politics to the farm.[7] He always believed that rural surroundings in boyhood were a great advantage. "The truth is," he once wrote, "that the old fashioned country homestead has produced nearly all of the successful men of this generation, because it produces health of body and mind, as well as of moral disposition, three things that are the chief conditions of success."[8]

In Jonathan's case the religious habits of his parents had far more to do with producing "moral disposition" than did the location of his home. For the Dollivers, Christianity was a way of life, not a garment to be displayed on special holidays or a sop to social convention and economic expediency. Their emphasis was upon the individual's daily relationship to God and fellow man rather than upon theological dogma or on future rewards and punishments. The whole family ordinarily gathered morning and evening for prayer and Bible reading, and the children studied and memorized important selections of the Scriptures. "I often rejoice that I learned to love home," Jonathan wrote in 1880. "I sometimes imagine that I hear Ma calling me down to prayers. If I could only get beside that desk with someone to call me down to prayers, with all our books and all our faces under one roof again!" [9]

Unquestionably the power of evangelical religion, reinforced by the happy memories of his home life and enriched by his wide reading in Biblical literature, made a lasting impression upon Jonathan Dolliver. His father, whom he adored and revered, was of particular influence in molding Dolliver's character and thought. Although forty-two years old when Jonathan was born, the elder Dolliver preceded his son in death by only five years. With the exception of intervals of various lengths between 1875 and 1881, the two lived under the same roof almost the whole of Jonathan's life. As a little boy he accompanied his father upon occasion when the itinerant minister was conducting a prolonged revival. They rode from settlement to settlement, sometimes remaining a week at a time in a community in order that the entire population might have an opportunity to attend services. The child was impressed not only by his father's preaching but also by the way in which he moved the people with the "earnestness of the message from a mind and soul inspired from on high." [10]

This earnestness and sincerity impressed more mature and more impartial observers also. After Jonathan went to Congress, his father, who usually accompanied him to Washington, where he was widely known as "Father Dolliver," was often invited to act as chaplain in the House or the Senate. Once a Senator remarked to him, "Father Dolliver, I love to hear you pray, for you seem to be talking to somebody that you know." [11]

Jonathan indicated his appreciation of the influence of his parents when he wrote to his father: "You will let me say that there are five of us who will bear through life the constant blessing of your example and Mother's — an example of piety, of labor, and usefulness." It was, indeed, a constant example. Even when the boys were away from home, the letters from their parents invariably contained such admonitions as: "Let your companions be few and well selected, and don't let the world of the flesh or the devil come in and rob you of your home in Heaven"; "Honor God in all that you do. Acknowledge Him in all your ways and He will direct your paths"; and "Be sure to avail yourselves of the privileges of the church and try to form characters worthy of imatation [sic]." [12]

Because their religious commitment was natural, unaffected, and patently sincere, and because they sought to "practice what they preached," James and Eliza Dolliver succeeded in rearing a family dedicated to the basic principles of Christianity. Jonathan as an adult was to be a tolerant Trinitarian, inclined to an optimistic predestination. A loyal Methodist layman, he was devoid of prudery, cant, and hypocrisy and was sufficiently well grounded in the fundamentals of the Judeo-Christian tradition that he never fell into the common heresy of confusing fundamentalism, Sabbatarianism, prohibition, or anti-Darwinism with Christianity.

Love of country was emphasized only slightly less than love of God in the rearing of Jonathan Dolliver. His father and mother, his grandparents, his uncle, and his great-uncle among whom he lived all during his childhood were ardent patriots and, whether Union Democrats or Republicans, were politically articulate. In his most impressionable years Jonathan heard from the lips of his loved ones of the struggle to save the Union. His great-uncle, William G. Brown, told him how, as a Jacksonian nationalist, a delegate to the Secession Convention at Richmond, he was ousted for speaking against war and disunion and how he barely escaped from a mob of men massed under his hotel window brandishing ropes and yelling, "Let's hang Bill Brown."[13] Jonathan later read that speech and always listened with mingled awe and pride to "Uncle Billy" when the Congressman came to the farm at Kingwood to talk of war and politics.

James Dolliver's view of the importance of patriotism is best comprehended from these words which he wrote to his sons: "Hold high the banner of the Cross and just below it nail the stars and stripes of your country and the day shall be yours."[14] Had it not been for his bodily disability, a diseased leg which finally had to be amputated, James Dolliver would have been the first volunteer chaplain of the loyal mountaineers in the Civil War. His wife shared the love of country which flamed in the hearts of her kinsmen, and she imparted it to her children. Jonathan's sister wrote him that his "loyalty and patriotism are due largely to mother."[15]

The Civil War and its aftermath conditioned to a marked degree the environment, political, economic, and intellectual, in which Dolliver spent his youth. According to his oft-repeated statement, the most impressive memories of his boyhood were associated with the end of that tragic conflict:

> I can just remember the day when the bells tolled for the dying Lincoln, and all the neighbors were crying, as if their own hearthstones had been bereaved. And then I remember a few days later, how it was said about the family altar of a quaint old homestead, down among the loyal mountains of West Virginia, that the war was over and the life of the republic saved. And when the boys kept coming back and used to tell to listening groups their thrilling story of the service, I remember how strong and splendid it all seemed — this defending the flag of the nation.[16]

Abraham Lincoln was the boy's hero, and throughout his life he habitually referred to Lincoln as "the grandest man of all time." John James Brown shifted his political allegiance to the Republican party during the war, and Dolliver's father had been pro-Republican since the mid-fifties. The latter, in fact, came to regard Lincoln and his party as "agents of God in America."[17] It is not amazing that Jonathan was long a narrow partisan. Nor is it strange that he was to be almost as slow as Theodore Roosevelt, born in the same year, in realizing that the forces which controlled their party had abandoned many of Lincoln's more liberal principles shortly after his funeral.

————————

During the last months of the war Jonathan began his formal education at Pleasant Dale school, a one-room building which had been erected by his Grandfather Brown in a thicket of laurel near Kingwood at a time when there were no public schools in the county. In fact, a free-school system was not attempted in West Virginia until 1864, the year Dolliver was in the first grade. Jonathan described his first teacher, Burgess Parks, as "a typical Dickens Gradgrind, devoted to facts."[18] Little else is known about Schoolmaster Parks, but Jonathan, despite this seemingly disparaging comment, developed a great respect for facts and mastered a remarkable array of them in many realms of knowledge in the course of his life.

Dolliver probably studied McGuffey's *Readers* during his four years at Pleasant Dale. They were popular and widely used in similar schools in the state at that time. As Mark Sullivan so aptly said, the *Readers*, McGuffey's and others, were "the backbone of education in the common schools of America — so far as it aimed to impart ideas, standards of individual and social conduct and the like."[19] Teaching children to be resigned to what was called "God's will" was one of the aims of McGuffey, and none of the contents of his books was inconsistent with the religion of John Knox or the Wesleys. Patriotism was inculcated not only by the selections of biography, poetry, and rhetoric found in the *Readers*, but also through the teaching of American history. Liberty, independence, resistance to tyranny, and the glorification of the heroes of the American Revolution were major themes.[20] Thus, in his first years in school, Jonathan received training which aimed at implanting religious, moral, and patriotic principles not unlike those emphasized by his family.

————————

If the records of Jonathan's early school days are scant, those of his years in preparatory school and college are quite adequate. In 1868, for the purpose of providing his sons better opportunities for education, James J. Dolliver moved his family to Granville, a settlement on the outskirts of Morgantown, West Virginia. They settled themselves in the brick parsonage in the "quiet little village," where the boys soon found new friends and new adventures. Jonathan and his brother fished in "the pool below the roots of the old sycamore tree," played on island and sandbar, swam in the Monongahela River, and occasionally raided their "Uncle Billy's wine down at the mill."[21]

In the autumn following his tenth birthday, Jonathan entered the preparatory department of what was soon to become West Virginia University. This "prep school" was designed for those who were too young or insufficiently advanced to begin college work. The academic year consisted of three thirteen-week terms. Tuition was five dollars per term plus a general fee of one dollar. Jonathan and Robert spent three years in the preparatory department before entering the University. In accordance with the rules, each day opened with Scripture reading and prayer, at which all the students had to be present. All were likewise required "to attend regularly some place of religious worship on the Sabbath, and on all occasions to treat the institutions of religion with respect."[22]

Jonathan began with the study of geography, arithmetic, English, grammar, Latin, and Greek. His grades the first year were average: his highest mark was 3.99 in geography and his lowest 3.28 in arithmetic, the scale being 1.00 to 5.00. The second year he completed algebra and began geometry, read Caesar and Cicero, continued Greek, and studied United States history and bookkeeping. His marks improved in his second year, and when he finished his courses at the end of his third year, his grades in a scale of 10 were 9.7 in both Latin and Greek, 9.0 in literature, and 8.5 in geometry.[23]

In addition to the specific classes, there was a general requirement consisting of "regular lessons in writing, spelling, elocution, and English composition."[24] It was there that Jonathan Dolliver, the future master of oratory, received his first training in the preparation and delivery of speeches.

In 1871, at thirteen, Jonathan entered West Virginia University as a freshman. His brother, Robert, was in the same class. It had been the custom of the Brown family to send the most promising scholar in each generation to college. James and Eliza Dolliver, however, both having been denied higher education, determined that all of their children, boys and girls alike, should have an opportunity to earn a degree. Even the small inheritance which Eliza received upon the death of her parents was used to help Jonathan and Robert through college. Duly appreciative of these sacrifices, Jonathan later wrote his parents that he would rather have his college education "than the best farm in Preston County," adding that "your idea of giving your children the benefit of good schools is the soundest."[25]

West Virginia University, established as "The Agricultural College of West Virginia" in 1867, was in the fifth year of its existence when Dolliver enrolled. Although small and of recent origin, the University was well organized in 1871, and it was said to offer "facilities for educational training and culture surpassed by few institutions in adjoining states." At least three of the ten faculty members held the Ph. D. degree, and there was a strong emphasis on sound scholarship and rigid discipline.[26]

The University "Code of Laws and Regulations" forbade the students to use tobacco, intoxicants, and profanity, to dance, play billiards, and attend theaters or circuses. Occasionally an example was made of some luckless boy caught in one of the prohibited activities. Such was the fate of Philander C. Knox, future Attorney General and Secretary of State of the United States, a junior when Dolliver was a freshman. Knox, discovered playing billiards, was expelled, but not before he and Jonathan had developed a friendship which culminated in their service together in the United States Senate more than thirty years later. "We were together that night," Dolliver recalled, speaking of Knox. "They caught him. In the confusion, I escaped."[27]

During his four years in college Jonathan pursued what was known as the literary course which led to the A. B. degree. This curriculum, while preponderantly classical, was rather broad in scope. In his first year he studied European history, the United States Constitution, English literature, algebra, geometry, and trigonometry. In Latin class he read Cicero's *De Senectute* and *De Amicitia*, Horace's *Odes* and *Epodes*, and Vergil's *Georgics* and *Bucolics*. The Greek reading included the *Iliad*, the *Odyssey*, and Herodotus. His marks were excellent, the lowest being 9.18 in Greek and the highest, a perfect 10, in the United States Constitution. Chemistry, botany, analytical geometry, philology, rhetoric, and logic, in addition to Greek and Latin, constituted the work of the sophomore year. His reading in the classics included Plato's *Apology* and *Crito*, Xenophon's *Memorabilia*, Horace's *Satires* and *Epistles*, and selections from the works of Livy. The third year he continued Greek and Latin and began the study of French. Other subjects were astronomy, physics, mental philosophy, English history and political economy, calculus, zoology, human anatomy, and military science. As a senior, Dolliver registered for the history of civilization, astronomy, geology, German, and moral, political, and sacred philosophy. His marks remained consistently high, and his four-year academic record was distinctly superior.[28]

He participated each term in that college activity designated as "literary." The rules of the University specified that "Declamations and exercises in oratory shall be had every week" and that "these shall be assigned to the students in rotation; nor shall any student be exempt."[29]

His major extracurricular activity was in the Columbian Literary Society which he joined in the spring of 1871. This organization met weekly for the purpose of conducting oratorical contests and debates and hearing student essays. Jonathan participated actively and served for a time as secretary of the Columbians. He was fined only twice in four years for failing to take part in scheduled activities, but so vigorous and intense was his interest in the proceedings that he was fined at least nine times for entering into debates, in moments of excitement, without recognition of the presiding officer.[30]

The Columbian and other literary societies presented public performances each year for the entertainment and enlightenment of the faculty, students, and townspeople. Jonathan represented the Columbians in the Brown Contest of

1872, attempting a humorous declamation entitled "Daniel vs Dishcloth." Its content was not as inane as its title, but he lost to his opponent from the rival Parthenon Society. The Morgantown *Post* generously commented that both orations were "admirably delivered" and that "the young gentlemen evinced excellent qualities that go far toward making good speakers."[31]

Manuscripts of several of Dolliver's college essays and orations have survived.[32] Some offer clues to the development of ideas which were to characterize his later thinking. In "The Republic Is Peace," an 1874 oration, Jonathan concerned himself with certain defects of the "Gilded Age." Why, he wondered, did the majority of the American people feel as they seemed to "towards the Negro and the poor man? Are these esteemed here in this land of equality and of freedom . . . on a plane of equality with all men?" He thought not, and added that "so long then as we refer to the Declaration of Independence as the corner stone of our governmental fabric, and at the same time deny any class all rights of citizens, little can be expected except social and political disorder."

The following year he touched upon the most obvious results of the unbridled laissez-faire capitalism of the Grant era. "The nature of worldly masters in the United States would almost seem incompatible with morality and decency," Dolliver asserted. "Success in business has come to be a symbol of robbery and fraud." If his analysis of the contemporary scene was superficial, if he failed to perceive the relationship between politics and the new industrialism, the young student at least did realize that all was not as it should be in his beloved country.

Chosen "philosophical orator" for his graduating class, Dolliver spoke at commencement in 1875 on "A Phase of Social Philosophy." It was, he said, one of the lessons of all history that "the efforts of a part of humanity to rise, and the determination of the other to subject them, destroy or ignore their rights, and degrade their character and position, have strewn the shores of time with the ashes of ruined cities and empires overthrown." He asserted the Jeffersonian belief "that the individual is inviolable, that force is no longer an object of worship, that man cannot be governed without his consent." In concluding his oration, Jonathan revealed his hatred of race and class distinctions: "Let the last prejudice on the ground of accidental condition of being be swept away forever. . . . Then shall we have no aristocracy of race, no privileged class . . . but a just government, deriving its powers from the consent of the governed." He was a democrat, if not a Democrat, and his strong belief in the basic tenets of democracy was characteristic of him throughout his life.

In an essay entitled "Time Tests Worth," Jonathan exposed himself as a devotee of the "great man" theory of history — Thomas Carlyle was admittedly one of his favorite authors. Expressing the view "that, the Bible excepted, the pen and voice of the Christian statesmen have wielded a mightier influence for man's elevation than any other agency," Dolliver stated that it was his conviction that men may lift themselves to the highest positions of public trust and honor "by patient toil and persevering labor, by unremitting efforts for the good of the country, and by gradually ingrafting their worth on their age."[33]

More important by far than his training as an orator was the influence of the broad liberal education to which Jonathan was exposed during his years in Morgantown. Although deficient in music and the other fine arts, the curricula which he so diligently studied afforded Dolliver a deep understanding of many areas of knowledge. He discovered an abiding interest in literature — classical, Biblical, and English — and a passionate devotion to history and biography. "Be careful to read only classics," he wrote his sister Mollie when she started to college.

> You will find that in the use of language, in the mastery of English style, the old poets are the best — like old friends. Read them studiously, remembering and laying up intelligently all those fine turned sentiments of which so great use is made by our best writers. Get the masterpiece of each and put it among your mental resources. . . . Study the sacred Scripture. It is the ornament of culture. Look to it that the lessons and language of the Bible be made part of your life.[34]

His own speeches and articles bear eloquent witness that he faithfully followed this advice.

Jonathan's fondness for reading was almost legendary even in his college days. Known for his silver tongue and for his daring as a swimmer, he was famed also as the fisherman who habitually hastened after classes to the Monongahela, where he would bait a hook and then stretch out "to employ the intervals between bites in translating portions of Caesar." One of his classmates recalled that he often saw "Prent stumbling down the road reading as he walked to the campus each morning."[35]

Certainly his years at the University did nothing to undermine Dolliver's religious or political convictions. He continued to live at home, where loyalty to the Union, nationalism, and an ardent attachment to the Republican party were second only to devout commitment to the religious precepts of Methodism. The college was to some extent dominated by the personality of the president, the Reverend Alexander Martin, "a kindly, shrewd Scotchman whose real scholarship was mellowed by humanity and intuitive understanding of the needs of youth,"[36] despite his approval of the regents' puritanical "Code of Laws and Regulations." A Republican as well as a Methodist minister, President Martin had no objection to Jonathan's making his debut as a political speaker in 1872 when the youth urged any who would gather and listen to vote for President Grant.[37]

President Martin was a long-time friend of the Reverend James Dolliver, and for that reason as well as others, he had the respect and admiration of Jonathan. Usually the president taught the senior course in philosophy, but in 1873 Martin took over the chair of astronomy and physics, and in 1874-1875 he was relieved of all teaching duties in order to devote his full time to administration.[38] Thus, Jonathan did not have Martin's notable course in philosophy, which so impressed Albert J. Beveridge in later years at De Pauw, where Alexander Martin became president after leaving West Virginia. Beveridge, a brilliant youth, was to become one of Dolliver's dearest friends. One of Beveridge's biographers has asserted that "to Doctor Martin must be attributed, in part at least, Beveridge's strong belief in a Divinity which shaped the destinies of nations as well as men, and his fearless insistence upon ethical integrity."[39] These same traits were characteristic of Dolliver, and it is not unlikely that Dr. Martin was of some significance in reinforcing and nourishing them.

Jonathan Dolliver, four months past his seventeenth birthday, was graduated from West Virginia University with honors in 1875. He ranked third in his class, his average in his senior year being 9.34 out of a possible 10.00. "His conduct was praiseworthy everywhere, his social manners commendable to others, and his diligence and zeal not to be surpassed," said one of Jonathan's professors.[40]

Probably the most succinct and accurate appraisal of the young man as he was at the close of his college years is found in the words of President Martin, who described Dolliver "as a young gentleman of superior natural ability, sound Education, and strict integrity, & as likely to do honestly and well whatever he undertakes."[41]

-III-

Choosing A Career, 1875-1878

*The teacher was often an ambitious young man bound upward toward
some other career, giving a few years of his life to a folk-service, as,
so to speak, a liaison between the older generation and the new, passing on accumulated wisdom, traditions and precepts of the race.*
Mary Sullivan, Our Times.

THOSE FINAL WORDS, "whatever he undertakes," in the letter of reference
given Dolliver by Dr. Alexander Martin suggest more than merely the
president's abounding confidence in the young graduate. Jonathan had completed his college days without having decided on a vocation. He felt no "call"
to the ministry as his parents had hoped that he might. He considered a career
as a banker but found no job available when he made application. Nor could
he yet definitely make up his mind to study law, although he had thought of
that profession because of his interest in the careers of John James Brown and
William G. Brown, and because of his fascination with oratory.[1]

Desperately in need of money, Jonathan found his first opportunity after
commencement in a rather unorthodox enterprise. The Monongahela River
had reached flood stage in mid-June. As it spread beyond its banks, its roving
current picked up saw logs lying hewed and ready for mill. Knowing that the
law provided 5 per cent of their value to those who salvaged the logs, young
Dolliver decided to turn a profit from his prowess as a swimmer. "I removed
my clothing and jumped into the river," he recalled, "where ever and anon I
would seize a likely log and steer it into calm water."[2] A newsman who observed this performance reported that Dolliver "captured" twelve logs bare-
handed, "a feat we are satisfied that was never equalled in this part of the
country. We are proud of that young hero; we admire his pluck, and challenge
any county in the State to produce a 'live steam tug' to equal him."[3]

When the floodwaters receded, Jonathan secured temporary employment in a
brick kiln as a day laborer. Then, toward the end of summer he heard
through his father's sister, Maria Van Fleet of Sandwich, Illinois, of the need
for a schoolmaster in the neighboring village of Victor Center.[4]

19

Walking part of the way, but riding in a stage most of the distance, Dolliver reached Connellsville, Pennsylvania, the first day. There he saw P. T. Barnum's show, bought a ticket for his first train ride, and "in the evening, full of strange thrills" continued his journey to Illinois. He long remembered that railroad trip, and in the last year of his life, he recorded his recollections of it:

> I raised the window of the day coach and let the cinders and smoke from the locomotive get in my mouth, nose and eyes, but principally into my eyes. The sensation of gliding in the moonlight through the woods and fields, past towns and sleeping houses, kept me alert and keen all night. I remembered the oxen and the round-bellied and big-footed horses back in the yellow dust of West Virginia, and prying a piece of coal from my eye, I said to myself: "This, then, is real life."

He stopped in Columbus, Ohio, to change trains, and in his innocence of the hazards of urban travel, engaged in seemingly intimate conversation with a well-dressed stranger in the station. A kindly policeman beckoned to the young man, so obviously from the country, and quietly informed him that he had been talking with the "most dangerous pickpocket in the United States." Jonathan's amused reaction was that this eminent criminal had been wasting his time with "a country boy who hasn't a red cent."

Arriving in Illinois the first week of October, Dolliver was welcomed at the home of his aunt and her family, and within a short time had succeeded in securing the teaching appointment. He discovered, however, that school would not open until corn husking was completed. It was then the custom in the rural Midwest not to begin the fall term as long as the weather permitted the boys to be of use in the autumn harvest and plowing. Waiting to begin his duties, Jonathan worked on the farm of one of the Van Fleet neighbors, where, as he put it, he "whiled away the time in various healthful exercises incident to practical agriculture." [5]

If anything of unusual interest happened in connection with his brief term as schoolmaster at Victor Center in the winter of 1875-1876, time has erased all record of it. He lived in the home of his Aunt Maria,[6] and undoubtedly spent much of his spare time in reading, in hunting and sleighing with his cousins, and in participating in such community social activities as spelling bees and box suppers which were customarily held in the schoolhouse. His status was quite enviable, for as one of his friends, later Governor of Illinois, was to relate, the country school of the seventies "was the centre of a genuine community life. The country school-teacher was a very important person, a leader in the intellectual and social life of the community." [7]

During this period of his life Jonathan wrote out a set of "Rules" to guide him in his daily conduct. In some respects similar to the "Resolutions" which Benjamin Franklin drew up for the regulation of his own life and to the young George Washington's "Rules of Civility," Dolliver's "Things to be Avoided" and "Everyday Rules" reveal something of the nature of their author, age eighteen.[8]

THINGS TO BE AVOIDED:

1st . . . Assume no attitude or posture for the sake of attracting attention, or that is liable to attract attention, and invite criticism from observers; be natural, be yourself in your actions, be modest not ostentatious. Unless you particularly guard yourself in these matters, you lay yourself liable to just criticism from others and your influence with others is weakened and you are liable to become an object of ridicule. . . .

2nd Don't tell anything that is liable to be taken for the truth when in reality there is some falsity in it, when talking with a person who is depending on you for the truth, for even though it may not be any injury to another, it will blunt your own sense of exact truth. . . .   ..

3rd Do not permit time, place or circumstances to cause you to falter in the discharge of known duty. . . .

4th Use no deceit in your dealings with your fellow men in any kind of transactions. Be thoroughly honest with every man. . . .

5th Never willingly or unnecessarily express an opinion concerning any one whereby such a person may suffer injury. . . .

EVERYDAY RULES

6th Have a definite number of things to do, these to be done systematically according to an arranged program, permitting nothing to arise to prevent the accomplishment of a prescribed amount of work.

7th Completely master and subdue all inclinations to mingle in society for the mere gratification of personal ends, until having acquired a proficiency in all necessary branches of knowledge.

8th Overcome all tendency to acquire the admiration of people, especially young ladies, simply for personal gratification and for improper reasons. . . .

9th Make the deportment not ostentatious or obtrusive, but retiring, reserved and dignified.

10th Cease all correspondence and intercourse with parties who care little for you or what you say except as it may further their personal and selfish plans.

So far as can be determined, Dolliver succeeded reasonably well in following this youthful code of conduct throughout life.

With the close of the five-month term at the Victor Center school in the early spring of 1876, Jonathan returned to West Virginia. He had saved more than $200, which he presented to his mother to be used for the needs of the family. Having had a taste of teaching, he decided to spend the next year in the study of law, and arrangements were made for Jonathan to "read law" in the law offices of his uncle, John James Brown, in Morgantown. State Senator Brown had an excellent law library, including sets of the *Congressional Globe*, the *Congressional Record*, and the Supreme Court *Reports*. Dolliver studied diligently, and nearly every evening his uncle examined him on the day's reading. "He gave me good instruction," Jonathan asserted.[9]

This legal education continued until the summer of 1877 without major interruption. Even though he made progress satisfactory to his instructor, the young man was more interested in reading the proceedings of Congress, past and contemporary, and in memorizing and practicing the perorations of various speeches of Daniel Webster and other orators than he was in studying law. The fact was, as Brown suspected, Jonathan was more attracted to politics than to law, more interested in becoming an orator than an attorney.[10]

The summer of 1876 provided an exciting interlude in Dolliver's legal training. "I walked, begged rides of farmers and beat my way on steamboats to the Republican National Convention in Cincinnati," he wrote. "I was for Blaine and cheered as loudly as I could. . . . In fact I strained my voice for Blaine."[11]

That convention, which met June 14, 1876, was the scene of the first great effort of James G. Blaine of Maine to secure his party's presidential nomination. Blaine was supported by politicians dissatisfied with President Grant's administration, and by a large number of enthusiastic younger Republicans attracted by Blaine's brilliant qualities and personal charm. At the outset more delegates were for him than for any other candidate. He was opposed, however, by Roscoe Conkling of New York, Oliver P. Morton of Indiana, both candidates themselves, and by other leaders of the so-called Stalwart faction of the party. On the other hand, Blaine was not acceptable to the out-and-out reformers who were for Benjamin Bristow of Kentucky, former United States Attorney General and Secretary of the Treasury, a man of integrity and ability.[12]

Blaine's faction was known as the "Half-Breeds." They were neither wholehearted reformers nor blind reactionaries, but rather were practical politicians looking for power and patronage. That the young Dolliver, idealistic but fiercely partisan, was drawn to the Blaine camp is understandable. He certainly did not want the corrupt gang around Grant to be continued in office, yet to plunge for thoroughgoing reform might seem to reflect too directly upon the party record of the General in the White House. Moreover, Dolliver was much attracted by Blaine's personal magnetism and renown as an orator. Indeed, it was characteristic of Dolliver's early political career that strong attachments to persons and to party would sometimes conflict with his concern for principles. Starting out with the Half-Breeds, he tried for many years afterward to walk a middle path between reaction and reform.

Robert G. Ingersoll presented Blaine's name to the convention in a speech which provided quotations for Jonathan Dolliver (and almost everyone else) for a generation. Jonathan seems to have been thrilled more by Ingersoll's thundering assertion that the American people "call for the man who has torn from the throat of treason the tongue of slander — for the man who has snatched the mask of Democracy from the hideous face of Rebellion" than by the more famous "plumed knight" simile. The young West Virginian had heard much of treason and rebellion, of course, and had little interest in knights, plumed or otherwise.

Despite the enthusiasm and the oratory, Blaine was defeated, his enemies casting their votes on the seventh ballot for Ohio's favorite son, Governor Rutherford B. Hayes.[13] Blaine himself could hardly have been more downcast than was Dolliver, but as he was to do so often in the future when disappointed with the outcome of a Republican convention, Dolliver gallantly asserted that the nominee "suited" him fine. He returned to Morgantown "full of new joy and fresh noise," and in the fall he "naturally made speeches for Hayes" in the campaign against the Democratic candidate, Samuel J. Tilden.[14]

Dolliver's major speech, the first important political address of his life, was delivered at Morgantown in early September. Speaking from the same platform with, and immediately following Waitman T. Willey, one of the founders and first United States Senators of West Virginia, Jonathan delivered a typical bloody-shirt harangue.[15] Quoting from Hooker's *Ecclestiastical Polity* the dictum that "he who goes about to persuade a multitude that they are not so well governed as they ought to be will never lack attention and favorable hearers," Dolliver sought to refute the Democratic argument that it was time for a change in Washington. Unwilling either to defend or explain the corruption of the existing regime, he devoted his efforts to attacking the Democratic party and insisting that its "only claim to be considered honest is that it has had no chance to steal for sixteen years." Predicting that "the result of S. J. Tilden's assault on the presidential chair will be very much like the time Satan laid claim to the 3rd estate of Heaven and God Almighty disallowed the claim," Dolliver concluded his tirade amid the cheers and applause of a partisan crowd stirred by his unusual eloquence. The tone of his speech was no lower than that set by many older and abler campaigners in the 1870's. The not unbiased Morgantown *Post* termed it "a most excellent speech," and called "J. P. Dolliver, Esq., one of the ablest stump speakers . . . of his age in the state. He has an admirable voice for public speaking and his manner was free and easy. He made a masterly charge upon the enemy and was loudly applauded during his scathing review of the Negro-massacring Democratic party."[16]

Jonathan spoke several times in various smaller communities in northern West Virginia in the following weeks, and by October newspapers called him "the young Demosthenes."[17] His enthusiasm was not dampened by the outcome of the election, despite the disappointment of seeing the Democrats carry West Virginia and the circumstances under which Hayes finally won the presidency.

Dolliver's experiences at the national convention and in the campaign of 1876 played a major part in his decision to seek a political career. The applause and the laudatory comments lavished on his speeches were heady wine. Not that he was conceited — he remained modest even in moments of greatest triumph. But he found politics interesting, and he had enjoyed the excitement of electioneering. Furthermore, his close association with his uncle during these months, and in the year following, as he continued the study of law, was likewise significant in contributing to his growing desire to seek through law and oratory a path to political power.[18]

Impecunious as he was, Jonathan found it necessary to return to teaching in the fall of 1877 in order to support himself, help his family, and accumulate the capital needed to establish a law office. As early as April he had applied, unsuccessfully, for the principalship of the Rockford Conference Seminary in Illinois. His letter of application stated that he proposed to make teaching his life work and that he would "prefer to serve the church rather than the secular public, as a teacher." He gave his age as "twenty-two years old," although in fact he was barely nineteen.[19] This violation of his rule of scrupulous adherence to the truth in these references to his age and to his "life work" is indicative of the desperate financial circumstances in which the Dolliver family found itself in 1877. By July 4 impatient creditors had secured judgment against James J. Dolliver, forcing the sale of much of his property to satisfy debts.[20]

Four days later Jonathan left for Illinois, where his popularity as a teacher at Victor Center in 1875-1876 and the influence of his Van Fleet relatives aided his appointment as assistant principal and instructor in the Sandwich High School for the term beginning in September, 1877. His brother Robert, who had also studied law and had taught in Indiana, obtained a teaching post in Sandwich, and the two young men rented a room at a Mrs. Sampson's during the fall and winter. Sandwich, located in the extreme southeast section of corn-rich DeKalb County, was a pleasant little town of "about 3000 inhabitants with good churches and good schools."[21]

Soon in demand as a speaker, Jonathan was especially popular with the local chapter of the "Red Ribboned Temperance Movement." His cousin reported that "Prent is doing nicely down to town. I went last Sabbath evening to listen to him deliver a temperance lecture. He had a *crowded* house & a very nice lecture. . . . The people of Sandwich think they have got *the* teacher. He is generally liked, & I think he is much pleased with his position." [22]

Jonathan wrote his mother in January of having been "called out by about 500 people, without notice or any regular preparation. I never had such an enthusiastic call for my services as a haranguer. I have taken pains to fill my head with the temperance question and I found no difficulty in making a speech." [23] His brother was enormously pleased with "the golden opinions from all sorts of people" which Prent had won as a result of lectures depicting the evils of drink. [24]

In addition to his teaching and speaking activities, Jonathan occasionally played football and constantly continued his reading. "I have learned more this year by study than I ever learned before in a year — in school or out," he informed his younger brother. [25] He also took an active part in the work of his church but apparently was not impressed with the enthusiasm of the local congregation; he wrote his father that he believed "that this is the foremost age of infidelity and that the foremost cause of it is the lukewarmness of the church." [26]

Busy and happy though he seems to have been at Sandwich, Dolliver had not lost sight of the law. Not long after school started he told his friend, William Van Horn, that he intended to become a lawyer and "go to Congress." [27] In December, 1877, he wrote his father that he and Robert were planning to buy a law library and open an office in the spring. "We have not settled upon a place yet, but *think* Fort Dodge in Iowa is the eligible spot — thither we propose to bend our steps." [28]

Preparatory to this move Jonathan obtained a law license from the Monongalia County Court in West Virginia, although, as the friend who mailed it to him pointed out, this document contained a "slight discrepancy" inasmuch as Dolliver was not yet of legal age, nor had he been a resident of the county for one year immediately preceding the date of issue. [29] Complying with a request from Jonathan for a statement certifying that he had completed the study of law, John J. Brown wrote that in his thirty years as a lawyer

> . . . among the many young men, who during that long period, have been under my preceptorship in the pursuit of legal knowledge, no one has been more diligent and faithful in his legal studies, become more thoroughly acquainted with . . . the elementary principles of the law, nor was more guarded and exemplary in his general conduct and moral deportment than young Dolliver. [30]

By mid-January, Jonathan and Robert had definitely decided to move to Fort Dodge as soon as the school term ended. "We will have three hundred dollars altogether," Jonathan told his mother. "It will take of that sum one hundred to fit us out with professional clothes. Over one hundred must be spent for Books and of our little 'cash on hands,' less than $100.00 for office rent and food. . . . We are poor but by the force of *Work* we mean to get into *Business* and make it go."[31] When John J. Brown heard that his nephews had bought a set of law books, he observed that they had done wisely, adding the revealing comment: "I don't think Prent will need it for he can assert law as he goes along no matter whether it is in the book or not."[32]

At the high school commencement exercises the last of March, Jonathan Dolliver, serving his final day as a teacher, delivered an address on Abraham Lincoln, the first of many eulogies he would live to deliver on that subject. A day or two later he set out for Iowa to begin in a new land a career in the profession Lincoln had followed.

In West Virginia, John J. Brown had just written Eliza Dolliver, who was worried about her sons' going so far from home: "There is no danger whatever but they will succeed, and I have no doubt if Prent has his health he will be a Representative in the Congress of the United States before ten years. He is perfectly irrepressible. The whole world cannot keep him down."[33]

-IV-

Neophyte Lawyer in
Fort Dodge, 1878-1879

We have not been entirely successful. . . . More study and more time will put us even with the profession. . . . God has been with us in Fort Dodge. It is plain that our coming West has been providential.

Jonathan Prentiss Dolliver, letter to his father, 1879

IT WAS EARLY APRIL, and the farmers of Webster County, Iowa, had not yet finished their spring plowing when the train carrying Jonathan Dolliver and his brother westward from Illinois chugged across the plateau, which slopes gently down to the Des Moines River, and braked to a stop in Fort Dodge. Iowa seemed to Jonathan to be a land of plenty. Her rich black soil, her invigorating climate, her broad prairies were in marked contrast to the poverty-ridden mountains of his native West Virginia, where the valleys were too narrow and the soil too thin to permit much profitable agriculture. "I hail from the Mountain State of West Virginia," he later told a Fort Dodge audience, "a State in the minds of whose people have been most beautifully mingled the highest ideals of liberty and profusest employment of the promissory note principle, in whose land the sound of few hammers but the Sheriff's is heard, and the main employment of whose citizens is a laborious and judicious dodging of old creditors." [1]

According to Jonathan, he and Robert had decided to establish themselves in the Hawkeye State after having "borrowed an atlas and studied the geography of the country." They noticed that Iowa was between the Mississippi and Missouri rivers, and one of them "hit upon the phrase that Iowa held a commanding position" in the West. The city of Fort Dodge "would be lapped," they thought, "by the waves of prosperity flowing inward from each river." [2]

Fort Dodge, erected in 1850 as a frontier outpost to protect pioneer settlers from Indian raids, became the Webster County seat in 1856. From the first, the citizens seemed to have "a genius for politics." In some of the early years

27

there were as many as four elections per annum. For decades John F. Duncombe of Fort Dodge was the uncrowned head of the Democratic party in northwestern Iowa. Opposing Duncombe was his friend, Cyrus C. Carpenter, also of Fort Dodge, whom the Republicans had twice elected Governor before 1878.[3] The county was generally Republican, but the Democrats were a strong minority. The congressional district, however, was safely Republican. Not until 1956 did the Democrats elect a Congressman from the district in which Fort Dodge is located.[4]

Fort Dodge and northwestern Iowa were thus attractive, economically and politically, to Jonathan and Robert Dolliver. They had determined to locate in a county seat town, and Jonathan, particularly, wanted to be in a congenial political atmosphere. Reasonably near Des Moines, the capital, Fort Dodge was still far enough away from any major city to enable the fledgling lawyers to avoid competition with urban attorneys. A new town of some 3,500 population in a prosperous and rapidly growing state, Fort Dodge was an ideal spot for a well-educated, politically ambitious young Republican to begin his legal career.[5]

On April 5, 1878, less than a week after his arrival, Jonathan appeared before the presiding judge of the Fort Dodge judicial circuit to receive his certificate of admission to the bar, "as Attorney and Counsellor at Law in the Several Courts of the State of Iowa."[6] He and his brother opened their offices the next day. "We are nicely fixed — Two rooms on Sixth St., right opposite Court House. We sleep in our office," R. H. wrote his father. They spent their last $25 for office equipment and furniture for their living quarters, but they had no immediate need for money as they had made arrangements to take their meals with a Mrs. Cheeny and were "very pleased to have so pleasant a boarding house."[7]

On his first Sunday in town, Jonathan attended Sunday school at the Methodist Church. The teacher of the young men's class was Cyrus Clay Carpenter, former Governor of the state (1872-1876), an honest and kindly Methodist with a long record of loyalty to the Radical Republican cause.[8] Carpenter invited Dolliver home for dinner and at the end of the day made this entry in his diary: "Had a talk with a Mr. Dolliver who is coming here to practice law. Find he is quite a great young man."[9] Noted as a good judge of human nature, Carpenter was attracted by Dolliver's qualities of character, not merely by his facility of speech.[10]

Governor Carpenter — he carried the gubernatorial title the rest of his life — became Jonathan's first important friend in Iowa. The Governor had no children, and he came to regard Dolliver almost as a son. Few men had a greater influence on Jonathan or played so important a part in promoting his political career. "[Carpenter] was a politician," Dolliver later wrote, "and in many respects the wisest and most successful that has ever lived in Iowa. . . . He knew how to approach those whom he wished to influence and guide, and while he could neither use base and questionable weapons for himself nor protect himself against them in the hands of others, he was throughout his public career the ideal type of the upright American politician."[11] Carpenter had powerful friends and useful political connections. Such men as James S. Clarkson, editor of the Des Moines *Iowa State Register* and chief cog in the Republican machine then known as "The Regency," United States Senator William Boyd Allison, and General Grenville M. Dodge, railroad builder, state and national political manipulator, and wheel horse of the Grand Army of the Republic, were among the ex-Governor's allies.[12]

From the beginning of his residence in Fort Dodge, Jonathan — "J. P." as he usually was known in Iowa — was in almost daily contact with Carpenter, frequently dining at the Governor's house, where he entertained Mrs. Carpenter with his witty conversation, talked politics with her husband, and borrowed books to carry to his room for reading while waiting for clients to appear. Carpenter wrote James J. Dolliver: "I see your boys usually every day." He described J. P. as "a natural born orator. I have never seen his superior and I have heard others, whose advantages for observation have been superior to mine, express the same opinion."[13]

By the latter part of April, five clients had retained the Dolliver brothers, and they had collected $20 in fees. The brothers felt insecure, however, and asked their father to try to borrow $100 for them in West Virginia (where they thought the interest was lower) in order that they would not be embarrassed in meeting their obligations in the weeks ahead while getting "cases that would pay right away." The first years, the "starving time" for young lawyers, are often difficult, and there is much evidence that the Dolliver boys did little more than make ends meet during the early months of their practice. J. P. observed that the summer time is the "deepest winter in a lawyer's purse" in Iowa, because "everybody is at home in the corn," and few had any need of an attorney.[14]

In September they found near the center of town in the Garmoe building over a barber shop a "fine office and two private apartments at a rental of ten dollars monthly, to be paid in ways to be afterwards agreed to." They "fitted up" one of the rooms "at a cost of $50.00 with carpet and furniture and stove and all the conveniences of life." They intended to cook their own meals, but Mrs. Cheeny "forbide it positively" and volunteered to feed them both "for $4.00 a week." Thus they continued to enjoy "a fine table and company for a mere trifle."[15]

Despite financial hardships Jonathan and Robert were sure after six months that they had located in "the best State in the Union. We see new evidence of

that each day. . . . Our friends are the wealthiest and most influential men in
this county. We have through our acquaintance and friendship with Governor
Carpenter . . . a passport to the acquaintance with all the first men of Iowa."
The brothers planned for their parents and younger children to move to Fort
Dodge as soon as possible.[16]

Meanwhile, Jonathan worried about the family debts and the problem of
getting his sisters through college. "It makes me mad sometimes to reflect that
the M. E. Church has impoverished us," he lamented, referring to his father's
pathetic stipend, always less than $50 a month. "They have promised and re-
fused to pay more than enough to have paid every conscientious dollar of our
indebtedness."[17] It was up to the boys in Iowa to raise the money to send
Gay, the younger sister, to Beaver College in the fall of 1878. She wrote them
that she could not go unless they "could furnish the cash," as her father could
not do so. Fearing lest they be too concerned, however, she assured them that
since "tomatoes are getting ripe, and butter is only six cents a pound, we can
eat all we want without stint." By signing notes for her tuition, her brothers
arranged for Gay to enter college. They likewise helped Mollie through her
last year, and she was able to graduate in 1879.[18]

In an effort to encourage the family, Jonathan wrote his father, "I know you
and Mother will live to see us all five doing well in the world. And more than
that we will all live together in the same house and we are now preparing for
our reunion."[19] Young as he was, he frequently sent long letters to his sisters
at Beaver, "advising" them as to their studies and their beaux. He suggested
that they study psychology with great care, predicting with unwitting accuracy,
"it will doubtless be one of the battlegrounds of future scientific investigation."
He told Mollie she was fortunate to be rid of a suitor who was wealthy but
"brainless" and whose mother did not think Miss Dolliver was "well enough
off" for her son. "You will live to teach them that poverty with sense is better
than the wealth of a father and nonsense therewith." When he learned that
his sisters were being snubbed by certain campus social butterflies, Jonathan
was infuriated yet sympathetic. Understanding that the reason for their humiliation was their "lack of collateral," he wrote that the girls who offended them
were of that class of "intellectual and moral deadbeats" who believed "that a
little display of unearned wealth covers a multitude of defects." He sought to
console his sisters by telling them to pay no attention to the snobs and by explaining that "one of the problems of society is the right of men and women
who have never worked an hour, who have never done any valuable thing for
society, to dress up at the expense of a dishonest father and Lord and Lady it
around among their equals with the air of self home-made royalism."[20]

Dolliver had some experiences of his own with the antics of small-town
cliques in the legal profession. "There are people out here who fight us for
intruding on the preempted territory of this county," he wrote, "but . . . no

sneer, no slight, no enmity, no open or underhand opposition can engloom and sadden and overcome a genuine vertebrate of the Dolliver family."[21] A few were understandably jealous of Jonathan. He had hardly settled in town before he became known as the protege of Governor Carpenter. The Methodist church, socially and politically powerful in Fort Dodge, provided him opportunities to secure the "confidence and friendships of the best part of the community," taking "more stock" in him, as he put it, than he deserved.[22]

Jonathan and Robert took an active interest in the church and gave liberally of their small income to support its activities, pledging $100 to help pay for the new church building being erected in 1878. "We intend to discharge the duties of citizens to the church better than they have discharged them who have starved our father on a death rate salary," J. P. promised. He made an address before the local missionary society in August, and straightway the brethren arranged to have him speak at the National Sunday School Assembly in the following year.[23] Although sincerely religious, Dolliver realized quite clearly that being identified with the Methodists was politically advantageous. Furthermore, participation in the work of the church afforded him opportunities to enhance his reputation as a speaker.

His interest in oratory, reading, and politics was unflagging, and as his law business was not burdensome, he devoted much of his time to improving himself through systematic study. To his younger brother, J. P. confided his belief in the importance of being "a fluent and attractive orator. It is the best hold a man can get in the world. It is the sure forerunner of influence among men." As for reading, he borrowed or bought every book he could and informed his sister that he "must have books if we have to live on corncob soup til blackberry time." By 1880 he could boast: "You ought to see my library. I am sitting now in a room three sides of which are piled with books. Every week puts new volumes on my shelves."[24]

He kept a small notebook in which he wrote summaries and quotations from his readings. In these years he also began the practice of copying lines or paragraphs from classical literature and pinning them on the walls of his room, where he could glance at them as he walked about and thus commit them to memory. His letters and lectures in this period contain quotations from or references to his reading of Burns, Byron, Bacon, Burke, Emerson, Lowell, Whittier, Goethe, Schiller, Aristotle, Homer, Plato, Cicero, Tennyson, Longfellow, Macaulay, Fox, Chatham, John Quincy Adams, Jefferson, Daniel Webster, Gladstone, and others. By 1880 he had secured all the *Congressional Records* printed, as well as "all the public documents, the reports of all congressional committees, the reports of commercial relations; a perfect record of American politics for more than twenty years."[25]

While, of course, his studies in Iowa had no connection with it, Jonathan undoubtedly merited the Master of Arts degree conferred on him in absentia by West Virginia University in 1878. Not an honorary degree in the usual sense, this M. A. was customarily granted to alumni two or three years after their graduation if their behavior had been exemplary and they had pursued some professional training such as reading law and gaining admission to the bar, as Jonathan had done.[26]

A letter describing his weekly routine gives a clear picture of his continuing effort to deepen and broaden his education:

> Each day between 7 A. M. and 6 P. M. we study Law and our cases. On Monday evening from 7-8, exercise and "visiting," from 8 to 9, Young peoples' meeting at the church . . . from 9 to — Shakespeare. Tuesday evening Greek Grammar and Plato's *Apology* and other Greek literature. Wednesday evening, Latin grammar and literature. Thursday evening from 8 to 9, Prayer meeting at church, from 9 to 10 Sunday School Teachers' meeting, from ten to — Milton (Par. Lost). Friday evening, History. Saturday night, Politics. Sunday, *The Bible.* We have a very busy time.[27]

While this schedule of study may have represented a goal not always attained, Jonathan did read widely, and he systematically selected from his reading ideas, expressions, and phrases for incorporation into his own speeches.

The first opportunities for Dolliver to gain further experience in speaking and politics came in the fall of 1878. His friend, Governor Carpenter, Republican nominee for Congress in the "Big Ninth District," faced an unusually stiff fight because of the rapidly growing Greenback sentiment in northwestern Iowa. Jonathan was delighted at a chance to take the stump for Carpenter and the Republican ticket. "We will go out through the state under the pay and direction of the State Central Republican Committee to speak against the Greenback heresy that is threatening the old party out here in the Northwest," J. P. wrote his father, referring to his brother and himself. "We will speak in the county seats of our own District & in the principal cities of the State."[28]

The year 1878 marked a high point of the Greenback movement in Iowa. The resumption of specie payments, as provided by the Specie Resumption Act of 1875, was to take effect on January 1, 1879, and the campaign of 1878 afforded the last opportunity for protest. In the Ninth District, the Greenbackers nominated Colonel Lucian Q. Hoggatt, a former Republican, to make the race against ex-Governor Carpenter. This normally Republican district was in a state of political upheaval, and conditions were especially unsettled in Webster County.[29] Thus Carpenter had to fight a combination of political forces led by a candidate advocating popular policies.

The campaign managers decided that Dolliver should confine his speaking tour to Webster County, where he was known and where his friend needed the most help. Consequently, he did not speak throughout the state as he had hoped to do. In preparation for his participation in the campaign, Jonathan read the history of the legal tender acts and studied the *Congressional Record* to see what had been said on the currency question in the debates of preceding years. Then he wrote out and memorized a speech which he used with slight variations as he spoke in the towns and country schoolhouses. Although he advocated a specie-backed currency, J. P. made no distinction between silver and gold as the metallic standard. He cited the sound money views of Alexander Hamilton, Andrew Jackson, Henry Clay, and Lincoln, and repeated some of the warnings of those revered statesmen as to the dangers of inflated currency. He believed that the honor and good faith of the nation were at stake in the battle against cheap money. As could be expected, he devoted segments of his orations to waving the bloody shirt and appealing to the traditionally Republican voters to stand by their party.[30]

"We will elect Gov. Carpenter," Dolliver predicted a few weeks before election day. "He is a good friend and helper of ours and will do us good service in the future." Such, indeed, was the case. Jonathan also benefited from the campaign in that his study of the currency question provided a foundation for his comprehensive knowledge of that subject, while his stump speeches helped him to gain a local reputation as an effective political orator.[31]

Intending to increase his contacts and improve his speaking techniques, Jonathan prepared a lecture entitled "Wine Among the Poets" which he delivered during the winter of 1878-1879 in several towns and in Des Moines. "It is just for advertisement and nothing else much," he wrote his father.[32] Although sentiment for control of the liquor traffic was rising in Iowa at the time, "Wine Among the Poets" was not a plea for prohibition but rather was designed to entertain audiences. He discussed the tendency of soldiers to imbibe too freely and felt he would not be misunderstood when he said that "you could no more start a temperance society in the army of the Tennessee than you could raise a preacher's salary in the hot hereafter." His quotations to illustrate his main point — "If wine has inspired some of the best poetry, it has damned some of the best poets" — were drawn from Shakespeare, Vergil, the *Iliad*, and from Robert Burns, to whom J. P. was distantly related. The lecturer concluded "that behind every intoxicated adventure there are strong and prevailing motives — deep-seated in the very nature of man and in the most fascinating relations of life."[33]

Despite the realistic appraisal of the temperance question, one probably not altogether expected from the son of a Methodist preacher, "Wine Among the Poets" was well received and frequently repeated. The Algona *Republican*, in reporting Dolliver's engagement in that town, commented: "The speaker is but a young man, and he looks like a mere boy on the platform, but his manner is good and his thought mature, indicating a generous culture and talents which ought to give him a high position in the years to come."[34] Certainly this lecture was a far cry from the youthful dogmatism which characterized his "temperance harangues" in Illinois.

Dolliver's most notable speech during his first years in Iowa was at Jefferson on July 4, 1879. Headlined by the Jefferson *Bee* "as one of the grandest orations probably delivered in the state on that day," it was printed in full in several hundred extra copies of the *Bee*, quoted widely in Iowa, and reprinted in three West Virginia papers.[35] The speech was an appeal to Americans to bury the bitter memories of the Civil War and to stand for national unity. "What motives can be stronger than the unity and brotherhood of the people?" he asked. The war was all in vain, he thought,

> . . . if the battle of sections is to go on until the enmity of generations, and the chance of politics shall have worked the disintegration of the country. . . . Would that the voice of Iowa might be heard above the rhetoric of custom-made platforms in favor of inter-sectional good will and a common understanding. Let us remember that men and parties are but means to the end of good government — that the means are not greater than the end . . . and above all, whatever the fate of men or parties, may the flag that covers us all with its benign shadow, command forever our undivided confidence and support.

Prepared a few months after his twenty-first birthday, this address indicated Jonathan's increasing maturity of thought and gave some promise that he might grow away from the bitter partisanship which marred his political oratory.

Dolliver continued to "wave the bloody shirt" to some extent in the 1879 campaign, however, and for several years thereafter. This was due in part to his border-state upbringing and in part to the fact that in the late seventies and the eighties the Grand Army of the Republic became active in Iowa politics. Having only 119 members in the state in 1878, the G. A. R. began a vigorous effort to increase its membership, and by the middle of 1879, with 435 dues-paying veterans on the rolls, the permanent Iowa Department of the Grand Army of the Republic was established. Within five years 16,500 "old soldiers" had enrolled. Practically all were Republicans, and many were intensely interested in keeping alive the memories of the Civil War. They, and thousands of veterans who did not join the G. A. R., were enthusiastic supporters of any speaker who would extol their virtues and blast the rebels, Copperheads, and Democrats — those three being synonymous in the minds of many Iowans.[36]

Thus, when Jonathan was invited to take part in the gubernatorial campaign in 1879, his stump speeches, while dealing thoroughly with the currency issues, showed something of the flavor of those he delivered in West Virginia in 1876.

Governor John H. Gear of Burlington, known as "Old Business," was the Republican nominee for re-election, and again the main threat was the Greenback movement. Dolliver, already developing an acute ear for political undertones, had written Congressman Carpenter before the state convention that "Gov. Gear will be nominated by acclamation and will have a clear field. We think he looks forward to the Senate." [37] Both statements proved to be accurate.

Jonathan was in demand as a speaker in the fall of 1879. A Greene County committeeman wrote, "I am asked fifty times a day — 'When is Dolliver coming?' — We *must* have you make three speeches before election." [38] A candidate for the legislature urged J. P. to come to his aid, "as I am a business man and not likely to be an able advocate while my opponent is a Greenbacker of the Strongest Sect." [39] Dolliver spoke nearly every day in September and October, sometimes accompanying Carpenter, who was "mending his fences" for 1880. The Congressman, recording their appearance together at a meeting in Boone, stated: "J. P. Dolliver led off in an eloquent speech of about an hour. . . . He is a marvel as a talker." [40]

On several occasions Dolliver participated in "joint debates" with one or another of the Greenback leaders. At one such affair in the coal-mining town of Lehigh, where the Greenback sentiment was especially strong, he achieved a notable victory. As a newsman put it: "J. P. did himself proud and walked away with the spoils. Half a dozen of the Greenback boys . . . walked up like little men and joined the Old Guard." Taking notice of him for the first time, following his joint debate with the Greenback chairman of Greene County, the powerful Des Moines *Iowa State Register* reported that Dolliver had "acquitted himself with great honor." Another paper asserted that J. P. fully deserved to be called "the boy orator of the Northwest" and described his "flights of eloquence as soul-stirring and grand." [41]

His hometown paper, reporting an end-of-campaign rally in Fort Dodge, at which Dolliver and Carpenter were the principal speakers, accorded Jonathan a cherished tribute:

> Mr. J. P. Dolliver . . . for an hour held a most delightful [*sic.* delighted?] audience with one of the most brilliant addresses ever delivered in this city. The people were eager to hear him, expected a great deal and were not disappointed. He is today one of the most effective stump speakers in Iowa. . . . His work in this campaign has done as much, perhaps more, to inspire Republican effort and puncture the soft money bubble as that of any other man.[42]

Governor Gear was re-elected, and the Republicans not only carried Webster County, which they had lost in 1878, but also kept control of the General Assembly. Jonathan had been partly right when he wrote before the election that he was not worried about the outcome because "the Greenback party can't stand the corn crop of this year."[43] Such a statement indicates that he had gained some insight into the relationship between economics and radical politics.

When the tumult and the shouting had quieted, Congressman Carpenter wrote to James J. Dolliver, expressing appreciation for Jonathan's efforts in the campaign and informing the father that J. P. had "good health, a good education upon which to build, good habits, and good ability . . . and so far as everything like oratory is concerned he carried off the palm every time."[44]

Before the close of his second year in Iowa, Dolliver had succeeded to a remarkable degree in carving a niche for himself in his favorite realms of endeavor — oratory and politics. He had not distinguished himself as a lawyer, however, nor was he satisfied with his achievements as a public speaker. "I propose to make a strike for a more extensive repute next year," he confided to his sister as the decade of the 1870's drew to a close.[45]

-V-

Gaining A Firm Foothold in Iowa, 1880-1883

Life is a search after power, and this is an element with which the world is so saturated — there is no chink or crevice in which it is not lodged — that no honest seeking goes unrewarded.

Ralph Waldo Emerson, "Power"

IN HIS MID-TWENTIES when he first attained state-wide fame, Dolliver was already a man of impressive physical stature. He was solidly built, seeming larger even than he was — and he was a full six feet in height. His shoulders were broad, his chest was massive, his head unusually large and crowned with thick dark brown hair which he parted on the left and combed slightly back from his low forehead. Fine eyes, very brown in color, eyes which were lively, keen, and piercing, and fairly danced when he spoke, were the striking feature of his round, ruddy face. A heavy mustache sprouted luxuriantly beneath a broad but not too prominent nose and drooped obliquely downward to the corners of his well-shaped mouth. He affected no beard or sideburns and was always scrupulously clean, although his clothes often appeared rumpled, as if the effort to contain his bulk and vitality were too great for cloth and crease.[1]

His laugh was hearty and infectious, his smile radiant with friendliness, his sense of humor keen and sparkling. One who knew him in the 1880's called him "a master of conversation" from whose lips fell in torrents "wit and humor, stories and incidents, snatches of poetry and excerpts from his own speeches. . . . He was still a bubbling boy, and it was a sense of boyhood that never became wholly extinct in him."[2]

When speaking in public Dolliver appeared at ease, and his delivery, usually informal, was clear and distinct. His voice was deep, melodious, rich, and resonant and was so loud that out-of-door audiences numbering up to six thousand could hear him without difficulty. He virtually never spoke extemporaneously, for he thought that "a man can only speak worthwhile when he has worked and thought worthwhile beforehand." As a youth he spent many hours in the woods near Morgantown rehearsing orations and seeking to learn "the best pronunciation of words and to be correct in small matters." A contemporary described Jonathan in the mid-eighties as a speaker who "united the most appropriate gestures and a play of features that expressed every emotion." Often he clasped his hands behind his back or stood with one hand in his pocket. When excited or trying to impress an important point upon his audience, he moved about the platform or leaned forward and gesticulated vigorously, using his head and shoulders as well as both arms for emphasis.[3]

In the composition of an address Dolliver was most particular, believing as he did that "little or nothing worth remembering has ever been spoken in the world without the most painstaking preparation entering into the very language and arrangement of the speech."[4] He sometimes worked several weeks on an important address or lecture before putting it in final form for memorizing. His memory was prodigious, and he held at his constant command all sorts of humorous anecdotes, statistics, political lore, and Biblical quotations and classical allusions he knew in such profusion. He never spoke from notes or manuscripts. Having labored diligently in phrasing a speech, he was able to commit it to memory word for word by reading it through two or three times in advance of his scheduled appearance.[5]

A friendly newspaper commenting on Dolliver's oratory in the eighties stated: "He shuns stage glitter; is disdainful of prettiness, does not pad with large words of portly breadth, but marches his phrases in solid files — alive with spontaneity and plainness." Jonathan told his younger brother "my idea is to get a 'picture' from the words if possible."[6] He did just that. Using similes, metaphors, and symbols, he painted word pictures which enabled his audiences to see the point he wanted to make. "No man approached him in the art of expression," a distinguished Iowan wrote of Dolliver. "His language was plain and simple, but it had a fundamental quality that made it the best possible garb for the idea he was seeking to convey."[7]

Although his genial personality, his commanding presence, and his charm as a conversationalist were important factors, his brilliance as an orator was the gift which helped most to pave the way for Dolliver's success. Like Odysseus he enchanted multitudes with the majestic sweep of his eloquence, and thus, with the aid of powerful and devoted friends, he quickly became a force to reckon with in Iowa politics.

Warm-hearted and generous, Jonathan won friends easily, and his loyalty to them inspired their willingness to concern themselves intimately with his welfare and advancement. Ex-Governor Carpenter was but one of several important Iowans whose affection for Dolliver was deep-seated and of lasting significance. Another was George Evan Roberts who moved to Fort Dodge in 1879 and bought the *Messenger* which, under his editorship, became one of the foremost small-town papers in Iowa.[8] Roberts had learned the newspaper business as well as economics and politics from the scholarly George D. Perkins, publisher of the Sioux City *Journal* and member of the Iowa Senate. While city editor of the *Journal*, Roberts became a profound student of finance and developed an ability to write with clarity and logic. By 1880 he was one of Jonathan's closest companions and most trusted advisers, ever ready to give him unstinted support in the widely-read *Messenger*.[9]

Scarcely less intimate was Dolliver's friendship with Stillman T. Meservey, ten years his senior, who was mayor of Fort Dodge in the early eighties. Meservey, a banker and businessman, was a leader in the development of the gypsum industry in Webster County and was active in Iowa Republican politics.[10]

There were other Fort Dodge friends, of course, many of them very devoted to Dolliver. But Carpenter, the politician, Meservey, the businessman, and Roberts, the editor, were his favorites, and each played a key role in Jonathan's life from 1880 on.

————

Dolliver was not merely an orator of unusual brilliance nor was he simply an attractive youth fortunate in the choice of friends. He was able and ambitious. He loved history and yearned to play a part in shaping the affairs of his era. Undoubtedly his predilection for history helped make him more than a self-serving politician — helped him, as Frank Luther Mott suggested, to gain the perspective needed for statesmanship.[11] Regarding history as the handmaiden of government, Jonathan accepted Sir J. R. Seeley's aphorism: "History without political science has no fruit; Political Science without history has no root." He rated an American history book second only to the Bible as a necessity for every home, and he wrote of England's past: "If a man actually feels that he has a part in the inheritance that has fallen to men wherever the English tongue is spoken, it is asking a good deal of him to entirely subdue his admiration for the sources from which we have derived our language, our literature and our laws."[12]

Dolliver's study of history enriched his rhetoric and accounts in part for his love of the political arena. He seldom missed a Republican convention — city, county, district, state, or national. At one or another of these, in the days before primary elections, delegates drafted resolutions or platforms and selected candidates for virtually all public offices from councilman, coroner, and Congressman, to Governor and President.

At their annual city convention in February, 1880, the Fort Dodge Republicans nominated Dolliver for city solicitor, an office then held by A. F. Meservey, brother of Stillman, who fought hard for renomination. When the exciting contest ended with Jonathan's defeat of "his very popular competitor by 23 votes," Maurice D. O'Connell, a prominent attorney, offered a motion to make

the decision unanimous. Meservey, however, bolted the convention and persuaded the Democrats to nominate him, thus precipitating a heated city-wide
campaign.[13] Robert Dolliver hastily informed his father that J. P. would "undoubtedly become the salaried attorney of the city in which he lives — his
prospects are the best in the world."[14] This optimistic report ignored the fact
that the Democrats and Greenbackers had formed a "Citizens Union" ticket
and that some Republicans were backing Meservey. A carefully preserved affi-
davit, indicating a type of opposition not altogether political, quotes one A. E.
Clarke's assertion "that he would support anybody rather than J. P. Dolliver
— that he would do all he could to defeat J. P. Dolliver — that the Methodist
Church had to be beaten."[15]

The convention fight, Meservey's defection to the Democrats, and Dolliver's
youth made the race for city solicitor the center of interest in the campaign.
George Roberts now found his first opportunity to use his paper in Jonathan's
behalf, and he wrote strong editorials urging the voters to support Dolliver.
Although the Democrat-Greenback combination elected the mayor, the assessor,
and a majority of the city council, Dolliver won the office of solicitor by a
twelve-vote majority, and his friend, Stillman T. Meservey, gained a seat on
the council as a Republican.[16] Thus barely twenty-two years of age, and only
twenty-three months after his arrival in Iowa, Jonathan assumed his first public
office.

His salary as solicitor was a nominal $200 a year, but the legal experience
was useful, and he took pride in being a part of the town government.[17] Two
of the three manuscripts which indicate anything about Dolliver's ability in
pleading a case in court have to do with his service as city solicitor, and these
briefs reveal that the attorney was more concerned with entertaining the jury
and appealing to the emotions of the jurors than with the marshaling of evidence and the elucidating of legal principles. Probably that is as it should be
in a frontier courtroom.

As Jonathan well knew, the quaint observation of the old English judge that
the law is a jealous mistress and brooks no rivals has never been entirely discredited. While he loved the law, he was not as devoted to it as to politics, and
he felt that the legal profession usually merely sharpens without enlarging the
minds of its diligent votaries.[18]

In February, 1880, at the time when Jonathan was winning his first nomination to public office, his brother Robert decided to abandon law for the ministry.
Their partnership had lasted through the first two of Jonathan's difficult early
years, a period during which they had "cut their own hair and pulled their own
teeth" to make ends meet. Now Robert was sure that he should follow his
father's footsteps as a preacher. The parents expressed delight at Bob's decision, and they continued for some months to hope that J. P. also would "yet
lay by the law and become a preacher."[19]

James Dolliver had no objection to the law as a profession and no doubt as to Jonathan's ability to succeed, but the fond hope of the old circuit rider was for all of his boys to become preachers. Nevertheless, he allowed each to choose his own career, and he encouraged Jonathan in his political ambitions even while preferring that he enter the ministry. Writing to Robert in early 1880, Father Dolliver predicted that J. P. "may stand in the halls of Congress — and his voice may be heard in the Senate of the United States — and who knows but what he may be President of these United States. This is not fancy, and I know it will not puff him up — he has more sense than that." In the same vein, he informed Jonathan of his belief that "you will step by step climb up the ladder of fame and at last claim your place in the Congress of the U. States."[20]

Robert's withdrawal from the partnership after his ordination in September, 1880, did not end his close contact with Jonathan. Year after year his long letters came regularly to Fort Dodge, expressing confidence in Jonathan's future and offering advice on many matters. Robert urged Victor, who moved to Fort Dodge in April, 1880, "to follow hard upon the footsteps of J. P. who under God is destined to be *facile princeps inter pares* — the foremost man of his generation."[21] Not long after arriving in his new pastorate, Robert wrote Jonathan:

> I expect to see you as you pass upon merit from one honor to an-
> other at the hands of your fellow men until you reach the highest
> within their gift. God has set before you here just such a destiny.
> . . . I expect through you to see our name . . . made by you one
> of the illustrious names of history's annals — "one of the few immor-
> tal names that were not born to die."[22]

If the expectations of family and friends stimulate honorable ambition, Jonathan Dolliver, boy and man, never lacked an abundance of such stimuli. Nor was he wanting in faith in his own destiny — and although destiny may be an unfashionable word in the twentieth century, it was not in the nineteenth. Whether, in fact, the Governor of the Universe cared what befell Dolliver is not ascertainable, but the point is that Jonathan thought that "our ways are in the hands of Him who careth for us."[23] Despite his upbringing in the parson- age and his deep reverence for his father, Dolliver believed his destiny lay in politics not in the pulpit. Thus he did not wed himself to the law at the ex- pense of political advancement.

Before Robert left Fort Dodge permanently, he and Jonathan had attended the Republican National Convention in Chicago. Arriving on June 2, 1880, in plenty of time to attend the first session, they secured promised tickets of ad- mission from friends in the West Virginia delegation and then visited General

Grant's headquarters at the Palmer House, where they mingled with the "vast surging mob of humanity — wild with excitement." As the opening hour of the convention approached, they made their way to the Exposition Building, where they found "a whirl of excitement worse than a tornado." Their gallery seats were "very good" and after watching the "vast throng of politicians" mill around while completing the preliminary organization, the Dolliver brothers witnessed the beginning of "the battle which can not be adequately described on paper." Robert did not remain for the end of the fight, but J. P. stayed all week.[24]

As in 1876, the party was bitterly divided. The Stalwarts led by Conkling had made great efforts to round up enough delegates to nominate Grant. Aided by Don Cameron's Pennsylvania machine and by General John Logan's Illinois organization, Conkling and company argued that Grant was needed to insure party victory and reverse the trend which in 1878 had given both branches of Congress to the Democrats. Blaine, regarded by many moderates as the only man who could save the party from the Grant-Conkling movement, was again a strong contender, with Secretary of the Treasury John Sherman a third active aspirant. Dolliver favored Blaine, but the eloquence of "Lord Roscoe" Conkling's speech placing Grant's name before the convention impressed him greatly. Before concluding, however, Conkling so insulted Blaine that there was no chance of winning Blaine delegates for Grant, and the convention deadlocked for six days and thirty-six ballots. Then the Blaine and Sherman forces combined to nominate James A. Garfield of Ohio, who had attracted favorable attention as leader of the anti-Grant forces opposed to the unit voting rule at the beginning of the convention and who had made the nominating speech for Sherman.[25] Garfield's nomination pleased Jonathan. He liked the Ohio General for his "humble earnest Christian faith" and because he was "among the only professing and active Christian men in public life."[26]

The episode of this convention which made the most lasting impression on Dolliver was not the great battle between the forces of his heroes, Blaine and Grant, nor the political maneuvering which brought forth the ticket of James A. Garfield and Chester A. Arthur. It was rather the presentation to the convention of a Negro leader, Frederick Douglass, who in the course of his remarks said: "I have been a slave and a fugitive slave. I am a man. All that I was I owe to the Democratic party. All that I am I owe to the Republican party." Jonathan secured an introduction to Douglass, shook his hand, and then swore, as he later stated, "that until the last veteran Democratic leader is laid upon the shelf prepared for political antiquities, I will not put a pencil mark [i. e., "scratch"] upon a Republican ticket."[27] Although it is unlikely that he would have voted other than a straight Republican ticket had he never heard Douglass, Dolliver's experience at the 1880 convention deepened his partisanship and contributed to his lifelong sympathy for the Negro.

Following his return to Iowa, Dolliver delivered the Fourth of July address at Lehigh. When introduced as "the Hon. J. P. Dolliver," he corrected the chairman, saying he was not distinguished by that title and had no honor but that of addressing the gathering. Whereupon the master of ceremonies explained that J. P. was "a Congressman of the future." Victor, who accompanied Jonathan to Lehigh, wrote their mother that "the people all treat the Dolliver Bros. with the greatest respect."[28]

Four days later, to Jonathan's delight, the Ninth District congressional convention renominated C. C. Carpenter by acclamation.[29] Before the autumn campaign began, Dolliver spent several days at a large religious assembly at Clear Lake, Iowa, where he lectured and conducted a swimming class for young ladies. His major address was "The Basis of Equal Rights Among Men," an appeal for just treatment of Negroes, the poor, and women, which he delivered July 19 to "an 'immense' and friendly audience . . . of College professors, Ministers, teachers, and educated men from all parts of the Northwest." He recorded that he "lectured for two hours without a note and without a joke and my audience insisted so urgently that I 'go on' that I was compelled to fill in at the end with all that I knew and some things that I could not 'swear to.' I regard 'these few practical remarks' as the most beneficial move I have made in the West." The Fort Dodge Messenger reported that Dolliver's lecture was "unanimously pronounced the best thing on the course."[30]

As a result of his series of talks at Clear Lake, Dolliver received an invitation to spend a year lecturing in Europe and was advised to become a professional lecturer in America. He thought he might consider such a proposition if he could make it pay. "Do not think that I am 'puffed' up about this," he wrote his sister. "God knows I am humble in view of my total failures to realize my ambitions. I have devoted my whole life to public speaking and know exactly how many cents on the dollar my efforts are worth."[31] He never made the tour of Europe, but the idea of lecturing in the United States as a way of earning money was a seed which soon sprouted in fertile soil.

Meanwhile, the national campaign was at hand. Governor Carpenter's diary reveals that Jonathan visited him with great frequency in August, 1880, to talk "upon politics, schools, man, and the churches . . . especially politics. He is a brilliant young man." The Congressman's admiration for his protege steadily increased, and he remarked that it was a "splendid thing" that J. P. was "so attached to the church and leads such a correct and religious life."[32]

When the time came to "take the stump" for Carpenter and the Garfield ticket, Dolliver was in great demand. The State Central Committee requested him to travel under its auspices and at its expense. He spoke almost every day from early September until election day. "The politicians have foreclosed a mortgage on my lower lip," he informed his sister.[33] The Des Moines Register paid much more attention to him than in the two previous campaigns. Describing one of his two-hour orations, the *Register* reported that the hall "proved quite inadequate to accommodate the multitude who poured forth to listen. . . . The speaker is known throughout this part of Iowa as the young man eloquent and his ability to define and defend the doctrines and principles of the Republican party are known and acknowledged by all."[34]

Perhaps his repute and his success as a political speaker in 1880 are best illustrated by an experience which occurred at Scranton on a rainy night in October. Jonathan delivered his address, and the audience then enjoyed a social hour and refreshments. As the rain continued to fall in torrents, the cry arose that Dolliver should give another speech. He responded and for "one half-hour dealt with the tariff, a subject which usually is dull to the average hearer, but was highly interesting and instructive in the manner treated by Mr. Dolliver."[35] This, as far as can be determined, is the first indication of his having studied the tariff and is his first speech on that question.

The outcome of the election, which sent the ill-fated Garfield to the White House and returned C. C. Carpenter to Congress with "the second best Congressional majority in the U. S.," was eminently satisfactory to Dolliver. He had again addressed a rally in Fort Dodge, "the great event of the campaign," and he believed that he had "succeeded in doing what I aimed to do — that is establish my reputation as a public speaker in my home town."[36] November 2, 1880, marked the first national election held since Dolliver had reached his majority. He was proud not only to be able to cast his vote for a winning Republican ticket but also to support an amendment to the Iowa Constitution which provided for striking the word "white" from the qualifications specified for a representative in the state legislature.[37]

From State Republican Headquarters came welcome praise: "Your services to the party in the Ninth District were signally successful," Jonathan read, "and the most flattering reports have followed your meetings. In behalf of the Committee the thanks of the Republicans of the Ninth District are rendered you."[38] When asked by an influential politician whether he wanted a federal office, J. P. declined because "there was probably no office except among the lowest that I could get and none except among the highest that I would have." He wrote his mother that he had "been asked by all the Republicans here to run for the Senate of Iowa next year. I replied that I lacked three years of being old enough for the office. I have been urged to run for the House of Delegates of Iowa next fall but, the salary is so small and the labor so great that I do not feel like losing the time from study."[39]

———

Just at the end of the campaign a fire destroyed a large portion of the business section of Fort Dodge, including the building into which Dolliver had moved his law office after Robert's departure. Friends wanted to contribute to a fund for Jonathan's use in replacing his law books, but he refused consent to their doing so. Instead, acting upon the suggestion made at Clear Lake in July, that he try earning money by lecturing, he arranged to deliver "The Basis of Equal Rights Among Men" in several Iowa towns during the winter of 1880-1881. Friendly editors publicized Dolliver's plight and urged people to attend his lectures.[40]

When he lectured in Des Moines at the First Street Methodist Church, the *Register* reported that "at times his portrayal of the wrongs of the weak and oppressed was beautiful, so much so that he held his audience of 300 people without any disposition to grow weary for nearly an hour." The admission fee was twenty-five cents, and Dolliver filled engagements in Webster City, Jefferson, and Manson, as well as Des Moines. He also gave this lecture at Sandwich, Illinois, and Pleasant Hill, West Virginia, to help pay expenses on his trip to West Virginia at Christmas time, his first visit home since 1877.[41]

Seeing his parents after more than three years caused him to give immediate consideration to implementing the long discussed plans of a home in Fort Dodge for the family. The old circuit rider's health was obviously failing, Jonathan thought, and a letter received in April after his return to Fort Dodge substantiated that belief. "This will be my last year in W. Va.," lamented the once vigorous parson. "It is hard for me to look to you my dear boy to take care of us in our old days but so it is."[42] By July, J. P. had bought a house and the necessary furnishings — all on credit. Robert agreed to help pay the mortgage, and Mollie supervised the details of moving — bearing in mind Jonathan's plea — "for mercy sake, Mollie, keep an eye on the economics of the situation." The arrival of the family in October, coinciding with a visit from Robert, provided the reunion which Jonathan had so often desired.[43]

Although preoccupied during much of 1881 with preparations for his family, Dolliver also devoted himself to his law practice and to participation in the Fort Dodge Literary Society which he had helped found the preceding winter. The Methodists sponsored this organization, sometimes called the Lyceum, but all citizens were welcome to attend the debates and discussions. Such groups were common in Iowa in the eighties. The meetings provided much in the form of fun and nonsense, but the officers were usually serious in their treatment of parliamentary practice, and many young lawyers and orators received valuable forensic experience and opportunities to increase their fame. The Fort Dodge *Messenger* asserted that the local society did "more to arouse the pride and develop and foster the latent energies and thinking powers of our young and middle-aged men and women than anything heretofore inaugurated in our city."[44]

In his first appearance on the programs of the Lyceum, Jonathan argued that the legislation and politics of the United States were not unduly controlled by the legal profession, that Asiatics ought to be excluded from this country, and

that women should be allowed to vote in all elections on a basis of equality
with men. Subsequently he spoke in favor of state liquor control, defended the
purchase of Alaska, and delivered a brilliant oration on the value of classics in
education.[45] On this last effort the *Messenger* quoted a "glowing critic" of the
speech, who said that if Dolliver "continues to improve, he will weave from
the genius of his own brain the robes of immortality."[46]

By 1881 Jonathan was sufficiently well known politically for candidates of
significance in the state to seek his aid and his opinion as to their strength in
northwestern Iowa. In addition to filling the offices of Governor and Lieutenant Governor, the selection of members of the legislature greatly concerned
Iowa Republicans in 1881. The venerable United States Senator Samuel J.
Kirkwood resigned in March to become Secretary of the Interior. Thus the
General Assembly elected in the fall had to choose two Senators when it met
in January, 1883 — one to finish Kirkwood's unexpired term, and one for a
full term beginning in March, 1883.[47] James F. Wilson of Fairfield and Governor John H. Gear were the leading aspirants for the long term. Wilson,
supported openly by Kirkwood and secretly by Senator W. B. Allison, wrote
Dolliver, asking for "sympathy and influence" and informing him, "I will be
very glad indeed to have you as an 'out-look committee' for the 'tall grass
region' and will be glad to hear from time to time as to the promise of the
canvass."[48]

Governor Gear also wrote J. P. concerning the contest for Senator, suggesting that if he were "not committed" on the senatorship, he would be "grateful
for any aid." Jonathan, doubtless after consultation with Carpenter, who was
close to Kirkwood and Allison and who had told Gear in 1880 that he could
not support him for Senator, replied to the Governor that he was already committed to "another candidate." He added tactfully that "while I shall not be
able to aid your friends in their work, I shall not on the other hand be found
doing you damage."[49] Carpenter's diary records his interest in Wilson's candidacy. On May 16, the Congressman "went to J. P. Dolliver's office and had
a talk with the boys about a representative" — that is, a candidate for the
state legislature. Friends of Wilson, possibly including Carpenter, urged Jonathan to make the race, but he declined, largely because he lacked the money
and felt obliged at that particular time to get his parents' affairs settled. He
did, however, play an active part in the campaign to nominate Republican candidates favorable to Wilson. Enclosing a check for use in the pre-convention
maneuvers, Wilson wrote Dolliver, "Your report is a very clear and satisfactory
one, one of the best in detail I have received. I will act on your suggestions in
all cases not already attended to."[50]

Meanwhile, the race for the gubernatorial nomination warmed up. Buren R.

Sherman and William Larrabee both sought this honor. Larrabee asked J. P. for support and, although defeated in the convention, expressed appreciation for the "efficient and powerful work" Dolliver had done for him.[51]

In the fall campaign Dolliver spoke extensively, contributing to some extent to the election of Sherman to the governorship and of a General Assembly favorable to the selection of Wilson. Never overconfident, however, Wilson asked J. P. to go to Des Moines when the legislature met in January and to remain there until that body had disposed of the senatorships — "I want some of my good friends from the outside to be present during the canvass," he added. Whether Wilson's need of "outside" observers was necessary to insure fair play in the legislative caucus is uncertain, but in due time the General Assembly sent him to the United States Senate. Carpenter, writing from Washington, rejoiced with Dolliver in Wilson's success, pointing out that J. P. would be "entirely *en raport* [sic] with a Senator who in my judgment will take his place among the statesmen of this century."[52]

As he began his fifth year in his adopted state, Dolliver had reason to feel that he was making headway. Recognized by powerful politicians and known far beyond his own county as an orator and lecturer, J. P. was apparently not without honor in his home town. He had helped arrange the little city's memorial service for President Garfield and had served on a committee to aid the Governor in raising the Garfield monument fund in Iowa.[53] "It is wonderful the way the people hand Prent around," Mollie wrote shortly after her arrival in Fort Dodge, "if he were President, there could not be more fuss over him."[54] Renominated for city solicitor by acclamation in February, Jonathan won re-election without opposition, for, as the *Messenger* observed, "his services have been as satisfactory to Democrats as to Republicans, and J. P. is as popular personally among Democrats as among Republicans — no matter how widely they may differ from him in political views, even over matters of local legislation, they know that he is incorruptible, and that he has no sort of sympathy with lawbreakers."[55]

Dolliver's legal practice increased slowly. It still consisted largely of routine business such as collecting overdue bills, drawing deeds and mortgages, and representing out-of-town insurance firms. Railroads or other large corporations did not retain his services, but by 1882 he was earning a fairly adequate income which together with his salary as solicitor and occasional lecture fees netted about $200 monthly.[56]

The year 1882 afforded several opportunities for Jonathan to consider the advice offered by his elder brother, who urged him to confine himself "to new and original thought."

> Do not I beg of you be a poll-parrot in anything you have to say
> — but like O. P. Morton give the ideas for the campaign and take
> position just ahead of every other man. Let me say to you the people

do not propose to perpetuate the quarrel between sections or to keep
up the present spoils seeking corruptions of the Republican party.
. . . Take up the great issues of monopoly and temperance. . . .
You will never rise by harping over the old war issues that are dead
and ought to be burried [*sic*].[57]

If Robert misjudged the continuing appeal of the bloody shirt in Iowa, he was
quite accurate in his choice of the new "great issues" which were soon to rise
in the Hawkeye state.

The General Assembly, which met in January and elected Wilson to the
United States Senate, debated two bills dealing with the questions of monopoly
and prohibition. One, a proposal to forbid the issuing of free passes by railroad companies to public officials or delegates to political conventions, was
defeated. Discussion of it, however, highlighted the free pass practice as "a
dangerous evil in the influence such valuable favors were likely to have upon
such officials as were called upon, in the discharge of their duties, to act upon
measures in which these corporations were interested parties." On prohibition,
the legislature adopted a joint resolution agreeing to the constitutional amendment proposed by the preceeding General Assembly prohibiting the sale and
manufacture of intoxicating liquors in Iowa.[58]

Proponents of prohibition immediately launched a propaganda drive to secure popular ratification of the amendment at the special election set for June
27. They pressed Dolliver into service, somewhat against his will. When
asked, even before the legislature had met, whether he would speak for the
amendment if the politicians submitted it to the people, Dolliver replied, with
a "wiser look" than his questioner "ever saw on so young a face" before: "I
think I shall go to Europe about that time."[59] J. P. finally agreed to support
the amendment, and later asserted that he spoke "in behalf of the amendment
mainly because I am unwilling by failing to speak for it, to seem to utter an
insinuating speech against it." He obviously knew that statutory prohibition
was not a satisfactory solution of the problem of intemperance and may possibly have foreseen that it would be a political liability to the party supporting
it. As a matter of expediency, however, he did not wish to seem out of step
with his party or to incur the ire of the Methodists and other powerful pressure groups whose advocacy of prohibition verged on fanaticism. Also, of
course, stumping the state for the amendment was a good way to increase his
acquaintance and keep his name before the public.

Since he had spoken often on the subject of temperance even while a young
teacher in Illinois, Jonathan was quite familiar with those aspects of the topic
which appealed to the "drys." His principal argument is of interest, however,
mainly because it discloses his view of the limitations of property rights:

The liquor traffic is in itself a fraud and a wrong against society.
Therefore, society has a right to control and prohibit it because soci-

ety is greater than all commerce and it has the right to control illegitimate business. The legal basis of such right is simply self preservation. When property takes the form of a public damage and peril, the right of it ceases to be a right that is guaranteed and becomes a wrong to be met with all the machinery of the law.[60]

Dolliver's efforts in behalf of ratification won the admiration of reformers, and even a newspaper opposed to prohibition commented favorably: "Though we cannot always agree with what he says . . . we must admit his power as a speaker."[61]

The *Messenger* expressed the sentiment of the majority in Fort Dodge when reporting that "Mr. Dolliver's eloquent tongue was never put to worthier use, than in thus championing the cause of the homes and firesides of Iowa against the invasion of the greatest social curse in the age." The voters approved the amendment, but the courts soon declared it invalid because of a technicality. Prohibition thus became one of the "burning issues" of Iowa politics for the remainder of the decade.[62]

In March the General Assembly acted to re-district the state into eleven congressional districts in accordance with the population increase shown by the 1880 census. As a result, Webster County and several neighboring counties of the old Ninth District were combined with others to form the new "Big Tenth."[63] One consequence of the rearrangement was the defeat of Cyrus C. Carpenter for renomination in the congressional convention. Despite all that Dolliver and Carpenter's other friends could do, Major Adoniram J. Holmes of Boone won the nomination which in the strongly Republican Tenth, as in the old Ninth, was tantamount to election. Carpenter's defeat was a bitter disappointment to Dolliver, whose part in the fight for his friend can be judged from a letter the Congressman wrote him soon afterward: "I thank you, from my heart for what you have done for me! . . . I don't know how I will ever repay you."[64]

If humiliation was his lot at the congressional convention, Jonathan's triumph at the state convention in August did much to restore his spirits and enhance his party standing. Attending as an alternate delegate, Dolliver agreed to make the nominating speech for Gilbert B. Pray, a candidate for clerk of the Iowa Supreme Court.[65] Thus, toward the end of the day, when nothing much remained on the agenda except the selection of Supreme Court officers, Dolliver received recognition from the chairman, moved down the aisle, and turned to face the delegates. Beginning with a pun upon the name of his candidate, he remarked that there ought not to be any question among those who have been attending to their religious devotions as to the desirability of nominating Gilbert Pray. Then, by identifying Pray with northwestern Iowa and with the young men of the party, Jonathan whipped up such enthusiasm that within ten minutes the convention made Pray's nomination unanimous.

One who heard this speech reported that the words of the young orator "strangely stimulated the imagination and fired the heart. Tall and muscular, his flashing eyes and glowing cheeks, his forceful gestures and clear-cut, fast-flowing eloquence, together admirably embodied the ideal young men of Northwestern Iowa for whom he pleaded." Another eyewitness described Dolliver's address as "the chief incident" of the convention, one which created a furor and reminded people of Robert Ingersoll's nomination of Blaine in 1876.[66] This brief address delivered in the presence of the hierarchy of the party was an important milestone in Jonathan's struggle for political recognition on a state-wide basis.

Hence, in the autumn campaign, he was urged to speak in several congressional districts. The tide was turning against the Republicans nationally in 1882, and several incumbent Congressmen were "running scared" in Iowa. One leader in the Sixth District appealed to J. P. to help Congressman Marsena E. Cutts, shrewdly emphasizing the advantage that might accrue to him from aiding others:

> *I* want you to come — for *your own sake* and the *future, come.* Two years ago this dist. was the battlefield of the state and this year it will be so hotly worked that the eyes of the whole North West will be drawn toward it. This is your opportunity — buckle on your armor — come with your whole equipment and you will find your-self at the end of the contest with a State reputation that will take off several of the years that lie between you and the U. S. Senate.[67]

Dolliver went, and Cutts won, but by so narrow a margin that the Democratic nominee contested the election.[68] Dolliver's engagements outside of his own district won the praise he was accustomed to nearer home. One newspaper suggested that he had "the making of one of the nation's leading men."[69]

Probably for Jonathan the most interesting event of the season of political activity was the visit of Senator William Boyd Allison to Fort Dodge. If Dolliver had ever met Iowa's senior Senator before, the fact is unrecorded. On Friday, September 8, 1882, Cyrus Carpenter entertained Allison and noted in his diary that "Geo. E. Roberts and J. P. Dolliver called at our house to see him."[70] There is no contemporary record of what the Senator and the solicitor talked about at the home of the lame-duck Congressman, but in 1907 Dolliver stated that Allison had been his friend for a quarter of a century and had been among the first to encourage his ambition to seek a foothold in public life in Iowa. Allison, a suave and cautious politician, had entered Congress in December, 1863, and was serving his second term in the United States Senate when this meeting with Dolliver occurred.[71]

Probably Senator Allison's major concern during his Fort Dodge visit was his desire to succeed himself in 1884. The legislature elected in 1883 would decide that matter. Inasmuch as Carpenter was soon to leave Congress, he was free to run for the Iowa House of Representatives if needed, and his decision to make the race in 1883 suggests that the Republicans were not overconfident and that Allison wanted the strongest men available to seek the Republican nominations in each district. Their loss of three congressional seats in 1882 and the blame they were getting for the prohibition debacle furnished sound reasons for wariness, and the state campaign of 1883 turned into one of the most spirited political contests in the history of Iowa.

Prohibition was the chief issue. Sorely disappointed by the Iowa Supreme Court's invalidation of the 1882 amendment, the prohibitionists turned their efforts toward influencing all political parties to take definite action on the question at their conventions. The Greenbackers declared for prohibiting the manufacture and sale of liquor and denounced Governor Sherman and the Republicans for mismanaging the matter. The Democrats opposed constitutional prohibition but advocated a well-regulated license law. They nominated W. I. Hayes, the judge who had first declared the prohibition amendment invalid, for Justice of the Supreme Court, thus doubly challenging the Republicans to go all out for statutory prohibition. The Republican convention found no alternative to an outright pledge to enact prohibition legislation. Congressman John A. Kasson, the temporary chairman, asserted that the Republican party would not "take the side of the saloon," and Lieutenant Governor O. H. Manning coined the slogan: "A school house on every hill and no saloon in the valley." [72]

The hard-fought campaign featured joint debates between the Republican and Democratic gubernatorial candidates, Sherman and L. G. Kinne, and scathing attacks on both by General James B. Weaver, the Greenback nominee. The Republican strategists, comforted only by the knowledge that the Democrats and Greenbackers were not able to combine, pressed into service all available orators. Dolliver spoke extensively, being especially interested in the election of Carpenter and other pro-Allison Republicans to the General Assembly. The outcome was a narrow victory for Sherman, but the Republicans kept control of the legislature by a comfortable margin, and Carpenter won a seat in the lower house. [73]

As the snows of mid-winter deepened, and the politicians turned their thoughts to the 1884 presidential sweepstakes, Eliza Dolliver wrote her daughters in Cincinnati Wesleyan College that J. P. seemed happy and successful and had been "very busy with law and politics" all year. [74]

-VI-

National Fame for the
Fort Dodge Orator, 1884

J. P. Dolliver is the oratorical revelation of 1884.
Utica (N. Y.) *Tribune,* 1884

CYRENUS COLE, editor and politician turned historian, avowed that "the year 1884 [was] a marked one in the history of Iowa."[1] On January 17 statesmen and leading citizens gathered in Des Moines to dedicate the new state capitol. They listened to John A. Kasson's address "pointing up the national problems inherent in the great accumulations of wealth on the one hand and the growth of poverty on the other, emphasizing the dangers inherent in reckless political demagogy, political libellers, and irresponsible newspapers."[2] Six days later the members of the General Assembly met in their new chambers to elect William B. Allison to his third term in the United States Senate.[3]

The most important legislation passed that year, in terms of immediate political consequences, was the enactment of a prohibition law in accordance with the commitments made by the Republicans in the preceding campaign. This law provided drastic penalties for violators and awarded informers with one-half of the fines collected. With prohibition already unpopular in many areas, this system of making law enforcement a matter of profit instead of principle outraged the public so much that whole counties ignored the law, while in others there were reports of the tarring and feathering of officers who attempted enforcement.[4] The blame for the legislation and its consequences fell squarely upon the party in power at Des Moines, and in the year of a presidential election such conditions caused the Hawkeye Republicans much uneasiness.

If 1884 was a "marked one" for Iowa, it was no less so for Jonathan Dolliver. In February the Fort Dodge Republicans gave him a third nomination for city solicitor, and he defeated his Democratic opponent, G. T. Peterson, in the March election by a vote of 487 to 395. The following month J. P. attended the state convention at Des Moines, called for the purpose of choosing delegates to the Republican National Convention. He was selected to nominate

52

James S. Clarkson for delegate-at-large, an indication that Dolliver and Clarkson were already on friendly terms and that J. P. was a "coming man" in Iowa politics.[5]

Just when Dolliver first met Clarkson is unknown. Their correspondence began in November, 1878; Clarkson heard Jonathan's 1882 convention speech; and they were apparently well acquainted before April, 1884, for J. P. would scarcely have been chosen to nominate Clarkson for delegate-at-large without prearrangement. Clarkson's 1910 statement that he first saw Dolliver in the winter of 1884 "working in a ditch in his bare feet, working out his poll tax" is not credible — certainly not *that date* nor *that season*, although such an incident might well have happened in 1878 or 1879 when Dolliver was impoverished.[6]

Clarkson's affection for Jonathan became as great as Carpenter's, and his interest in and ambitions for the young attorney at least equaled that of any of Dolliver's other close friends. A dominant figure in Iowa politics since he had helped to engineer Allison's first nomination for United States Senator in 1872, Clarkson had made the Des Moines *Register*, which he and his brother owned, the recognized organ and oracle of the Republican party in Iowa. Known as "Ret," the signature he used on copy he wanted his printers to return for correction, Clarkson was a florid-faced man of sturdy body and medium height with "an imperial head on a short neck."[7] His editorial style was partisan and personal, positive and aggressive, and he had few peers as a political organizer.

One of Clarkson's obsessions was James G. Blaine, whom he had supported for the presidential nomination in 1876 and 1880. Despite the preference of such Iowans as Congressman John A. Kasson for the nomination of President Chester A. Arthur in 1884, the Clarkson followers in the state convention secured adoption of a resolution instructing the Iowa delegation for Blaine. Dolliver, pro-Blaine as usual, nominated Charles T. Morris for district delegate to the national convention and helped secure his election.[8]

The Republican National Convention which assembled in Chicago on June 3, 1884, lacked some of the enthusiasm of previous similar gatherings of the party. President Arthur, having satisfied neither Half-Breeds nor Stalwarts, found to his disappointment that there was no great demand for his continued service in the White House. Some of the young delegates like Theodore Roosevelt and Henry Cabot Lodge, and reformers such as Carl Schurz, Charles Eliot, George W. Curtis, and Andrew D. White, worked for the nomination of Senator George F. Edmunds of Vermont. Edmunds' strength and the sixty-one votes held by Illinois's favorite son, General John A. Logan, a Grant era Stalwart, were sufficient to prevent the nomination of Arthur, but no combination of forces was found to stop the well-organized Blaine movement. Thus, on the fourth ballot, after Logan had withdrawn in his favor, James G. Blaine, who appears not to have wanted the honor in 1884, became the Republican nominee despite the protests and against the better judgment of many of the best men in the party. General Logan, a Grand Army of the Republic politician whose name was besmirched because of alleged involvement in the Credit Mobilier scandal, received the second place on the ticket by acclamation. The platform adopted outraged even the Republican New York *Times*, which branded it an "insincere and senseless hodgepodge." [9]

Dolliver, attending the convention as a spectator, was overjoyed that the long-sought prize had come at last to Blaine, and the platform was surely no shock to a politician of his 1876 vintage.[10] Intellectuals and reformers, however, looked with dismay upon the results of the Republican convention, described by the *Nation* as a "mass meeting of maniacs." The New York *Times* declared it could not support Blaine, for reasons "perfectly well understood by everybody," and other important papers abandoned the party. *Harper's Weekly* and the *Nation* led the protest of independent journals against Blaine's candidacy, and President Charles Eliot of Harvard publicly wished for the formation of a new political party, "a party of principle." A conference of Independent Republicans met in New York, denounced Blaine's selection, and called upon the Democrats to do better. In Boston, Charles Francis Adams, Jr., addressing the Massachusetts Reform Club, expressed the hope that the Democratic party would nominate Governor Grover Cleveland of New York.[11] To thousands of Republicans, the nomination of Blaine, tainted as he was with dubious railroad transactions while Speaker of the House, was "an affront which made them turn anxiously toward the Democratic party." When the Democrats did make Cleveland their standard-bearer, disgruntled Republicans, proudly accepting the name "Mugwumps," endorsed him as an exemplar "of political courage and honesty and of administrative reform." [12]

To the Blaine Republicans in Iowa, already sorely burdened with the prohibition problem and a perceptible lack of interest in the national ticket on the part of the pro-Arthur faction, the Mugwump movement was disconcerting. Ret Clarkson, now an important member of the Republican National Committee, was especially anxious to whip up enthusiasm for Blaine at the state convention, called to nominate state officials, scheduled for August 20. He sought, above all, an orator who could put a thrill into that convention and head off any revolt on the part of those who blamed "The Regency" for the party's troubles.[13] Dolliver, Ret decided, was the man for the task at hand. The State Central Committee agreed to name J. P. temporary chairman of the convention, thus giving him the first chance to address the delegates.

Realizing the importance of his opportunity, Jonathan wrote and rewrote his keynote speech and rehearsed it many times in the woods near Fort Dodge. Clarkson and his lieutenants in the state organization outdid themselves in efforts to make the convention "one of Iowa's great political gatherings." When Dolliver, at 11 A. M. on August 20, ascended the rostrum in the Grand Opera House in Des Moines to assume the chairmanship, he saw seated round about him the elite of Iowa Republicanism. Even the old Civil War Governor, Samuel J. Kirkwood, was there. Most impressive of all to Jonathan was the arrival of General William T. Sherman, honored guest of the convention.[14]

As the young orator stood waiting for the "perfect storm of applause" which greeted him to subside, he appeared "strikingly handsome, tall and agile . . . in the very vigor of health and in the bloom of young manhood."[15] James B. Weaver, who attended the convention, later recalled that the appeal of Dolliver's personality was instantaneous, "from the moment he began, the thrilling sentences held his audience as by spell."[16] His address was splendidly designed to serve its intended purpose. Opening with a compliment to the "magnificent assembly" and a tribute to the party veterans, Jonathan launched into an arraignment of the Democrats and a eulogy of Blaine which produced the very effect Clarkson sought.

Within a few seconds the partisan crowd was roaring approval of such seemingly spontaneous gems as:

> The Democrats of Iowa are the farthest removed from office of any part of the human race except our Greenback brethren. . . . A Democrat has not been seen on the streets of an Iowa city after 9 o'clock on election night for a quarter of a century. The music of the telegraph office has been their annual elegy of grief. They look upon a bulletin board as an enemy of free government, and accept the first half of Franklin's maxim, "early to bed," when the returns are coming in.

Paying his respects to Grover Cleveland, Dolliver asserted that "Four years ago his name could have been prudently used as an alias under which to travel incognito all over the known world outside of Buffalo. To elect him President would be like lending money to a stranger on the train."

Although an eminent historian recently wrote that the Democratic and Republican platforms in 1884 "offered no real points of contrast,"[17] Dolliver's view of the matter was that

> . . . Democrats of the practical school have no creed except the oath of office. All the important Democratic principles are unfit for use. ,
> They have been left out in the field just where they were used last, with not even a bunch of swamp grass thrown over them. . . . It is true they talk piously of the need of reform. They work their classical allusion to the Augean stables for all there is in it. These, they assert, must be cleaned out. Yet from the general appearance of the

crowd that is on hand to do the business, the average citizen is likely to conclude that their intention is to steal the fork rather than clean out the barn. It is true, they pre-empt all sides of the tariff question. . . . You might as well try to fit the hundred headed dog of the ancient fable with a straw hat as to place a candid and intelligible tariff platform under the feet of the Democratic party. They approach that question and nearly every other like a man emptying hard coal ashes in a high wind, with their eyes shut and their backs to the subject.

The Mugwumps likewise received attention as Dolliver lambasted the "saints of Beacon Hill and Franklin Square" and "those who would have the country govern itself by the advice of persons whose names . . . are written in the herd book of high political grades." Alluding to the rival claims of purity made by advertisers of a product then much used in every kitchen, J. P. scoffed: "There are Republicans who treat their conscience as if it were the stock in trade of a baking powder factory — they solemnly protest that everybody's conscience has alum in it except theirs."

After listing, with poetic license, Republican achievements since 1861, Dolliver concluded with a tribute to Blaine, "a man who bears the grandest brain ever covered by an American hat, and the best heart ever wrapped up in an American vest . . . a man who comprehends with a serene faith the mission of the Republic and its sublime destiny in the midst of the nations and the ages."[18]

Young Albert Beveridge, in Iowa for the summer selling books to earn his way through college, stood far back in the crowded auditorium and "listened in wonder to this amazing address." When Dolliver sat down, Beveridge, who had been pro-Arthur, was ready to take the stump for Blaine, and all signs of apathy in the convention had vanished. The delegates stood in their chairs waving hats and handkerchiefs and cheering wildly as they applauded "one of the most brilliant specimens of convention oratory ever delivered in Iowa." This thunderous ovation, said the jubilant Clarkson, "shows how heartily the great Republican party of the State has united on the ticket given the party at Chicago."[19]

The *Register* printed the entire text of Dolliver's speech, and the Associated Press obligingly telegraphed it to all parts of the nation. The Morgantown *Post* and the Chicago *Tribune* quoted it extensively, and scores of papers throughout Iowa and neighboring states carried news or editorial comments. The Fort Dodge *Messenger* reprinted many of these, commenting that the keynote address placed "Mr. Dolliver at once in the front rank of campaign orators. We at home long recognized his abilities as a speaker, and he now bids fair to win something more than a state reputation in this particular line."[20]

Robert Dolliver read of his brother's triumph and wrote Jonathan that the Dakota papers "were filled with your success. . . . To say I was rejoiced does not express it. I may have been the only one who had perfect confidence in your doing what you have done but I think not. . . . Iowa has use for you, the nation has honors for you." With his letter Robert enclosed a clipping from the Democratic Chicago *Times* which attacked Jonathan and asserted that the Republicans had no desire for an orator who would give serious discussion to great public questions. "What they want is magnetism and fun. That is why they hail Dolliver as the rising sun." Knowing that there was much truth in the *Times's* article, Robert advised J. P. to ponder it carefully: "It shows what your enemies say of you — that is more important than what your friends say. Get all you can from your foes."[21]

News from the East reaching Iowa in late August indicated the urgency of the need for "magnetism" as well as money to insure a Republican victory. In the exclusive New York City clubs, Whitelaw Reid could find practically nobody who expressed the intention of voting for Blaine. The almost solid support given Cleveland by the independent papers, the anti-Blaine cartoons in *Harper's Weekly* and *Puck*, and the daily announcement for Cleveland of men prominent in business and the professions, were ominous. Some men of great wealth contributed to the Democratic campaign chest instead of to the Republican; other capitalists donated to both parties. The relative poverty of the Republicans at a time when the Democrats were reasonably affluent was an unusual feature of the 1884 contest.[22] Cleveland assured industrialists that business would not be disturbed by a Democratic victory, and many took him at his word. Unemployment, a falling stock market, and other symptoms of depression were harmful to the Republicans. The Mugwumps grew stronger and more active; young men everywhere rallied to Cleveland, a young man himself.[23]

Under these circumstances it was not difficult for Ret Clarkson to persuade Stephen Benton Elkins, Blaine's campaign manager, that J. P. Dolliver should be invited to speak in the East and North under the auspices of the Republican National Committee. Dolliver left for New York in mid-September, stopping overnight in Cincinnati to visit his sister at Wesleyan, where he addressed the daily chapel service. "I am now advertised as the only stump speaker in the United States that in addition to his other duties got invited to open a female seminary with prayer," he wrote, after enduring weeks of joshing.[24]

Perhaps such an incident was symbolic of the whole campaign. There were no important partisan issues, or, at least, as Henry Adams put it:

> No one talks about real interests. By common consent they agree to let these alone. We are afraid to discuss them. Instead of this, the press is engaged in a most amusing dispute whether Mr. Cleveland had an illegitimate child, and did or did not live with more than one

mistress; whether Mr. Blaine got paid in railroad bonds for his services as Speaker.[25]

For the young Iowa politician to begin a six-weeks stumping tour in behalf of "Boodle" Blaine by offering prayer in a Methodist school was not more ludicrous than for Henry Ward Beecher to appear in public defense of Cleveland's chastity, nor for the old spoilsman Roscoe Conkling to explain his refusal to speak for Blaine on the grounds that he did not "engage in criminal practice." [26] Truly, the "canvass of 1884 was a succession of dramatic spectacles and mass demonstrations into which men in all walks of life, and even women, were drawn by the contagious excitement." [27]

When Dolliver arrived in New York City, the papers were headlining the results of the September election in Vermont which indicated a smaller Republican majority than expected. For the moment, however, J. P. was not concerned with the significance of those statistics. Like any country boy in New York for the first time, he found the city "bewilderingly large" and was impressed with the "fine houses on 5th Avenue — Mrs. A. J. Stewart's marble palace stands there like a monument," he wrote his sister, "while Vanderbilt's houses . . . stand along the avenue perfect gems of architecture and perfect models of luxury." [28]

At Republican headquarters Clarkson introduced Jonathan to the members of the executive committee of the Republican National Committee. They assigned him to speak with Garret A. Hobart at the opening of the New Jersey campaign in Paterson on September 19. Several members of the National Committee attended this rally, as did a crowd of more than 10,000. Hobart asserted that Dolliver's address was "the best and most effective political speech ever made in New Jersey," and those on the committee who had questioned whether a "mere western boy" ought to receive the sponsorship of the national campaign organization ceased to doubt.[29] Later in the week Blaine, said to have "taken a great liking to him," introduced Dolliver to a group of distinguished men as "the young Iowa orator who is showering the land with epigrams." [30]

During the remainder of September and throughout all of October, Dolliver spoke nearly every day, and often two or three times daily, as he toured New York, New Jersey, Connecticut, and Ohio, "where the real fight is on." He traveled part of the time on Blaine's special train and on October 25 addressed the Union League Club in Philadelphia with the presidential nominee. The Philadelphia *Press* commented that Dolliver "speaks from conviction, and, with his epigrams and funny comparisons, carries his audience where he pleases." [31]

One of Dolliver's most successful meetings was at Utica, New York. There he made a blistering attack upon Democratic notions of government finance and suggested that the United States ought to use surplus revenue for the rehabilitation of the Navy. "Our commerce demands the restoration of the

Navy," he asserted. As to the policies of the opposition, Dolliver quipped: "In my judgment when American slavery died, the Democratic Party was too old to marry again."[32]

At Norwich, Connecticut, Dolliver urged his listeners to be sure to vote: "The man who, having the right to vote, is too lazy or too high-toned to mingle with his fellow citizens at the polls is the merest ape and echo of a citizen. . . . No man can turn his back on the election without openly deserting the duty of a citizen." He also denied the Democratic charge that long tenure in power had corrupted the Republicans. "A political party is nothing but an organization of the people bound together by great ideas and great principles," he argued. "Its moral character is the exact moral character of the people who compose it. . . . It can not escape an occasional scoundrel since scoundrels are very numerous on this planet."[33] Senator Orville H. Platt pleaded in vain with the National Committee to direct Dolliver to spend an entire week in Connecticut.

On October 26 Jonathan made his first visit to Washington. He met President Arthur and his Cabinet "and others very numerous and eminent," but, as he confided to Mollie, he had "lost much of the awe with which one looks at the figure of a *great man*."[34] After a brief respite at the capital, J. P. spoke at rallies in Brooklyn, Jersey City, New Brunswick, and Camden before departing for Iowa to participate in the final weeks of the campaign.

"Dolliver has completely captured the East," Clarkson reported. "It is impossible for the national committee to resist the demands for him. We have fifty applications for him to one for anyone else. His success is absolutely marvelous."[35] Naturally the citizens of Fort Dodge watched with prideful interest the remarkable progress through the East of their favorite son. They prepared a great welcoming celebration to greet him when he returned on the eve of the election to make an address at the final Fort Dodge rally. "People from all over the state are coming," Gay wrote. "They have gotten out handbills the size of one side of our house. You never saw anything like it."[36]

Five special trains helped bring the three thousand people who met Dolliver at the railroad station in his home town. The throng placed him at the head of a torchlight parade which included units of cavalry, bands, floats, and several marching clubs. The procession moved to the town square for the speeches, and there was much "spontaneous enthusiasm for Dolliver, thoroughly nonpartisan in its genuineness."[37] He wrote soon afterward: "The people turned out in great numbers to see me and gave me a most cordial and hearty welcome. That reception was altogether the most remarkable thing in my life."[38]

The election returns soon cast a pall of gloom over Dolliver and his friends. Swamped by conflicting appeals of Mugwump and spoilsman, Greenbacker and

Prohibitionist, Democrat and Republican, and swayed by unfathomable prejudices and preferences, the American voters at last ended one of the vilest presidential campaigns in history by sending Grover Cleveland to the White House.
Many have written explanations of Blaine's defeat. Jonathan blamed the Prohibition party, feeling with good reason that votes cast for that party's presidential nominee cost the Republicans New York State.[39] He also asserted that
the Republican betrayal of the Southern Negro since 1876, permitting that race
to be disfranchised, had helped to create the political situation of 1884. Thus,
as he put it, the nation's "foremost statesman went down before the candidacy
of a common hangman — a thing without example in the history of the human
race since Clodius gave Cicero twenty-four hours to leave town."[40]

Much as he regretted the outcome for Blaine and his party, Dolliver did not
regard the Democratic victory as harmful to his own plans. In a long letter to
Mollie he revealed his understanding of the advantage of being in the opposition at the beginning of a political career:

> I feel deeply this national disaster — not for myself. I sought no
> office in any man's gift. The only office I shall ever hold will come
> directly from the people. In that honorable search for office I am
> benefited and not injured by the successful candidacy of Mr. Cleve-
> land. Not only can I better pursue my purposes with a democratic
> administration but having reached office I can better make the fight
> for distinction. So that I have no personal grief to ventilate. But I
> shall not live long enough to see this nation regain the riches squan-
> dered by the folly of the people in the restoration of the Southern
> Confederacy at Washington.[41]

In October and November several newspapers suggested "the young War
Eagle of Webster County" as the next Republican nominee for Governor of
Iowa. Both the *Iowa State Register* and the Des Moines *Capital* endorsed that
notion, while the Marshalltown *Times* boomed him for Lieutenant Governor.
George Roberts put a stop to such nonsense by pointing out in the *Messenger*
that Dolliver was not old enough to qualify for those offices and that Webster
County wanted to send him to "the House to grow."[42]

From his new friends in the East also came undisguised encouragement.
Garret A. Hobart of the Republican National Committee, a future Vice President, wrote:

> Last night I dined with the "old man" [Blaine]. He wanted to know
> all about you again — How you got through the campaign, &c. Mr.
> Whitelaw Reid also seemed to have much interest in questions about
> you — all of which I could and did answer. Mr. Blaine was in great
> spirits & is about as lively a corpse as I have ever seen. . . . They
> predict great things of you & always count you "in" — So don't go
> back on your name or your *luck* & be with us when we get together
> again. I will take a lively hand in keeping you where you belong —

and nothing will please me more than to hear of your success. I so confidently expect it that I predict it at every opportune time.[43]

In less than seven years Dolliver the orator had made a favorable impression on powerful friends in his home town, in Iowa, and in the national councils of his party. Many thought the time was at hand for him to seek a greater office than that of city solicitor of Fort Dodge. As his letter to his sister and the unmistakable hint in Roberts' *Messenger* clearly indicate, Jonathan had decided to make a bid for the Tenth District's seat in Congress at the earliest opportunity.

-VII-

Hat in the Ring, 1885-1887

Caress the ear of the voter, and cultivate the county, finding the influences that control it, and making the men who do control it see that you rely on them. A good natured contest inspires belief in success.
James S. Clarkson, letter to J. P. Dolliver, 1886

MAJOR ADONIRAM HOLMES's defeat of Governor Carpenter for the congressional nomination in 1882 probably opened the way for Dolliver's candidacy for the House of Representatives at an earlier date than he otherwise could have arranged. Had Carpenter received a third nomination and election in that year, he most likely could have retained the Tenth District seat as long as he desired. With the anti-third-term tradition broken — only one Congressman, from the area encompassing the Big Tenth, was given a third nomination in the period 1850-1886 — Carpenter might have entrenched himself in the counties newly added to the district, thus virtually insuring repeated renomination. The Dolliver-Carpenter relationship being what it was, Dolliver would never have opposed his old friend. Even if Carpenter had planned to step aside in due time in favor of Dolliver, there would be a prejudice against giving the nomination successively to two men from the same county.[1]

Major Holmes, renominated by acclamation in accordance with the tradition of giving a second nomination without much contest, was re-elected in 1884.[2] If Holmes, a Boone County man, were to desire a third nomination in 1886, as Carpenter had in 1882, he could expect strong opposition on the "no third term issue." There was no valid reason, sentimental or otherwise, for Dolliver to refrain from a contest with Holmes.

Two questions, however, worried Jonathan in the winter of 1884-1885 as he pondered his political future: How could he finance a campaign for Congress? And did anyone else in Webster County intend to be a candidate for the Republican nomination? No immediate answer to either question was available. Nevertheless, in January, 1885, Jonathan wrote his younger brother, a student at Iowa's Cornell College: "My stake is the 50th Congress and that I propose to make at all hazards." At the same time he clarified his position on the governorship: "Of course, I am no candidate for that office. . . . The *Register* and other newspapers of Iowa have been thusing [sic] up the boys on that subject more for diversion than for any actual purpose . . . [and] indulging in a little free advertisement of my name in connection with that office." [3]

A month later Dolliver discovered one "hazard" to his plans for 1886. Maurice D. O'Connell, the man who offered the motion making unanimous Dolliver's first nomination for city solicitor, had become his law partner in 1882.[4] The following year the President had appointed O'Connell United States Attorney for the Northern District of Iowa, a post he expected to lose in 1885.[5] The possibility of Dolliver's being in the 1886 congressional picture was no secret to his partner, for the idea had received extensive public airing in 1884-1885. Therefore, Jonathan was amazed when O'Connell let it be known that since the Democrats were soon to take control of the United States Attorney's office, he himself would like to run for Congress. Dolliver's reaction was to dissolve the law partnership forthwith. While recognizing O'Connell's perfect right to become a candidate, he felt that O'Connell ought to give him help instead of competition. Dolliver explained the situation to his sister:

> My partnership with O'Connell is at an end. I am proposing to put the knife into him about a year from now and I thought in the meantime I had best withdraw from all business relations with him. He has been crazy to go to Congress for ten years. His wife shares this insanity. For five years of our residence here, they treated me and mine with serene indifference. Two years ago they got an idea that I was liable to be useful to them or dangerous and so they formed an alliance with me. It was a transparent device. Last year, by a lucky strike I got a grip on the people of Iowa of the most remarkable kind. They have given me the most generous confidence and applause. The people of this town have been specially kind in recognizing me. . . . Everybody in this County was convinced that I should have a chance for Congress next year, letters poured in on me, newspapers began to boom me some for Governor of Iowa others for Lieutenant Governor others for the State Senate others for the House of Delegates and others for Congress. I prefer Congress. I saw that I must get away from O'Connell and so I "made way for liberty" and today I am free. This week I shall organize the new law firm of Dolliver and More — Charlie More is anxious to go in with me and willing to give me all the time I want for politics and so I go in with hands free to make a strike for life. I may fail to realize on this investment, but whether I do or not I shall at least feel that I have made a proper effort to seize this opportunity that only comes to a man once in a life time.[6]

Having decided to seek the nomination, Dolliver, aided by Carpenter, Roberts, Meservey, and other close associates, began quietly making plans to sound out the sentiment and win the support of politicians likely to be delegates to the congressional convention. In March, Robert Dolliver expressed the hope that Major Holmes would not desire renomination and that J. P. was "now the heir apparent." If so, Robert was confident his brother could win the election, for "of course, all our Methodist people will be a unit for you regardless of politics."[7] Holmes gave no indication of his intentions, and it was too early for Jonathan to do anything about launching a drive for delegates until the 1885 state elections were safely out of the way.

Lacking federal patronage for the first time since before the Civil War, the Republicans of Iowa viewed the gubernatorial contest of 1885 with misgivings. Adlai E. Stevenson, Cleveland's First Assistant Postmaster General, was replacing Republican postmasters with "deserving Democrats," and the leaders of that party in Iowa, having arranged a fusion with the Greenbackers, had high hopes of gaining control at Des Moines after more than a quarter of a century of biennial defeats. The Democratic State Convention nominated Charles E. "Copperhead" Whiting for Governor and E. H. Gillette, a former Greenback Congressman, for Lieutenant Governor.[8]

The leading Republican candidate for the governorship was State Senator William Larrabee, a wealthy Clermont miller and landowner, who had first sought the nomination in 1881. Dolliver had supported Larrabee in that year, and in April, 1885, he received a letter in Larrabee's practically indecipherable scrawl, asking for aid and advice. Larrabee said he found "many Reps in various parts of the state entertaining many doubts of our ability to hold the state this year — I expect it will be our up hill year, yet I think with a good organization & hard work we can be reasonably sure of a victory."[9] Larrabee's forensic abilities were reported to be not much superior to his penmanship; hence, his managers enlisted Dolliver as the official orator of their campaign. So serious was the outlook for the Republicans that Ret Clarkson warned Jonathan not to overuse humor in his speeches![10]

Dolliver's first major address in the pre-convention warm-up was a Memorial Day oration at Fort Dodge. Although the occasion was nonpolitical, there were partisan overtones in the speech appealing directly to the Grand Army of the Republic, which by 1885 was becoming a force in Iowa politics.[11] The Republican aim in the campaign was to revive Civil War issues in order to divert attention from the prohibition question and fire the interest of the war veterans in the "party of the Union."

Larrabee received the nomination he desired at the August convention, and Captain John A. T. Hull, backed by the G. A. R., was nominated for Lieutenant Governor. The platform berated President Cleveland for removing Union soldiers from office, chastised the "Rebels" for infringement of Negro civil rights, and endorsed the establishment in Iowa of a home for disabled veterans.[12] The "bloody shirt" waved again when the stumping started in September. Dolliver, Captain Hull, and Colonel William Peters Hepburn, Congressman from the Eighth District, headed the list of Republican orators.

Jonathan repeatedly asserted his confidence in victory, assuring his audiences that "Iowa will go Democratic when Hell goes Methodist." He worked, however, as if he feared the devil was on the verge of serious embarrassment. One who met him for the first time during this campaign wrote of Dolliver:

> He filled my eyes and my ears to the brim, and also all my expectations. He was good to look at — a tall, leonine fellow. . . . As he spoke he paced up and down the platform, gesturing with his body and his head as much as with his arms and hands. His mind seemed to be on fire and the flames leaped out of his eyes and from his tongue. He passed from jest to pathos so rapidly that his auditors might still be laughing when they had to begin to wipe away their tears.[13]

Dolliver appealed for the labor vote as well as for that of the veterans. He accused the Democrats of being antilabor because they were not willing to erect a tariff to protect the wages of the workingman. "From the very nature of things," he told a Des Moines rally, "the new problems growing out of the rights of labor, would be committed in God's providence to the destroyers of slavery, and not to its funeral procession." [14]

The Larrabee-Hull ticket won by a narrow plurality. But for the rallying of the G. A. R., it is likely that the Democrats would have tasted victory in 1885. Dolliver's role in this campaign, enabling him to speak extensively in the Tenth District, dovetailed neatly with his personal political plans. His friends moved into places useful as lookouts and listening posts. Still Meservey was elected to the legislature, relieving Carpenter, and George Roberts became secretary of the State Central Committee.[15]

Three days before the year ended, Dolliver addressed the Iowa State Teachers Association in Des Moines. His subject was "The Public Virtue in Its Relation to Secular Politics." The speech was "devoid of the sarcasm and vehemence" which often characterized his political efforts.[16] In it Dolliver, his mind filled with his own hopes for national service, stressed the relationship of an educated electorate and an enlightened participation in politics to the maintenance of liberty and equality of opportunity. He would "throw open the doors of every institution of public education to every man, woman and child in the Republic," said Dolliver, not for any one group's rights, "but for the inalienable right of society to prepare for its service every hand which in the providence of God is called to promote the national progress."

> I would make the school house a kindergarten of patriotism, teaching to every child in the Republic the history of the country so that if in an evil hour he should be called, as thousands were called yesterday, to lay down his life he would know exactly what he was dying for. . . . I believe in the school houses. Let them flourish in this country until demagogues of every political party shall tremble and local politicians forget their kind.

In the final paragraphs of this address Dolliver spoke briefly of some of the new problems of American industrial and urban society. The following quotation indicates why certain great corporations in Iowa were not among his enthusiastic political admirers:

> The material progress of the last half century has resulted in an unexampled increase of the national wealth. Already the demand is heard from the producers of wealth for a larger share of the product of their skill. The remaining years of this century will be devoted to an intelligent application of the precepts of justice to the individual and commercial life of the nation. We shall live to see that property is something more than a mere possession. It is a moral trust. So that every man who owns a railroad, or a coal mine, or a cotton factory, or anything whatsoever, is in a high sense the trustee of the community and under a high law to use his estate without violating the public welfare. . . . The day is coming when the reckless tyranny of money must come to an end. For years the Chambers of Commerce and Boards of Trade at the great centers of American business have been managed in utter contempt of public rights; . . . for more than a generation owners of railroads of the country through the common weapons of corporate despotism, the pool, the special rate, the bogus issue of stocks and bonds have learned and practiced upon the people the most odious measure of extortion. The day is at hand when the real sovereignty of this country will learn the art of bringing to nought the devices of extortion.[17]

In commenting on the economic power of the railroad corporations, Dolliver approached a subject of increasing interest in Iowa. By the mid-eighties, when he was at the beginning of his career, the railroads had become a dominant force in Iowa politics, especially in the southern and central sections of the state. Their aim was to prevent regulatory legislation and tax policies unfavorable to their monopolistic operations. Although concerned with the selection of the Governor and the Executive Council of Iowa (which fixed property valuations), the railroad managers considered it of paramount importance to have a majority of the General Assembly subservient, or at least sympathetic, to them in order to defeat "discriminatory" bills and to assure the choice of friendly United States Senators. Through the granting of free passes to officeholders, G. A. R. members, delegates to nominating conventions, newspaper editors, and ministers; by providing rebates to politically powerful businessmen; and by arranging free excursions to Florida, Canada, or California for politicians and their families, the railroads won and kept the favor of large numbers of those Iowans who had most to do with the selection of nominees for state offices in both major parties.[18]

People who accepted these favors did not regard them as bribes. Few, if any, saw anything wrong with taking whatever they could get from the railroads. After all, had not the government granted these companies more than

4,360,000 acres of Iowa soil? As "Uncle Henry" Wallace put it, "A man was a very green one in those days who paid fare to a political convention, passes being furnished by the railroads."[19] Cyrenus Cole remembered that the "trains were crowded with those who rode on passes." They "were issued to business men to get their business, to politicians for their votes, and to editors and reporters for their influence. Even judges rode on free tickets."[20]

Dolliver used free passes for years, but he warned in 1885 that "this pass business must not be overdone."[21] Although he began condemning the financial "extortions" of the railroads as early as 1885, there is no reason to believe that he yet clearly realized the extent of the subtle political influence of railroad attorneys like Joseph W. Blythe of the Burlington and N. M. Hubbard of the North Western in southern and central Iowa politics. For one thing, of course, the Tenth District was far from the "Burlington Reservation" in southern Iowa and was never brought under the control of Blythe or Hubbard as were many of the other Iowa Republican strongholds.[22]

As an intimate of Carpenter, who had been Iowa's Governor when the so-called Granger Law of 1874 was passed, and as a supporter of Larrabee, who soon became the most ardent advocate of railroad regulation, Dolliver, the critic of corporate greed, was fortunate to be a resident of a congressional district outside the domain of the Blythes and the Hubbards. No well-oiled political machine dictated policies, granted favors, or inspired fears in the "Big Tenth." Warring factions, county pride, Scandinavian minorities, prima donna editors, and the G. A. R. were the factors for a congressional candidate to compute in attempting to balance a convention equation so that x minus the divided delegates of his rivals equaled a nomination for himself.

As winter snows melted and the lengthening days signaled the approach of spring in 1886, Dolliver devoted more and more of his time to preparation for the congressional convention, where, as he had written his sister, he proposed to "make a strike for life." He had saved some money during the preceding year, and he hoped to make an additional $500 before summer by lecturing. This, supplemented by some promised aid from his brother Robert, would constitute his campaign fund. Robert, who had accepted a church in Cherokee, Iowa, reported in March that "J. P. has the lead for Congress."[23]

Jonathan was not so sure. The G. A. R. was more active in Iowa politics than in 1884, and Congressman Holmes, who had decided to seek renomination, had "worn the blue" and risen to the rank of Major when J. P. was still an infant in old Virginia. Dolliver, unwilling to burn any bridges behind him, accepted renomination for city solicitor in February and won a fourth term by defeating J. B. Butler in the March election.[24]

An additional reason for uncertainty appeared when leading Iowa newspapers began urging the legislature to reorganize the congressional districts. The Democrats had won three Iowa seats in the national House of Representatives in 1882 and in 1884, and Republican editors thought that this was most deplorable. Clarkson's *Register* argued that Iowa was a Republican state and ought to have a Republican delegation in Congress and that redistricting was especially desirable in a year when the party had a reasonable hope of gaining control of the next Congress. On April 10, 1886, the General Assembly enacted a gerrymandering bill described as "the most obvious disregard of the principles of democracy in the history of Iowa representation. By the switching of a few boundaries, the Republican party gained five congressional districts and the Democrats were left in control of but one." [25]

In this rearrangement the "Big Tenth" lost six Republican counties and gained five Republican and two Democratic counties. [26] The district was left safely Republican, but Dolliver's efforts in the six counties removed from the Tenth had clearly been wasted. Furthermore, he faced the problem of making friends in the seven new counties. Holmes and the other candidates had the same problem, of course, but Holmes had the advantage of being in office. The franking privilege and free garden seeds were useful weapons available to the Congressman but not to his opponents. Despite some doubts of success, Dolliver announced his candidacy on April 12. [27]

Dolliver was still concerned about "Trouble from O'Connell," but by late April the Fort Dodge *Messenger* had "no hesitancy . . . in stating to the Republicans of the tenth congressional district that Mr. Dolliver will appear before them through the Webster county delegation as the unanimous choice of the party, irrespective of faction, and trusting to the favor of the convention upon the solid basis of an earnest and enthusiastic home support." [28] O'Connell, unable to get a single Webster County delegate, did not enter the contest.

By May 1, thirty-nine of forty-one Republican newspapers in northern and central Iowa had commented favorably on Dolliver's candidacy. [29] The Pocahontas *Record*, however, suggested that Webster County was not entitled to the Congressman again, but if she were,

> . . . there are better men there than J. P. Dolliver — M. D. O'Connell, C. C. Carpenter, R. M. Wright and L. S. Coffin. What has J. Prentiss ever done that he is entitled to so exalted a position? He has never fought, bled, and died for this noble country but his only recommendation seems to be "a gift of gab," which constitutes the side show to the large circus in Congress. [30]

In addition to his lack of a Civil War record, Dolliver's opponents claimed he was too young to go to Congress. Governor Carpenter, who was managing the campaign, arranged with A. D. Bicknell, a pro-Dolliver editor, to raise this issue in order that Carpenter might answer it publicly. Thus Bicknell wrote to Carpenter, suggesting that Dolliver's youth was against him, and that Carpenter himself should be the Webster County candidate. Carpenter's reply, immediately published in the Humboldt *Kosmos*, stated that he was not a candidate for Congress but was "advancing J. P. Dolliver." Then, getting to the matter of Dolliver's age, Carpenter continued:

> I desire to say, that to my mind, the objection which you say has been urged against his nomination is one among the strongest arguments in his support. I think I may say without fear of successful contradiction, that no public man in the history of this country has ever attained great distinction and usefulness who did not enter public service early in life.

The Governor cited the examples of David Wilmot who entered Congress at thirty-two, and Galusha Grow who was not yet twenty-seven when elected and "who immediately came to the front as a leader in the free soil struggle . . . was speaker of the house of representatives, and was the author of the homestead bill." Carpenter pointed out that Dolliver

> . . . will be 30 years old when sworn into office, five years beyond the age which the wisdom of the fathers fixed as the limit of eligibility. . . . If being comparatively young is an objection to support for public office under any circumstances, it is when the aspirant for public favor is not only young, but lacks the training which equips for public duties, or the balance which comes through moral stability. But neither of these exceptions can apply in the case of Mr. Dolliver. He is an educated, thoughtful man of rare good judgment and unfaltering industry. He is also a man of highest morals and purest private life, and withal a modest, unassuming and generous-hearted citizen.[31]

Carpenter wrote letters to the party leaders in all parts of the district in an effort to line up delegates favorable to Dolliver's nomination. Many pledged support, others wished to remain uncommitted, and a few took the view of Huitt Ross who saw no reason "to discharge a faithful servant for one who has never been tried," and suggested that Dolliver wait two years.[32]

Senator Allison explained to Jonathan that he could take no part in the campaign. "I am your good friend & have rejoiced at your steady growth & popularity, & if I could in any way I would cheerfully promote your plans, but Mr. Holmes has always been my friend. . . . Should you receive the nomination it will give me pleasure to aid you in any way that I can."[33]

A week before the convention met at Algona, the Fort Dodge *Messenger* discussed the situation and predicted a close race. In addition to Holmes and Dolliver, State Senator John J. Russell of Jefferson, W. L. Culbertson of Carroll, a member of the legislature, and Colonel J. M. Comstock of Algona were seeking the nomination. The *Messenger* anticipated that Dolliver would be the leading candidate but warned that this did not assure him the victory. It was gratifying, however, that "a majority of the counties, having no home candidates, and therefore the only counties free to choose from all the candidates for their value to the whole district, will send delegates directed to vote for Mr. Dolliver . . . because it completely protects him from the charge of being a too eager candidate." The *Messenger* then expressed for Webster County and Dolliver's friends everywhere the hope that the Algona convention would

> . . . put the banner of its cause into the hands of this young champion. . . . All the people of this county know that whether J. P. Dolliver goes to congress this year or not, he is, if spared his life and health, a man of great future. . . . Put him by the side of Henderson and Hepburn, and we pledge he will be found a worthy colleague.[34]

At 10 A. M. on August 19, 1886, Phil Livingston, the chairman of the Tenth District Central Committee, called the convention to order at the Kossuth County courthouse in Algona. Upon perfecting their organization, the delegates began to vote on the candidates for the congressional nomination. On the first ballot Dolliver received 31 votes; Senator Russell, 26; and Major Holmes, 15; while 25 votes went to various county "favorite sons." There were 97 delegates, thus 49 votes were needed for victory. Dolliver's strength lay in the unwavering loyalty of the ten delegates from Webster County and of the eight from Calhoun, six from Humboldt, four from Winnebago, and three of the five from Pocahontas County.[35] The balloting continued all afternoon, and when the 75th ballot showed Dolliver with 31 votes, Russell with 26, and Holmes with 19, the convention adjourned for dinner.

Public interest in the proceedings was intense. The courtroom was thronged with spectators when the balloting resumed at 7 P. M. It was soon clear that Dolliver had lost none of his following during the dinner hour. As the night session dragged on, his lead climbed until at one time he had 45 and 10/11 votes. Had he received 1 and 1/11 more votes, he would have won, because two delegates friendly to him had agreed not to vote for him until he could attain 47 votes, when these two "reserves" would put him over. After the 164th ballot, the convention adjourned until Friday. Jonathan still led with 38 votes, but the outcome remained uncertain. The field had narrowed to Dolliver, Holmes, and Russell when the voting began the next morning. Major Holmes apparently used the night's recess to perfect his tactics. On Friday's first ballot Holmes's Boone County delegates cast their 13 votes for Senator Russell. This indicated an agreement between the forces of the two veteran candidates: if Russell could not be nominated with the aid of Holmes's home county, his cause was demonstratively hopeless. Russell's maximum vote was 47. Dolliver could easily dictate Russell's nomination, but the Dolliver delegates stood firm; they had made no deals. Then, on the 188th ballot, Russell's delegates all switched to Major Holmes, giving him 63 votes to 34 for Dolliver. It is said that Governor Carpenter wept while R. M. Wright of Webster County moved, on Dolliver's behalf, to make Holmes's nomination unanimous.[36]

The convention was free of acrimony throughout. The candidates had finally combined forces to defeat Dolliver largely because all feared that if he were elected he would remain in Congress year after year, and no one else would get a chance to serve. Following an acceptance speech by Major Holmes, the chairman presented Dolliver to the convention as "a future Congressman from this district." Jonathan had prepared two speeches before going to Algona — one for victory, one for defeat. The latter, which he delivered, was "one of the most captivating speeches that ever came from a man under such circumstances." He began by describing a Dore illustration in Dante's *Inferno* which depicted a man holding his own head at arm's length. He suggested that "we whose heads have been amputated by the amiable warrant of this convention might fitly adopt this work of art as a faithful sketch of the exercises in which we are now engaged." After thanking the delegates who had faithfully supported him, Dolliver expressed the opinion that

> . . . all personal considerations are swallowed up in a genuine enthusiasm for the chosen candidate of the Republican party. I leave the convention, as I entered it, with the most cheerful sentiments toward everybody, and especially toward those whose superior skill in the practice of the movement cure has enabled them to cover me up; and in the same cheerful frame of mind I promise them that I shall dig out, and with the platform of the republican party pasted in my hat, and the straight ticket in my hand, I shall have no trouble in finding an open field for such service as I may be able to render to the common cause.[37]

It was a witty and eloquent speech, carefully thought out and skillfully delivered. Several people remarked that if he could have made it at the beginning instead of at the end of the convention, he would have won the nomination. The Webster City *Freeman* predicted that within four years Dolliver would win a unanimous nomination and thereafter "have a series of re-elections," because "a man with such broad and generous culture at his age, with a character so pure, and a personality so magnetic . . . can never be kept down in this free country."[38]

Five days after his defeat at Algona, Dolliver attended the Republican State Convention in Des Moines, and as his "silver tongued eloquence" was considered "indispensible to an Iowa convention," the delegates insisted that he speak, although he was not scheduled to do so.[39] Greeted with great applause and cheering, Dolliver, alluding to the result of the congressional convention, began: "It looks as if I ought to have taken a change of venue." He sought to arouse the party for the fall campaign by attacking the Democrats and appealing to the Republicans to pursue liberal policies. There were two kinds of Democrats in Iowa, he shouted, "the copper-heads and sore-heads. The first are Democrats because they had a delicacy about tendering their services to the country during the war, and the last because the country had a delicacy about accepting their services since the war." As for the Republicans, Dolliver predicted:

> If the party shall wisely put itself in harmony with the new and living issues of justice that concern the problems of labor and industry of the country, if it shall wisely take a stand in favor of the right and the helpless and against those who whether right or wrong are not helpless, if they do that faithfully and interpret in the future as they have in the past the best brain and conscience of the country, there is living to-day no one of us that shall set a limit to the prosperity and power of the party.[40]

This address was received with enthusiasm, and "it fully sustained the speaker's reputation as being the foremost young orator of Iowa." The convention then elected Dolliver as one of four delegates from the Tenth District to attend the Republican Anti-Saloon meeting in Chicago on September 16.[41]

After he returned from Chicago, Jonathan prepared to participate in the fall campaign. He offered to take the stump for Major Holmes and agreed to speak in several towns outside of the Tenth District.[42] In 1886 the Democrats and Greenbackers again effected a fusion in Iowa, and despite all the Republicans could do, the Democrats retained two congressional districts. In the Sixth District, General James B. Weaver won re-election, and in the Second, a Democrat won over the venerable Governor Kirkwood. The defeat of Colonel W. P. Hepburn in the Eighth by a so-called "Independent Republican" was an unexpected reverse. Major Holmes won, however, and the Republicans carried all the state offices.[43]

On Washington's birthday, 1887, Dolliver attended the annual banquet cf the Michigan Club in Detroit as one of the guests of honor. This affair, a Republican pep rally, featured as orators of the evening Representatives John S. Wise of Virginia and C. A. Boutelle of Maine, Governor C. G. Luce of Michigan, Senator Joseph R. Hawley of Connecticut, and Dolliver.[44] The Detroit *Tribune* printed the text of Dolliver's speech, entitled "Washington the Soldier," and described the "Hawkeye spellbinder" as follows:

> In conversation Mr. Dolliver is very entertaining. He talks quietly, yet in a convincing way, and is chock full of information on public questions. In appearance he is tall, angular, and stoop-shouldered. His head is large and well formed, and covered with thick brown hair. A heavy mustache of a like color is his only facial ornamentation. . . . Dolliver [is] a picturesque figure that reminded many of the elder Republicans of that eloquent young orator who nearly half a century ago electrified the then youthful West — the Abraham Lincoln whose masterly addresses from the stump first called the attention of the country to that man of genius and destiny.[45]

Except that any comparison of Dolliver and Lincoln either in appearance or in oratorical ability required a vivid imagination on the part of the reporter, this word picture was quite accurate as of 1887. Another paper, in detailing Jonathan's activities in Detroit, mentioned his "lighting a cigar and fixing it in the corner of his mouth." This item caught Robert Dolliver's eye. He irately dispatched a sermon-length letter depicting the evils of smoking and inquiring whether J. P. was "still a Christian!"[46]

After his return from Michigan, Dolliver seems to have spent the spring and summer of 1887 rather quietly. His correspondence indicates that several candidates for state offices consulted him or sought his support and that he was keeping in touch with political affairs in the Tenth District.[47] He did not participate actively, although he was present, in the Des Moines convention of August 24 which renominated Governor Larrabee and adopted a platform favoring a protective tariff, effective regulation of the railroads, and liberal pensions for veterans.[48] When the campaign began in October, Dolliver spoke almost every day in behalf of the state ticket, and following the Republican victory at the polls, he received the thanks of the state chairman for "abundant services."[49]

Dolliver was determined to try again for the congressional nomination in 1888. Not all of his friends agreed that this was a wise course. On Christmas Day, 1887, Ret Clarkson wrote J. P. a sixteen-page letter urging him to consider becoming editor of the *Iowa State Register* to "keep up its power & increase it." In time, Ret more than hinted, Dolliver could use his "trained strength" for a "larger field," and Clarkson "could open the way for that." Just what Clarkson had in mind for the future is not altogether clear. He expected a renomination of Blaine in 1888, and apparently planned to accept an appointment which would remove him from Iowa. Possibly he hoped that Dolliver could gain sufficient political stature from editing the *Register* a few years to enable him to secure election to the Senate or appointment to the Cabinet.[50] A Pennsylvania lawyer had written Jonathan the preceding year, "I think your Congressional defeat is a blessing — if you would spend a winter around Washington & see the kind of cattle that go to Congress, you would be ashamed to associate with such a crowd. Nine-tenths of them are dead beats."[51]

Jonathan did not agree. He declined Clarkson's plea that he become an editor, just as he had his father's that he enter the ministry. He had tried and failed to "make the 50th Congress"; he aimed next at the Fifty-first.

-VIII-

Twofold Victory: The Election of 1888

In choosing Dolliver the Convention has made no mistake. . . . As a brilliant orator and a clear thinker, he has impressed himself upon public opinion very strongly, and given evidence of special fitness and qualifications for Congressional duties. It is apparent that he is beginning a career which will be honorable to himself and to his District and State.

Des Moines *Register*, August 22, 1888.

As THE YEAR 1888 approached, both parties turned their attention to the presidential and congressional contests near at hand. In his annual message to Congress, December 6, 1887, President Cleveland had discussed only one subject, the tariff. He blamed high import duties for a Treasury surplus which was keeping out of circulation money needed for an expanding economy, a situation which might soon produce business stagnation. Pointing out the relationship between the tariff and the development of trusts, "which have for their object the regulation of the supply and price of commodities," the President charged the protective system with increasing the living costs of the poor in order to give immense profits to favored manufacturers. As a remedy, Cleveland proposed a reduction of the import duties on necessities and a general readjustment of rates to eliminate "hardships and dangers."[1]

The tariff immediately became the issue of the 1888 campaign, the salvation of the Republicans who lacked any other important issue. Cleveland's attitude had "the effect of committing his party unreservedly to a policy of opposition to the existing protective system, and so of making this question more distinctly a party matter than it had been at any time since the Civil War."[2]

The Democratic-controlled House, after months of debate, passed the Mills bill which provided for mild reduction in duties upon manufactured goods and placed a few raw materials on the free list.[3] Since the Republicans had a majority in the Senate, Congress enacted no tariff legislation. The Senate leaders kept that body in session until late October, while Allison of Iowa, Nelson Aldrich of Rhode Island, and others framed a substitute measure under the guise of amending the Mills bill. Their strategy was to prolong the session, get a tariff bill set up in the Senate, and then adjourn shortly before the election, leaving the impression that if the Republicans won in November the tariff would be left protective and the problem of the surplus disposed of by reducing internal taxes on whisky and tobacco.[4]

While the politicians in Washington prepared for battle over the tariff, those in Des Moines became embroiled in the equally thorny and politically explosive question of railroad regulation. Governor Larrabee devoted much of his second inaugural address in January, 1888, to an arraignment of the transportation monopolists. He specifically requested legislation fixing maximum passenger fares and freight rates, and empowering a state-financed board of commissioners to reduce excessive rates. "Overnight the State was thrown into a turmoil" with one set of extremists proposing the re-enactment of the Granger law repealed in 1878, while on the other hand railroad spokesmen raised the cry that Larrabee's proposals would bring disaster if adopted.[5]

The terrific controversy aroused by Larrabee's program threatened to split the Iowa Republicans at the very time the state leaders were laying plans to secure the presidential nomination for Senator Allison. Ret Clarkson, knowing the probable reaction of Eastern industrialists to any revival of "Grangerism," was furious at the Governor's ill-timed attack on the railroads. "This will alienate many friends," he wrote Allison.[6] The *Register* came out in opposition to the reformers in the statehouse who naturally resented the lambasting given them by that organ.[7] In the midst of these political storms and of a northwestern blizzard, the Republican State Convention assembled at Des Moines for the purpose of selecting delegates to the national convention and of perfecting an Allison-for-President movement.

Doubtless recalling 1884, the State Central Committee selected J. P. Dolliver as temporary chairman of the state convention. His task was to bring harmony to the party. He was known to be an intimate friend of Larrabee who wanted him on his staff and whose daughter later married Dolliver's younger brother, Victor.[8] Likewise, everyone knew of Clarkson's regard for J. P. and believed that if anyone in the state were acceptable to both hostile chieftains, it was Dolliver. He had the good will of all factions in Iowa politics and the eloquence to persuade the convention to unite in choosing a strong slate of pro-Allison delegates.[9]

Dolliver, although in deep mourning at the unexpected death of his beloved mother on March 1, accepted the invitation to preside and prepared his address with the usual care. His keynote speech, delivered March 21, emphasized the thesis that a Westerner could unite the national party and that the state should forget its bickering and get solidly behind "William B. Allison, the log-cabin student of Ohio — the statesman of Iowa." If Allison won the nomination, Jonathan concluded, the Republican party could face a new era of American politics — "an era of peace, of fraternity, of commercial expansion, of industrial growth; an era that shall emancipate labor; that shall control the basis of wealth; that shall sanctify the rights of citizenship; that shall perfect popular education; that shall realize in the mission of the Republic all the dreams of patriotism."[10]

One who heard this speech recorded that it accomplished its purpose and that he would never forget Dolliver's "kindly eye, flashing with good humor, and at times kindling with the glow of prophetic vision and the fire of a great purpose; the resonant voice responding to all the lighter shades of humor and on occasion stirring the assemblage to a pitch of enthusiasm such as in medieval times, under the stirring appeal of Peter the Hermit, impelled men to march to the rescue of the Holy Sepulchre."[11] Congressman David B. Henderson, later Speaker of the House, wrote of his "delight over your grand speech at the convention. . . . You drew me closer & closer & closer to you until you had me wholly under the spell of your thrilling power."[12]

During the afternoon session, when the time came to elect the permanent chairman of the convention, the news spread that the committee on organization intended to report Governor Larrabee as the choice for that honor. This, of course, was completely unacceptable to those who were managing Senator Allison's campaign. They did not want Allison in any way associated with Larrabee, whom Eastern Republicans regarded as the reincarnation of the spirit of Grangerism. The Governor suddenly found that he was "ill," and some quick-witted soul arose to offer a motion from the floor that the temporary organization be made permanent. This carried easily, and Dolliver presided throughout the two-day convention.[13]

But the end was not yet. When the balloting for delegates-at-large began, enthusiastic pro-Allison men nominated Dolliver. He immediately protested that he was not a candidate and must not be voted for. Nevertheless he was elected, defeating John Y. Stone, the Attorney General, who was slated for the place. "The Convention," wrote Cyrenus Cole who was present, "literally went Dolliver mad."[14] A delegate later informed Clarkson that had it been necessary to do so, many would have insisted upon supporting Dolliver even as against Clarkson himself.[15]

In February, Dolliver had written Senator Allison: "I assure you that the great pleasure of my life will be the opportunity of giving you a hearty support in the arduous months that are before the Republican party. I have the most perfect faith in your nomination and election as President of the United States."[16] Blaine, the logical nominee of the party, if it were to choose its real leader, had removed himself from the race. The Iowa Republicans therefore felt confident that Allison had a good chance for the nomination in 1888. Congressman D. B. Henderson urged Carpenter to try to get Iowa united behind Allison and to discourage any movement for Blaine, because "the nomination of Mr. Blaine means another defeat for us."[17]

Clarkson, still a member of the National Committee and a Warwick by inclination, was the leader of those working in Allison's behalf. His chief aides were Representative Henderson and Jacob Rich, president of the Dubuque Linseed Oil Company and an intimate friend of Allison's. Dolliver, in addition to his work in Iowa, which included a major address at the first annual convention of the Hawkeye Republicans, also went to Minnesota, where he attempted, unsuccessfully, to "sew-up the Minn. delegation" for Allison.[18]

The leading aspirants for the nomination were John Sherman of Ohio; Walter Q. Gresham of Indiana; Chauncey Depew, president of the New York Central Railroad; Senator Joseph R. Hawley of Connecticut; ex-Governor Russell A. Alger, the Michigan match king; and Benjamin Harrison of Indiana, a dark horse secretly supported by Stephen B. Elkins as Blaine's choice for the nomination.[19]

Clarkson, Dolliver, Henderson, and Rich arrived in Chicago two weeks before the convention, to open Allison headquarters in the Grand Pacific Hotel. At the same time a large number of railroad men gathered for an annual meeting in the Windy City. From them Clarkson heard disturbing reports that certain tycoons of transportation were "very angry" at the action of Iowa's railroad commission in lowering maximum rates. "Some of the Eastern men are inclined to take revenge on you," Ret wrote Allison, who, of course, had had nothing to do with the railroad reforms of Governor Larrabee's administration.[20]

By Wednesday, June 18, the opening day of the convention, there were about 3,000 Iowans in Chicago to parade, shout, and carry banners for Allison. The Senator remained in Washington, where the "great tariff debate of 1888" raged on. Dolliver helped manage the Allison headquarters. A young Wisconsin Congressman, Robert M. La Follette, drifted into the Grand Pacific Hotel, where, as he recalled many years later, he first saw Dolliver

> . . . mounted on a table, addressing the crowd of delegates. . . . I see his commanding figure as plainly now as then, and again I hear his animated and stirring appeal . . . pleading with visiting delegates to nominate Allison as the Republican candidate for the Presidency. For several days before the balloting began this remarkable young orator made the Iowa headquarters the center of interest when the convention was not in session.[21]

It was strange, if not stupid, in view of Dolliver's widespread fame and popularity as an orator, that the Iowans did not select him to present Allison's name to the convention. Instead, they chose Colonel William P. Hepburn, merely a better than average speaker. Hepburn had suffered defeat for re-election to Congress from Iowa's Eighth District in 1886, and he had also failed in his effort to supplant Allison's friend, James F. Wilson, for the sena-torial nomination in 1888.[22]

Perhaps it made no difference who spoke for Allison at Chicago. Iowa was not a "doubtful" state, to be awarded a nomination for the sake of electoral votes in November. Her senior Senator never received as many as one hun-dred votes on any ballot, yet he almost emerged as the winner when a group of leading delegates met after the third indecisive ballot and agreed to try to swing their states to Allison as a compromise candidate. This agreement was blocked by Chauncey Depew of New York, who had withdrawn from the race because of the bitter opposition of the agrarians to the nomination of a railroad president. The "Allison" arrangement was dropped. If it had worked, New York, Illinois, Wisconsin, Pennsylvania, Massachusetts, and California would have joined Iowa and Tennessee, and possibly Missouri, in voting for Allison. "I think," recorded Senator George F. Hoar of Massachusetts with historical inaccuracy, "no other person ever came so near the Presidency of the United States and missed it."[23]

When on Monday the sixth ballot showed that Allison had no chance, Clark-son had Henderson withdraw Allison's name, cast Iowa's votes for Harrison, and release Allison's non-Iowa delegates. Clarkson, a Hoosier native and a devotee of Blaine, played an important part at a crucial moment in swinging a block of delegates to Harrison on the seventh ballot, and thus starting a band wagon movement which pushed the Indianian to victory over Sherman and Gresham on the eighth roll call. Levi P. Morton of New York, a state almost as "doubtful" of going Republican as was Indiana, was the first-ballot choice for the vice-presidency.[24]

The platform placed the Republicans on record as "uncompromisingly in favor of the American system of protection," denounced the Mills bill "as de-structive to the general business, the labor, and the farming interests of the country," and advocated "the entire repeal of internal taxes, rather than the surrender of any part of our protective system." The party also favored "the use of both gold and silver as money."[25]

Shortly after the convention adjourned, Ret Clarkson became vice-chairman of the Republican National Committee and chief assistant to Matthew Quay, whom the great industrial interests demanded as chairman of the committee and generalissimo of the Republican campaign.[26] The Democrats had already renominated President Cleveland and adopted a platform advocating tariff re-form and the reduction of the surplus. Although the campaign was languid until late in the summer, behind the scenes the Republicans were raising a huge slush fund from manufacturers desiring a high tariff.[27]

Meanwhile, back in Fort Dodge, Dolliver and his friends prepared for their third convention of the year. His service at the state and national convention had increased Dolliver's prestige and encouraged his supporters in their efforts to forward his nomination for Congress.[28] The formal announcement of his candidacy had appeared in the Fort Dodge *Messenger* on April 12, 1888, and in May, George Roberts ran a forceful editorial endorsing Dolliver and urging that Major Holmes, having had three terms, should step aside, as "the honor should be passed around."[29]

Holmes, however, was eager to remain in Congress. Dolliver's friend, A. J. Barkley, a Boone banker, wrote that Holmes was seeing to it that "large quantities of garden seeds are being distributed where they will make friends, and to fickle fellows who like attention."[30] Clarkson did not think it wise for Dolliver to run against the Major again, but said if J. P. wanted the nomination, "we must all help you to get it."[31] Possibly Clarkson still hoped to persuade Dolliver to take over the *Register*. More likely he felt that Major Holmes deserved renomination because he was a war veteran. The Iowa G. A. R. and the *Register* had been crusading for months against Cleveland's pension vetoes and his order to restore captured battle flags to the Southern states, and in behalf of sending more G. A. R. members to the House and Senate. It was taken for granted in the late eighties that any Republican with a Civil War record was entitled to votes, and eight of Iowa's eleven Congressmen in the Fiftieth Congress were Union veterans.[32]

Nevertheless, Dolliver was determined to make a greater effort in 1888 than he had in 1886. He wrote scores of letters to leading men in all occupations in each county of the district, asking their support in the township caucuses and county conventions. Ex-Governor Carpenter and George Roberts attended many of the county conventions to look after Dolliver's interests. The excitement was so great at the Humboldt County meeting that a man who was for Dolliver deposited a "receipt instead of a ballot," thus making J. P.'s majority "twenty-six instead of twenty-seven."[33]

Dolliver's lack of money was a handicap. A. J. Barkley sent him $50 and wished it "could be ten times as much."[34] Despite all obstacles, however, it was clear the week before the convention assembled that Dolliver had almost enough pledged delegates to insure his nomination. The delegations from Webster, Hamilton, Humboldt, Hancock, Winnebago, and Calhoun counties and two to five of the Pocahontas County delegation were for Dolliver, thus assuring him at least forty of the forty-eight votes needed for victory. Congressman Holmes had the eighteen votes of Boone and Kossuth counties, with possibly three from Emmet County. Judge J. P. Conner was Crawford County's "favorite son," and either he or Captain Albert Head of Greene County would get Carroll County's seven votes. Of the only other candidate, the *Messenger* observed: "Captain E. J. Hartshorn has just been married and ought to have enough to make him contented and happy, and will doubtless be at the convention in a very tranquil frame of mind. He will be supported by Palo Alto County with four votes and perhaps by Emmet County."[35]

The convention met at Webster City on Monday, August 20, the opening session beginning at 3 P. M. to effect a temporary organization and then adjourning until 8 P. M. By unanimous consent there were no nominating speeches. On the first two ballots Dolliver received 42 votes; Holmes, 18; Head, 17; Hartshorn, 12; and Conner, 8. Eight of Dolliver's votes came from Hamilton County, the home of the popular State Senator John L. Kamrar of Webster City. In an effort to prevent Dolliver's nomination, his opponents persuaded Kamrar to become a candidate, and on the third ballot the Hamilton County delegates began voting for him. As a result, Dolliver's total on the following 34 ballots seldom exceeded 34 and was sometimes as low as 32.[36]

The session adjourned before midnight, and many county caucuses took place before sun-up. The balloting continued Tuesday morning without decisive results. Dolliver received 45 votes on the 56th ballot, but his total dropped to 39 on the 58th. Judge Conner's highest vote was 42 on the 77th roll call; Senator Kamrar's maximum never exceeded 45. In the afternoon session, Major Holmes, who had only one vote on the 92nd ballot, boomed ahead to 47, one short of victory. When Holmes did not find that needed vote on subsequent ballots, the Hamilton County delegates abandoned Kamrar and in concert with Judge Conner's Crawford and Carroll County men and the delegations from Pocahontas and Palo Alto counties, joined Webster County on the 110th ballot to cast 55 votes for J. P. Dolliver. A motion making Dolliver's nomination unanimous immediately carried. He and Major Holmes were in a nearby barbership getting shaved when the news reached them. They sat up in their chairs and shook hands. A reporter recorded that "Major Holmes acquiesced very cheerfully in the result."[37]

Explanations of Dolliver's victory in 1888 were numerous. Two accounts taken together give a valid picture. First, according to the *Register*:

> The end came when it had been completely demonstrated that Dolliver had enough votes for him, either as first or second choice, to hold the convention in deadlock and that these delegates were disposed to hold it in deadlock until frost came rather than nominate anyone but J. P. His safety lay in the fact that the delegates were for him after their home candidates, and were too earnestly for him to be willing to trade him off for some distant possibility of nominating their first choice.[38]

For example, the eight Hamilton County delegates left Dolliver for Kamrar, but voted for no candidate except these two, and when they saw Kamrar could not win, they returned to Dolliver.

Secondly, Judge Conner, long Dolliver's friend, wrote him years later:

> I some times think you never understood fully just how much your first nomination depended upon the effort of your friends [in Crawford County]. This county had been promised to Maj. Holmes long before the convention and the plan of Hon. J. Fred Myers both in and out of his paper was to minify your qualifications for the office and magnify those of Mr. Holmes and with this fact against you and the further fact that the Grand Army people were marching to the same tune there was little hope of your being able to prevent Holmes getting the delegation. . . . I am sure you understood at Webster City that while some from this county favored my nomination there was a further purpose demonstrated that you were not to be beaten by anyone else and *certainly* it was within our power at any time to have nominated some other party had the disposition existed.[39]

Judge Conner's statement is particularly significant in view of the fact that Holmes could have won the nomination had he received the Crawford County delegation vote as he had anticipated before Conner became a candidate. Further evidence supporting Conner's story is a news item which appeared two days after the convention, praising Judge Conner "for his integrity and character and for his manly action in declining to enter a combination to sacrifice Dolliver for the sake of the chance, good though that chance was, to nominate himself."[40]

There was great interest throughout Iowa in the outcome of the Tenth District contest. The *Register* devoted its entire front page, except for advertising, to news of Dolliver's victory, and other papers in all sections of the state gave it extensive coverage. Major Holmes's home town paper, the Boone *Republican*, commented: "If we were to have a change no one could suit us any better than Mr. Dolliver."[41] Robert Dolliver, overjoyed at the nomination, wrote from Cherokee: "Your victory fills our people here with jubilation." The headline in George Roberts' *Messenger* most nearly expressed the feeling of the victor: "The Battle is over and J. P. Dolliver goes to Congress."[42]

When J. P. arrived home from Webster City, a heart-warming welcome awaited him. "There are precedents for the nomination of a Fort Dodge man for office," an observer wrote, "but no precedents for the royal and whole-hearted reception given to Dolliver yesterday. . . . He was met at the depot by the Young Men's Marching Club, drum corps and band, and an enthusiastic crowd. In the evening a magnificent reception was held at the rink."[43] There was little time, however, for Dolliver to relax and enjoy the felicitations of his fellow townsmen.

The national campaign was in full swing in the East. Clarkson, as well as Republican leaders in Maine, where elections came in September, insisted that Dolliver take the stump for Harrison in that state not later than August 27.[44] While touring Maine, J. P. renewed his acquaintance with Blaine, and met, probably for the first time, Congressman Thomas B. Reed of Portland and Senator Nelson W. Aldrich of Rhode Island.

By late September, Dolliver was back in Fort Dodge preparing to campaign in his own behalf. His Democratic opponent was Captain J. A. O. Yeoman, a distinguished Fort Dodge lawyer, who had been his party's nominee for Lieutenant Governor of Iowa in 1879. His fame as the "only officer who had actually risked his life" in the efforts to capture Jefferson Davis, an exploit for which Congress awarded Yeoman $3,000 of the $100,000 granted for the arrest of the Confederate President, made Yeoman a foe capable of attracting many G. A. R. votes. To offset this, Major Holmes and Governor Carpenter toured the district for Dolliver, and no effort was spared to link Yeoman with the head of his ticket who had vetoed pension bills for Union veterans.[45]

Since Dolliver and Yeoman were friends, and since neither possessed abundant resources, they agreed to conduct their campaign as a series of joint debates. During October they appeared together throughout the "Big Tenth" at approximately twenty towns. Their meetings were usually three hours in duration, with each candidate speaking an hour and each taking a half-hour for rebuttal. For the most part they confined their speeches to the tariff. At Algona, for example, Yeoman supported the Mills bill and attacked the high tariff policies of the Republicans, which he thought were responsible for the "frequent and excessive robberies perpetrated by the bloated manufacturers of the East through the enabling power of the Protective system." Dolliver's reply was that there were far more "gigantic trusts" in free-trade England than in America, and he attacked the Mills bill as being sectional in character and inadequate in scope. Admitting that tariff revision was probably needed, Dolliver ridiculed the Democrats for calling the existing rates "highway robbery" and then proposing a bill which reduced the "robbery by about 4%." His view was that revising the tariff could best be accomplished by the friends of protection, and he suggested that "the difference between giving the revision of the tariff to the Democratic party and giving it into the hands of the Republican is just the difference between having your barbering done by a butcher and having it done by a barber." The *Register* described these debates as being "of a high order, both speakers demonstrating a thorough familiarity with the tariff controversy from their respective standpoints, and using the arguments suited to their views with force and effectiveness."[46]

Dolliver, a far abler speaker, seems to have fared better than Yeoman, but on the whole their joint meetings were characterized by friendliness and good sportsmanship. One of Victor Dolliver's friends wrote: "I went to hear the joint discussion between J. P. and Yeoman. It was decidedly *rich*. I heard the next day that some of Yeoman's friends would not speak to him because he did not succeed better."[47] A few years later Captain Yeoman wrote J. P.: "Our common contests . . . to me were an intellectual delight if not of triumph. We have been ancient but honorable political foes, but have always taken our wounds in front. The scars I have born[e] away from these contests are of pleasant memory."[48]

Clarkson, busy with the presidential campaign in the East, gave Dolliver little if any aid. The vast sums which John Wanamaker raised for the Republicans by "frying the fat" out of manufacturers interested in a high tariff were not squandered in Iowa or other "safe" states. The need for funds to "influence the vote" in New York and Indiana was great, and Clarkson reported it unlikely that the national committee could afford money to "help in the Districts," although he promised to do what he could in close contests in Iowa.[49]

From Leigh S. J. Hunt, publisher of the Seattle *Post-Intelligencer*, Dolliver received unexpected financial assistance. Hunt, a fabulous character, had been superintendent of schools at Mount Pleasant and at East Des Moines in the early eighties, and had served in 1885-1886 as president of the Iowa State Agricultural College at Ames. He admired Dolliver as an orator, and the two had become close friends before Hunt moved to Seattle, where he quickly amassed a fortune in real estate, banking, and publishing.[50] Although money from Hunt apparently did not reach Dolliver until late in the campaign, the amount, unrecorded, was in Dolliver's view, quite significant. Years later he wrote Hunt:

> When I had to make my first campaign I had lots of people to speak well of me and cheer me on, but you alone took in my whole problem and put your money at my disposal. I might possibly have been elected without your help, but that is doubtful; and with it I was able with small draft on my own resources to make a gentlemanly and high toned campaign and cover all the weak points.[51]

Dolliver defeated Yeoman, 20,864 to 15,496.[52] John J. Brown's 1878 prophecy that J. P. would be in Congress within a decade was accurate enough to satisfy practical politicians. Harrison carried Iowa by a large majority, and his party elected Congressmen in all of Iowa's districts except the Second. Control of the White House and of Congress passed to the Republicans as a result of the national elections, despite the fact that President Cleveland received 100,476 more votes than did General Harrison.[53]

Dolliver's victory brought him congratulations from all sections of the country — and also immediate problems. He had wisely hoped in 1884 to enter Congress during a Democratic administration, when he could make a name as a critic of the majority and would be free of the plague of patronage. It happened, however, that his career in the House began when, for the first time since the Civil War, his party was returning to power following a Democratic President. All sorts of office seekers waited expectantly and impatiently for the ousting of the incumbents.

In December, Dolliver wrote Harrison, recommending the appointment of Ret Clarkson as Secretary of the Interior "or some other post of equal dignity in the new Cabinet." Dolliver emphasized the part Iowa had played in Harrison's nomination and informed the President-elect that Clarkson had "the unanimous support of the Republicans of Iowa. He represents them as no other man among us can and will take into your Cabinet the fighting weight of the Republicans of this state." Actually, Clarkson hoped to be Postmaster General, and Harrison apparently had no objection to him for that office, but the party bosses had promised it to Wanamaker.[54]

The real stumbling-block in Clarkson's path to the Cabinet was Senator Allison. Harrison offered Allison the Treasury, but Allison delayed either accepting or refusing. It was not feasible to give Iowa two Cabinet seats. Allison knew this. He also must have known that he would refuse to leave the Senate to become Secretary of the Treasury. Dolliver wrote Allison in late December, expressing the satisfaction of Iowans that the Senator was not going into the Cabinet and telling him that his best chance for the presidency lay in remaining in the Senate. O'Connell and other Iowans made it clear that if Allison went into the Cabinet, a fight between Governor Larrabee and Colonel Hepburn for the senatorship would wreck the Iowa organization.[55] Still Allison did not inform Harrison until February that he would not accept appointment to the Cabinet. By that time, no Cabinet post suitable for Clarkson remained unfilled.[56] He finally accepted appointment as First Assistant Postmaster General.

Meanwhile, Dolliver was interested in the identity of the new Speaker of the House. He urged Representative David B. Henderson to become a candidate, and Henderson replied that he had decided to do so and that Dolliver's "warm and enthusiastic nature will be of great service to me, especially among the new members."[57] Joseph G. Cannon of Illinois also coveted the speakership, and he asked Carpenter to get Dolliver to support him if Henderson withdrew.[58] The outcome of this contest was uncertain, and, of course, a freshman Congressman would have little to do with it.

Other matters, such as public curiosity as to his attitude toward the admission of Chinese to the country, required Dolliver's attention as the year ended. The day after Christmas, J. P. wrote a long letter answering an inquiry from the New York *Herald* as to what his position as a Congressman would be on the question of restricting immigration. He held the view that "this country is the asylum for the oppressed of all nations" and that the "Northwest still welcomes industrious people without inquiring what language they speak or

from what country they come." This was especially true of immigrants from
North Europe without whose help the Northwest "would today be a half-
settled wilderness." However, recognizing that certain types of immigrant
labor were undesirable, Dolliver suggested that legislation might be needed to
prevent the importation of laborers under contract and to prohibit "the un-
loading on these shores of the paganism of Asia and the outcast population of
Europe." Expressing himself as unwilling to join in "the crusade against sound
American traditions" which welcomed immigrants, Dolliver denied the argument that the United States must close her doors to foreigners lest they bring
in ideas of anarchy and socialism. "If those of us who were born here and
those of us who already live here," he concluded, "are faithful to the moral
precepts upon which the national safety rests and diligent in the application of
the spirit of the working man of Nazareth to the industrial life of the people,
we have little to fear from the honest immigrant who sees in this form of our
government the pledge of justice and the promise of prosperity for himself
and his family." [59]

As he concluded his last year as a private citizen, Dolliver thus revealed his
liberal and humanitarian spirit, his faith in man and in the Great Republic.
For him all social problems had a moral basis and all citizens a responsibility
to seek solutions in the light of the hopes and needs of human beings and in
accordance with Christian principles.

- IX -

Advocate of Pensions
and Protection, 1889-1893

*I have never heard any subject discussed here for any length of time
that did not in some strange way land at last at the gateway of the
tariff question.*

Jonathan P. Dolliver, March 29, 1892

JONATHAN P. DOLLIVER was by 1889 a professional Republican politician; for
him, being a Congressman was a vocation. Shortly after his first election to
the House, he closed his law office permanently without ever having made a
serious effort to distinguish himself at the bar. The law had provided him a
living and had helped prepare him for his chosen career, but having entered
upon that career, he felt no further need for a profession which he regarded
primarily as a means to an end. Love of money was not one of his vices;
what he needed in the future, his salary as a Congressman would supply.[1]

In his thirty-first year when he took his seat in the Fifty-first Congress, Dolliver had had no experience in legislation. He had no political machine; no
clique or faction controlled him, much less owned him. The Republicans of
the Tenth District had sent him to Congress, and he apparently expected to
stay, despite the inability of any of his predecessors to do so. The voters
knew where he stood on the issues of the day. For ten years he had delivered
lectures and campaign speeches in the whistle-stops, county seats, and cities of
northern and central Iowa. He was on record in favor of state prohibition,
pensions for veterans, and the protective tariff. He had advocated regulation
of railroads before Larrabee became Governor and long before Albert Baird
Cummins ceased to be a railroad attorney.

An ardent nationalist, Dolliver believed that "state boundaries are really no
more important to the new American people than line fences."[2] He repeatedly urged federal aid to education and vigorous enforcement of those constitutional amendments protecting the civil rights of Southern Negroes. As early
as 1884 he had suggested the wisdom of enlarging the navy. His first stump

86

speeches in Iowa established him as a strong proponent of sound money. From his college days, his political addresses and his lectures had revealed his strong sympathy for the laboring man and for the weak and helpless who found themselves exploited by what he called "the tyranny of the money power."

Dolliver knew of the many economic and social ailments in his country at the end of the eighties. He may have read the *Methodist Review's* analysis of the causes of those ills, summarizing views widely held in reform circles in 1888:

> . . in the unhallowed temple of Mammon men are taught how to frame plausible theories in defense of gambling, speculation, "corners," "trusts," "combinations," "pools," briberies, railway wrecking, betrayals of official obligations, adulterations of food, fraudulent manufacturing, dealing in things injurious to health and public morals, and similar methods of gaining wealth by wronging other men.[3]

If he did not read it, Dolliver could well have written it, for it expressed his own observations.

To Dolliver "the most weighty question of practical politics in every quarter of the earth is the simple question of equal chances for men to win in the race of life." But the answer was not socialism. "Society has outgrown the dogma of state ownership," he repeatedly asserted. "The sober claimants of social justice have *never* urged a practical communism of property. . . . They see in communism the suspicious science of giving to each a satisfactory share of nothing." He rejected all radical solutions: "No theory of government can bring about actual equality," he wrote. "What is demanded is not equal wealth — but an equal chance to pursue wealth; not equal influence — but an equal chance to pursue influence — not equal happiness, but an equal chance to pursue happiness. . . . The sameness of rights and not sameness in the result of the exercise of rights."[4]

He stood squarely upon Cicero's ancient doctrine of natural rights and accepted as among those rights the main body of existing laws relative to the ownership and distribution of property. He was a Jeffersonian agrarian, assuming, as Merle Curti has put it, "that if no unfair or objectionable practices intervened, under these laws individuals would attain a state of well-being representing a high degree of social justice."[5] Defining the ideal society as one "in which every member is secured equally from wrong from the government and from private persons," Dolliver held that "a government that places unequal shields before the violated rights of its citizens is a false pretense, and a government which stands idle while private persons trample upon the forms or substance of the People's rights is in the same sense totally unworthy."[6]

Dolliver never doubted that government might endanger the rights of the individual. Although he had little use for laissez faire, he did not, on the

other hand, believe that all the problems of the age could be solved by legislation. He was no Benthamite reformer. Like Jefferson, he had great faith in
the people and a great concern that they have sufficient education to enable
them to maintain their freedom. He knew that tyranny thrives on ignorance
and that every exploiting group fears popular education. "The people — free,
intelligent, upright — are the best conservators of the political order," Dolliver
wrote, "better than armies and navies, better than courts and prisons, better
than a multitude of Congresses." [7]

Laws existed against polygamy, the saloon, murder, looting, and "those
mercenary organizations of the money power, as when capital combines in a
bloodless conspiracy to practice the arts of extortion," Dolliver told a West
Virginia University audience the year he entered Congress. Yet "in spite of
codes and courts" these evils persisted because, as he thought (with Edward
Gibbon), "the operation of the wisest laws is in their very nature imperfect
and precarious; they seldom inspire virtue, they do not always restrain vice,
their power is insufficient to prevent all that they condemn, nor can they always punish the actions they prohibit." He did not "disparage the gospel of
legislation," but he did urge "a mighty revival of the old fashioned spirit of
law abiding citizenship." This, together with "the conservative influences that
belong to time, and an enlightened and purified public opinion," would bring
into being a better social order. [8]

The clue to his approach as a Congressman to the solution of most national
problems is found in that phrase, "the conservative influences that belong to
time, and an enlightened and purified public opinion." As his close friend
Meservey observed, Dolliver had "confidence in the people . . . all the
time." [9] Of fundamental importance also was his religious concept that God
rules the world. To Dolliver the history of the founding and the development
of the United States was evidence that God sanctioned the principles of democracy and guided the destiny of the American people. "A universal fidelity to
the precepts of upright living" was, he held with Edmund Burke, "essential for
the life, health and strength of popular institutions." [10] Thus, he was not an
enthusiast for mere legislative reform. The Grangers, Greenbackers, and Populists had little more attraction for him than did the theories of Henry George
or the doctrines of the collectivists.

There is no reason to doubt the sincerity of Dolliver's belief that a revival
of religious faith and educational endeavors (schools for all, colleges, libraries,
lyceums, Chautauquas, and periodicals) designed to provide an enlightened
citizenry were the best means of improving society. One wonders, however,
if Dolliver really understood the difficulty of attempting to defend the political
ideals of Thomas Jefferson through means sanctioned by Edmund Burke and
within a party headed by Benjamin Harrison at a time when the new industrialism posed unprecedented challenges to individual liberty and equality of

economic opportunity. But, of course, Dolliver was neither a philosopher nor a critic, and, as Vernon Parrington has shown, "most of the critics were singularly ill equipped" to deal with "the problem whether an undisciplined people, wedded to an old-fashioned agrarian democracy, could cope with an ambitious industrialism that was quite cynically buying and selling the political state."[11]

Whatever the inconsistencies of his intellectual position, Dolliver succeeded as a politician in the 1880's and 1890's because he usually articulated the beliefs and aspirations of a majority of the voters of Iowa's Tenth District. Their emotional attachment to the Republican party, their nationalism, their love of liberty, their yearning for equality of opportunity, their emphasis on Christian ethics, and their adherence to a competitive capitalistic system of individual enterprise — all were personified in their young Congressman. Claude Bowers was perfectly right in thinking that Dolliver's "intense humanity, his love and understanding of the mind and heart of ordinary folk, made him a perfect interpreter of the plain people."[12]

To a degree he was guided by public opinion, for he believed that enlightened public opinion should be the true basis of government. If, however, on certain issues his "ear to the ground" informed him his constituents were not with him, he would not hesitate to attempt to "enlighten" them and convert them to his position. Nevertheless, he did not get too far ahead of his followers, realizing quite clearly that the politician who makes that error may find himself on election day a chief without enough Indians.

When Dolliver entered Congress the tide of national politics was conservative. It had been so since 1869, and there would be no shift until after the turn of the century.[13] Despite his strong liberal strain, Dolliver joined the ranks of the moderate conservatives, where, without apparent discomfort, he remained during his service in the House. Again, as in 1876 when he cheered with the Half-Breeds, he was neither an ardent reformer nor a reactionary. The "influences that belong to time" and the development of an "enlightened public opinion" might bring liberalism to the fore again; meanwhile Representative Dolliver would bide his time within the party he loved and served so well.

"J. P. started for the Capital of our country Friday night," Gay Dolliver wrote Victor on February 10, 1889.[14] He went to Washington to witness the counting of the electoral vote and the official declaration of the election of Benjamin Harrison, "a very solemn and stately proceeding," Dolliver thought. He remained for the inauguration of the new President and to learn his way about Washington from the amiable Major Holmes, whom he would replace in December. "I believe I shall enjoy the work of the House," Dolliver informed his family, "though I confess it is a little in the nature of a bear garden to the uninitiated observer."[15]

The novelty of life in Washington soon wore off, however, and by the end of February he confided to Mrs. Carpenter:

> I do not like this town as much as I did, but the flowers here keep me from getting homesick. I like the flowers better than the people. I have been so homesick that I have hardly known what to do. Even the fair faces on the street and in the hotel parlors . . . have failed to interest me and I would have given half a year's salary to be back where people wear common clothes and say what they mean.[16]

Demands for patronage troubled him as early as February. As a result of the change of administration, the rush of Republican office seekers was "almost like the march of the Barbarians on Rome."[17] Carpenter advised Dolliver to "help the fellows whose shrewdness and influence as politicians will help you in the future." He also recommended that J. P. consider hiring the stenographer who had worked for Carpenter in Washington, as she was "probably between fifty and sixty and your connection with her of course could not be a matter of comment."[18]

Dolliver's first concern was to secure Carpenter's appointment as postmaster at Fort Dodge. Everyone knew that the Governor really needed the salary, and all realized that Carpenter was Dolliver's mentor and a dear friend. J. P.'s reply to all applicants for the postmastership was: "I will say to you candidly, as I have said to others, that it is my intention . . . before considering the claims of any other candidate, to offer the Post Office to our friend and distinguished townsman, ex-governor Carpenter." With Ret Clarkson as Assistant Postmaster General, Dolliver had no difficulty in expediting Carpenter's appointment, although the old Governor worried lest undue haste might discommode the Democratic incumbent for whom he felt sympathy.[19]

While in Washington in March, Dolliver also aided his ex-partner, M. D. O'Connell, to regain his former post as United States Attorney for the Northern District in Iowa. O'Connell thanked J. P. for the "kind, manly, and generous treatment," and expressed pleasure that "notwithstanding conflicting interests in the past, we find today no reason for other feelings than of respect and esteem each for the other."[20] Thus, one potential future rival became a faithful ally.

Dolliver returned to Iowa in mid-April, intending to spend the summer and autumn in attempting to cope with the patronage problem. His private correspondence indicates that he regarded "the swarm of place seekers" much as did Henry Cabot Lodge who wrote: "I am harassed to death and if this accursed patronage does not kill me politically and destroy my health and temper nothing will."[21] The distribution of spoils, however perplexing, was not the only worry of a professional politician in Iowa in 1889. It was time to choose a successor to Governor Larrabee and a General Assembly which would elect a United States Senator in 1890 when Allison's term expired.

The Republicans nominated a weak gubernatorial candidate, J. G. Hutchison, and adopted a platform reaffirming the past utterances of the party on prohibition. Many Republicans, especially in the river cities, had "had enough" of the prohibition experiment. Some of the railroads withheld the usual support in order to punish the party for Larrabee's regulatory legislation. The Democrats chose Horace Boies, a first-class lawyer and farmer, as their gubernatorial nominee. Their platform denounced prohibition as a failure, proposed a local option license law for control of liquor, and advocated the adoption of the Australian ballot and the continued regulation of railroads.[22]

The issue was prohibition, and the Democrats waged a well-organized campaign exploiting all the weaknesses of their opposition. To the surprise of Dolliver and many others of the bloody-shirt brigade, Boies won by more than 6,500 votes, and the Democrats gained exactly one-half of the seats in the lower house. But with their hold-over members in the state senate, the Republicans were able to control the General Assembly in the election of a United States Senator, and Allison was safe by an eight-vote margin.[23]

Two weeks after the Iowa Republicans, "stepping on a corkscrew," suffered the election of a Democratic governor, Jonathan Dolliver arrived in Washington to begin his first term in the House of Representatives.[24] He arranged for room and board at the residence of one William A. Woods, the rate being $100 a month. Writing his father and Gay of his intention to send them $50 a month, he advised them to live well and economically: "Economize on everything except coal. The man who tries to save coal when the thermometer is at 40° below deserves to freeze to death."[25]

On Thanksgiving Day, Dolliver dined with the Clarksons at noon and with Senator Allison in the evening. In his weekly letter to his father on December 1, J. P. described his experiences on the eve of the opening of the session:

> Well, the caucus is over and Mr. Reed is elected Speaker. He is the greatest man in the House and I am glad he is in, if Henderson could not win. I secured with the aid of the Delegation the election of Holmes as Sergeant at Arms of the House — I thought it would be well to get him out of Iowa. Tomorrow Congress meets and I feel a sort of solemnity in taking my seat for the first session of my first Congress.[26]

The President's message was read in the House on December 3, 1889. He suggested a revision of the tariff law without impairment of "the just and reasonable protection of our home industries." Other recommendations included: liberal pensions for veterans, a large appropriation for the navy, and federal control of congressional elections to prevent the suppression of the suffrage among the Negroes of the South.[27]

For two or three weeks after receiving this presidential program, the House did very little. "We are not yet organized for the reason that Mr. Speaker Reed required considerable time to make up his Committees," Dolliver informed his father. Meanwhile, the Congressmen investigated the theft by the cashier of their Sergeant-at-Arms of money due members of the House. J. P. was "short $300 salary . . . which this infernal rascal stole," but he expected to recover it. Aside from this diversion, Dolliver visited the Smithsonian Institution, the Art Gallery, and the Botanical Gardens. He liked Washington better than he had in the spring. "Everybody treats me kindly and I am becoming quite satisfied with things here," he reported. "We have lots of callers and I presume we shall have to go into society a little, though my double barreled coat is as yet on the same peg I hung it on when I came here."[28] Mrs. Carpenter, knowing his unconcern in the matter of clothes, wrote him "to be careful to dress properly for state functions."[29]

During the third week of the session Speaker Reed completed the committee appointments, and William McKinley of Ohio received the chairmanship of the Ways and Means Committee. Dolliver considered his own assignments to the Naval Affairs and War Claims committees as "good ones." He was especially pleased with the former, which he regarded as "important because of the universal demand for a new and strong navy," and because he enjoyed the company of Charles A. Boutelle, the chairman, and Henry Cabot Lodge, who shared his enthusiasm for a great navy. In his second speech in the House, Dolliver supported building "a Navy that can fight" if necessary "to keep other people from disturbing either our prestige or our rights."[30]

Even after the organization of the committees, the House did not get down to business. The Republican majority was slim, and Democrats frequently refused to answer a quorum roll call, even though present in the chamber. To end this scheme of filibustering by silence, the Speaker, on January 29, 1890, directed the clerk to record the names of those present who refused to answer and to count them in completing a quorum. The House immediately exploded in a storm of verbal violence comparable to the scene enacted therein the night of Dolliver's birth. When an irate Southerner arose to deny the right of the Speaker to count him present, Reed replied: "The Chair is making a statement of fact that the gentleman from Kentucky is present. Does he deny it?" The uproar lasted three days, but in the end the House adopted rules giving the Speaker the power to count members present in making up a quorum and to refuse to entertain dilatory motions.[31] Dolliver enthusiastically supported "Czar" Reed and expressed pleasure "that we have a man in the Chair of the House of Representatives great enough in body and brain to deliver that curious assembly from the control of the seedy statesmen who have for so many years kept famous on motions to adjourn."[32]

If the enactment of a large body of legislation is a test of parliamentary procedure, Reed's policy was successful. During its first session, the Fifty-first Congress passed the Sherman Antitrust Act, the Sherman Silver Purchase Act, and the McKinley Tariff, and attacked the problem of the surplus by increasing the veterans' pensions and voting large appropriations for the navy. Dolliver supported all of these measures, but, as befitted a freshman Congressman, he played no significant part during the early months of the long session.[33] He wrote his father in February, 1890, that he was preparing three speeches — one on the pension question, one in favor of retiring General Fremont, and one on the tariff — but so far had made none, preferring to strengthen his "position in the House by observing a becoming silence."[34]

His opportunity to "violate the golden rule of silence" came on April 4, 1890, when the chairman of the Committee on Invalid Pensions asked him to reply to a Missouri Democrat's attack on the pension bill. Dolliver's maiden speech in the House was "a really fine oration."[35] He spoke for "the men born since 1850," saying that they, "without distinction of party politics, recognize that . . . in fighting for the unity of the Republic the armies of the nation carried on their swords the welfare of centuries and in their hearts the great hope of posterity." He ridiculed the existing pension system under which "$8 a month is the accepted unit for total disability" and wondered at "the delicate shading of disease that is relieved by the payment of $2 a month, now received by nearly 27,000 men . . . while in one case the Law has cut a penny into vulgar fractions and passed to the pensioner's credit the quaint and princely allowance of $2.33 1/3 per month."

In his fervid peroration, which brought him "loud and prolonged applause," Dolliver exclaimed:

> The old soldiers stand before the public Treasury, not as paupers, not as mendicants, not even as beneficiaries. They are the preferred creditors of the nation of America. . . .
> I shut my eyes while the busy fingers of calculation compute the cost. It makes absolutely no difference what it costs. The defense of the Union was an undertaking so vast that no worldly arithmetic can estimate its expense. But the American people, with eager patriotism, were ready to pay all that it cost . . . that the flag of the great Republic might live through the storm of battle.[36]

Throughout his public career Dolliver was a tireless advocate of adequate pensions for war veterans. In addition to supporting all general pension legislation, he personally introduced 498 bills to grant or to increase pensions for private individuals or special groups of soldiers or sailors.[37] A vast amount of his correspondence concerns the desires or needs of his constituents for such relief, and it was Dolliver's custom to call at the Pension Bureau frequently, often on his way to the Capitol of a morning.[38]

On Lincoln's birthday, 1890, Dolliver addressed the New York City Re-

publican Club's annual banquet at Delmonico's. At the speakers' table he sat
by John C. Fremont and chatted with Chauncey Depew, Stephen B. Elkins,
and Senator Shelby Cullom. His speech was light and humorous for the most
part. He praised Ret Clarkson, "a man who not only has Democratic blood
on his hands, but good Republican blood in his veins," for his efforts to clean
the Democrats out of the appointive offices, and admitted that "if in the
process we happen to see the awkward squad of reform on its way to the
rear, we can moderate our distress by considering that while they rest from
their labors, their works do not follow them." Ending on a more serious note,
Dolliver attacked "the great centers of American wealth and business" for
having "set the dogs of avarice and of bloodless greed to guard the national
treasury against the worn-out veterans of the Union Army." He urged the
Republican party to "go back to the grave of its greatest leader . . . and re-
consecrate its service to the plain people of the United States" to the end that
all should have "an unfettered start and a fair chance in the race of life."[39]

This address was well received, and it won Dolliver much attention in the
New York and Iowa papers.[40] Consequently, the commander-in-chief of the
G. A. R. invited him to deliver the principal address at the Memorial Day
exercises at the Metropolitan Opera House in New York on May 30. This
was a great affair in the 1890's, and Dolliver prepared himself carefully for
his appearance before an audience which he anticipated would be larger and
more important than any he had yet addressed.[41] His speech was one of rare
beauty, pathos, and eloquence. Including an inspiring tribute to the valor and
sacrifice of the Union soldiers, Dolliver also devoted several passages to discussing the significance of the Civil War as "a moral spectacle" and the national victory as "the mark of God's providence." He concluded with a plea
for an abandonment of sectional animosities, telling his Northern listeners that
already in the South "in business, in politics, in literature, men are coming
forward who breathe the air of a new and better era."[42] Dolliver, by 1890,
was through with waving the bloody shirt, and the nation was well along the
road to reunion.[43]

Describing this New York trip to his father, Dolliver wrote of the "great
and enthusiastic audience" which cheered his speech to the echo, and of his
visit to Grant's tomb. The latter greatly disappointed him. He thought it was
"a disgrace to the country, being a low squatty brick structure about like a
smoke house in the rear end of a butchershop."[44]

Not long after returning to Washington, Dolliver dined one evening at the
home of Senator Allison. There were no other guests. According to a friend
to whom Dolliver related the conversation, Senator Allison remarked that he
was beginning to worry because people were frequently referring to the

"brilliant Mr. Dolliver." The Senator agreed with that characterization, but he had been in Washington long and had seen many brilliant men come and go. He wanted Dolliver to stay, and he advised him not to rely merely on his reputation as an orator, not to make too many witty speeches on too many subjects. The way to a long and useful career in Congress, suggested Allison, was to "select some thing in government in which you are particularly interested, and master it." Dolliver took this advice seriously. He decided to concentrate on mastering the tariff question, a subject on which he had spoken occasionally since 1880 and which had been the chief issue of the election of 1888.[45]

The year 1890 was an opportune time for a young Congressman to turn his attention to the tariff. Having won control of the government largely because of their promise to maintain and extend the policy of protection, the Republicans under the leadership of William McKinley of the House Ways and Means Committee began work on a new tariff law shortly after the convening of the Fifty-first Congress. Taking the 1888 Allison-Aldrich "substitute" for the Mills bill as a point of departure, McKinley and his cohorts prepared a measure which embodied a radical extension of the protective system. It raised the general level of duties from 38 per cent to nearly 50 per cent, gave "protection" to nonexistent industries, such as tin-plate manufacturing, and placed higher rates on eggs, potatoes, wheat, corn, barley, hemp, and flax in an attempt to fool the farmer into believing that he as well as the manufacturer profited from a high tariff.[46]

There was little, if any, justification for this type of tariff legislation in 1890. The United States had few "infant industries" needing protection, and as her productive capacity was rapidly outgrowing the demands of her home markets, her surplus grain, meat, and manufactured products sought outlets through foreign trade. James G. Blaine, Secretary of State, although still a protectionist, seems to have grasped the elementary notion that if the United States were willing to make tariff concessions to other nations, especially the Latin American countries, they in turn might be induced to adjust their tariffs to admit more American products. Blaine, urging the principle of reciprocity, attempted to convince Congress that it should leave a duty on raw sugar and allow the President to offer its abolition in return for free admission of American goods to the ports of sugar producing nations. But the House, intent upon reducing the Treasury surplus by cutting off revenue, removed the sugar duties and passed the McKinley bill without provision for reciprocity agreements. Blaine, aided somewhat by Harrison, was barely able to get the Senate to insert into the bill a section giving the President power to impose certain duties on sugar, molasses, tea, coffee, and hides, if he found that countries exporting those items to the United States were imposing "unjust or unreasonable" exactions on American products.[47]

Congressman Dolliver's mastery of the tariff question was insufficient to enable him to speak against the McKinley bill. Indeed, he spoke eloquently in its behalf, although he preferred, as he told the House, "to be a hearer and I had hoped, a learner." In his first defense of the bill, May 16, Dolliver posed as an Iowa nationalist who looked "to the American market for the sale of substantially all that we raise and for the supply of substantially all we need."[48] He said not a word about the difference between the "prosperity" of the farmer and of the manufacturer, nothing about the plight of the consumer, and made no comment on Blaine's reciprocity proposals. His confidence in the mercantilist theory of self-sufficiency resembled that of Colbert in the age of Louis XIV.

At McKinley's request, Dolliver spoke again on September 27, when the House was in the last hours of debate on the conference committee report. Frankly admitting the Democratic charge that the McKinley bill sought not only to protect old industries but to create new ones, he stated that the bill "openly proposed to establish . . . the tin-plate and the linen industry." He defended the lifting of duties on sugar and the granting of bounties to sugar producers, thus indicating his rejection of Blaine's argument for reciprocity despite a reputed widespread interest in it in Iowa. The main purpose of the speech was not to change any votes in the House. It was rather a transparent effort to whitewash the tariff bill by presenting it as "a measure covering the whole field of American interests." Dolliver sought especially "to emphasize the fact that the time has come when the corn country and the wheat country have as much to say about the tariff as the cities and villages. . . . That is what it means when the products of the farm for the first time take their proper place in the list of protected industries."[49] Either he had his tongue in his cheek, or he had more to learn about the tariff than one of his constituents who wrote him that if the McKinley bill "becomes law both Iowa and the nation will go Democratic by astonishing majorities."[50]

A second aim of Dolliver's September 27 address was to defend the record of the Fifty-first Congress. Democrats and old-time reformers like Carl Schurz charged that the Sherman Antitrust Law was nothing more than "a lightning rod to prevent the popular feeling against the trusts from striking the tariff," that the act was designed not to give effective control of combinations in restraint of trade, but merely to meet the cry that the tariff was the "mother of trusts."[51] Dolliver asserted that the Sherman law was an answer to the American farmers' demands "that the exactions of avarice and greed shall be removed from the American market place." It was a step "in the right direction," he argued, "and if it finally fails in reaching the result, the farmers of the United States will see that it is perfected and that no measure is spared to restore to American business the principle of honorable competition."[52] His hint of its possible failure indicates his real feeling that the law was a

futile gesture. His effort to credit it to the agrarians was part and parcel of
the scheme to sell the work of the session as advantageous to the farmer and
worker.

Likewise in his comments on the Sherman Silver Purchase Act, which he
inaccurately described as "providing for the free coinage of the whole product
of the American silver mines," Dolliver boasted of the monumental "wisdom
of this Congress." He knew, of course, that this act frightened the Eastern
advocates of the gold standard without completely satisfying the Western
silverites or the inflationists, and that the Senate had passed it as a part of a
deal whereby the high tariff proponents secured the votes of the Silver Senators needed to enact the McKinley bill. He professed to believe, however,
that the Silver Act "has solved the silver question and made the way to the
free coinage of the world's silver supply easy and plain." Venturing into the
hazardous sphere of prophecy in his appeal to the November voters of the
great West, Dolliver uttered a sentence which returned to haunt him many
times: "I predict that before the administration of President Harrison ends
silver will be coined by the United States without limit, as gold is now
coined."[53]

A few hours after concluding this speech, Dolliver voted with 150 of his
colleagues to adopt the conference report on the McKinley bill. Four days
later, after its adoption by the Senate and approval by the President, the bill
became law, and the first session of the "Billion Dollar Congress" came to an
end — but the tariff issue was by no means laid to rest, nor was the silver
question.[54]

The Tenth District Republican Convention renominated Congressman Dolliver by acclamation on June 20, 1890. "It was simply immense!" his brother,
Victor, who attended, wrote: "J. P. can never hope to have a convention more
unanimous in its sentiment or loyal in its devotion and enthusiasm." Jonathan,
with no serious opposition, did not even go to Iowa for the convention.[55]

He hurried home after the adjournment of Congress in October, however,
for it was becoming increasingly evident that many voters of the country were
pleased neither with the new tariff nor with the Republican administration.
Civil service reformers were outraged at Harrison's spoils system, but the
patronage-hungry politicians were not satisfied with the distribution of the
plums.[56] Even Ret Clarkson resigned in 1890, when the President made public
professions in favor of reform yet insisted on placing his own relatives and
personal henchmen in government posts, regardless of both the Civil Service
Commission and the exigencies of practical politics. Writing Dolliver of the
President's shortcomings, Clarkson charged that Harrison had "broken the
party's spirit, humiliated its workers & leaders & brought out nondescripts,

drones, mugwumps & unknowns to have the party's honors & administer the
party's power."[57] Theodore Roosevelt, whom Harrison appointed to the Civil
Service Commission, felt that "the little grey man in the White House" had
no real convictions regarding reform and had "never given us one ounce of
. . . backing." But Roosevelt, caring much more for office than Clarkson
ever did, stayed with the administration.[58]

More dangerous to Republican success at the polls than the disgruntlement
of reformers and spoilsmen was the idea rapidly spreading in the West that
the party was serving the manufacturing East at the expense of the agricultural sections. The high rates prescribed by the new tariff were immediately
reflected in increased retail prices, causing widespread discontent among consumers. The silver law did not satisfy debtors that they would obtain the
relief which they believed lay in an abundance of cheap currency. Demands
made in the name of the National Farmers' Alliance, supported in part by
the Knights of Labor, for the issue of irredeemable paper currency, free silver
coinage, prohibition of the "alien ownership of land," and taxation which
would not "build up one interest or class at the expense of another," had no
favor with the Fifty-first Congress.[59]

In Iowa the Farmers' Alliance went on record in 1890 in favor of free silver,
the issuance of all money by the government without the intervention of national banks, eventual government ownership of railway, telegraph, and tele-
phone lines, and direct election of United States Senators. Alliance officials
and local groups took an active interest in the congressional contests, and in
the Tenth District, as well as in the Seventh and Eighth, they endorsed the
Democratic candidate.[60]

Dolliver made a vigorous campaign, but his margin of victory was the nar-
rowest he was ever to have — 1,311 votes out of more than 35,000 cast. Five
Iowa Republican Congressmen, including ex-Governor Gear and Major John F.
Lacey, met defeat, while J. T. Flick and D. B. Henderson barely won re-elec-
tion by 198 and 116 votes respectively. These three were the only Republican
members of the Fifty-first Congress returned to office. Captain John A. T.
Hull and George D. Perkins, both elected for the first time, were the other
Republicans in the new Iowa delegation.[61]

Elsewhere a "tidal wave" swept Democrats into control of the national
House of Representatives by a huge majority but left the Senate in Republican
hands. Among the victims were William McKinley and Joseph G. Cannon.
In Nebraska an unknown young Democrat, William Jennings Bryan, won a
seat in the House, as did two candidates of the new Peoples party — which
also elected five Congressmen and a United States Senator in Kansas. The
"Peoples Movement" even infected the South, where in Georgia the Southern
Farmers' Alliance helped send Thomas E. Watson to Congress and made Benjamin R. Tillman governor of South Carolina.[62]

James J. Dolliver

Eliza Jane Dolliver

JONATHAN PRENTISS DOLLIVER ABOUT 1889

FATHER DOLLIVER WITH JONATHAN AND MOLLIE

Dolliver took no significant part in the debates of the second session of the Fifty-first Congress which convened in December. He succeeded in getting an appropriation for a new federal building in Fort Dodge in January, 1891 — not a difficult task in a Congress bent upon abolishing the Treasury surplus.[63]

No issues of importance came before the House in this "lame duck" session. The Senate rejected the "Force Bill," providing for the supervision of congressional elections by federal officers in certain circumstances, which had passed the House the preceding July. At that time Dolliver had spoken in behalf of the measure, believing that it might accomplish its intended purpose of giving the Negro of the South "the prospect of citizenship under national protection." He knew the dangers of any effort to provide federal supervision of elections and that many members of his party preferred not to risk it, but Dolliver insisted that "the Republican party stand faithful to the obligation laid upon it by the providence of God in the emancipation of an unfortunate race — united as one man to defend the sanctity of American citizenship."[64] Republican Senators had used the "Force Bill" to bargain for passage of the McKinley Tariff in the first session; they used it again in the fight for a free silver bill in the second.[65] The result was fatal to the Federal Elections measure.

After spending the summer and fall in Iowa, where he campaigned unsuccessfully to prevent Governor Boies's re-election, Dolliver returned to Washington for the meeting of the new Congress in December, 1891. He rented a second floor room in the Hamilton Hotel on K Street, where George Perkins and several other Congressmen lived. Although Dolliver took a greater interest in the social life of Washington than he had during his first term, he wrote that he intended to spend much time studying and to take "more or less part in the debates of the House."[66] He was no longer a "freshman." As a result of the large turnover of membership since the election of 1890, Dolliver acquired seniority rather quickly.

With the opposing parties in control of the House and Senate, the Fifty-second Congress was a "do-nothing" body. Attempts to repeal the McKinley law took the form of bills aimed at particular details rather than an outright effort to enact comprehensive substitute tariff legislation. Such bills of this nature as passed the House were killed in the Senate. Dolliver defended the McKinley Tariff on February 15, 1892, in a brief speech in which he denied that the tariff had had any adverse effect on the West. His most telling point was a quotation from the recent inaugural address of Iowa's Democratic and anti-protectionist Governor Boies, asserting that "at no time in the history of Iowa have her people been blessed with a more general prosperity than they now enjoy."[67]

The truth was that Iowa was more prosperous in 1892 than she had been. The agrarian discontent which swept the states farther west was much less in Iowa. Real estate mortgage debts were smaller in Iowa than in Kansas, and most of the Iowa mortgages were of the investment type which did not suggest either distress or frequent foreclosures. Interest rates were lower. The population increase during the preceding decade was slight — only 17.68 per cent — smaller than that of any other western or north-central state except Indiana and Ohio.[68] Iowa, in short, was no longer a frontier state subject to the radicalism of a frontier section. Furthermore, the price of corn, oats, and wheat, Iowa's most valuable agricultural products, was much higher than it had been at the end of the eighties.

Dolliver assumed that Iowa's prosperity was due partly to the Republican tariff policy. Thus, his long address on March 29, an answer to Bryan's attack on the McKinley Tariff, was aimed especially at "educating" the Iowa voters on the question which was obviously to be the main issue of the 1892 campaign. He had that speech reprinted and sent it into thousands of Iowa mailboxes. The burden of his argument was that home industries should be encouraged in order to provide larger markets for American agricultural products. When interrupted by a request that he explain the apparent paradox in the Republican statements that removal of duties on sugar had resulted in lower prices while the placing of higher duties on other products likewise caused prices to go down, Dolliver instantly replied:

> The removal of a revenue tariff from a thing which we do not and cannot produce in a supply equal to our wants, the price of which is necessarily made in markets outside of our own, relieves the public of a tax. The free admission of goods the like of which we do or can produce in quantities commensurate with our demand, the price of the domestic article being fixed by the conditions of our own markets, would, while holding out to us for a time the promise of cheap merchandise, so speedily prostrate our established industries as to leave us at the mercy of foreign merchants, and so ruinously degrade the level of American life as to cripple the people's ability to buy at whatever price the bargains might be offered.[69]

The assumption that American industry could not compete with foreign and that unless aided by a protective tariff domestic manufacturing would face destruction and leave the American consumer at the mercy of foreign monopolists (he usually cited the "English") was the crux of his defense. Regardless of its merits, Dolliver's argument seemed plausible to Iowans, and the volume of correspondence favorable to his position, as well as the Tenth District election returns, indicated its effectiveness.

Although there was little question but that the tariff would be the principal issue of the 1892 campaign, Republicans were not in agreement on the matter of their presidential nominee in the months prior to the nominating convention. Ret Clarkson, then chairman of the Republican National Committee, desired to defeat President Harrison for renomination. Clarkson was again supporting Blaine, whom he thought was the only man able to "draw from the Farmers' Alliance the necessary votes to keep the party in power in the States of the Northwest."[70] Some professed to believe that Clarkson himself should be nominated. This annoyed Senator Allison, who gave out an interview in which he belittled Clarkson and intimated that Clarkson was not even strong enough to obtain a Cabinet post in 1889.[71] Allison, the very man who had stood in Clarkson's way in 1889, did not want any Iowan other than himself mentioned as a presidential possibility in 1892.[72]

Dolliver publicly supported Clarkson and authorized newsmen to quote him as stating: "I am impressed with the belief that [Clarkson] is the best available presidential timber, and I believe that he could be nominated and elected."[73] Privately, of course, J. P. knew that Clarkson had no hope and no chance of being nominated. He wrote Clarkson of the "nearly universal desire" for a candidate other than Blaine or Harrison, one with no past ties to Blaine, and expressed the conviction that "three out of four of the politicians want McKinley and the other fourth Sherman." According to Dolliver's estimate, the "aggressive forces among younger Republicans wanted William McKinley."[74] Allison supported Harrison, and the Iowa delegates cast twenty votes for the President, five for Blaine, and one for McKinley — more evidence that Clarkson was not the "boss" historians have depicted him as being.

The story of the fiasco of 1892, including Blaine's futile eleventh-hour bid for the nomination by resigning as Secretary of State, and Harrison's first-ballot victory, needs no repetition. The Democrats made Grover Cleveland their standard bearer for a third consecutive time, while the new Populist party chose General James B. Weaver of Iowa to run for the presidency. Weaver, a former Republican whom Clarkson had helped drive into third-party politics by euchring him out of the gubernatorial nomination in the mid-seventies, had no significant following in his own state.[75] The campaign of 1892 was relatively quiet and dignified, one of measures rather than of men. The record of the "Billion Dollar Congress" and the tariff were the principal national issues.[76]

The paramount issue of the election, so far as Iowa was concerned, was the tariff. The Hawkeye Republicans refused to endorse prohibition in 1892 and placed Albert B. Cummins, an uncompromising opponent of prohibition, at the head of their list of presidential electors. Hence, that question was not as important as it had been in preceding years. The Republicans attacked the war record of Cleveland and Adlai Stevenson, Democratic candidate for Vice President, and revived the question of Cleveland's pension vetoes. Neither major party said much about silver.[77]

Although Dolliver had thought early in 1892 that Holmes, Head, and Kamrar, individually or collectively, might attempt to contest his renomination, he was informed by his supporters that the efforts of his rivals to "down Dolliver" were proving futile. Actually, Dolliver was renominated without difficulty, and the anti-third term tradition was broken for himself and for his twentieth century successors. "It is your ability to help yourself that makes easy work for your friends," Roberts wrote in April.[78] That, plus the power and skill of those "friends" and the lack of unity among his rivals doubtless accounts for Dolliver's easy convention victory.

Partly because of his narrow victory in 1890 and also because Clarkson insisted that Iowa would be "hard to carry" in 1892, Dolliver "worried all the time" over the fall campaign.[79] Hindsight indicates that this anxiety was largely unwarranted, although "running scared" may have made victory more certain. Dolliver carried the Big Tenth by 4,974 votes — an increase of 3,663 over his 1890 total — and Republicans won nine of the other ten congressional districts and all state offices contested.

Although defeated for re-election, President Harrison received more votes in Iowa than the combined total cast for Cleveland and Weaver. Populism made little headway in Iowa, where "Calamity Jim" Weaver polled barely 20,000 votes. The Fort Dodge *Messenger*, ardent advocate of protection, asserted that the reason for the Republican state victory over the Democrats and Populists "is found in the universal prosperity which is enjoyed in Iowa. The cries of the calamity howlers were unavailing against the positive knowledge that times were never so prosperous before." There were other reasons, of course, including the G. A. R. resentment against Cleveland's first-term pension vetoes, the unswerving devotion of the Scandinavians to Republicanism, and the success of speakers in defending the tariff.[80]

When Dolliver began his third term in 1893, the Democrats were in control of both houses of Congress and of the executive department for the first time since before the Civil War. Dolliver had won his spurs as an advocate of pensions and of the protective tariff during the Harrison administration. In the Fifty-third Congress he found himself a member of "the opposition," a situation he had thought in 1884 would be advantageous.

- X -

Politics and Romance, 1893-1895

You really in love and engaged seems like a myth and yet by your own confession it must be true. . . . Lou is a dear good girl besides being capable, and above all she has common sense.

Mollie Dolliver to J. P. Dolliver, 1895

WHEN BENJAMIN HARRISON succeeded Grover Cleveland in the White House in 1889, he found a full treasury. Four years later, after the Republican administration had exposed the nation to the folly of the McKinley Tariff, the waste of the Dependent Pensions Act, and the extravagance of the Sherman Silver Purchase law, Cleveland resumed the reins of government to face the most disheartening state of affairs since Lincoln's time. The country was at the threshold of the great panic of 1893.[1]

The fundamental causes of this panic are obscure, and the suggestion that it was an inevitable curve of the business cycle is not enlightening. One factor contributing to the collapse was the prolonged agricultural depression which had begun in 1887 and had resulted in serious curtailment of the purchasing power of farmers as well as in a reduction of the income of important railroads. The failure of the great English banking house of Baring Brothers in 1890 had led to the withdrawal of much British capital invested in America and also had precipitated business distress in Europe and Australia which led to a decline of American markets in those continents. The economic upheaval abroad as well as foreign distrust of America's monetary policy following the enactment of the Silver Purchase Act of 1890 caused European creditors to dump their American securities on the market, thus depressing stock values and draining the nation of its gold. The loss of gold, especially the depletion of the Treasury's gold to redeem silver certificates issued to purchase silver bullion, created fears in sound money circles that the government might abandon the gold standard. This uncertainty was, in the opinion of President Cleveland, a major cause of the panic.[2] Hence, in an effort to restore confidence in American fiscal policy, the President called a special session of the new Congress for August 7, 1893, for the purpose of repealing the Sherman Silver Purchase Act.

The President's message, read to the assembled lawmakers on August 8, reviewed the results of the existing silver policy, which required the government to purchase 4,500,000 ounces of silver bullion monthly and to pay for it in Treasury notes virtually always redeemable in gold. Cleveland believed that unless repealed the Silver Purchase Act would lead to "the entire substitution of silver for gold in the Government Treasury and that this must be followed by the payment of all Government obligations in depreciated silver." Hence, "at this stage gold and silver must part company and the Government must fail in its established policy to maintain the two metals on a parity with each other. . . . I earnestly recommend the prompt repeal of the provisions of the act passed July 14, 1890, authorizing the purchase of silver bullion."[3]

Enormous pressure was brought to bear upon Republicans, who had enacted this measure "to prevent something worse" and to insure the passage of the McKinley Tariff. The Eastern gold wing of the party and the great industrial and financial interests urged them to rise above the plane of party politics and as patriots to hasten to the rescue of prostrate business. On the other hand, the West demanded free-silver coinage and bimetallism. The increasing value of money and its scarcity made it necessary for the debtor everywhere to pay his obligations in a dollar far dearer than he had received and gave the Western producer a diminishing return for his crops.[4]

As a freshman Congressman, J. P. Dolliver had voted for the Silver Purchase Act and had approvingly predicted that it would lead to a free-silver policy.[5] He represented an area where the need for an expanded currency was great, and he knew full well that the Greenbackers had carried Webster County in 1878. As a partisan Republican he felt no inclination to support a Democratic President, but as a patriot and a believer in "sound money," he would do so if he thought such action were necessary.

He was not yet convinced when he arrived in Washington, where he again took "a room on the second floor at the head of the stairs in the Hamilton." The political atmosphere in the capital reminded him of the carnival at the Columbian Exposition in Chicago, where he had stopped on his way East. J. P. wrote his father of his ride on a Ferris wheel, "but it does not begin to compare with the wheels that are revolving in the heads of statesmen."[6]

Dolliver's mail from the "Big Tenth" was heavy in August, and most of the letters strongly advised him to vote against repeal. "Whatever you do — do not support Cleveland," an Iowa editor wrote. "Do not become a volunteer fire brigade to put out Democratic fires." Another advised: "Keep in the middle of the road. . . . Let the democrats do the talking and voting. This is their funeral." Numerous articulate and literate farmers, merchants, lawyers, and editors warned their Congressman not to be snared by the "Eastern Cleveland Republicans."[7] Some were even more emphatic and wrote in the tenor of S. A. Wolcott:

We do not think there is any more sense in the people of this country decrying silver as a money metal than there would be in Americans decrying corn as a food product. . . . The people of this section will kill any man politically who votes either for a gold standard or for the issuance of any more bonds to get gold.[8]

S. J. Bennett, a Fort Dodge banker, dispatched a long letter on August 18, which reveals the strong pro-silver sentiment of a most orthodox Western Republican in 1893. He had just returned from the state convention, Bennett informed Dolliver, and there could be no question but that "the Reps of Iowa are in favour of the use of silver. We want the silver dollar to be the equal of any other dollar and when it is so arranged we *cannot* have to[o] many of them." The businessmen have not lost confidence in Congress, Bennett continued, "for the very good reason that we never had any . . . hence we have nothing to loose [sic]." This Fort Dodge banker suggested that "confidence will not be restored by the repeal of the Sherman bill, but when the threatened legislation on the tariff is accomplished and the business [men] of the country can know upon what basis they can do business."[9]

Not all of Dolliver's correspondents took a position against repeal, but it is pertinent to note that the ablest advocate of the President's policy who wrote the Iowa Congressman resided in New York. Edward O. Leech, cashier of the National Union Bank in New York City, explained that "every other civilized country in the world had closed its Mints to the coinage of silver" when the United States passed the Bland-Allison Act. Hence, as the United States minted more and more silver, the price fell, "showing conclusively how incapable we were alone to handle the vast product of silver which was being poured upon the world." As a result, the banker continued, the United States has "between 500 to 600 millions of dollars of silver . . . worth about half what it cost, with our gold stock enormously reduced."[10]

An Iowa labor leader sent Dolliver a resolution adopted by the Dubuque Trades and Labor Congress urging repeal or amendment of the Sherman Act, but "only upon the condition that we shall have in its stead free and unrestricted coinage of silver at the ratio of 16 to 1."[11]

Dolliver made up his mind slowly. On August 20 he wrote his brother that it was "exceedingly doubtful if the Sherman law is unconditionally repealed," and stated that he was preparing to make "a speech on silver this week." He was studying and working hard on the question, despite the excessive Washington heat, and had "not got away even for a day's fishing."[12] He spent every day in the House, listening to the discussion and endeavoring to profit by it.

Late in the afternoon of August 25, Representative Henderson rose in the House to request unanimous consent "that my colleague [Mr. Dolliver] be allowed to speak for twenty minutes."[13] Colonel Henderson was Senator Allison's close friend; they were neighbors in Dubuque. Allison, co-author of the

Bland-Allison Act and supporter of the Sherman Silver Purchase bill, was one of the leaders of the Senate conservatives. Aldrich, Orville Platt, Sherman himself, and Allison were now backing President Cleveland's demand for repeal.[14] There is no written evidence other than Dolliver's speech, but it seems safe to assume that Allison's influence was decisive in determining the position Dolliver finally took. The letter of his New York banker friend was also effective, as the opening paragraphs of Dolliver's address indicate.

> There is one central problem that includes the whole field of the controversy, and that is: Can a nation situated like ours, under circumstances such as obtain now, invite to its mints the whole silver product and the whole silver stock of the world without creating a coin that shall partake of the fluctuating and depreciated character of silver bullion? That question has not been answered.

Referring to Bryan's three-hour speech on the 16th in behalf of free coinage, Dolliver said: "I will not conceal the disappointment with which a plain and perplexed man, anxious to be right and seeking to know the practical effect of the theory of free coinage on our monetary system, has sought in vain for that grain of wheat in the midst of so vast and entertaining a display of chaff." Dolliver reviewed the Greenback movement and his stand in the seventies against an unstable system of currency. "I stand," he said, "where I have always stood, for a national currency every dollar of which shall be equal in value to every other dollar issued by the Government. . . . I would not dare to cast a vote here which might have the effect of destroying the prosperity of American business by an experiment which, for all that has been said, presents itself to my mind in the form of an unlimited manufacture of short-weight dollars."

In brief, he rejected the plea for free and unlimited coinage of silver on the grounds that it would lead to the same evils he had feared in unsupported greenbacks. He continued, however, to advocate "the use of both gold and silver in our coinage," as he had in the seventies.

As for the Sherman Act, Dolliver admitted that he was not convinced that it was "the sole cause of the troubles that now afflict us." He advanced the view expressed in Bennett's letter, and by many other Republicans, that fear of tariff revision was the chief cause of the panic. Alluding to the antirepeal sentiment in Iowa, Dolliver expressed his faith in his people and his concept of the duty of a Representative: "I believe that the people of the United States will in the long run respect a man who refuses to betray them even for the sake of their applause." He had no fear about what would happen to Congressmen "who in the discharge of a high responsibility exercise their own judgment and obey their own convictions on this question." It was his hope that the Brussels conference would in its future meeting "restore the monetary status of silver." Meanwhile, following the example of Senator Allison, who "knows more about this question than any man in public life," Dolliver announced that he would vote for repeal. He held with Allison "that the road to a larger use of silver in the coinage of the world lies through the repeal of that part of the Act of 1890 which now compels this Government to bear the burden of silver alone." He suggested no alternative solution. He ignored the need of his section for adequate currency and evidently desired to follow the sterile advice of those who wrote him to let the Democrats do the proposing, as this was "their funeral."

"If anybody supposes that our decision here ends the controversy about silver, he is mistaken," Dolliver concluded, "and if anybody thinks that our action in suspending the purchase of bullion is in any sense the 'doom of silver,' it only shows that he does not comprehend the movement of the mighty forces that are at work."[15] This was better prophecy than he had indulged in when he spoke for the passage of the bill in 1890.

Three days after Dolliver's speech, the House voted to adopt the repeal bill offered by William L. Wilson of West Virginia. One hundred Republicans, led by ex-Speaker Reed, voted with 139 Democrats to grant the President's request. The Senate finally acted in October to accomplish repeal.[16]

Typical of the criticism Dolliver received following his speech and vote was a letter from a constituent:

> Is it fair to the debtor class to legislate so that their burden of debt or interest shall be heavier to bear? . . . I don't think our soil would refuse to yield grain or grass, or that our people or any other people would want any less of our products if we were to have practically a single silver standard of value. . . . If somebody must suffer loss because it is impossible to preserve a stable double standard, let the creditor stand it, he is best able and can recover more quickly.[17]

J. Fred Meyers sent Dolliver a marked copy of an editorial in his Denison *Review* which lambasted Western Republicans for supporting the President, and ended with this bit of verse:

> We are coming, Father Cleveland —
> We come a hundred strong,
> To register thy dear command;
> We know we have been wrong.
>
> With patriotic hearts we come,
> Let Democrats rejoice —
> Republicans we are at home —
> But here we're Grover's boys.[18]

Dolliver replied that he felt the "pressure of social and industrial problems" and observed that some steps must be taken to restore the rights encumbered "by what is vaguely called the money power."[19] He suggested no "steps," however, and his use of the adverb "vaguely" strongly hints that he was uneasily leaning toward a defense of business, for he had used the term "money power" without qualification for a decade.

Perhaps J. P. took some comfort from ex-Governor Carpenter's note saying: "I think you voted right on the Silver question. Whether the repeal . . . will help the country to prosperity or not, the people think so; or at least a majority of the business community think so, and it is just to try the experiment."[20]

Dolliver may have believed he was placing patriotism above partisanship, nationalism above sectionalism, when he cast his vote for unconditional repeal. Unquestionably his action was courageous in view of the known prosilver sentiment of his district. It is fair to question, however, whether in following the lead of Reed and Allison he rose above partisanship. An overwhelming majority of the Republicans in the House voted for the Wilson bill. Without their vote it could not have passed. Why did not Dolliver and other Western Republicans insist upon a substitute for unconditional repeal which offered some solution to the needs of the West and South for an adequate and flexible currency system? Dolliver's speech suggests an important clue, one which seriously damages the Republican claim of "rising above partisanship." In a brief paragraph he revealed the thinking of the party-firsters:

> Either the repeal of this law will help us or it will not. It it does, we shall all rejoice. If it does not, we shall all be nearer knowing what the matter is, and the Democratic party will be brought face to face with the omens of the disaster that must follow their tariff policy, with no cover to hide them and no subterfuge of explanation to keep them from an open responsibility. Therefore, as a partisan, I am in favor of clearing this issue so that every man may know that whatever follows the tariff act of this Congress comes from that act, and not from imaginary sources in another field of legislation.[21]

By permitting outright repeal, the Republicans eliminated a dangerous law for which they stood responsible. They allowed the Cleveland Democrats to shoulder the blame for "downing silver," a "crime" in the eyes of many voters which might well split the Democratic party in 1894 or 1896. Finally, by demanding no *quid pro quo* of the administration on the tariff, the Republicans left the way open for a wrangle on that question which might result in an unsatisfactory revision and thus provide the party of protection a winning issue as had the Mills Bill in 1888. This may have been good politics for Dolliver and his party. It was neither patriotism nor statesmanship.

President Cleveland and the Democrats likewise failed to provide a reasonable solution to the currency question. Cleveland, like Dolliver, was remarkably "courageous" in the negative matter of repealing a law which both knew ought never to have been passed. Neither displayed any great courage or forcefulness in the positive sense of fighting for the establishment of a banking and currency system adequate for the needs of the day. While the greatest blame for the failure of the government to solve the currency problem probably rests on the extremists of the silverite bloc to whom no solution short of free and unlimited coinage seemed acceptable, the fact remains that the forces mustered to repeal the Sherman Act were not rallied to pass any other measure aimed at accomplishing effective financial reforms.[22]

Dolliver, of course, was a mere Congressman. His responsibility as a member of the minority in the House was limited. His position as a Representative of an agrarian state prosilver in sentiment explains his resting quietly in the period 1893-1895 upon the unrealistic perch of the advocates of international bimetallism. Nevertheless, when able and moderate men bungle a serious problem, they open the way for radicals and reactionaries to squabble over extreme measures. The people, meantime, suffer unrelieved.

While Dolliver was in Washington for the special session, political developments in Iowa destined to concern his future were taking form. For one thing, the State Republican Convention abandoned the policy of supporting state-wide prohibition in an effort to unite the party for the gubernatorial and legislative election. This was a relief to Dolliver, who felt that "experience, our only guide in these things, shows that prohibition is only possible in spots" — as the Democrats had long asserted — and that to continue to stand for the old policy would weaken Republican candidates.[23] A direct result of the convention's action was Frank D. Jackson's victory over Governor Boies in the November election and the safe margin of control given the Republicans in the General Assembly. Probably of equal importance in accounting for their success at the polls was the Iowa Republican platform statement advocating equal legal value for gold, silver, and paper money.[24]

Of no less interest than the state election was the problem of the choice of a successor to United States Senator James F. Wilson, who had announced that he would not seek a third term in 1894. As early as January, 1893, the names of Jonathan P. Dolliver, George D. Perkins, John F. Lacey, James S. Clarkson, John H. Gear, Albert B. Cummins, William P. Hepburn, David B. Henderson, and John Y. Stone appeared as possible candidates. The suggestion that Clarkson should replace Wilson met with favor, and Dolliver, Cyrenus Cole, and others urged Ret to enter the race. Clarkson declined, feeling that those in the party who still "think prohibition is the *only* question in politics" would oppose him because he was advocating that the Republicans abandon "missionary work . . . and merely moral hobbies."[25]

Opposed to the election of Gear, and knowing that Henderson was "geographically unavailable," since he resided in the same city as Senator Allison, Clarkson advised Dolliver to seek the senatorship. "I see no reason why you should not take a fly at it," Ret wrote J. P. in February. Dolliver had "more senatorial timber" in him than Gear, Perkins, Lacey, Hull, or Hepburn, Clarkson thought. "But it all depends on what your friend Wm. B. Allison & the railroads back of him, should say or wish."[26] What W. B. Allison desired is not a matter of record, but it is not difficult to surmise that he did *not* want anyone who might rival him as *the* spokesman for Iowa in the United States Senate. The man selected by J. W. Blythe and the railroad magnates "back of" Allison was ex-Governor John H. Gear, Blythe's faither-in-law, aged seventy.

Others besides Clarkson peppered Dolliver with letters urging him to make a bid for the Senate. Carpenter informed him that "the boys are talking about making you United States Senator, and if you let them alone I think they will do it." Meservey and O'Connell both wrote that J. P. must consider himself "in the field for Senator." They expressed the belief that his chances were very good as there would be eight to ten candidates before the caucus and very likely a deadlock between the forces of the older aspirants which might well open the way for an agreement on Dolliver. "No other man has as large a following; no other man can arouse equal enthusiasm; and no other man can do as much as you to hold the state in the Republican line at this impending crisis," wrote another Iowa politician.[27]

Dolliver refused to announce any interest in being a candidate. Carpenter's view was that J. P. should "stump the state" for Republican candidates for the legislature, "win friends and do favors and then if the caucus gets tied up they will think of you."[28] Possibly Dolliver's following his old friend's advice explains his failure to enter the contest. More likely he realized that with the Allison support behind Gear, and R. P. Clarkson and the *Register* backing A. B. Cummins, the only chance he had was as a "dark horse" in a deadlocked legislative caucus.

When formal announcements of candidacy appeared, only Gear, Cummins, Lacey, Hepburn, Perkins, and Stone were in the race. The real struggle was between ex-Governor Gear and Albert B. Cummins, a brilliant lawyer who had won fame as an opponent of prohibition and as a foe of the barbed wire monopoly. In August, Cummins asked Allison for support, writing at the same time to Dolliver for his aid, unless Dolliver himself were a candidate, adding: "Whether you are 'for me' or 'agin me' be assured the placid waters of our friendship will not be disturbed."[29] Perkins, then one of Dolliver's closest friends in the House and a candidate Roberts favored, also requested Dolliver's backing. John F. Lacey, the former West Virginian whom Dolliver's father had baptized and greatly admired, wrote J. P.: "I would like to have you help me for your district holds the key to the [senatorial] situation."[30]

Dolliver's course was one of benevolent neutrality. His personal relationships with most of the candidates were such that he could not help one as against another. In September, Cummins wrote again saying that he had the impression that Dolliver might decide to run. This disturbed Cummins, who felt they ought not to oppose each other and said he would not have announced had he thought J. P. would be a candidate. "It won't be hard to induce me to make an assignment — and to whom rather than you? — but if nothing unexpected happens I have an instinct that I shall win."[31] This clever letter must have tickled Dolliver's sense of humor. Everyone knew Cummins wanted to be a Senator. His device of appealing to Dolliver on the grounds of "I would not oppose you, and might give you my strength if you ran, so you ought not to oppose me," was one Dolliver could easily recognize and enjoy.

Equally ludicrous was a proposal from L. S. Coffin, a Fort Dodge philanthropist and temperance leader, who had decided he should be a Senator. His approach was that the temperance people would oppose both Gear and Cummins, but that Cummins was the stronger candidate and might win. Therefore, Dolliver ought to support Coffin, an old man, because if Cummins were elected "it will mean 12 to 24 years of Cummins," whereas if Coffin could have the seat for six years then "you will be the logical candidate for this office."[32]

When the Republican caucus met in Des Moines in January, 1894, the chances of a deadlock were strong. Seven names — Gear, Cummins, Perkins, Lacey, Coffin, Stone, and Hepburn — were presented for consideration. But the strength of all except Gear and Cummins quickly vanished, and Gear won by two votes on the third ballot. He then defeated the Democratic nominee, former Governor Boies and became Allison's colleague.[33]

This was a significant senatorial contest. Gear's election was a clear-cut victory for J. W. Blythe and the railroad managers. But Cummins had demonstrated his strength as a politician determined sometime to have a seat in the Senate. The widespread sentiment favorable to Dolliver as a compromise nominee and the respect shown for him by the leading aspirants in their efforts to win his aid and keep him out of the race marked him as a powerful factor to reckon with in future dispositions of Iowa's senatorships.

While the maneuvering for the senatorial succession was at white heat in Iowa, Dolliver returned to Washington for the regular session of Congress in December, 1893. As expected, the President called for tariff reform including a reduction of duties upon "the necessaries of life" and "the removal of restrictions upon the importation of the raw materials necessary to our manufacturers." Cleveland believed that reduced tariff duties would in due time help "produce sufficient revenue to meet the needs of the Government."[34]

Congressman William L. Wilson, former president of West Virginia University, introduced the administration's tariff bill in December, and as chairman of the Ways and Means Committee he opened the debate on January 9, 1894. On the whole the Wilson bill began as a moderate compromise measure which aimed, as Wilson stated, to leave no duty high enough to enable anyone to get a monopoly of the home market for his product, but rather "to permit enough competition from without to protect American consumers from exaggerated prices and from combinations, and at the same time contribute some revenue to the public treasury."[35] Although the free list contained more than 340 subdivisions, including coal, iron, lumber, wool, cotton, raw silk, raw sugar, salt, and other raw materials, this was by no means a free-trade bill.[36]

There were, however, three important innovations: the adoption wherever practicable of ad valorem instead of specific rates; the remission of all duty on common necessities and raw materials for manufacturing; and a provision for a personal income tax of 2 per cent on incomes of $4,000 and above. The propertied classes of the North and East viewed the income tax proposal as a socialistic scheme supported by both "the shirtless Populist barbarians of the West" and the "Carl Schurz barbarians of the East." Spokesmen of special interests attacked the whole Wilson bill as "an extreme, insane measure." The truth was that this bill, as it stood in the House, represented a wise and conservative revision which left the American tariff "still more highly protective than that of any other country."[37]

Dolliver's position on the Wilson bill was extremely weak. He spoke at length on January 11, but instead of discussing the proposed revision he denounced "free trade" and the Walker Tariff of 1846, and attempted the impossible task of showing that the panic of 1893 was caused by the as yet unenacted tariff law of 1894. He did not comment on the income tax provision. The best that can be said of his remarks is that they were humorous and harmless and resulted in one of the few instances in which an opponent squelched him in debate. J. P., after ridiculing Wilson's so-called "free trade" theories as typical of the professorial mind, related that he had graduated from West Virginia University shortly before Wilson became president and had thus narrowly escaped being his student. "Sir," Wilson replied, "I have always regretted that the gentleman was not a pupil of mine. It was said by Dr. Johnson that you could make a great deal of a Scotchman if you caught him when he was young. And I have always believed that I could have made a great deal of so brilliant a youth as my friend from Iowa, if I had been able to teach him economics before he got to be a Republican politician."[38]

The sordid tale of the emasculation of the Wilson bill in the Senate, after its passage in the House, needs no repetition. The failure of the Congress, abetted by the "maladroit tactics" of President Cleveland, to reform the tariff along the lines of the original Wilson measure was one factor contributing to the defeat of the Democrats in the congressional elections of 1894 and is another example of the lack of statesmanship characteristic of the early nineties.[39]

Dolliver spoke frequently during the remainder of the session, which lasted until late summer. He was especially interested in larger appropriations for the navy and in preventing any decrease in pensions for veterans.[40] His greatest concern was to secure an appropriation to indemnify the settlers of the Des Moines River lands who had lost title to their homesteads because of complicated conflicts in grants made by the federal government to railroads and to the Des Moines River Improvement Company. This appropriation had been urged by Iowans in Congress for some twenty years, and Dolliver at last succeeded in tacking it on to the Sundry Civil Expenses bill. In July he wrote his father that the River Land appropriation "had been a hard thing to manage. But I have got it managed."[41]

Regardless of what was said or written in 1893 concerning Dolliver's position on the silver and tariff questions, by the late spring of 1894 his standing in his own district was better than ever. He had won friends by his vigorous efforts to get justice for the settlers of the upper Des Moines valley, and his success in the "Billion Dollar Congress" in securing appropriations for public buildings was in evidence, as wood and stone replaced news releases and blueprints. O'Connell wrote in March that he and Roberts were confident that Dolliver would have "no substantial opposition" for a fourth nomination. This was a conservative prediction, for the convention renominated Dolliver by acclamation on July 10.[42]

By 1894 the Iowa Republican party was conspicuously increasing its solidarity after years of dissension over the prohibition question. The enactment of the "Mulct" law by the legislature that year permitted a satisfactory type of local option and reduced the importance of liquor control as a political issue. The state platform pledged Iowa Republicans "to work for bimetallism" and for the "largest possible use of silver as money" consistent with parity of values. The Democratic stand on silver was more qualified, and that party in Iowa was showing signs of divisions between conservative elements supporting Cleveland and elements favoring fusion with the Populists. In the Tenth District the Democrats and Populists effected a fusion in an effort to defeat Dolliver. One result was that antifusion Democrats either voted for Dolliver or refused to vote at all. After an intensive campaign, Dolliver won by 14,356 votes, the largest majority he ever received.[43]

His re-election by nearly 10,000 more votes than he had in 1892 is indicative not merely of Dolliver's local popularity but also of the national trend which swept the Republicans into control of Congress. Republican candidates carried every district in Iowa and won seats in such Democratic strongholds as North Carolina, Tennessee, Virginia, Kentucky, West Virginia, and Missouri.[44] Dolliver's good friend, Champ Clark, one of the Missouri Democrats defeated, called the election "the greatest slaughter of the innocents since Herod." Congressman Wilson's West Virginia friends regarded his defeat by the Republicans and machine Democrats as making "the state the absolute property" of

Stephen B. Elkins and his father-in-law, Henry G. Davis, who respectively dominated the Republican and Democratic state organizations.[45] Nationally, the Democrats, blamed for the repeal of the Silver Act, the passage of the mongrel Wilson-Gorman Tariff, and the continuing depression, and beset with such problems as Coxey's Army and the Pullman strike, had been "found wanting in unity, efficiency and good sense in the sight of the country."[46]

Dolliver rejoiced in the great victory and planned a celebration dinner for his friends in the House as soon as they returned to Washington for the December session. Thomas B. Reed, in his note accepting Dolliver's invitation to this affair, lamented the loss of Champ Clark, "son of thunder," but expressed glee at the public's change of attitude toward the President. Reed observed that even the Boston papers now "speak disrespectfully" of Cleveland, "him whom Russell Lowell compared living with Abraham Lincoln dead." Cleveland "seems actually to be a man who will die like the rest of us," wrote Reed, "which is lucky for he would be heavy to translate."[47]

Reed's reference to Lowell was doubtless inspired by Dolliver's article entitled "A Glance at the Early Life of James Russell Lowell" which had just appeared in the November *Midland Monthly*, an Iowa magazine edited by Johnson Brigham. This essay was Dolliver's first serious literary effort, although he had earlier written news items for weekly papers in West Virginia, Illinois, and Iowa, and had impressed Clarkson and others as a writer of promise. Theodore Roosevelt thought this piece on Lowell was unusually fine. Teddy wrote Dolliver:

> I confess that I am a little surprised and disappointed that so admirable an article, one from a new standpoint, should not have appeared in one of the bigger magazines. I wish you had given me a chance to submit it to the Forum or the Atlantic. Magazine editors are kittle-cattle and often fail signally to see what is best; but I cannot believe they would all have been blind to so admirable an article. It is one of the best I have seen anywhere.[48]

Dolliver's observations concerning the factors which contributed to Lowell's development reveal at least as much about the Dolliver of 1894 as about the youthful Lowell:

> Two things enter into the building of Lowell's character which make the whole world his kin, — two genuine touches of nature, poverty and love. The one taught him to work, the other transfigured the world and opened for him the upper chambers of the imagination. . . . It surely puts him nearer to us to see him eagerly picking up odd chances to earn a little money . . . even postponing his union with the girl he loved that he might not bring her into the midst of a struggle to which she was not used. She was a woman of extraordi-

CYRUS C. CARPENTER

JAMES S. CLARKSON

GEORGE E. ROBERTS

ALBERT B. CUMMINS

JONATHAN PRENTISS DOLLIVER

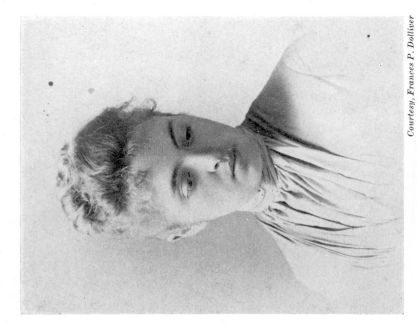

LOUISE PEARSONS DOLLIVER

nary personal endowments. It is not too much to say that the "white and gracious thoughts" which the poet found in her dominated his life, enlisted his early ambitions in the willing service of the right, making the very appearance of evil hateful to his eyes.[49]

Poverty Dolliver had known — and the love of family and devoted friends. But until he was thirty-six he paid no serious attention to the various young women who hoped he would fall in love with them. "No girl of my acquaintance has ever appealed to me as the 'fairest among ten thousand,'" young Jonathan had written his mother in 1878. "I will find some one later, as Father found you, by accident or providence. I only hope to have as good fortune as he had."[50] The following year, writing of a wedding he had attended at the Carpenter home, Dolliver told Mollie: "I have plenty of chances to 'yoke up' with fair and sprightly maidens, but am giving them the 'go-by.' None of us can afford to prospect a family of our own for many days — we must not think of it. We have reputations and standing in society to make first."[51] In the summer of 1881 a Miss Jennie Berry attracted Jonathan's attention briefly, but he corresponded with her for less than a month after she moved from Fort Dodge to Minneapolis. He ended the affair abruptly when he discovered that she was as interested in one of his friends as she professed to be in him. In his final letter, a carbon copy of which he kept, Dolliver asserted that it would be "unaccountable insanity for me to cast off my aged father and mother for the love of a school girl."[52]

His association with Governor Larrabee's daughter in the mid-eighties was not a love affair, as far as Jonathan was concerned, nor were his attentions to the daughters of Congressmen C. A. Boutelle of Maine and Philip C. Post of Illinois in the early nineties. He enjoyed the company of women, and his correspondence indicates that he was popular not only with the young ladies but also with several mothers who quite obviously encouraged his interest in their marriageable daughters.[53]

It was sixteen years from the time of Jonathan's boyish letter to his mother describing the qualities he sought in a bride until, "by accident or providence," he discovered Louise Pearsons. Propinquity and prosperity probably had much to do with this match. Louise was an intimate friend of Gay Dolliver, and was often in the Dolliver household; poverty no longer prevented Jonathan from considering marriage. Jonathan and Louise had known each other for many years, although, as she was eight years his junior, they were not often together until 1893 or 1894. Her father, George R. Pearsons, a native of Bradford, Vermont, had settled in Fort Dodge in 1868 and had become mayor in 1873. A brother of D. K. Pearsons, the Chicago philanthropist, George Pearsons was himself a well-to-do landowner, prominent in various business enterprises in Iowa.[54]

Louise Pearsons received her early education at Dana Hall and was graduated from Wellesley College with the class of 1889. She then taught in the Presbyterian College at Fort Dodge for two years and at Northwestern Academy in Evanston from 1893 to 1895. The first evidence of Jonathan's having given her more than the courteous attention he showed to all of his sisters' friends is found in family letters of 1894. At Christmas time he gave her a book, and the first letter which she wrote to him was to thank him for that gift.[55]

By July of 1895 they were secretly engaged, but the secret was ill kept. Gay wrote Louise, shortly after J. P. returned from a visit with Louise at Lake Okoboji, that Jonathan "seems to be absent-minded with a far-away look in his eye. . . . You must write me what went on at the lake last week so I may know just how hard an *attack* he has." Robert learned the news in August and rejoiced "in the prospect that the tone and character of the family circle will be thus elevated" by the marriage. When the public announcement of the engagement appeared in the newspapers, letters and telegrams of congratulation poured in. George Perkins wrote his colleague that the news "is in line with the best testimonials to your judgment I have met and should settle the question of a unanimous renomination next year without a further word." All agreed that Dolliver was fortunate in his betrothal to a mature, well-educated, gracious woman who shared his interests and ambitions. "This is the most sensible act of your sensible career," wrote State Senator A. B. Funk, distinguished editor of the Spirit Lake *Beacon*.[56]

The aged James J. Dolliver officiated at the wedding on November 20, 1895. It was a great social event, attended by notables from all over the state as well as by people of the most humble walks of life. Workmen, weary and soiled, walking home at the end of day, stopped by the church to listen to the music, and Dolliver had them invited inside to shake hands and to meet his bride.[57] "It does not seem possible that millions of people have been married before us," J. P. wrote Louise, "that millions of hearts have felt the strange emotions of the wedding rites, that millions of feet have kept step to poor old Mendelssohn's great popular air . . . and that we are only joining the procession. . . . Such a sweet experience was never in my heart before. Oh! Louise, let us pray that no shadow may ever fall on our love."[58]

Champ Clark, writing a friendly letter of congratulations, concluded: "A good wife is a good thing."[59] This was especially true in Dolliver's case. He was the kind of man to whose career the character of his life companion made a great difference. He needed a woman's love, understanding, and encouragement, and he wanted a home and children. Louise was noted for her sound judgment, her business ability, and her fine touch in social and political relations. The surviving comments of their contemporaries indicate a unanimous opinion that Jonathan and Louise were unusually happy together and that her influence on his career was very great. Senator John C. Spooner of Wisconsin told Dolliver: "You never amounted to anything until Mrs. Dolliver took hold of you; your speeches have been better and your life on a better level since you got married." Dolliver frequently wrote, as he did in 1900, that their years together were "not only the best years of my life — they are the only real life I have lived — all before was vanity and vexation. You are the making of me."[60] Perhaps the words of an humble old German woman, "Grandma" Kliendof, who loved them both, were not wide of the mark. She told Louise that "if you and Mr. J. P. had both hunted the world over you could not have done so well."[61]

- XI -

The Battle of Silver and Gold, 1896

So far as the State of Iowa is concerned, the men who follow the plough all day long in the hot sun, thinking over questions of political economy, have a record for conservative prudence in these complex national affairs from which many of their critics could derive useful lessons.

Jonathan P. Dolliver, 1896

FOLLOWING A BRIEF wedding trip, Dolliver and his bride established their first Washington home at the Hamilton Hotel. J. P. seems to have been completely happy, and he had reason to feel that he had "arrived" both politically and socially in Washington. When the new Congress met in December, 1895, he received a coveted place on the Ways and Means Committee, the most important in the House, as well as retaining his seat on the Naval Affairs Committee.[1]

The President's annual message, read to the Congress on December 2, gave especial prominence "to the condition of our foreign relations and the exigencies of our national finances." Dolliver, as yet not greatly interested in foreign policy, expressed no opinion on the Venezuelan controversy which provided the major topic of conversation as 1895 turned into 1896. Of greater concern to him were the "exigencies of our national finances." In brief, the problem of maintaining the government's gold reserve remained unsolved despite the repeal of the Sherman Silver Purchase Act and the efforts of the administration to replenish the Treasury's supply of gold through the sale of bonds. On December 3, 1895, the gold reserve stood at $79,333,000 and was steadily falling, and the economic depression which had begun in 1893 continued.[2]

The new Republican House, of which Thomas B. Reed was the Speaker and in which Nelson Dingley, Jr., former Governor of Maine, was chairman of the Ways and Means Committee, at once began work on an "Emergency Revenue Bill." The committee met "day and night and even on Christmas" in order to frame this measure. Strange to say, however, this so-called Dingley bill was

118

not designed to establish an orderly currency and banking system nor even to implement requests of President Cleveland and Treasury Secretary John Carlisle for authorization to issue low-rate gold bonds. Instead, the Republicans, holding to their 1893 line that the Democratic tariff was the cause of the trouble, proposed to repeal the Wilson-Gorman Act. Their "Emergency Revenue Bill," built largely around a tariff on wool, was supposed to "reassure manufacturers who would employ the workingmen and start the wheels of industry; while bringing in needed revenue it would end business depression." [3]

Dolliver enthusiastically supported the Dingley bill which passed the House on December 26. Nothing came of it, however, as the Silver Senators refused to act on a tariff bill unless something were done for silver. The administration turned a fourth time to a bond sale to increase the gold reserve, and the Dingley Bill became a "mere campaign document, a statement of what the Republican leaders would do if they could" — an assertion of the theory that the issue of 1896 was the tariff. [4]

Although Dolliver continued to hold that the depression was a result of the election of a "free trade" Democratic government in 1892, he had, by 1896, crystallized his thinking on the silver question. In 1890 he had voted for the Sherman Silver Purchase bill and had favored the free coinage of silver. Three years later he helped repeal that act, but stood for bimetallism. With the failure of the International Monetary Conferences to reach agreement on bimetallic standards and the rise of the radical free-silver element in American politics, Dolliver moved into the ranks of the gold-standard advocates. His vacillating course on the currency question in part reflected the failure of the Republican party to adopt any consistent policy on the issue until the midnineties. Likewise, his change of position was partly due to his careful study of financial theory and his growing conviction that an unlimited coinage of silver would lead to uncontrolled inflation disastrous to farmers and workers as well as to creditors. Representing a district which favored flexible and abundant currency, Dolliver risked his political life by coming out squarely for the gold standard before the Republican party was committed to it — and certainly no such commitment existed to the extent that he could defend his position on grounds of party loyalty until after the national convention of June, 1896. [5]

The influence of George E. Roberts was undoubtedly great in leading Dolliver to think through the money question. Since the Greenback fight, Roberts had been against "unsound money." In 1895 he published his famous pamphlet entitled *Coin at School in Finance.* This was an answer to William H. Harvey's free-silver tract, *Coin's Financial School,* which was attracting an immense amount of attention. [6]

Roberts wrote in the language of the kindergarten. His book was crudely

Dolliver flatly denied that free coinage would meet the need for an expanded currency.

> You say that you wish to have more money in circulation in the United States. . . . It will take you fifteen years, working the mints of the United States at their full capacity, to make as many new coins of silver as the enactment of a law for the free coinage of silver will drive out of use in gold in the United States in three months. . . . Your proposal . . . will destroy an element in the monetary volume of the modern business community more precious than either gold or silver — the character and commercial integrity, without which no business prosperity is possible.

Recalling the views of Thomas Hart Benton, which had won that great Missouri Democrat the nickname "Old Bullion" in the age of Andrew Jackson, Dolliver reminded the free-silver Democrats that Benton had "wanted the humblest workingman in the United States to be paid for his labor with a coin as good as the money of the crowned heads of the Old World."

Dolliver attacked the silver advocates at a weak spot when he pointed out that if a monetary system were established which raised prices the workingman would suffer because his pay would not rise accordingly. Thus for Americans to vote for such a program "will manifest a lack of common sense that has never characterized the working people of any country in any age."

Furthermore, as to the immediate effect on the debtor, Dolliver emphasized a practical point when he asserted that "long before the name of a President of the United States could be signed" to a free-silver bill, creditors would demand immediate payment of all short-term notes and refuse to renew mortgages or to extend credit. This "loss of individual credit and of national character would be beyond the remedy of time," he thought, and he quoted Daniel Webster's statement that "credit has done more a thousand times to enrich nations than all the mines of the world." Hence, Dolliver warned of the danger of trying to increase the number of coins by means that tend to impair the exercise of commercial credit. "Credit commands all commodities exactly as the coin itself commands them," he asserted, "and, therefore, must be reckoned as a part of the volume of money in any intelligent estimate of the relation of money to prices. The great economists from Adam Smith and John Stuart Mill until today, admit that credit has substantially the same effect on prices as money itself."

When asked if he were in favor of the coinage of silver dollars, Dolliver replied that he was, providing every one of them was "equivalent in value to the dollar of gold." Frankly admitting that he had changed his views since 1890, he stated: "For myself I have made up my opinion in this matter slowly and deliberately, not only contrary to my sympathies, but also to my prejudices, guided at every step by the experience of the nations of the world." [9]

This address was well received and widely read. It was one of the most effective replies to the silverites delivered in the House, and it put Dolliver on record for the maintenance of the existing monetary standard months before the Republican party and such men as William McKinley decided whether to be "gold-bug," "silver-bug," or "straddle-bug." The one defect of the speech and of Dolliver's stand on the whole question was his failure to offer any alternative to the 16 to 1 formula other than the status quo. At least he was candid enough to confess this. "It is vain to talk of the hardships that now surround us," he told the House. "I know something of them; but hard as the place is in which we stand, nevertheless we are able to stand, and if you ask me what we propose to do, I will assure you that we intend to stay where we are, unless some one can tell with some degree of certainty whether the leap proposed is toward the solid ground or into the bottomless pit."[10] This frank and concise statement, free of hedging and hypocrisy, unequivocally defined the position of intelligent conservatism.

Less than a month after his currency address in the House, Dolliver arrived in Des Moines to preside as temporary chairman of the Republican State Convention called to choose delegates to the National Convention and to endorse Senator William B. Allison for the presidential nomination.[11] Allison's defeat by Harrison in 1888 did not cause him to give up hope of being President, nor had his shoddy treatment of Ret Clarkson caused that would-be Warwick to abandon efforts to put the Iowa Senator in the White House.

As early as October, 1894, Clarkson had written Allison, advising him to be a candidate for the 1896 nomination and assuring him of support. Clarkson also warned Allison to secure re-election to the Senate when his term expired in 1896 before concentrating on the presidential race. This was because Clarkson believed that Albert B. Cummins, "whose ambition is so great as to be surprising," was thinking of the Senate seat for himself.[12] Undoubtedly Clarkson was right about Cummins. As a matter of fact, Cummins had already urged Allison to seek the presidency several months before Clarkson did. "I believe the effort can be made successful," Cummins wrote. He suggested that Allison would be the best man in the party to give the Republicans "a distinctive position upon the silver & currency questions." Cummins believed that the party needed to be relieved from "adhesion to the single standard," but he was opposed to "unrestricted coinage of silver."[13]

Allison replied that while he was not eager for the nomination, he did not feel he had any right to deny Iowans the use of his name if they desired to do so. The money question will be brought forward as the unsettled problem & will be uppermost in the North & West," he predicted, without commenting on Cummins' position.[14]

Throughout 1895 Clarkson, now an absentee Iowan in business in New York, sought Eastern support for Allison and also stirred his Western friends to action. He commissioned Cyrenus Cole to prepare a campaign biography of Allison and guided the efforts of Blythe, Cummins, Rich, Gear, and other Hawkeye politicians who for one reason or another hoped to promote the old Senator to the presidency. In Clarkson's opinion, William McKinley was the man to beat, if Allison were to win the nomination. Ret professed to believe that McKinley was spending too much money, especially in rounding up Southern delegates. "There is something in the average Republican that recoils against the use of money to gain a Presidential nomination," wrote Clarkson — the same Clarkson who had helped Wanamaker elect Harrison in 1888! "It is so high and exalted an office that a mercenary hand should never touch it," he continued. "Allison is gaining strength all the while. . . . The most powerful men in the East are for him either first or second, while we are also going to have in my judgment the best States in the South pretty nearly solid and many of the best delegates in the worst States. The men who buy and sell we do not want."[15] This was a pretty song, but a rather strange tune for the old spoilsman! If he were sincere, and there is reason to believe he was, he certainly had much to learn about garnering Republican delegates in 1896. He was right on one point — McKinley was the leading contender, the man to stop.[16]

In January, 1896, the Iowa General Assembly re-elected Allison to the Senate as had become customary every six years. The State Republican Convention met on March 11 to endorse him as Iowa's candidate for the presidential nomination. Dolliver's task as temporary chairman was to set the stage for an enthusiastic pro-Allison demonstration. There were McKinley men in the ranks of the Hawkeye Republicans, and Clarkson *et al.* were taking no risks of losing even one Iowa delegate at the National Convention.[17]

Dolliver received a thunderous ovation upon taking the chair, and "each telling point of his hour-long address was heartily cheered." Placing the blame for the depression on an unfavorable balance of trade which he attributed to the Democratic tariff, Dolliver asserted that the first duty of a new Republican administration would be to make prompt provision for an adequate national revenue. "It is a pitiful and wicked thing to leave so good a man as Uncle Sam, who has always done a middling good business in his own name, standing in front of an empty safe, talking in a whisper with a group of gentlemen with an appetite for fresh bonds," he told the applauding delegates. "It is an interesting fact that this country never had a protective tariff that did not produce a sufficient revenue," he said. "A community that has sense enough to buy what it needs at home always has money enough left to gratify a reasonable taste for luxuries and novelties of foreign production." The Republican hope of making the tariff the main issue of the campaign partly accounts for his devoting so much attention to that subject. Nevertheless, he did not ignore the monetary issue, and, although he knew many in the convention opposed his stand, Dolliver did not soft-pedal his criticism of free silver. "For one, I want that exact equality of paper with coin, and of all existing coins of the same denomination with each other, inviolably preserved," he said as he began an attack upon Populist financial theories.[18]

Dolliver's keynote address served its intended purpose. A solid Allison delegation was elected without opposition, and A. B. Cummins, the permanent chairman, piloted the convention to a peaceful adjournment without any effort on the part of the McKinleyites "to bust the slate."[19]

Dolliver's participation in this convention is interesting for three reasons. In the first place, his speech, when compared with those he made under similar circumstances in 1884 and 1888, reveals his development. Gone is the unfettered partisanship of his youth. He seems almost kind to the Democrats. Perhaps Mrs. Dolliver was responsible for this improvement. Secondly, Dolliver demonstrated his courage in standing solidly for a principle — sound money — which was not yet supported by his party in Iowa. It is significant that he was not chosen as a delegate to the Republican National Convention in 1896, although eight years previously the state convention had gone "Dolliver mad" and elected him a delegate-at-large. Thirdly, much as he admired Allison, he did not think the Senator could win the nomination. Dolliver had seen the beginning of the movement for William McKinley in 1892. It was Dolliver who, in 1895, had hailed the Ohio Governor as the "Advance Agent of Prosperity," a phrase that caught the fancy of reporters and cartoonists who used it repeatedly in 1896.[20]

By the time the Republican National Convention met in St. Louis on June 16, the nomination of McKinley was a foregone conclusion. Even Clarkson admitted as much in late May, and so did the supporters of Thomas B. Reed, a stronger rival of McKinley than Allison ever was. Dolliver attended the convention for the fun of it and to "do a little politicking" for Allison. At the end of the first day he wrote his wife, with apparent satisfaction, "Sound Money goes in the platform."[21] The nomination for the vice-presidency of his old friend, Garret A. Hobart of New Jersey, also pleased Dolliver. With the party platform of June embodying the monetary principles for which he had spoken in February and with two men whom he had long known at the head of the national ticket, Dolliver returned to Fort Dodge to attend to some pressing personal politics.

As soon as J. B. Romans had become convinced that Dolliver meant what he said about sound money, he began a campaign to organize the silver Republicans of the Tenth District for the purpose of preventing Dolliver's renomination. In March a county chairman wrote Dolliver that "J. B. Romans is the new Moses who is offering to lead our farmers out of the wilderness." Romans was "storming the school districts" trying to get the voters to pledge themselves to support no candidate, from President to constable, who was not for free silver. He soon decided that his best chance of beating Dolliver was to join the free-silver Democrats, get the congressional nomination of that party, and hope for support of silver Republicans in November. To aid him in undermining his former friend, Romans secured the services of William Jennings Bryan of nearby Nebraska.[22] Bryan, no longer in Congress, was very popular with the free-silver people in Iowa. Known as the "Boy Orator of the Platte," he was one of the few men in America who approached Dolliver in oratorical ability.[23] From mid-March until June, when not otherwise engaged in promoting his own interests within the Democratic party, Bryan filled speaking engagements in the Tenth District of Iowa.

On June 25, J. B. Hungerford of Carroll, a warm supporter of Dolliver, wrote of Bryan's speeches in that vicinity during the previous week. "The coinage feeling is rampant," Hungerford informed J. P., "and we need someone to answer [Bryan] — and one as good as Bryan or not at all." [24] Dolliver's reply, written less than two weeks before Bryan's dramatic nomination for the presidency in the Democratic Convention, indicated the Iowan's assessment of the "Peerless Leader," and his own determination to win renomination and reelection:

> I suppose that Bryan's talks will catch a good many of the people, though, as you say, there is a long summer before us for thought and meditation, and I do not believe that the damage to our cause will be great. I know the young man [Bryan] very well, and have heard him, in Congress, describe all the evils which we now suffer, attribute them to the protective tariff, and promise all the relief needed by the speedy adoption of the policy of free trade. I do not believe his talk, in the long run, will amount to anything. He was afraid to run for Congress, in his own District, two years ago, and I do not believe that he will very seriously promote the candidacy of our friend Romans. I will send you some silver literature. . . . I intend to make a thorough canvass of this District, holding meetings in nearly every village, taking with me maps and tables and literature. . . . We must not allow the prosperity of the American people to be totally ruined without making an honest and earnest appeal to the intelligence of the community to prevent it. I do not believe that we shall fail, or come any ways near failing, but I have the most perfect confidence in the good sense of the public.[25]

On July 29 the Tenth District Congressional Convention met at Jefferson, Iowa. After electing George E. Roberts chairman of the congressional committee and perfecting the organization of the convention, the delegates adopted a resolution expressing their "appreciation of the faithful, intelligent and efficient service rendered the district by our present Congressman, Hon. J. P.

Dolliver," and recommending "that he be renominated." Immediately thereafter every delegate voted for a motion declaring Dolliver to be the nominee
by acclamation. Including Dolliver's brief speech of acceptance, the session
lasted just twenty-five minutes.

Upon adjournment those present joined a large crowd waiting at the east
side of the courthouse for the opening address of Dolliver's campaign. The
Jefferson *Bee* regarded it "as the best possible evidence of the high esteem in
which Mr. Dolliver is held by the people of Greene County that, in the face
of the fact that 'The Greatest Show on Earth' gave a performance at the same
time he spoke, more than 2,000 people should assemble to have some of the
dark spots in the financial question made clear, and hard knots untangled."
Dolliver's speech was similar in most respects to the one of February which he
delivered in the House, and was typical of the scores of campaign addresses he
made in the three months before the November election. "I have come to instruct, if possible," he began. "I find the people want to know facts, and so I
am here to stand face to face with my friends and neighbors and discuss matters that concern us all." He urged his listeners to get rid of whatever prejudices they had acquired, because the money question was one "requiring investigation and thought." Expressing his confidence in the people to decide
wisely, he asserted that the "counterfeit orators" of the free-silver stripe would
discover that they were "not dealing with a weak and feeble people, but with
thinking men whose judgment upon serious questions may be depended upon."

Dolliver used twenty large charts illustrating the statistics he quoted as he
reviewed the history of the currency question and the relation of the price of
silver to gold and of each to commodities. One point stressed in his campaign
speeches which he had merely mentioned in the February debate in the House
was the "Crime of 1873." According to Bryan and his adherents, the demon-
etization of silver in 1873 "destroyed one half the metal money of the country." Dolliver bluntly denied the truth of this.

> I know how much there was then and how much there is now.
> . . . The total output of standard silver dollars from the foundation
> of the mint in 1792 to 1873 was 8,031,000. . . . Since 1873 there
> have been coined over $500,000,000 in silver dollars. . . . So that
> since that "one-half" was destroyed the mints of the U. S. have pro-
> duced more than 75 times as many silver dollars as were made from
> the foundation of the government up to 1873.
>
> Now what is left of Bryan's argument when he said the government
> had destroyed half our metal money? They say the effect was to
> double the value of the other half and thus drag down the value of
> silver and with it all merchandise and produce. Whatever it may be
> that has destroyed the bullion value of silver it was not the Act of
> 1873. You say, what then has sent silver down? Here is one thing:
> In 1873 there was produced 63,000,000 ounces of silver; in 1894,
> 167,000,000 ounces; in 1896, 200,000,000 ounces. With this extraor-

dinary output we have seen the price of silver fall from $1.30 per ounce to 63 cents per ounce. This is the chief reason.

Citing historical examples to prove his point, Dolliver showed that there was no necessary connection between the decline of the price of goods and the decline of the price of silver. He suggested that the use of improved machinery and the opening of so much land in the Northwest had brought overproduction and that the unemployment and low wages of the urban laborer led to under-consumption. These factors, he thought, plus the conditions of the world markets, had much more to do with low prices than did silver.

Of this opening address an editor wrote: "Other years farmers may have gone to political speeches to be amused and entertained . . . but they are not doing it this year. . . . They want facts and figures. . . . They came to get a few points . . . and they went home with a wagon load. . . . That tent and those charts will do the business."[26]

The reference to the "tent" pertained to an announcement that Dolliver had "hired an immense tent and proposes to go from district to district expounding the truth." That was precisely what he did, for he was advised by his party lieutenants in Webster, Crawford, Boone, Hamilton, Carroll, and Kossuth that those counties might vote Democratic.[27] Even Mark Hanna, McKinley's manager, became alarmed after a private poll indicated that there were 30,000 political bolters in Iowa and that the Hawkeye state appeared likely to go for Bryan. In efforts to calm the pro-silver Republicans, Iowa's national commit-teeman, A. B. Cummins, stated in late August: "I favor the coinage of silver upon the ratio of the real or intrinsic value of the two metals," while Senator Allison and Representative Hepburn emphasized the meaningless statement in the Republican platform favoring an international agreement for the use of silver and gold as money. Ret Clarkson wrote Dolliver to tell the voters that the Republicans "do not mean gold monometallism" despite the wording of the St. Louis platform.[28]

Dolliver wisely rejected Clarkson's suggestion of resorting to double-talk. Much of his strength and popularity lay in the fact that his people believed in his integrity and sincerity even when they might doubt the wisdom of his stand on a specific issue. The campaign of 1896 was the most strenuous of Dolliver's entire career, but there is not the slightest evidence in that contest or in any other in which Dolliver engaged that he ever stooped to dishonest, shoddy, or underhanded tactics to secure a vote. His papers and those of his contempo-raries in Iowa politics reveal no trace of deceit or double-dealing on Dolliver's part, and even hostile newspapers never accused him on that score. He told the people the facts as he saw them. He tried to convince them that his posi-tion was sound, not fool them into believing that his party platform did not mean what it clearly did mean. Time and again in the 1896 contest Dolliver told his audiences:

If I have not told you the truth in this matter I urge you not to vote to return me to Congress. If I cannot tell the truth when talking to my friends and neighbors I deserve to be retired to private life. . . . All I ask is that men will take time to examine the facts upon which the campaign is based; investigate; take counsel of your wife; talk; think and reason, and if you honestly conclude that it is for the best interests of the people to place the affairs of state in the hands of Mr. Bryan, then you have my permission to vote for him.[29]

Dolliver, unlike Theodore Roosevelt, Henry Cabot Lodge, William Allen White, and numerous editors, preachers, and Republican stump speakers, did not stoop to name-calling and vituperation in the fight against Bryan and free silver.

As the campaign wore on, Dolliver undertook to show the Iowa farmer that free and unlimited coinage of silver would produce an inflation which would increase not only the price of the things the farmer had to sell but likewise of what he had to buy. Furthermore, the farmer would soon find that the industrial wage-earner, who consumed agricultural products, could not secure wage increases commensurate with the rise in prices. Thus, the farmers' market would be glutted and agricultural prices would drop. Finally, Dolliver suggested that when debtors began paying off loans and mortgages in debased currency, interest rates would naturally rise and credit for the farmer who needed it in the future might be difficult, if not impossible, to get.

Dolliver traveled tirelessly, speaking daily throughout every county, town, and nearly every township in his huge district. He wrote his wife regularly of his progress in giving the people "the gospel truth of politics for two and a half hours" at each meeting. In addition, he did yeoman service for the national ticket and for other congressional candidates throughout Iowa and in neighboring states. He received valuable aid from Leslie M. Shaw, a Denison lawyer and banker, who entered politics as a speaker for sound money in 1896, and, of course, from George Roberts and his Coin at School in Finance.[30] The National Committee allotted $10,000 for expenses in the Tenth District, more money than Dolliver had ever had before, but the need seemed great. Important also was the attitude of the gold Democrats. John McCarthy, the Tenth District member of the Democratic State Central Committee, offered his services "in any place in the district" and promised that many Democrats would vote for Dolliver. Citizens of German birth who had gone Democratic over the prohibition question in the 1880's were for sound money.[31]

It was a remarkable campaign. As Jesse Macy observed, the 1896 contest in Iowa was "characterized by earnest and sincere discussion of the issue — viz., the free coinage of silver. . . . Old party lines and former issues were in large part ignored."[32] Dolliver, faced with what even the "experts" of the East regarded as almost certain defeat and with the problem of overcoming marked public hostility to the course he advocated, took his case to the people in an

effort comparable to that of President Harry S. Truman in 1948. If the test of
campaign oratory and straightforward argument on the issues is the result secured on election day, Dolliver's speeches on silver must be ranked among his
greatest, and his work in the crucial "battle of the standards" must stand in
significance next to his service in fighting for railroad regulation in 1906 and
as an Insurgent in 1909-1910. His victory was a smashing vindication of his
trust in the wisdom of the people to choose sensibly if given the facts. He
defeated Romans by 10,968 votes — next to the highest majority he ever received. McKinley carried Iowa, and the Republicans won control of the White
House and both branches of Congress.

Bryan and his followers failed to make the most of what ought to have been
their basic issue, namely, "that the people, not the corporations and men of
wealth alone, should control the government, and that the government should
suppress the tendencies of the plutocrats to exploit the poor." [33] Getting side-
tracked on the currency question, the Bryanites found it impossible to convince
thinking people that the free-silver panacea would not in the end hurt the
farmer and laborer more than it would the plutocracy.

Like Jackson, Benton, and Lincoln, Dolliver was first of all a nationalist.
He appealed to the voters on the grounds of national interest and the welfare
of all classes. His blindness to the threat of plutocracy and his pious conservatism are revealed in such statements as the following:

> I have made up my mind that the Lord in His own good time has
> methods of scattering the wealth of the world; that no unscrupulous
> money power can long dominate the human race; that this world will
> in the end be governed by the manhood and womanhood there is in it,
> and that no syndicate of avarice can drive the integrity out of Ameri-
> can politics and American business.[34]

Dolliver offered no program for controlling plutocracy in 1896, partly because he underestimated its strength, partly because he believed that the "conservative influences that belong to time," and providence would solve the
problem, and partly because his opponents did not force him to consider the
matter seriously. The Bryan party set up the straw man of free silver; Dolliver
took that apart and scattered the pieces. He merely had to ask the people to
choose between sound money and unsound money, between gold and silver,
between probable prosperity and possible panic. His position would have been
weak if challenged by an intelligent liberal alternative, but it was strong enough
to swamp the radicals of the silver crusade.

It is inconceivable that Dolliver would have agreed with a recent assessment
of the election of 1896 as "a contest between a highly efficient machine and an
emotionally aroused rabble, frankly a class and sectional struggle." [35] Certainly any slight acquaintance with editorials in conservative newspapers and
journals, sermons in "respectable" churches, and campaign literature distrib-

uted by agents of industry and finance provides proof positive that Bryan's "rabble" had no monopoly on aroused emotions.[36] As to the so-called "class and sectional struggle," Dolliver stated specifically time after time:

> This is one nation and one people. When I find a man going about trying to incite one section of the country against another, I put him down as an enemy of his country and a dangerous man. . . . I do not want labor paid in a 50 cent dollar. . . . Neither do I want pensioners, depositors in banks, or creditors paid in 50 cent dollars. . . . I don't want the credit of the United States destroyed.[37]

The debt-ridden Iowa farmers described in Romans' letter heard and read their Congressman's speeches. Their emotions may have been aroused by Bryan, but they voted for Dolliver, who believed that the true interests of farmer and wage-earner, creditor and debtor, businessman and banker could be best protected in a strong nation with a sound money policy.

Generalizations about a national election seldom explain very much. The rise of the price of wheat between August and November of 1896 may have helped the Republicans, but it surely meant more to the farmers of Kansas than to the corn-growers of Iowa — yet Kansas voted for Bryan. There undoubtedly was "a class and sectional struggle," but the fact that the Solid South voted as usual for the Democratic nominee (although in some Southern states Bryan's vote was less than Cleveland's had been in 1892) while all the border states, except Missouri, went Republican is not convincing proof of sectionalism. Nor is the discovery that eight of the Midwestern states gave their electoral votes to McKinley with four going to Bryan. Enough wage-earners voted for McKinley and the "Full Dinner Pail" to carry all of the industrial Northeast for the Republicans in the "class struggle" of 1896, but the Rocky Mountain states, dominated by millionaire mine-owners, were solidly for Bryan.

Whether laboring men voted for McKinley because their employers told them the "whistle would not blow on Wednesday" if Bryan were elected or because they believed in sound money and reasoned that no matter who won the factories would open, lest stockholders lose dividends, is a matter of some importance. The assumption that the explanation was the coercion of the workers carries the implication of a degradation of democracy which one having Dolliver's faith in the common man could not accept. It was alleged that agents of the great insurance companies owning mortgages on Iowa farms attempted to come to an understanding with every farmer "that if McKinley were elected they would grant five years' extension of the loan at a low rate of interest." If this were true, Dolliver would not have believed that many of his constituents could have been thus bought — and conclusive evidence that they were is probably nonexistent.[38]

The personal equation is important but frequently neglected. Whatever may have determined the outcome elsewhere in 1896, the evidence in the Tenth

Iowa District suggests that Dolliver's personal leadership was of paramount significance. There Bryan himself discussed the issue upon which he chose to stand or fall and spoke on it with great frequency and over a long period of time. At the beginning of 1896 and of the campaign, sentiment in the Tenth was clearly pro-silver. Nevertheless, between the last of July and election day, Dolliver, speaking almost exclusively on that issue, offering no new economic remedies, and making no promises, won a decisive victory.

Albert Cummins who had succeeded Clarkson as a member of the Republican National Committee wrote Dolliver: "You will not suspect me of flattery when I say that I believe that your personal campaign was the best that was carried on in the United States." The Republican state chairman asserted that Dolliver's "strong campaign . . . had as much as any one thing to do in turning the tide our way." Many others expressed the belief that the Fort Dodge Congressman played a major role in carrying the Hawkeye State for the national ticket.[39]

Dolliver's influence on the campaign outside of Iowa can not be assessed. His speeches in other states were said to have been effective and to have placed the Republican National Committee "under great obligations to the [Iowa] State Campaign Committee."[40] His christening McKinley "The Advance Agent of Prosperity" provided the Republicans with an important and widely used phrase, but the vote catching value of such intangibles escapes calculation. The same is true of the quotations and arguments taken from his currency address of February 12 and used in the campaign literature which Mark Hanna's agents scattered profusely throughout the nation.[41] William McKinley was one who knew of and appreciated Dolliver's efforts. The President-elect wrote in mid-November, expressing his thanks for Dolliver's services and inviting him to "drop in on me" at Canton.[42] It is not without significance that McKinley appointed Dolliver's closest friend, George E. Roberts, Director of the Mint, and named M. D. O'Connell of Fort Dodge, J. P.'s former law partner, Solicitor of the Treasury.[43]

It has been the custom of scholars and publicists to attribute the outcome of the 1896 campaign to various economic factors, one of which inevitably is the vast sum of money spent by the Republicans. Similarly, the Democratic victory of 1936 is explained in terms of "reliefers" refusing to bite the hand that doled out government checks. In each case these "pocketbook" theories probably have much validity. Nevertheless, Dolliver's experience in the "Big Tenth" in 1896 justified his Jeffersonian belief in the ability of the people to vote intelligently in the national interest if properly informed on the issue at stake and if they would put aside their prejudices to think and reason. Naturally, in the Old South and the silver states such rising above prejudice was unlikely in 1896, just as it was in 1936 in Maine and Vermont. Elsewhere, in both elections, one with Jonathan Dolliver's faith in democracy would not hesitate to suggest that in 1896 for the conservatives and in 1936 for the liberals, the majority of Americans voted as they did in the sincere conviction that they safeguarded the welfare and advanced the best interests of the nation — regardless of the money distributed by a Mark Hanna or a Harry Hopkins. Perhaps Dolliver, the classically-educated agrarian, unfamiliar with the boss-ridden corruption of urban politics in the immigrant-infested industrial centers, was merely naive in 1896. But certainly his faith in the integrity of man was greater than his fear of the venality of the masses.

- XII -

Making a Tariff and a Governor, 1897

The fact is that a great many things get in a tariff bill and a great many things get out of it without the consent of those who are finally called upon to answer for the defects and shortcomings of the law.
Jonathan P. Dolliver, Speech in the House

AS VIEWED IN RETROSPECT as well as by some contemporaries, the election of 1896 symbolized the triumph of industrialism over agrarianism, of Hamilton over Jefferson, of capital over labor. To Henry Adams, McKinley's victory meant that the bankers became "the greatest single power in the country and infallibly control the drift of events."[1] President Cleveland, relieved at the defeat of his own party, wrote that "recent events may well cause those who represent business interests to rejoice on their escape from threatened perils."[2] On the other hand, the fact that Bryan polled 6,467,946 votes signfied the magnitude of the dissent and presaged a future resistance which, unencumbered by monetary heresy, would revitalize democracy.

Jonathan Dolliver, traveling the Chautauqua circuit for the Rocky Mountain Lyceum in early November, 1896, told his audiences the election returns indicated that the American people wanted an end of the free-silver agitation and a return "to sound tariff policies" which would restore prosperity.

> There will indeed always be room for complaint and room for reform. It will tax the wisdom of the approaching century to deal with the problems arising out of great riches on the one hand and great poverty on the other, without violating or rudely disturbing the law of property, which we have inherited from our ancestors. But in the solution of these problems it is well that the country should be on its guard against the sorcery of the demagogue and the arts of the political adventurer.[3]

Dolliver's implied belief that the reforms would await the "approaching century" proved to be accurate. The discussion of the currency problem died

away as prosperity returned. Nature and science provided an increased supply
of gold for money, as new mines were opened in Alaska, Colorado, South
Africa, Canada, and Australia, and as the cheap cyanide process for extracting
gold from low-grade ore was perfected. Meanwhile, with the balance of power
in the Senate still in the hands of the silverites, the Republicans, although
having won the election on the sound-money issue, had no stomach for attempting any monetary legislation. Instead, McKinley and his friends in Congress determined to bring "sound tariff policies" to the forefront.[4]

Strictly speaking, until the new Congress met, no existing group in the
Fifty-fourth Congress had authority to prepare legislation for action by the
Fifty-fifth. Nevertheless, even before the final session of the Fifty-fourth Congress assembled in December, 1896, Nelson Dingley, chairman of the Ways
and Means Committee, called his Republican colleagues on that committee to
Washington to begin work on a tariff bill. He knew that Speaker Reed intended to reappoint him chairman and that the membership of the committee
was to remain substantially unchanged so far as his party was concerned.[5]

Dolliver received a telegram from Dingley asking him to be in the capital on
November 15 for a conference on the tariff. Later Dolliver wrote that the
committee began its deliberations immediately and "worked every day including Sundays . . . beginning at 9 o'clock each morning, taking 20 minutes off
at noon, one hour from 6 to seven for dinner, and continuing until midnight."
Until December, Dingley and his ten Republican colleagues studied together
"around a little table covered with a green baize cloth" in the privacy of a
"little room on the 4th floor" of the Cochran Hotel in downtown Washington.
"We have undertaken to revise the whole tariff schedule this winter," Dolliver
wrote his wife in mid-December. "Congress itself is dull and uninteresting but
the Ways and Means Committee is busy and industrious."[6]

In January, Dingley appointed Dolliver chairman of a subcommittee to prepare the agricultural schedule. "I take a good deal of satisfaction," Dolliver
later wrote, "in the fact that these duties as reported by my sub-committee
were adopted without alteration by the Ways and Means Committee and found
their way into the tariff law as reported by the Committee. They were not
subsequently disturbed either in the House or the Senate. In that sense, I may,
without unbecoming vanity, claim to be the author of the agricultural schedule
in the tariff law of 1897."[7] Dolliver was also a member of a subcommittee on
reciprocity and became a forceful advocate of reciprocal trade agreements, in
marked contrast to his attitude toward reciprocity when Secretary Blaine
urged that policy on the framers of the McKinley Tariff in 1890.

At the public hearings on the proposed Dingley bill, Dolliver was especially
active in questioning witnesses and pleaders for special interests.[8] As one who
desired to master the subject, he made the most of his opportunity to probe
into all phases of tariff making. Although he remained a sturdy defender of

protection in 1897, his enlightenment on the relationship between exorbitant duties and the growth of trusts and monopolies began during these months, as did his insight into the influence of powerful lobbies on the molding of legislation.

In his inaugural address President McKinley emphasized his belief that "the paramount duty of Congress is to stop deficiencies by the restoration of that protective legislation which has always been the foremost prop of the Treasury." To accomplish this duty, the President convened Congress in "extraordinary session" on March 15, 1897. As soon as the House was organized, Nelson Dingley presented "a bill to provide revenue for the Government and to encourage the industries of the United States" and moved its reference to the Ways and Means Committee.[9] The House agreed to Dingley's motion, and the Speaker then named the committee and referred to it the bill on which most of the members had been working since November.

Four days later Chairman Dingley reported a "favorable recommendation" from his committee, and on March 22 the House began discussion of the proposed measure.[10] The Democratic spokesmen, especially General Joseph Wheeler of Alabama, ably protested the procedure which the Republicans had followed in the preparation of the Dingley bill and demonstrated with statistics furnished by McKinley's Secretary of the Treasury, Lyman Gage, that there actually was currently no deficiency in the Treasury receipts and thus no need for the new tariff law.[11] The Republicans made no specific answer to these attacks; their primary aim was to enact a high protective tariff, not a revenue measure, and they knew that they had the votes in the House.

On March 23 Dolliver arose to speak in behalf of the bill he had helped frame. With his usual frankness, he began by stating that he liked the Dingley proposal because "for the first time since the first act of the First Congress, a protective tariff bill has had the candor to state the purpose of it in the title." That could be taken, he argued, as evidence of the "complete ascendency of the protective-tariff doctrine in the thought of these times." In his judgment, "the best thing about this bill is that no sectional influence has been heeded in the preparation of its schedules . . . it is neither Eastern nor Western, neither Northern nor Southern." Dolliver lauded the bill for its concern for the protection of all interests in the nation and for levying specific rather than ad valorem duties. The latter, he said, were subject to so much abuse that they merely encouraged importers to a "contest of skill in the falsification of invoices."

On the whole, Dolliver's position in 1897 was not unlike that of 1890. There were, however, two points at which his remarks revealed trends of thought indicative of his future. Of foremost importance in this respect was his statment that "we may with assurance look forward" to a time when the free list might be greatly enlarged "without injury to a single domestic interest." Secondly, his desire to find "a working basis for new reciprocal agreements" also indicated his growing belief that the rigid policy of the past needed modification.[12]

Dolliver's address on the Dingley bill attracted much attention. The Boston *Globe* described it as the "leading speech" on the measure and commented that Dolliver was "one of the most graceful, polished, and forceful orators in either branch of Congress," a man noted "as a master of the tariff question." A Des Moines paper called the speech "without doubt the greatest speech of the tariff debate."[13] Of more significance than the flattery of urban newspapers, however, was the lack of letters of praise from Iowa. Dolliver had received numerous letters complimenting him on his 1890, 1892, and 1894 tariff speeches. Not so in 1897.

In less than a week after Dolliver's address, the House passed the Dingley bill without major amendment and sent it to the Senate, where it was referred to Nelson W. Aldrich's Finance Committee. Aldrich's aim was to frame a measure upon which the silver and gold Republican Senators would agree, and one which would not so offend France as to lead that volatile Republic to torpedo the McKinley administration's plans for an international agreement for the establishment of bimetallism. The latter effort, of course, was a design on the part of the Republican leadership to appease the Silver Senators, heal the East-West rupture in the party, and head off any resurgence of another free-silver crusade in the next presidential election.[14]

Aldrich reported the Senate version of the tariff bill in early May. In general, his committee had lowered the rates specified in the House bill. Senator Aldrich claimed, in his opening speech, that industrial conditions generally did not demand a return to the rates imposed by the McKinley Act. "Without relinquishing a particle of our devotion to the cause of protection," he said, "we feel that we have a right to ask that the cause shall not be burdened by the imposition of duties which are unreasonable and excessive."[15] Aldrich may possibly have meant what he said. Apparently he did want to satisfy the French demand for lower duties on certain French exports to America. The New England woolen manufacturers, powerful in Rhode Island, opposed the levy of excessively high duties on raw wool. The Sugar Trust did not desire an increase in the rates on raw sugar, and the Aldrich Committee reported a "scheme of sugar duties, partly specific and partly *ad valorem*, complicated in its effects, and difficult to explain except as a means of making concessions under disguise to the refiners."[16]

The Senate, however, did not follow the recommendations of the Finance Committee. In the course of two months, the high protectionists, aided by the Silver Senators who demanded increased rates for lead, wool, and hides, forced through 872 amendments to the Dingley bill, most of which raised tariff duties.[17] When Aldrich was unable to get his sugar schedule adopted, "his health failed, and he quit the job for several weeks — delaying the passage of the bill while the sugar trust was bringing in enough raw sugar under the Wilson Bill to last several years."[18] Thus the Sugar Trust was well cared for, and the woolen schedule as finally adopted pleased the Far West and was "highly satisfactory to the woolen interests, especially in New England."[19]

Senator Aldrich's position is interesting in view of the events of a dozen years later. It is likewise important to note that in 1897 both Dolliver and Aldrich were considered tariff experts, both talked in terms of moderation of "unreasonable and excessive duties," and both played important roles in the passage of the Dingley Act. Ironically, Aldrich secured very nearly what the woolen and sugar interests wanted regardless of his apparent "defeat" in the Senate, while Dolliver, despite the long months of careful study and work with the Ways and Means Committee to frame a reasonably "scientific" protective tariff, had the disappointment of seeing the details of the Dingley Act patched up by the Conference Committee "in no less haphazard fashion" than had been the case with previous tariff measures. Nevertheless, Dolliver voted for it and spoke well of it for many months.[20]

When the Dingley Tariff became law on July 24, 1897, it was the highest ever enacted up to that time. It pushed protection "farther than the political situation fairly justified," wrote Taussig. "It disheartened many . . . and even good party members, loyal to the general policy of protection, doubted whether that policy had not now been carried too far."[21] Such doubts came in due time to Jonathan Dolliver but not to Nelson Aldrich.

———

While Representative Dolliver's education in the intricacies of tariff making as practiced in the United States Senate proceeded in Washington in the early summer of 1897, Republicans in Iowa engaged in an important struggle over the question of a nominee for Governor — a struggle which foreshadowed the Progressive-Standpat split in the party. In fact, in many respects the factionalism which came to be characteristic of Iowa Republican politics in the first decade of the twentieth century had its beginning in the summer of 1897. The political pot, which among Hawkeye Republicans seldom cooled, had begun to simmer late in 1896 and early in 1897 when there was talk of Allison's entering McKinley's Cabinet. In November, 1896, Albert Cummins wrote Henry C. Payne, a Wisconsin leader:

> There is one thing that I especially want to know a little bit sooner than anybody else in this state, namely, whether Allison is to be invited into the Cabinet; and inasmuch as he will be in Washington and I here [Des Moines], I shall have no chance to consult him. I want to know what the probability is of his acceptance in case the place is tendered him. You can readily understand the interest that I have in this question.[22]

Cummins obviously hoped to get Allison's seat in the Senate. Indeed, Cummins' ambition to become a United States Senator was to be a major thread in Iowa politics for the next dozen years. There had been talk of Cummins for Attorney General in the McKinley administration, but he informed Charles G. Dawes, "I started out with my eye on another seat, and intend, if I can, to keep it there until I have accomplished my purpose." More specifically, he wrote another friend: "So long as there was any chance that Allison would take a place in the Cabinet I did not want to interfere in any degree, inasmuch as I would a great deal rather take my chance of succeeding him in the Senate than to become Attorney-General." [23]

When Allison declined to enter the Cabinet, Cummins turned his attention to gaining control of the Iowa General Assembly. "I expect to be a candidate for the Gear succession," he wrote in February, 1897, "and am therefore interested in seeing that the State Senators who are nominated and elected this year are not hostile to me." [24] Senator Gear's term expired in 1900; thus, the state senators elected in 1897 would be in office and would help choose the United States Senator in 1900. Further evidence of Cummins' maneuvers came to light when O'Connell discovered that Cummins was supporting H. G. McMillan, the State Republican Chairman, for a federal appointment, and that McMillan "seemed to understand" that Cummins was doing so in order to get his help in a "fight against Senator Gear in 1900." [25]

The control of the governorship, of course, bore directly on the senatorial succession. This was true not merely because a Governor has great political power in his party organization, controls state patronage, and might himself be an aspirant for the Senate, but because Senator Gear was old and unwell. Should he die in office, the Governor would appoint his successor.

Cummins informed those who suggested that he enter the gubernatorial race in 1897 that he did not want to be Governor. Several other Republicans did, however. Among them were State Senator A. B. Funk, editor of the Spirit Lake Beacon; Lieutenant Governor Matt Parrott; and Leslie M. Shaw, a resident of the Tenth Congressional District who had won fame as a gold-standard advocate in 1896. The Blythe-Hubbard railroad "machine" preferred Parrott; Clarkson's Register, now managed by Richard P. Clarkson with Cyrenus Cole as associate editor, supported Shaw; and George E. Roberts favored Funk.[26]

Dolliver seldom meddled in pre-convention state politics, and in this case he had good reason to hesitate to do so, since Funk was a personal friend and Shaw a valued political friend. Nevertheless, immediately following his return to Fort Dodge after the adjournment of Congress, Dolliver received a letter from Shaw, asking with unmistakable bluntness: "Do you believe that the 10th district can be secured solid [for me]? In other words, do you believe you can secure it solid, for I appreciate that I shall have to rely very considerably upon your good right arm?" J. P. replied on July 31 that he thought Shaw ought to have all of the Tenth District delegates except those from counties in Funk's senatorial district. Shaw answered that his supporters "had it ciphered out that Mr. Funk could not be nominated; otherwise I don't think my name would have been presented. It was done without my knowledge or consent, however, but the argument that was used to secure my consent eliminated the possibility of Mr. Funk's nomination." What that "argument" was, Shaw did not say. He also asked Dolliver to get Roberts to endorse his gubernatorial candidacy in the Fort Dodge *Messenger*.[27]

Roberts had kept the *Messenger* out of the fight, doubtless feeling that, since he was Director of the Mint, he ought not to interfere in state politics and that anything the *Messenger* said would be taken to indicate Dolliver's views. In early August, however, the *Messenger* printed comments favorable to Shaw without formally endorsing him. Shaw's law partner thanked Dolliver for this and urged that Roberts "continue to write [Shaw] up."[28] Privately, Roberts maintained that Senator Funk was his first choice and that Webster County ought to support Funk until it was determined whether he or Shaw had the greater strength in the convention. In fact, Roberts wrote his view to Judge J. P. Conner, Shaw's next-door neighbor, a close friend of Dolliver and Roberts as well as of Shaw. Roberts' attitude did not please Shaw, who wrote Dolliver that the "10th District ought to support a 10th District man from the start, not an 11th District man" such as Funk.[29]

There was talk of a deadlocked convention and of the possibility of bringing out the aged James Harlan or Congressman Hull as a candidate. Cummins thought Harlan might be nominated in the mix-up but hoped Hull would not be.[30] He favored Funk, but as a national committeeman and a potential candidate for the Senate in 1900 he did not want to get into the fray.

Dolliver, evidently deciding that the party was heading for an unfortunate ruckus harmful to all concerned, informed Shaw on August 6 that he felt that he could control the Tenth District in Shaw's behalf and would try to do so. Shaw was delighted. "I shall appreciate your services very much," he wrote his Congressman. "I recognize, of course, that it won't do for you to antagonize other candidates in their home counties, but the mere suggestion of my strength and fitness to your friends throughout the state will be of great assistance when the time comes for the delegations to break away from political affiliations." A few days later Shaw, at Conner's suggestion, asked Dolliver to attend the state convention and make the nominating speech.[31]

The convention met on August 18 at Cedar Rapids, but there were no nominating speeches. On the first ballot, Parrott led easily, with Funk and Shaw in second and third place and only a few votes apart. The third ballot revealed that Parrott's strength had in large measure been transferred to Shaw, who won the nomination.[32] Thus, the meaning of Shaw's August 3 letter, relative to the "argument used" to persuade him to be a candidate, since Funk could not win, becomes clear. Although he did not tell Dolliver, and no positive evidence is available, it is apparent that Shaw had learned that the Blythe-Hubbard crowd were willing to transfer their support to him if they found on early ballots that they could not nominate Parrott.

The fact that Cyrenus Cole, a friend of N. M. Hubbard of Cedar Rapids, was for Shaw from the beginning is significant. He claims credit for the suggestion that the *Register* support Shaw as a means of defeating Parrott, whom R. P. Clarkson detested.[33] The Blythe-Hubbard group did not want Funk. If Cole could persuade them that Shaw was "safe" then they would not scruple to abandon Parrott, providing Shaw had enough strength of his own to win with Parrott's delegates. Shaw's problem obviously was to amass enough votes to enable him to rival Funk on the first ballot. To do that and to strengthen his personal position in the eyes of the state as a whole, Shaw must have the undivided backing of his own congressional district. He turned to Dolliver as the one man who could make certain that the "Big Tenth" would support Shaw instead of Funk.

Intrastate sectionalism was always an important factor in convention politics. Dolliver knew, and other politicians understood, that he could support Shaw on the ground that he was a "home district" man. Cole and others knew that Dolliver always sought harmony and deplored factionalism in party conventions — his role in 1884, 1888, and 1896 was familiar to all. Let somebody persuade him that a head-on collision between Funk and Parrott would divide the party, but that nobody seriously objected to Shaw, a new man in politics, and the path was smoothed for Dolliver to boost Shaw's candidacy.[34]

Dolliver's efforts contributed to, perhaps made possible, Shaw's victory. If harmony resulted, however, it was more apparent than real, more temporary than permanent. Although he bore Dolliver no ill-will whatever, Senator Funk, pondering his defeat, fostered among his supporters a feeling of animosity toward Blythe and Hubbard which boded no good for the future peace of the party. Albert Cummins expressed the greatest "gratification at the outcome of the convention," but he too was soon to join "Abe" Funk.[35]

Judged with the benefit of hindsight, the Republican gubernatorial contest of 1897 was of lasting significance in Iowa politics for three reasons. It marked the definable beginning of the division of the party in that state into what by 1901 came to be called the "Progressive" and the "Standpat" factions; for certainly at first that schism was one of personalities not issues, a matter of Cummins-Funk and Company *vs.* Blythe-Hubbard Incorporated. Secondly, Shaw's nomination and subsequent election began a political career which culminated in his service in Theodore Roosevelt's Cabinet. Thirdly, Shaw's obligations for his first nomination to the Blythe-Hubbard organization on the one hand and to J. P. Dolliver on the other placed the Governor in a peculiar relationship to the political future of both Dolliver and Cummins.

- XIII -

Defender of Imperialism, 1898-1900

This war is an incident, a noble and splendid incident, but only a transient incident in the life of a great community like ours.
Jonathan P. Dolliver, 1898

FAR MORE IMPORTANT IN 1897 and 1898 than the subdued rumble of future political warfare in the Hawkeye State were the reports of battle, murder, and sudden death which the Hearst and Pulitzer correspondents in Cuba dispatched from that unhappy outpost of Spain's misgoverned empire. The Cuban revolt, caused in part by the economic depression in the island resulting from the termination of a free market for sugar in America after the passage of the Wilson Tariff Act, began in 1895. From the start many Americans sympathized with the Cubans in their resistance to Spanish misrule, but President Cleveland, while insisting upon the protection of the treaty rights of American citizens and urging Spain to accept American mediation to end the rebellion, refused to be stampeded into intervention.[1]

The upheaval in Cuba came at a time when there was an increasing interest in the United States in territorial expansion, in the enlargement of the navy, and in the need of a Central American canal to increase the mobility of the navy in protecting both coasts.[2] Already the United States had revived the Monroe Doctrine in the Venezuelan affair and had exerted mild efforts to gain control of Hawaii and Samoa. Indeed, the rise of the "New Manifest Destiny" had begun in the late eighties at about the time Dolliver entered Congress. Stimulated by the writings of Captain Alfred Mahan, Rudyard Kipling, Henry Cabot Lodge, Theodore Roosevelt, Dr. Albert Shaw, and others, imperialist sentiment gained steadily in the 1890's.[3] By 1896 it received expression in the Republican platform:

> The Hawaiian Islands should be controlled by the United States, and no foreign power should be permitted to interfere with them; the Nicaragua Canal should be built, owned, and operated by the United States; and by the purchase of the Danish Islands we should secure a proper and much needed naval station in the West Indies.[4]

142

Dolliver was not, in the mid-nineties, an imperialist of the school of Lodge, Roosevelt, or Albert Shaw. He had always been an advocate of a larger navy, partly because of his sentimental regard for his ancestors' naval service, partly because of his ardent nationalism, and partly, no doubt, because of his chance assignment to the Naval Affairs Committee when he began his career in Congress. In April, 1896, Dolliver voted for the concurrent resolution favoring the recognition of Cuban belligerency and urging President Cleveland to offer Spain the good offices of the United States in the negotiation of a peace granting Cuba independence.[5] This, of course, was not binding on the Chief Executive nor did it necessarily indicate aggressive imperialism on the part of those who supported it.

When, after the election of 1896, Lodge, Roosevelt, Senator James D. Cameron of Pennsylvania, and others attempted to arrange for America's intervention in the war before Cleveland's term ended, Dolliver thought their plans ridiculous and dangerous.[6] However, at that time, he was too absorbed in tariff making to pay much attention to jingoism. There was no war declaration between December and March largely because of the unyielding opposition of Cleveland, Secretary of State Richard Olney, and Speaker Reed to any movement toward intervention.[7]

President McKinley also opposed American involvement in the Cuban affair. During the first year of his administration he succeeded in resisting various demands for recognition of Cuban belligerency or of Cuban independence and refused to consider intervening in the war. Thus, despite the mounting pressure of the imperialists, the sensational headlines of the yellow press, and the yammering of the sentimentalists, the American government avoided a showdown with Spain until the crisis of 1898.[8]

Unfortunately, a turn for the worse came in January of that year, shortly after Congress returned from the Christmas recess. On January 12, Consul-General Fitzhugh Lee reported "rioting" in Havana and suggested that the presence of American warships might be necessary "later but not now."[9] After determining that the "rioting" had ceased and after assuring the Spanish government that the arrival of a United States ship in Cuban waters was merely a "courtesy" visit, the administration ordered the *Maine* to sail for Havana. In reality, this gesture was pleasing neither to the Spanish nor to the Cubans, and it aroused immediate criticism in Congress.[10] On January 27, two days after the *Maine* arrived in Havana, David DeArmond, a Missouri Democrat, interrupted debate in the House on an appropriation bill to denounce the McKinley administration's Cuban policy. Referring to the *Maine*, he asked:

> Is she there to vindicate American manhood, to protect American citizenship, to proclaim . . . sympathy for the struggling Cubans and detestation and horror over the outrages perpetrated upon them? Oh, no! The *Maine* is in Habana harbor merely on a friendly visit

to the Spaniards. . . . Let not the country be deceived by this latest
move for Spain. Let not patriotic citizens anywhere over the country
be deluded with the hope that their Government is going to do something worthy of them or worthy of it.[11]

Before the applause of the Democrats and imperialistic Republicans had died
away, Dolliver arose to answer this stinging blast at the President's peaceful
policy. Although expressing his personal sympathy for the Cuban people,
Dolliver decried the daily Democratic "appeal to the country against us on the
question of patriotism in respect to Cuba." He cited the example of the Grant
administration in dealing with the Cuban insurrection of the seventies and
quoted Grant to bolster his own view that "any intervention in the affairs of
Cuba would be not only unwise but injurious."[12] More than a year later,
speaking of his state of mind at the beginning of 1898, Dolliver said: "I was
one of those who were very anxious to keep clear of Cuban intervention largely
on account of the enormous increase of responsibilities made necessary by a
successful war with Spain." In another speech he explained that in early 1898
he felt that it was his "duty to stand by William McKinley while he used all
the power of his great position to prevent the destruction of the peace."[13]

That William McKinley did use "all the power" of the presidency to prevent
the Spanish-American War is a matter of extreme doubt. In fact, "American
historians are today agreed that the war with Spain could have been avoided
with honor, if McKinley had been resolute enough to exercise a little more
patience with Spain and defy Congress."[14] The De Lome letter, the sinking of
the *Maine*, and the apparently overwhelming desire of the people for action
created a situation which the imperialists in the President's party exploited to
the utmost. Even William Jennings Bryan was demanding Cuban independence,
and preachers were praying for war.[15] Thus, after Spain had belatedly agreed
to the essential American demands regarding a Cuban armistice, President
McKinley yielded to the pressure of the warmongers and asked Congress for
authority to use the army and navy to make peace in Cuba.

Senator John Coit Spooner of Wisconsin thought "possibly the President
could have worked out the business without war, but the current was too
strong, the demagogues too numerous, the fall elections too near."[16] The
imperialists advised McKinley that Congress would declare war over his veto
and thus ruin his administration and his future if he did not ask for war. The
scene in the House during the debate over the war resolution was like that of
forty years preceding when the extremists brawled over the admission of Kansas. "There were half-a-dozen personal collisions; books were thrown; members rushed up and down the aisles like madmen, exchanging hot words, with
clenched fists and set teeth; excitement was at fever heat."[17] Finally, at about
2:45 A. M. on April 19, the House voted 311 to 6, with 39 members not
voting, to adopt a joint resolution "that the Government of Spain relinquish its

authority and government in the Island of Cuba and Cuban waters, and directing the President of the United States to use the land and naval forces of the United States to carry these resolutions into effect." Included in the resolution was the Teller Amendment whereby the United States disclaimed any intention of annexing Cuba. Dolliver was one of the 311 voting "yea."[18]

Unquestionably Dolliver would have continued to support McKinley had the President had the courage to withstand the clamor for war and to pursue the quest for a peaceful settlement of the Cuban affair. Speaker Reed would have done likewise. Chairman Boutelle of the Naval Affairs Committee voted against the resolution directing intervention. Even such an advanced imperialist as Lodge did all he could "to keep Congress from breaking away & acting" without the lead of the President. Business interests generally opposed the war, and many of the twenty-one Senators who voted against the resolution on April 16 were closely identified with great corporations.[19] On the final vote, however, all Republican Senators except six Silver Republicans either voted for intervention or abstained, and of the thirty-five votes against it, twenty-seven were cast by Democrats, twenty-five of whom favored the objective but not the form of the resolution. On April 25 both houses voted unanimously for the declaration of war.[20]

Three factors account for Dolliver's conversion to imperialism in April, 1898. Probably most important was his sincere belief that God guided the destiny of the United States, a conviction which he held from childhood to death and which was in no way a product of the ideology of the "New Manifest Destiny" of the nineties. His religious attitude in this respect made it natural for him to feel that it was America's mission to free Cuba and to assume responsibility for territories in the Pacific. Secondly, his loyalty to party and his deep-seated patriotism led him to an ardent support of McKinley's foreign policy, once the President had defined that policy in terms of war and national expansion. Thirdly, Dolliver was subject to the same pressures as were brought to bear on the President and all Congressmen in the weeks following the sinking of the *Maine*. In addition, his imperialistic-minded friends, knowing of his influence as an orator in the House, constantly pushed him to go along with them. For example, Dr. Albert Shaw, editor of the *Review of Reviews*, an outspoken expansionist, spent the entire evening of April 3 in Dolliver's home talking with him "of Cuba and of the U. S. position in the matter."[21] Also Secretary of Agriculture James ("Tama Jim") Wilson, an Iowa friend of long standing, visited the Dollivers frequently. Wilson, a persuasive Scot, looked upon the United States as "the instrument of the Almighty to alleviate the sufferings of a people oppressed for four hundred years" and saw "the finger of God leading the nation along the way to a greater work for humanity."[22]

Dolliver's first speech in the House following the declaration of war was in behalf of a revenue bill presented by the Ways and Means Committee on April 27. He advocated a "pay as we go" policy of war financing, because "it is hardly credible that we are going to belittle the great proceeding by leaving the expense of it to be borne by future generations." The bill Dolliver supported provided exclusively for internal revenue taxes on such articles of voluntary consumption as beer and tobacco, and special taxes on licenses for tobacco dealers and foreign ships entering American ports. The Democrats and Populists inquired how it happened that the miraculous Republican tariff of 1897 did not supply the needed revenue, and urged that enactment of an income tax law and the coinage of the government's silver bullion were the proper methods for raising additional revenue.

Dolliver defended the Dingley Tariff, pointing out that it had not been in force long enough for a fair test and, furthermore, that no tariff could be expected to produce the money needed for the exigencies of war. He did not oppose the income tax in principle but suggested, in view of the Supreme Court's recent invalidation of the income tax provision in the Wilson-Gorman Act, that the beginning of a war was not the time to experiment with that form of taxation. His scornful rejection of the silver coinage proposal was in line with his 1896 view of attempting to solve problems of government financing by opening the mints and starting the printing presses.

His concluding paragraphs brought "loud and prolonged applause" from his colleagues. Speaking of the war itself, Dolliver said:

> I do not pretend to be able to predict the size or the cost of the undertaking on which we have entered, but my conviction is that . . . in the end we will gain all that we lose and infinitely more. We have already gained the outspoken sympathy of that great English-speaking world of which we are a part. And more important than that, we have gained a new sense of the unity of our own people and our own country. . . .
>
> Nor do I think that our people will ever regret the part they have assumed. There are times in the life of nations when they move upon impulses so pure that the approbation of the national conscience is a full reward for all sacrifices, however grievous.[23]

Probably no speech he ever made in the House brought Dolliver such universal acclaim. The New York *Times* called it a "sincere and truthful statement of the sentiment of the great body of the American people" and asserted that Dolliver was the "real champion of the revenue bill." President McKinley, "with tears of gratitude in his eyes," thanked Dolliver for his "patriotic and inspiring words" and said his address was "the best of the session."[24] From each member of the Cabinet and from citizens in all parts of the nation came messages of congratulation and support. Clark Howell, editor of the Atlanta *Constitution*, wrote Dolliver that "even should this government be forced to the necessity of paying many more times the amount that has already been appropriated, the expenditure would be well worth the investment if its only result were to be found in the absolute annihilation of sectional lines, and in the assurance to the world as well as in the satisfaction of our own people, that the wounds of the Civil War have been absolutely healed." A prominent Missouri attorney thought that "in broad and unselfish devotion to principle, in patriotism, in wisdom and in eloquence," Dolliver's speech was "the equal of anything ever delivered in the halls of Congress."[25]

Historians a half century later agreed with the judgment of Dolliver and Howell that the Spanish-American War was a great factor in the reconciliation of North and South, the final step on the road to reunion after the tragic Civil War.[26]

While the short and popular war with Spain drew blood in Cuba, Puerto Rico, and the Philippines, the American Congress took up a matter of territorial expansion which had previously excited sporadic interest. From the days when Secretary of State Daniel Webster had declared that the United States could not view with equanimity the annexation of Hawaii by a foreign power, there had been Americans who urged their government to acquire these beautiful islands. President Cleveland blocked the most nearly successful move to secure Hawaii when, at the beginning of his second administration, he withdrew Harrison's treaty of annexation from the Senate.[27]

The Republican platform of 1896 gave new hope to those who wished to plant the Stars and Stripes in Honolulu. By June 16, 1897, the McKinley administration had signed a new treaty of annexation with the Hawaiian government, but determined anti-imperialist — or at least anti-administration — Senators blocked its ratification. With Admiral Dewey's conquest of Manila, however, came renewed demands for the prompt acquisition of Hawaii as a necessary link between America and the Philippines. Hence, the administration requested the Congress to pass a joint resolution of annexation, this requiring only a simple majority vote instead of the unobtainable two-thirds needed in the Senate for consent to the ratification of a treaty.[28]

Dolliver, long a friend of the navy, whose spokesmen were urging the need of Hawaiian naval bases, delivered an address on June 15, 1898, voicing powerful support of the joint resolution. When he arose to begin, the House greeted him with applause, "a thing said to be entirely unusual and without precedent," he wrote his wife.[29] His argument in favor of annexation was threefold. In the first place, he believed in it because "for nearly sixty years it has been the opinion of our great Secretaries of State that this thing ought to be done." Secondly, he suggested that the Americans must decide either to "get in" or "get out" of Hawaii. "We either have an interest in acquiring the islands or we have no interest in standing guard over them against others. If they are important enough to defend from others, they are important enough to acquire for ourselves." The weakness of the logic of these two points is obvious. The latter, if taken seriously, meant an end to the Monroe Doctrine and implied either splendid isolation or unlimited conquest of the Western Hemisphere, neither of which Dolliver believed in for a moment.

His third premise, that Hawaii was essential for American defense, was sound. He quoted General Scofield as saying "that from a military standpoint the annexation of these islands is a necessity to the United States." More to the point, he cited Captain Mahan, whom he called "in some respects the most influential living authority in naval matters, an authority on war recognized by the whole world." Dolliver accepted Mahan's view that the acquisition of Hawaii was "of immense importance now and hereafter to the successful naval operations of the United States."[30]

Dolliver's address came in the last hours of the debate on the Hawaiian question and was regarded as one of the major efforts to bring the matter to a conclusion satisfactory to the administration. A Democratic substitute providing for an American guarantee of the independence of Hawaii was defeated 204 to 96, and the joint resolution of annexation then passed the House by a vote of 209 to 91.[31] The United States, under Republican leadership, had resumed the pre-Civil War Democratic policy of manifest destiny. Dolliver wrote his wife that his speech was "exceedingly well received" and that his mind was "more at ease on the problem" of annexing colonies.[32]

If Dolliver gradually became a defender of imperialism because of religious, personal, and party influences, it is certain that he did not do so, as did others, because of any acceptance of the sociological theorizing based on Charles Darwin's evolutionary philosophy. He was not a disciple of Herbert Spencer, John Fiske, or even of Josiah Strong, although closer to Strong than to the others. During his address at the laying of a cornerstone at the State University of Iowa in Iowa City in June, 1898, Dolliver revealed his contempt for those who attempted to transplant from the laboratory biological truths applicable to plants and animals and apply them to the political and economic problems of mankind.[33] For Dolliver, America's venture into the arena of world responsibility was a duty thrust upon her by God, not a means of demonstrating her fitness to survive as a representative of some superior race.

Just a week before his arrival in Iowa City to participate in the building ceremonies at the University, Dolliver had received word of the death of his great friend and benefactor, C. C. Carpenter. This was a shock to Jonathan. "The news of the death of Governor Carpenter has filled my heart with sorrow such as I have not felt since death entered my own household," he wrote. "I loved Governor Carpenter next to my own father." Dolliver at once offered the Fort

Dodge postmastership to Mrs. Carpenter, as a "small token of my love for Governor Carpenter."[34] She accepted, somewhat to the disappointment of S. T. Meservey, who wanted the office should she decline. Dolliver was greatly relieved at her decision, for he hated squabbles over patronage, and he had heard from his brother-in-law that if Meservey were appointed, "the Spanish War would be secondary to the uproar in Fort Dodge."[35]

This comment implied that there was hostility toward Meservey, the man who, with the death of Carpenter and the removal of Roberts to Washintgon, had become Dolliver's chief Webster County political lieutenant. Such enmity, if any, certainly did not extend to the Congressman. The Tenth District Congressional Convention met in Fort Dodge on the last day of June and renominated Dolliver by acclamation. "Iowa is fast learning the wisdom of the Eastern states in keeping a good man in Congress, when a good one is secured, in order that the state and nation may profit by his ripe experience and the sharpened abilities which follow a long and useful service in the legislative branch of the government," observed one editor. "The Tenth District of Iowa has been represented in the National Congress for ten years by one of the brightest and brainiest young men in the nation, Hon. Jonathan P. Dolliver, and he should be returned." The Democratic Fort Dodge *Post*, virtually admitting that Dolliver was unbeatable, asserted that "if a political foe must serve the Tenth District, the *Post* prefers by long odds to have a brainy and heroic man who heads the front of his column . . . rather than some little politician."[36]

Following the convention, Dolliver invited the delegates to his home for a reception and refreshments. In the evening a nonpartisan banquet was arranged by the people of Fort Dodge. The Reverend James Dolliver gave the invocation; there were toasts from each of the fourteen county delegations, and then two of the most prominent Democrats in Webster County delivered addresses of tribute to Dolliver. Captain J. A. O. Yeoman, the opponent of 1888, speaking on "Patriotism Higher than Party," stirred the emotions of his audience as he praised Dolliver's work in the recent Congress. Following Yeoman, M. F. Healy, former chairman of the Democratic State Central Committee and potential nominee for Congress against Dolliver, spoke with apparent sincerity and geniality of "Our Fellow Townsman, J. P. Dolliver." Dolliver, obviously deeply moved by the whole affair, talked of the work of "The American Congress" and suggested that he believed the United States ought to retain the Philippines. Much of his address was devoted to eulogies of Captain Yeoman and of Congressman Joe Wheeler of Alabama, a former Confederate General, who had gone to Cuba to fight under the Stars and Stripes.[37]

This unanimous renomination and the banquet excited comment all over Iowa. Various papers noted that "a rather surprising feature of Congressman Dolliver's popularity is the high regard in which he is held by his Democratic friends in his home city."[38] Governor Shaw wrote Dolliver: "To represent a district like the tenth is a great honor, but to represent such a people year after year and term after term, and to receive the endorsement of a great party time after time by acclamation, and better still, to be worthy of it all, is something in which your personal friends and admirers are justly proud."[39]

An editor, booming Dolliver for renomination before the convention assembled, explained Dolliver's popularity as a Congressman. He was not only a great orator, a warm and generous personality, and an honest man, wrote the newsman, but Dolliver "continues to look after the individual affairs of his constituency. He always gives a prompt reply to letters and is successful in dealing with the small affairs which call for his attention in behalf of his constituents." He usually made patronage appointments early and announced them before contests developed, and thus he probably had as little opposition from disgruntled job-seekers as any Iowa Congressman.[40]

The election campaign of 1898 was not strenuous as compared to those of 1894 and 1896. So far as Dolliver was concerned, the main issues were the tariff and imperialism. Both in his Chautauqua lectures and in his campaign speeches, Dolliver spoke as an imperialist. "Whose fault is it that we are in possession of Manila?" he asked a Fort Dodge audience.

> I will tell you what I think about it. I think that our nation in the Providence of God, has fallen in with forces that nobody understands. . . . Without our knowing it and without our intending it, the good Lord above us intends to use this great united Republic as a frontier garrison of liberty, and to advance the cause of human freedom and to enlarge the boundaries of civilization.[41]

He said in a speech in New Jersey in August that "it may be counted as certain that the flag of the United States is in the Philippines to stay, and that whether our Government assumes sovereignty over the whole group or not, we will secure such a naval and commercial station there as will enable us to minister to the needs of our own commerce and become the agents and guardians of the peace and liberty of the islands."[42]

In November, Dolliver easily won his sixth term in the House, and the Republicans retained control of Congress, losing some seats in the House but gaining firmer control of the Senate. In New York, Colonel Roosevelt, having almost single-handedly won the war with Spain (according to unkind critics), won the governorship of the Empire State. Speaker Reed, disgusted with the imperialists, refused to stand for re-election in Maine. By all reasonable standards, the Republican party deserved defeat for getting the nation into an unnecessary war, for the incredible mismanagement of the War Department, and for enacting a tariff law burdensome to the masses of the people.[43] But times were more prosperous, the Democrats' performance in Congress did not entitle that party to victory, expansion was popular, and a "great war" had been won.

Finley Peter Dunne accurately depicted the mind of the American majority in 1898 in one of his priceless dialogues:

> "We're a gr-reat people," said Mr. Hennessy earnestly.
> "We ar-re," said Mr. Dooley. "We ar-re that. An' th' best iv it is, we know we ar-re."[44]

Within a few days after the last session of the Fifty-fifth Congress convened in December, 1898, the United States concluded peace with Spain. Whether the administration could muster two-thirds of the Senate for a vote permitting ratification of the treaty became the issue of greatest interest as the year ended.

The opposition to the treaty centered on the acquisition of the Philippines. McKinley and his spokesmen were hard pressed by the anti-imperialists who professed to believe that the forcible annexation of people against their will violated the Constitution and the Declaration of Independence. With great logic, those opposed to the treaty pointed out that by projecting herself into the Far East, America would become entangled in the affairs of Asia and of Europe. They also jeered at the inconsistency of those who had started out with the high moral purpose of freeing the Cubans and had ended up with the conquest of islands 8,000 miles away.[45]

The House, of course, had nothing to do with the ratification of the treaty, but it did have to appropriate funds to implement it and to provide for an army to pacify the Philippines. The opponents of imperialism in the House attacked the administration during the debate on a bill for the reorganization of the army, a measure sponsored by J. A. T. Hull of Iowa, chairman of the Military Affairs Committee. Dolliver come forward on January 25, 1899, to answer the critics of imperialism and to aid in the passage of Hull's bill.

In his long and carefully prepared address, Dolliver reviewed the circumstances which led the nation into war with Spain. Assuming apparently that Spaniards had sunk the *Maine*, he suggested that General Blanco "might have known that when they blew us up in that harbor we were likely to come down everywhere." Thus, as Dolliver explained it, the Americans were in the Philippines, having thought it wise to strike at Spain wherever they could find her. Admiral Dewey had done his duty; he still waited for Congressmen to do theirs and send him the aid needed to bring peace to those islands.

Dolliver replied to the "first-class statesmen . . . busy with their constitutional quibbles" by quoting John Marshall "that the power to make war and to frame treaties necessarily involves the power to acquire territory, and that the power to acquire territory implies the power to govern and control it." His conclusion was that America could not do else than stay in the Philippines. When asked if he advocated forcible annexation against the wish of the people of the islands, Dolliver replied:

If the matter rested with me, I would take possession of the entire Philippine group, and establish on the island of Luzon an American headquarters, a base of operations for the fleet that is to defend the increasing commerce of the American people in the Pacific Ocean, and from that headquarters spread the influence of American enterprise in all the market places of the East; and I would hold that whole territory in trust for the civilization of the islands. . . . To my mind it does not seem incredible that the Power which is over all the governments of men is about to take the great Republic, united and made strong in the devotion and loyalty of all its people, and use it as an instrument in His hand to enlarge the boundaries of civilization, to extend the frontiers of freedom in far-off lands, and to garrison new outposts of social progress in the ends of the earth.[46]

It is never possible to answer those who are committed to the theological view of historical events held by Dolliver. If their premise is wrong, no argument can shake their adherence to it, and it can not be proved wrong since the finite mind of man can never completely comprehend the infinite mind of God. But the terrible danger is that even those who sincerely believe what they say, as Dolliver unquestionably did, will allow the nation to play at being God instead of humbly and resolutely seeking to be His agent. The question which Dolliver and the other imperialists never faced squarely was whether the American people were willing then, and for the future, to pay the price of taking "possession of the entire Philippine group" and thus becoming an Asiatic power.

Dolliver, of course, said he would have the base of operations and the fleet needed to protect the islands if the decision were left to him — and he and men of his calibre might well have done so — but as he knew, the decision was not for him to make. The imperialists' mistake was not in advocating retention of the Philippines, for there was no other honorable alternative to that as Dolliver made clear in 1899 and 1900, but rather in having supported the war in the first place. Having made that blunder, they compounded it by failing to understand the implications of becoming a world power. Not understanding that themselves, the imperialists were unable to educate the people as to the absolute essentials and realities of international politics.

It appears from his speeches that Dolliver tried for two or three years in a general way to inform the people on America's new responsibilities. Speaking in Wisconsin in July, 1899, he discussed them as follows:

If imperialism means that we are going to build and control a great navy, why then we are. If by imperialism they mean that we are going to dig the Nicaragua Canal, they are right there. We are, too, to give a stable, free, and just government to the islands we have taken from the unjust monarchy of Spain. We are going to do that if we have to stay in them all the rest of our lives. . . . We are going to establish a government in Cuba that will protect the life and liberty of its people, we have spent four hundred million dollars for Cuba; shall we leave them to anarchy now? A military necessity compelled us to take Hawaii. The Philippines are a more difficult and troublesome question. . . . What we do in this case affects all the future.[47]

In October of the same year Dolliver told the faculty and students of the University of Michigan that "the United States for the first time in its history finds itself in a position to take its place in prestige and influence among the nations." He regretted the Philippine insurrection but asserted that the "war must now be carried on to a finish and until there is no man in the Philippine Islands who does not respect the flag." The United States could not leave the islands if she desired to, he argued, for "when a nation invades and destroys the government of another, she is responsible for the establishment of a new government" and for providing for the welfare of the conquered people.[48]

When the bill which became the Foraker Act providing civil government for Puerto Rico was before the House in February, 1900, Dolliver made one of the major addresses in behalf of the measure at the conclusion of ten days of debate. In addition to supporting the purposes of the bill itself and the constitutionality of creating a colonial government "of the old crown colony type," Dolliver sought to answer critics of the administration's policy in the Philippines. The sharpness with which he attacked the Democratic politicians for the bitterness of their arraignment of the President was reminiscent of his speeches of the mid-eighties. His appeal to anti-imperialist Republicans who had "gone into the labyrinth of the Constitution and are not expected back" was that they give "the old Republican party a chance for its life, by allowing this question to pass from this place, where it can be debated but not determined, to that tribunal where it can be both argued and decided." As for himself, Dolliver believed the Constitution allowed the nation to govern colonies as she saw fit, but he was willing for the Supreme Court to decide the matter. He challenged the Democrats who were standing so firmly against the constitutionality of the colonial experiment in governing peoples without their consent to show their sincerity by "denouncing the political movement which in five Democratic States has nullified the great amendments to our Constitution, taken away from millions of people the right to be consulted in the government of the community where they were born, and established a white man's oligarchy with hardly a principle of popular institutions left in it."

Dolliver concluded this speech, his last major address in the House, on a note of optimistic patriotism which was basic in his very nature and which in a certain sense had always characterized his service as a Congressman: "I believe in the United States of America; I back the old Republic of our fathers against the world. . . . Whatever may be in store for us, whatever political party may rise or fall, the Government shall live to scatter the riches of human liberty to races yet uncivilized and to nations yet unborn."[49]

- XIV -

The Hinge of Fate, 1900-1902

If one advances confidently in the direction of his dreams, and endeavors to live the life which he has imagined, he will meet with a success unexpected in common hours.

Henry David Thoreau, *Walden*.

AS THE NINETEENTH CENTURY drew to a close, Jonathan Dolliver, ranking member of the Ways and Means Committee, tariff expert, and spokesman for imperialism, was in the midst of his sixth term in Congress. Although still a relatively young man, he had long enjoyed widespread fame as an orator and lecturer and was among the very few members of the House having a well-established national reputation. He was not, however, altogether satisfied either with his personal achievements or with the political situation developing within his party in Iowa.

In the personal sense, Dolliver, anticipating the birth of his first child early in 1900, felt financially insecure. Deriving his income exclusively from the meager salary of a Congressman and from lecture fees, he found the costs of biennial political campaigns and of maintaining a home in Fort Dodge for his father and sister as well as one in Washington an increasing burden. Furthermore, with the election of his colleague, David B. Henderson, as Speaker of the House upon Reed's retirement, whatever ambition Dolliver may have had to attain that office in the future was thwarted. It was unlikely that two Iowans could hold the speakership within the same decade, especially in view of the desire of Joseph G. Cannon of Illinois to wield the gavel. This is not to say that Dolliver resented Henderson's selection or had any expectation of being his successor. On the contrary, he ardently supported his old friend. But in thinking of his own future, Dolliver apparently realized that he was nearing the top of the ladder in the House with little probability of succeeding to the paramount position in that body. According to his closest friend, George Roberts, Dolliver, in this period, "felt disillusioned of public life (by spells) and spoke of leaving Fort Dodge for a larger city, and devoting himself to the practice of law."[1]

154

In Iowa politics, Dolliver regretfully watched the Republican cleavage, which had begun at the time of the Funk-Shaw contest for the gubernatorial nomination in 1897, widen to dangerous proportions in 1899-1901. Albert B. Cummins, defeated by Gear for the senatorship in 1894, had immediately set to work to win that coveted office in 1900. Shortly after the nomination of Shaw in 1897, Cummins wrote Robert Mather, general counsel for the Rock Island Railroad, asking his help in the fight for Gear's seat and suggesting that Mather and his Iowa attorney, Carroll Wright, "occupy toward my contest the same relation that J. W. Blythe occupies toward Gear's."[2] It is pertinent to note that Carroll Wright was Cummins' law partner and that the Gear-Cummins contest was by no means merely a fight by Cummins against the domination of the railroads in Iowa politics. Blythe and the Burlington, aided by Hubbard and the North Western, backed Gear. The Rock Island politicians, Funk, and other anti-Blythe Republicans supported Cummins, who had long been attorney for the Chicago & Great Western Railroad in Iowa. Some writers on the Cummins-Gear contest seem to have overlooked this aspect of the Cummins support. Cummins' correspondence in the period 1892-1904 shows that he regularly accepted railroad passes and eagerly sought the support of railroad politicians wherever he could get it.[3]

Senator Gear was in his mid-seventies, and his health was rapidly failing in 1899-1900. He ought not to have been a candidate for re-election, and it is difficult to escape the conclusion that the Blythe forces pushed the old man into the race solely to maintain their control of the senatorship. The argument that they used Gear to beat Cummins is only partly true. They did not want Cummins, but if defeating Cummins were the only thing involved, other Iowans than Gear could have done that — notably J. P. Dolliver. Blythe, by his own admission, did not want Dolliver in the Senate.[4]

Governor Shaw, who had senatorial ambitions, also might have beaten Cummins had Gear and the Blythe-Hubbard organization backed him and if no third force had intervened. This would undoubtedly have been a pleasing solution for the Shaw-Blythe-Hubbard wing, but they dared not attempt it. Had they tried that scheme, they would have forced Dolliver into the race for the simple reason that Dolliver and Shaw were from the same congressional district, and Dolliver could not permit Shaw to become Senator without eleminating himself for many years, if not forever, from the senatorship. Blythe and his associates were certainly shrewd enough to understand that fact, and they could not run the risk of bringing out Shaw to beat Cummins lest Dolliver enter the lists to protect his own future either by aiding Cummins or, more likely, by rallying his vast horde of friends behind his own candidacy. Shaw, coming from the Democratic section of the "Big Tenth," had no personal Republican followers from his own section in the General Assembly, as did Dolliver, and inasmuch as he had needed Dolliver's aid to win the gubernatorial nomination, he certainly had no chance of defeating either Dolliver or Cummins, backed by Dolliver, in a senatorial contest.

Newspaper polls taken in the early months of 1899 revealed that Dolliver's popularity as a possible Republican candidate for Senator exceeded by far that of ten other well-known politicians including Gear, Cummins, Shaw, and ex-Governor Larrabee. In Webster County those polled were almost all in favor of Dolliver, but they likewise indicated that Cummins was their choice if Dolliver did not become a candidate. It is significant that in one poll Dolliver's Fort Dodge spokesman, S. T. Meservey, listed Cummins as his choice, thus indicating that he did not consider Dolliver in the race. Another close friend of Dolliver's, William S. Kenyon, an able young attorney serving as Webster County Republican Chairman, listed Dolliver first, Cummins second, and commented that "Iowa should send to the United States Senate a representative of the progressive sentiment of the nation."[5]

In July the Humboldt County Republican Convention unanimously passed a resolution favoring Dolliver's election to the Senate, and various newspapers and groups attempted to start Dolliver-for-Senator booms.[6] As late as the last week of July the Iowa City *Republican* observed:

> No one denies Mr. Cummins' ability and brilliancy, both of which
> are unusual. However, under existing circumstances he is in no sense
> a logical candidate for the United States Senate — nor would he be if
> Mr. Gear were not in the field. The line of succession passes through
> Mr. Gear's hands to Mr. Dolliver, who seems to be tightening his
> grasp thereon.[7]

Cummins' view of the "line of succession" was somewhat different. Writing to Harvey Ingham in 1898 of the possibility of Dolliver's being a candidate against him for Gear's seat, Cummins observed: "I sincerely hope that [Dolliver] will not be, for he is Allison's natural successor, and if he could look over the matter carefully, it seems to me that he must conclude that nothing could be better for him at the present time than to stand with me and with my friends."[8] Although Cummins had never held elective office, except for a seat in the lower house of the General Assembly, to which he was elected as an Independent Republican partly by Democratic votes in 1887, he seemed to feel from the early nineties on that he had a peculiar claim to a seat in the United States Senate. If there were such a thing as a "line of succession" to the Senate, Dolliver's long service in Congress and as a party worker would appear to have placed him well ahead of Cummins in that line, as the Iowa City editor suggested. Since, however, there was little likelihood of Allison's retiring in 1902, Cummins' proposal would have put himself in the Senate an unforeseeable number of years ahead of Dolliver.

Dolliver, however, was not a candidate. Having known Gear since 1879, and having served with him in the House for two terms, Dolliver refused to enter the contest against him in his old age after it became certain that Shaw was to confine himself to seeking re-election as Governor.[9] There is ample evidence that Roberts, Meservey, Kenyon, and other politicians in the Tenth District favored Cummins over Gear at the beginning of the campaign.[10] But as the bitterness of the battle increased, more and more people turned to Gear. This was in part due to the tremendous efforts of the Blythe-Hubbard machine and the influence of the officeholders beholden to Shaw, Allison, Gear, and the Congressmen.[11] There was also another factor as was explained by George E. Roberts in the Fort Dodge *Messenger*. Roberts stated that he had been friendly to Cummins for Senator and that:

> It has not been without regret that we have seen his chances of election pounded to pieces by the awkwardness of his managers. The general public likes a generous contest. There was at the outset a substantial point to be made against Senator Gear on account of his age. But it was a point that required, if not a delicate, at least a gentlemanly treatment. The people of the state were not ready to see one of the most famous and honored servants of the people chased into a graveyard by a band of political savages. It is hard to state the feeling that came over Mr. Cummins' more discreet friends in this part of the state when his chief organ at Des Moines pointed out with glee the probability of Governor Gear's breaking down under the burdens of the fall campaign.[12]

Roberts' point was well worth the serious consideration of Cummins and his backers, but as time would show, they learned nothing from the moderates. The outcome of the campaign was the re-election of Governor Shaw and the election of a General Assembly in which the Gear strength was predominant. When the Cummins forces in the lower house were unable to elect their candidate for Speaker, Cummins withdrew from the senatorial race, and the legislature elected Gear for a second term.[13] The Blythe-Hubbard-Shaw wing of the party had won again. The Cummins-Funk faction, more embittered than ever, turned their thoughts to the future and began a search for an issue. Moderates like Dolliver, Roberts, Kenyon, the Clarksons, and others hoped for harmony and feared that the jealousies and hatreds engendered by the extremists in both factions would seriously weaken the party. This is not to say that Dolliver and his friends considered either Cummins and Funk, or Shaw and Blythe, as extremists, but that many of the partisans of each side were so regarded.[14]

The Gear-Cummins contest raised in the minds of thinking Iowans the question of the wisdom of the method provided in the federal Constitution for choosing Senators. George Roberts observed that instead of the legislators selecting the Senators, as was intended by the founding fathers, the tendency had developed for aspirants to the United States Senate to determine the election of members of the legislature. Thus, "often no other matter is considered in nominating a candidate" for the General Assembly than his position on the choice of a United States Senator.[15] In due time this matter, already aired by the Populists, was to come to the attention of the Congress and the states in the form of a constitutional amendment. Meanwhile, in 1900 the interest of all parties turned to the presidential election.

A month before the Iowa legislature met to re-elect Senator Gear, the Dollivers returned to Washington for the first session of the Fifty-sixth Congress. Two events of a personal nature made the early months of 1900 memorable for the Dolliver family. In January their first daughter, Margaret Eliza, was born. Somewhat later a movement began, supported by practically all Republicans in the House, to make Dolliver his party's nominee for Vice President of the United States.

There was no question as to McKinley's renomination, but as Vice President Hobart had died in November, 1899, and Bryan was the probable Democratic presidential nominee, many Republicans sought a young and popular orator as McKinley's running mate.[16] The Dolliver boom began in April, after Elihu Root had positively refused the honor, and Theodore Roosevelt had issued a public announcement saying, "It is proper for me to state definitely that under no circumstances could I, or would I, accept the nomination for the Vice-Presidency. . . . My duty is here in the State whose people chose me to be governor."[17]

Senator Henry Cabot Lodge suggested in mid-April that Dolliver was the best Western man for Vice President, but Lodge was for Roosevelt first, last, and all the time, even though Roosevelt was allegedly out of the running and Lodge committed to support Secretary of the Navy John D. Long of Massachusetts.[18] Speaking before the Massachusetts Republican Convention on April 27, Dolliver announced that he, too, favored Long's nomination and that "here and now I resign as a candidate in the vice-presidential race in his interest." Dolliver did not take his own chances seriously and said that friendly colleagues and newspapermen were pushing his name forward.[19]

At first the Iowa papers had questioned the wisdom of advancing Dolliver for the vice-presidency. The *Register* feared that Dolliver's election would cost Henderson the speakership. It asserted that other states, especially Illinois, wanted to give Iowa the vice-presidency in order to be able to argue that Iowans should not preside over both houses of Congress, and thus open the way for Joseph Cannon to become Speaker.[20] Henderson, however, backed Dolliver, and both the Speaker and Senator Allison, who declined to be a candidate himself, professed to believe that Dolliver could be nominated.[21] George Roberts sent a special dispatch to Iowa, stating that Henderson was urging Dolliver's selection and that:

The House is practically solid for him and the members are actively advocating his nomination. The idea that in the event of Mr. Dolliver's nomination, Speaker Henderson would fail of re-election is given no weight among members of the House. They say that Speaker Henderson is assured of re-election if the next House is Republican.[22]

Iowans, therefore, were united behind Dolliver when the Republican Convention met in Philadelphia on June 19.[23] The Cummins faction supported Dolliver, hoping to eliminate him from Iowa politics before another senatorial vacancy occurred, lest he be in Cummins' way. Likewise, Shaw and the Blythe-Hubbard people realized that putting Dolliver into the vice-presidency would pave the way for Shaw, a Tenth District resident, to go to the Senate if an opportunity arose. Dolliver's personal friends, men like Roberts, Meservey, Secretary Wilson, O'Connell, and Perkins, wanted Dolliver to have the honor, and some of them felt that the vice-presidency in 1900 might be a stepping-stone to the presidency in 1904.[24]

Dolliver did not want to be Vice President and could not afford the costs of social entertaining which went with the office. He said that "one term would make me a beggar."[25] But unlike Root and Allison, who was McKinley's choice as a running mate, Dolliver did not decline to allow his name to be considered. In the first place, the impulse toward him was as much a surprise to him as to anyone else. In fact, he did not give much thought to the matter until Congressman Charles H. Grosvenor of Ohio, a politician close to McKinley, came out for Dolliver. Then, realizing that powerful administration forces might be behind his boom, Dolliver went to see the President to tell him that he did not want the vice-presidency and would not accept it. McKinley asked him to make no public statement but to allow the discussion to continue, as it could not possibly harm him. The President felt that the "introduction and inspiration of new names" was needed to prevent the vice-presidential situation from "drifting by default to a weak choice." Dolliver agreed to keep quiet on the subject, and McKinley made it clear that the administration did not intend to support anyone for the nomination.[26]

Some days after his conference with the President, Dolliver had a talk with Senator Marcus A. Hanna of Ohio, chairman of the Republican National Committee. Hanna indicated that he felt uncertain of being able to bring about Secretary Long's nomination, which Hanna desired. According to Dolliver, Hanna requested him to be a candidate and he refused. The Senator then "asked me if I would not help out by allowing the use of my name, and I consented to do this, on the condition that at the proper time, I should be protected. Senator Hanna promised that this would be done."[27] Hanna's opposition to the nomination of Theodore Roosevelt is well known, and it appears that he hoped to have several candidates in the race in order to head off any stampede for the New York Governor.

By the time the convention met in June, two things had become apparent to Dolliver. First, his candidacy was being seriously pushed by Iowans and others who assumed that his silence indicated his willingness to accept the nomination. The Washington *Times-Herald* reported on June 3 that there was for Dolliver "what appears to resemble a genuine, spontaneous demand — more perhaps than for any other man who has been mentioned in this connection." [28] Secondly, Dolliver came to feel sure that Theodore Roosevelt wanted the nomination. [29]

The story of Roosevelt's oblique campaign for the vice-presidency is all too familiar. He steadfastly "advanced backward" from his February 6 position that "under no circumstances" would be accept the nomination. McKinley, whatever he may have said, quite obviously did not desire either Roosevelt or Long as a running mate if he could prevent it without endangering his chances for re-election. After having told Dolliver he would support no candidate, the President on June 10 called Senator Allison to the White House to plead with him in the presence of Hanna and Charles G. Dawes to accept the vice-presidency. According to Dawes's diary, "Allison persists he will not accept the nomination for the Vice-Presidency." Three days later Allison issued a public statement: "I will not have the Vice-Presidency; it cannot be forced upon me. If I should be nominated at Philadelphia, I will decline, will refuse to run." [30]

Allison could have done nothing else, even had he wanted the nomination, and he did not want it. To have accepted after Dolliver had been publicized for weeks as Iowa's candidate would never have been understood. It would have appeared to be a betrayal of Dolliver, and it would have reopened the senatorial question in Iowa, something which Allison's backers in the "Burlington Reservation" certainly did not desire. The President's last-minute effort to get behind Allison for the vice-presidency was a blunder as stupid as it was futile.

Charles G. Dawes, Comptroller of the Currency, and one of McKinley's most intimate friends, now attempted to aid Dolliver's "cause" at the convention. McKinley had finally decided to keep out of the affair altogether. Allison and Dolliver's other supporters insisted that he stay in the race unless Roosevelt consented to accept, in which case Iowa would be for Roosevelt. [31] Mrs. Dolliver vigorously opposed any suggestion that her husband change his mind and seek the nomination. She wanted him to be President sometime but felt that the vice-presidency was not the best path to the White House and knew that they could not afford the office. [32]

Dolliver and his wife had rooms at a Germantown hotel during the convention. When it became clear that Senator Platt, aided for reasons of their own by Matt Quay and Boies Penrose, was going to try to force Hanna to accept Roosevelt's nomination, Dolliver went to see Hanna, reminded him of his promise, and advised him to make the best of the situation by accepting Roosevelt.

Popular sentiment among the delegates was for Roosevelt, as Hanna knew, and, of course, others besides Dolliver urged him to yield. In fact, Hanna had little choice, in view of the power of the New York and Pennsylvania bosses. After talking with Hanna, Dolliver and Lafayette Young, a Des Moines editor who had intended to make the nominating speech presenting Dolliver to the convention, went to the Walton Hotel in Philadelphia to see Governor Roosevelt. Dolliver recalled that "Mr. Roosevelt was very warm and looked worried. His face was flushed and he had his coat off." Roosevelt informed the Iowans that he was perplexed. It was very strange, he thought, that the men who could aid him in securing renomination as Governor of New York, his "real ambition," were proposing him for Vice President, while those who had it in their power to make him Vice President were disposed to advise him to confine himself to the governorship. Dolliver knew all about the attitudes of the men to whom Roosevelt alluded and also that Roosevelt had recently discovered that Platt had arranged to defeat him for Governor if he did not accept the vice-presidency. Hence, Dolliver suggested that if Roosevelt had changed his mind and wanted to accept the vice-presidential nomination, the three of them ought to go directly to see Senator Hanna. They did, and, according to Dolliver, Roosevelt explained to Hanna that he had been reluctant to consent to being a candidate because neither McKinley nor Hanna wanted him on the ticket. "On the contrary, we want you," replied Hanna.[33]

Having at last backed completely out of their much advertised positions, Hanna and Roosevelt were agreed upon one thing at least. That was that Roosevelt's nomination must come from the West and not from New York or Pennsylvania, lest the Platt-Quay-Penrose victory be too obvious. Hanna asked Dolliver to prepare a speech nominating Roosevelt, but Dolliver refused, saying that Young had brought a speech all the way from Iowa to use to nominate a Vice President and that "it would be a bad thing to let him go home without getting this out of his system." Hanna agreed and told Young to "put in San Juan hill and the proper coloring" and to nominate Teddy with the address intended for Dolliver. Thus, when the time came, Alabama yielded to Iowa, and Lafayette Young nominated Theodore Roosevelt for Vice President of the United States.[34] After a hard-fought campaign in which imperialism was a major issue and during which Dolliver toured the East and North, the Republicans won an easy victory in November.

Inasmuch as Dolliver did not want the nomination, and Roosevelt did, the result of the convention, fateful as it proved to be, gratified the two men most immediately concerned. Secretary of Agriculture James Wilson wrote Dolliver soon after the convention adjourned:

> The advertising you have had will be beneficial in many ways. It is well known that if the Rough Rider had not been in evidence with his big hat and all that, that you would have been the choice. It will not

hurt Roosevelt a particle to preside over the Senate of the United States, neither will it hurt you to be brought prominently before the people of the country. Everything said of you has been flattering to yourself and your friends and your future is in no way handicapped. I am well satisfied.[35]

The kindly old Scotsman was quite correct. Neither Roosevelt nor Dolliver was damaged by the events at the convention. Sooner than any politician dreamed, the hinge of fate turned again and altered forever the status of Vice President Roosevelt and Congressman Dolliver.

———

On July 14, 1900, less than one month after the meeting of the Republican National Convention, Senator John H. Gear of Iowa died. Governor Shaw immediately determined that he would not appoint a successor until thirty days after Gear's funeral. Since the General Assembly would not meet again until 1902, the man appointed would serve until January of that year, at which time the legislature would have to elect two Senators — one to complete Gear's term, and the other for Allison's seat.[36]

The funeral wreathes had not wilted on the grave of Senator Gear before the politicians began to speculate and maneuver in regard to his successor. The Cummins faction, with an amazing lack of political realism, asserted that the Governor ought to appoint Albert B. Cummins. Others mentioned the availability of E. H. Conger, Minister to China, and of Congressmen George D. Perkins, W. P. Hepburn, J. A. T. Hull, John F. Lacey, and Jonathan P. Dolliver.[37]

Governor Shaw wanted the seat for himself, and it had been Gear's hope that Shaw would be his successor. But Shaw realized that his chances of securing the senatorship for himself, should he call the legislature into session to fill the vacancy, were too slim to risk. He did not want to resign and accept appointment for two years, as he might then have even less certainty of an election. Joseph W. Blythe desired the appointment of Shaw or Congressman Hepburn. Judge Hubbard was for Shaw or Representative Hull. Blythe's brother, James, was for Shaw if Shaw decided to try for the office.[38]

The problem of the Blythe-Hubbard-Shaw group was simply this. They wanted to make either Shaw, Hepburn, or Hull United States Senator. Shaw declined to leave the governorship under existing circumstances, and none of his advisers wanted the General Assembly called, because that would reopen, at the beginning of the presidential and congressional election campaigns, the factional fight of the preceding January. The foremost aim was to prevent a victory for the Cumminsites. The Governor and his clique feared to appoint either Hull or Hepburn, feeling certain that Cummins could defeat either in 1902. Finally, a secret conference of the machine leaders with Senator Allison met in Chicago to work out a solution. The identity of all of those present is not known. Dolliver was not there, but he later learned of the purpose of the meeting and described it precisely:

> In solemn conclave, the name of every conspicuous public man in Iowa was canvassed, the test of availability being, not whether he had served the state faithfully, not whether he was prepared by training or experience for the high office, but whether, if appointed, he could hold his own in the Legislature in which the strength of Mr. Cummins had been fully demonstrated.[39]

Two or three letters written during these days of feverish political soul-searching indicate the trend of affairs. James E. Blythe advised Shaw in early August:

> I have arrived at the conclusion that the best thing for you to do for your own future, is to promptly make the appointment of whom you consider the strongest man in the recognized list of senatorial timber, and to make that appointment after an understanding with your friends that we should all stand together to see your appointment sustained by election in the legislature whenever it is convened.

Blythe then discussed each possible appointee. He considered Hepburn too old, Lacey too unpopular, Perkins too weak to hold his own district against Cummins.

> This narrows the field down to Hull and Dolliver. The appointment of Hull might result in a fight between him and Cummins and the one who got the most of the seventh district [Hull and Cummins both lived in the 7th] would have the advantage. I believe Cummins would have the advantage over Hull in the state at large. . . . I think Dolliver is the best man to appoint. He is located in the territory which has been favorable to Cummins and he possesses many of the elements which go to make Cummins strong with the people. I am sure that . . . the newspapers would take the position that the fight ought to be dropped if Dolliver was appointed.

Blythe added that he believed his brother, "the boss," would have to accept Dolliver and stand by Shaw's decision. The final paragraph contained the bait to attract Shaw's attention and appeal to his vanity. "With the prominence you have already attained nationally as an advocate of sound money, I should think we ought, with the help of Allison and Dolliver and your Iowa friends, [arrange it] that you might readily go into the cabinet." James Blythe, enclosing a copy of the letter to Shaw, wrote Dolliver to try to get Hubbard's support by showing him that if Shaw attempted to get the senatorship himself, Cummins would either be elected or use his influence to name another.[40]

On August 19 Colonel Richard Root, a close friend of Blythe, Gear, and Allison, wrote the Governor that neither Hepburn nor Hull could defeat Cummins and that if Shaw himself were not to take the senatorship, then the man to support was Dolliver. "I have made careful inquiries from Republicans from a large number of Districts in this state and they all say, if it cannot be Shaw then it ought to be Dolliver."[41]

Shaw finally reached a decision on August 22. At 5:45 P. M. he dispatched a telegram to Dolliver: "Have ordered commission made out appointing you to United States Senate."[42] The Governor immediately released the news to the press. The people of Fort Dodge turned out in large numbers, and soon Central Avenue was crowded. By dark "fireworks were flaring from every building and street corner . . . and at 8:30 all the whistles in the city commenced a joyous and noisy acclaim. The brass band emerged and discoursed some of the best music that has ever been heard in Fort Dodge" as the city celebrated "the promotion and preferment of its most prominent citizen."[43]

The person most concerned was among the last to learn the good news. Dolliver was in Allerton on the evening of August 22, debating imperialism with Champ Clark, and did not hear of his appointment until he stepped off the train in Des Moines late that night. Informed of the Governor's action, Dolliver issued a statement saying that he would accept the appointment, resign his seat in the House, and decline the nomination for a seventh term which had been unanimously tendered him in May. "In entering upon the office of United States Senator," he said, "I will have only one ambition, and that is to represent the whole state and in so far as its duties relate to party matters, the whole Republican party."[44]

Literally hundreds of telegrams and letters of congratulation poured in upon Dolliver from all parts of the nation. Every newspaper in Iowa "except two of Democratic leanings" endorsed his appointment, and his rivals, including Cummins, offered their best wishes.[45]

It has been assumed by writers of Iowa history that Dolliver's appointment came simply as a reward to a member of the Old Guard faction. Such was by no means the case, first of all because he was never a part of the Blythe-Hubbard organization. He finally got their support for his appointment in 1900, but only because they wanted to prevent Cummins' election. Once Shaw decided not to take the senatorship himself, there were several compelling reasons for him to appoint Dolliver. He was obligated to Dolliver for his 1897 nomination. He owed much to the railroad politicians, and by appointing Dolliver he aided them in keeping Cummins out of power. Dolliver, next to Speaker Henderson, was the senior Iowa Congressman and the only one with a national reputation. Had nothing else been involved, he was without exception the logical Iowa Republican to promote to the Senate in 1900. Shaw's friend, Judge J. P. Conner, wanted to go to Congress and would have a chance to do so if Dolliver went to the Senate. Finally, Shaw wanted a Cabinet post in 1902 and a presidential nomination in 1904. He knew Dolliver stood well with President McKinley and that if anyone in Iowa could heal the breach in the party it was Dolliver. If his own party were torn apart during an election, or if his appointee were repudiated by the legislature, Shaw's chances for a national political career would be damaged. Shaw, therefore, aided by Blythe's brother and probably by Allison, convinced Blythe and Hubbard that Dolliver was the only man to appoint.[46]

As an important pro-Cummins Iowa paper commented:

> Mr. Dolliver is an able, an honest, and an attractive man, and he will make an excellent Senator. It cannot be fairly charged that he is a member of the machine, or that he is controlled by the political elements in the Republican party of Iowa against whose continued domination the rank and file of the party rebelled. . . . He is the lucky heir of a train of favorable political circumstances. His location was right, his age was right, and his reputation for independence was right.[47]

Dolliver understood perfectly well why he was appointed, and he felt no obligation either to Shaw or to the Blythe-Hubbard machine. He wrote Clarkson:

> I was appointed after everybody else had been cancelled out and it was discovered that owing to my location and the general goodwill of the state towards me, I was the only man whose appointment would make the defeat of Cummins absolutely sure. . . . I was the only man in the state who could hold the old Gear strength practically solid and take any votes away from Cummins.[48]

Dolliver saw no reason for the Cummins faction to resent his appointment, since from any conceivable point of view Dolliver's standing in and service to the party, state, and nation exceeded that of Cummins and gave him as much claim to the senatorship as anyone.

The Cummins faction, however, immediately announced that Cummins would be a candidate against Dolliver in 1902. Dolliver instantly accepted the challenge. He wrote to all members of the General Assembly, to the Congressmen who had been his rivals, to Speaker Henderson, to James E. Blythe, to the Methodist Bishop of Iowa, and to various editors, lawyers, and political leaders asking their support. He began most of these letters as follows:

> I wish to have your help in holding on to the seat in the Senate, to which I have been appointed. . . . The question is whether I am a suitable person to represent the State, or whether after having resigned my seat in Congress in order to accept the Governor's appointment I ought to be retired to private life. . . .
> This is my emergency, the action of the Governor has compelled me to leave the ship I am on, and unless I can reach the deck on the other ship, I am left in the deep sea with all my belongings.[49]

Dolliver assured Senator Allison that he would make no arrangements harm-

ful to the old Senator's own chances for re-election in 1902. "It is my intention, with the help of my friends throughout the State, to defeat Mr. Cummins
if he tries to prevent the legislative endorsement of Governor Shaw's action,"
Dolliver wrote Allison. "In all that I do, I intend to keep in view your interests as well as my own, and I will give this gentleman a senatorial fight, if they
want it, which they will remember a good many years."[50]

To his friend Cummins, Dolliver wrote a cordial and frank letter which
ended with a pleasant hint. "Our personal relations have always been so
agreeable that I look forward to the future with the assurance that nothing is
likely to happen which shall disturb the friendly feelings which I have always
had toward you."[51]

Cummins knew, as did everyone else, that much of his strength lay among
those people who were also Dolliver's friends. In any contest between the two,
the odds were overwhelmingly in favor of Dolliver, who had a great popular
following of his own. In addition, choosing from their point of view the lesser
of two evils, the old Republican organization could be counted on to support
Dolliver, the independent, against Cummins, the head of a rival faction.
Hence, on September 7, Cummins withdrew his announced intention of con-
testing for the senatorship, having decided after due consideration to become a
candidate for Governor in 1901.[52]

Even before taking his seat in the Senate, Dolliver demonstrated his independence. J. W. Blythe naturally sought to establish a friendly relationship
with the man he had opposed for the appointment until the last hour. He was
accustomed to getting exactly what he wanted from his father-in-law, Senator
Gear, but Blythe realized, as he wrote Dolliver, that his wishes could no longer
"have undue weight." Blythe, Hubbard, and Allison all asked Dolliver to appoint Gear's private secretary as his own. Dolliver, knowing exactly why these
gentlemen wanted to have their man in a key position to screen his callers and
his mail, positively refused.[53]

Shaw, Blythe, and Hubbard insisted that Dolliver personally intervene in the
Tenth District Congressional Convention called to nominate his successor.
They wanted to be sure that a pro-Cummins man was not nominated. Dolliver
declined to do so. He wanted Judge J. P. Conner, his long-time friend who
had helped him win his first congressional nomination in 1888, to succeed him.
But in Dolliver's view, it was unwise for either himself or the Governor to be
involved in an "unseemly contention about my successor." He said the people
of the Tenth District would resent either his or Shaw's efforts "to dictate the
nominee." Dolliver bluntly told Blythe that it would not do for the Governor
and his forces to try to dominate the convention. Dolliver's Webster County
friends were for Conner, but they were not fighting other candidates in their
own counties.[54] Conner won, a fact pleasing to both Dolliver and Shaw.
However, Shaw and Blythe could take little credit for the victory, and neither

was happy at Dolliver's plainly evident intention of doing precisely as he thought best regardless of the wishes and suggestions of the Governor and "the boss." [55]

The real showdown between Dolliver and the Blythe-Hubbard-Shaw forces came in 1901. As soon as Cummins announced his candidacy for the gubernatorial nomination, the Old Guard organization began frantically hunting for a man to put forward against him. [56] They begged Dolliver to agree to back either George Perkins, Senator James H. Trewin, or E. H. Conger, and to pledge that he would come into Iowa and campaign against Cummins. Shaw and Blythe were particularly insistent that Dolliver must do this, and they as well as others tried to make Dolliver think that Cummins' real intention in running for Governor was merely to carry into office with him enough legislators to bring about his own election to the Senate in 1902. [57] This was a possibility, and there were those in the Cummins-Funk faction who planned to follow this procedure. [58] Cummins and Funk, however, both assured Dolliver and his associates that Cummins had no such intention and that he would use his influence to secure Dolliver's unanimous selection by the Republicans in the General Assembly. In fact, Cummins even asked Dolliver and Roberts to help him get the gubernatorial nomination. [59]

After giving the whole matter careful consideration and discussing it in detail with Allison, Roberts, Secretary Wilson, Barkley, Meservey, and others, Dolliver decided not to intervene against Cummins but to take him at his word on the matter of the senatorship. Dolliver did have Still Meservey run for the legislature and Barkley seek re-election as state senator in order that trusted friends would be on hand in the event trickery were attempted. [60] Funk agreed to having the county conventions in pro-Cummins territory pass resolutions directing the nominees for the General Assembly to vote for Dolliver for United States Senator. Having taken these precautions against a double-cross by the Cumminsites, Dolliver firmly informed the infuriated Blythe and his associates that he would not help them defeat Cummins for Governor. [61] Cummins was nominated on the first ballot at the convention in Cedar Rapids on August 7 and elected in November.

Few incidents in his career better illustrate Dolliver's sagacity as a politician or his skill in safely maintaining his independence of both factions in Iowa politics. He clearly saw Cummins' weakness in having "tied himself up so that even if he and his backers should want to attack me, they could make little headway unless he might gain sympathy from the fact that I had been active against his ambition to be Governor. . . . Curiously enough his strength is of such a character that much of it can be counted as friendly to me." [62] Thus, Dolliver realized that if he remained neutral, Iowans who otherwise would resent his interference would vote for Cummins for Governor and also for legislators pledged to elect Dolliver to the Senate. Dolliver, likewise, correctly

assessed the danger of allying himself with men like Blythe and Shaw, motivated
as they were by hate of Cummins and love of power for themselves. Half-
humorously, but with much truth, Dolliver wrote Ret Clarkson:

> Many of those who were instrumental in appointing me Senator
> had no interest whatever in my future but desired me to take a course
> that would reopen the Senatorial question for the purpose of filling
> the field with such an array of candidates as would make it possible
> for our good Governor to come on the field as a peacemaker and set-
> tle all trouble by taking the office himself. . . . [They] have been so
> zealous in my interest, so afraid that Cummins was going to beat me
> that at one time they had their preparations all made to attend to it
> themselves. Fortunately the people of the state from one end of it to
> the other recognized the wisdom of the course I have taken and have
> failed altogether to respond to the suggestion that I ought to be pun-
> ished for the crime of having failed to appear among them in the role
> of petty boss to dictate the management of their affairs.[63]

Dolliver put his faith in the people, not in political machines. He refused to
do anything in secret against Cummins either to eliminate him as a rival or to
win for himself the favor of the powerful Blythe forces. He told Blythe sharply
that if he ever found it necessary to fight Cummins on any issue he would do
it "in the open field in such a way as to square with my views" of honest political methods.[64] Blythe and Shaw never forgave Dolliver. Years later Dolliver
wrote Cummins: "When you were first a candidate for Governor, my sympathies were with you, and the pressure I resisted was such that I have to this day
to bear the burden of hatred for not opposing your nomination at Cedar
Rapids."[65]

The convention which nominated A. B. Cummins for Governor of Iowa,
August 7, 1901, also adopted a platform containing a statement regarding
national tariff policy which came to be known as the "Iowa Idea." George E.
Roberts was the author of the tariff planks, the significant phrases of which
were:

> We favor such changes in the tariff from time to time as become
> advisable through the progress of our industries and their changing
> relations to the commerce of the world. We endorse the policy of
> reciprocity as the natural complement of protection and urge its de-
> velopment as necessary to the realization of our highest commercial
> possibilities. . . . We favor such amendments of the interstate com-
> merce act as will more fully carry out its prohibition of discrimination
> in rate making and any modification of the tariff schedules that may
> be required to prevent their affording a shelter to monopoly.[66]

Roberts wrote these tariff planks in Dolliver's hotel room in Cedar Rapids.
In his recently published *American Epoch*, Arthur S. Link's statement, that
"After an epochal struggle in 1902 [sic], the Iowa Republicans nominated the

progressive Albert B. Cummins for Governor and wrote into their platform his proposal . . . the 'Iowa Idea,' as Cummins' suggestion was called," is very nearly devoid of facts. The date was 1901, Cummins was not yet a progressive, the proposal was not his, and he had nothing to do with suggesting it.[67]

Dolliver heartily approved Roberts' tariff planks, and they were naturally regarded as an expression of his views by virtue of their origin. A few days after their adoption, Dolliver, enroute to Washington, stopped in Canton to see President McKinley. The President was preparing the address which he was to deliver in Buffalo on September 5. On his desk lay a copy of the Iowa platform, parts of which he told Dolliver he was including in his speech. McKinley particularly commended the tariff declaration, asserting that tariff reform, especially through reciprocity agreement, was to be a feature of his second administration and that he hoped Dolliver would support reductions where needed. This conversation made a great impression upon Dolliver, and as soon as he reached Washington he repeated it to Roberts.[68]

The President delivered his address at Buffalo, and in it he advocated reciprocity and lower tariffs, observing that the nation could no longer repose in a "fancied security," forever selling everything and buying little or nothing from other countries. The next day an assassin shot McKinley. When Theodore Roosevelt became President, other matters than tariff reform moved to the fore.[69]

Although Albert Cummins had nothing to do with writing the platform and did not know of the tariff declarations until after the Cedar Rapids convention adopted them, he endorsed them wholeheartedly. During his campaign he popularized the "Iowa Idea" and in tariff reform he found an issue on which to fight the Blythe-Hubbard-Shaw organization in the future.[70] Shaw regretted "exceedingly" the prominence being given to the question of the tariff, "especially by Republicans." He argued that the party had "lost a Congress every time we have tried the experiment," and that "the reduction of the tariff as a remedy for trusts is a Democratic doctrine."[71]

Dolliver, speaking in behalf of Cummins and the state ticket in the autumn of 1901, urged immediate ratification of the reciprocal trade agreements known as the Kasson Treaties and advocated the reduction or repeal of any Dingley schedules which sheltered monopolies.

> I do not look upon the tariff rates established by the law of 1897 as immutable and sacred. On the contrary, it is evident that within the last five years changes have occurred in the conditions which surround both our industries and commerce which suggest, if they do not require, modification in some of the schedules upon the exact lines referred to in the Cedar Rapids platform. . . . In some of our industries, especially some of those which have to do with the products of iron and steel, the rates deemed essential in 1897 can properly be reduced, if not remitted altogether.[72]

When the General Assembly met in January, 1902, the Republican caucus by unanimous vote nominated J. P. Dolliver to complete the four years of Gear's term, and W. B. Allison to succeed himself in the United States Senate. In expressing his appreciation to the caucus, Dolliver referred to the factional differences within the party and remarked that he was especially gratified as he began his service as an elected Senator to have this "unanimous manifestation of the confidence and good will of the Republican party . . . because I have never found anything in this state except kindness and good will, and I have an ambition in my public service to feel towards the whole party and towards the whole community of Iowa a sentiment responsive to their expression of confidence and support." He also paid tribute to Senator Allison, for whom he confessed "almost a filial affection," and counted it "one of the great fortunes of my life that I shall have the benefit of his judgment and the guidance of his wisdom and of his experience." [73]

A week later the General Assembly elected Dolliver to the United States Senate by a vote of 119 to 20 over the Democratic nominee, J. J. Seerley.[74] In his speech of acceptance, Dolliver emphasized his position on the tariff question and placed himself on record for reform in the following unequivocal statement:

> The design of Protective laws is to prevent our home industries from being overborne by the competition of foreign producers, and it may be safely said that no American factory making an unequal or precarious fight with its foreign rivals will ever look in vain for help and defense to the people of Iowa. *But we are not blind to the fact that in many lines of industry tariff rates which in 1897 were reasonable have already become unnecessary and in some instances even absurd* [italics added]. They remain on the statute books not as a shield for the safety of domestic labor, but as a weapon of offense against the American market place itself. Without overlooking the dangers and evils of a general tariff agitation, I cannot believe that a correction of obvious defects in the present schedules, made by friends of the law in an open and business-like way, could be disastrous in any legitimate interest of the people — unless indeed we admit the claim put forward by some — that Congress is impotent and helpless in the presence of these questions. . . . How is it possible to put off very long the readjustment of our laws to the needs of the era? [75]

Dolliver's acceptance speech aroused much interest over the nation. The Minneapolis *Journal* thought that he "did not state the case too strongly" when he said "the defects of our tariff laws ought to be corrected," but the editor doubted that a Republican Congress would ever deal "intelligently, vigorously, honestly and fearlessly" with the tariff issue. "Congress is not helpless but it is indifferent," the Chicago *Tribune* observed in an editorial favorable to Dolliver's views. "The day will come when the people will be less prosperous than

they are now. Then they will become harsh critics of excessive customs duties.
. . . Then perhaps Congress will become interested in the subject which Senator Dolliver would like to take in hand now."[76] Time would prove the accuracy of each of these editorials.

In his remarks to the Republican caucus and to the Iowa General Assembly
in January, 1902, Dolliver mentioned the very factors which were to highlight
his career as Senator. His desire for party harmony, his expression of affection
for Allison, and his unequivocal endorsement of the Iowa Idea, emphasizing as
it did the need for revision of the Interstate Commerce Act and the Dingley
Tariff, were harbingers of Dolliver's greatest interests in the years ahead.

- XV -

Prelude To Greatness, 1902-1905

*Dolliver scorned to do injustice to the wealthy; he would have pro-
tected the rights of any rich man as quickly as those of any poor
man; and yet he steadfastly strove to bring about conditions which
should be in the interests of the plain people and should make this
country an economic and industrial, no less than a political, democracy.*

Theodore Roosevelt.

WHEN JONATHAN DOLLIVER took his seat in the United States Senate for the
first time in December, 1900, William McKinley had but recently won re-
election as President, the Gold Standard Act had been passed the previous
March, and Nelson Aldrich, "the manager," had just begun his second year as
chairman of the Senate Finance Committee. Senator Allison, the "conciliator
and adjuster," still presided serenely over the Appropriations Committee, and
his friend and fellow-townsman, David B. Henderson, was Speaker of the
House. On the surface, all power seemed safely in the hands of the conservatives. This was the moment, observed Nathaniel Stephenson, "when senatorial
power was at its peak."[1]

During his first eighteen months as a member of the Senate, Dolliver, in def-
erence to the tradition that new Senators should be seen but not heard, seldom
participated in debate. His first address, January 9, 1901, a tribute to Senator
Gear, was delivered at the invitation of those in charge of the Senate memorial
services. Even in this speech, however, at the very beginning of his senatorial
career and at a time when some Senators were little more than special agents
for great corporations, Dolliver set forth his personal view of the duty of
statesmen. Alluding to Bryan's famous statement in his "Cross of Gold"
speech, Dolliver said:

> A noted political leader of our day has broadened the definition of
> a business man to include workers in every field, on the farm and in
> the factory as well as in the bank and in the counting house; and
> while it may be a maxim of private life that every man should attend

172

to his own business, the statesman of today in the nature of the case attends to the business of all.[2]

Such a concept was not widely held in the Senate of the United States in the last years of the McKinley era. There were Senators who attended to the "business" of the silver mineowners, of the railroad, traction, oil, and banking interests, of the steel, sugar, textile, and other manufacturers, but relatively few statesmen who looked after the "business" of the laboring masses, rural or urban, or that of the farmers, the professional classes, or the small business-men.[3] Doubtless Dolliver's remarks passed unnoticed by his audience in 1901. Allison's colleague, delivering a memorial oration for "Old Business" Gear, would hardly arouse the suspicions of Aldrich, Foraker, Elkins, and the other leaders of the Senate.

By 1902, however, when Dolliver returned to Washington after his election by the Iowa General Assembly, Theodore Roosevelt was in the White House, the "Iowa Idea" had attracted national attention, the Muckrakers had begun their exposures, and, for whatever it meant, a great deal of political power was in the hands of Iowans. It was a matter of great pride to Dolliver and to his Iowa contemporaries that in the early years of the Roosevelt regime, Leslie Shaw was Secretary of the Treasury; James Wilson, Secretary of Agriculture; George Roberts, Director of the Mint; M. D. O'Connell, Solicitor of the Treasury; and that in addition to the positions of Allison in the Senate and Henderson as Speaker of the House, Iowans were chairmen of five committees in the House of Representatives. Partly because of his reputation in the House and in the party, partly because of his personal acquaintance with the Senate leaders as well as with the President, and partly, no doubt, because he was an Iowan, identified with the movement for tariff reform at a time when that sub-ject was becoming a distinct dividing line between Standpatters and Progres-sives, Dolliver quickly came to be regarded as a man of importance among the younger members of the Senate.

Within the party structure he was neither a Standpatter nor a Progressive, but he was much more in sympathy with the latter than the former. On such matters as tariff revision, the necessity for control of monopolies — especially railroad regulation — woman suffrage, child labor, federal aid to education, flood control, conservation, and pure food and drug legislation, Dolliver stood with, or in advance of, those who called themselves Progressives.[4] But, like Erasmus of Rotterdam in the Reformation era, Dolliver sought reform within the existing organization. He understood too well that in Iowa, at least, the so-called Progressive Movement in its initial stage was more a matter of dis-appointed personal ambitions and bitter political rivalry than a concern for great issues. Knowing that, and revering his party despite its faults, he could not unreservedly give his endorsement to the movement without, as he saw it, substituting demagoguery for integrity, sacrificing his independence for commitment to the demands of the "cause," and contributing to strife instead of harmony.

Furthermore, Dolliver's lack of faith in reform through legislation caused him to hold aloof from those enthusiasts who believed that antipass laws, the direct primary, and the initiative, referendum, and recall were necessities for the preservation of democracy. He had used passes for two decades, as had Cummins and most other Iowa politicians, and he knew that the very legislators who had enacted laws to regulate the railroads during the Carpenter and Larrabee administrations had ridden to Des Moines on passes.[5] Certainly Dolliver had nothing to fear from primary elections, for his greatest strength was with the people. He frequently stated that he had no objection to that method of nominating candidates, but for two reasons he did not support the movement to enact primary laws. First, he regarded this as properly a state matter and felt that a United States Senator ought not to presume to influence members of the General Assembly on such questions. More important was his belief, often expressed, that if a people could not conduct an honest caucus and an honest convention, they could do no better in managing a primary election. Hence, he regarded the primary as a dubious experiment if the end in view were reform.[6]

He likewise rejected such innovations as initiative, referendum, and recall as unnecessary, cumbersome, and probably futile. Writing in 1901 to his friend, Professor Richard T. Ely of the University of Wisconsin, concerning various reforms advocated by Ely and other Progressives, Dolliver said:

> In all these things the suggestions of your letter look in the right direction [maintenance of honest democratic government]; yet the more I meditate upon it, the more it looks to me that these reformations prolific of good as they will be, are in the nature of effects rather than causes. Somewhere above the statehouse, above the courthouse, and above the schoolhouse, society must find the influences which are to produce the good citizenship of the future. . . . I inherited the Christian faith as interpreted by our fathers, I am now approaching middle life, and I find that all other evidences of Christianity are beginning to appear insignificant to the one made prominent by the needs of modern society. Namely, that unless it be true that there is a Divine Force within reach, able to take men deformed by sin and leave them standing upright then there is no hope left for our race.[7]

One clue to the difference in emphasis between Dolliver and the early Progressives was that whereas the Progressives stressed that "if the laws are the right laws, and if they can be enforced by the right men . . . everything would be better,"[8] Dolliver, with a deeper insight into human history, realized that unless sinful men were "born again," as his father phrased it, no legislation imaginable could solve the basic social problems of greed, avarice, and lust manifested in the growth of monopolies, corruption in politics, and the exploitation of labor, of women, of children, of immigrants, and of natural resources. The difference, however, was one of degree rather than of kind, and it is doubtless true that many Progressives hoped to improve conditions without indulging in the illusion that problems could be finally solved. No Standpatter, Dolliver believed in applying human intelligence, based upon experience, in efforts to improve society and solve its problems. But he did not accept the heresy, born of the Renaissance, that man could attain perfection through his own efforts. He did not think that imperfect man could by legislation perfect society. He wanted to know where the Progressive reformer was going to get the "right men" to make and enforce the "right laws." He was willing, without any illusions as to complete success, to work for social justice through the "statehouse," "courthouse," and "schoolhouse" — and in Congress and White House, too — but somewhat like Reinhold Niebuhr in a later era, Dolliver was far from believing that the ills of the world could be set right if only men obey the law — even the law of Christ.[9] Rather, he regarded the problem of achieving justice in a sinful world as a very difficult task.

Dolliver had faith in man, but his faith in man was not a substitute for his faith in God, and he had a rather clear notion of man's limitations. Thus, he told Ely that "these reformations" were "effects" rather than "causes." Regenerated men with a serious sense of social responsibility were seeking solutions, and the "effects," that is, the results, of their efforts were the various reforms. But Dolliver's emphasis was upon the cause, upon the source of regenerated men, and he concerned himself deeply with the problem of apprehending that Divine Force "able to take men deformed by sin and leave them standing upright." Speaking at Saint John's Protestant Episcopal Church in Washington at a centennial celebration of Universal Bible Sunday in 1904, Dolliver told a great audience, which included President and Mrs. Roosevelt and most of the notables of the capital, that the Bible "contains the only light in this world throwing the slightest ray upon the problems without the solution of which human society everywhere is at its last resource." He thought that:

> The one central problem with which the world has grappled in all the ages has been the preservation of public morality without which a government like ours goes to pieces within a few generations; and the Bible will be cherished, and revered, and honored among men in all centuries because it alone among the sacred writings of the world exhibits a comprehension of the problem which lies at the basis of all government and of all society.
>
> We have, some of us, overestimated the importance of law in meeting the difficulties which concern the public morality in a country like ours and under a system of government like ours; for the law is hardly more than an expression of the general purpose and will of the community, sometimes feeble to begin with and often becoming helpless with time, and in the very nature of the case falls very far short either of inspiring virtue or restraining vice.[10]

If he did not rely too greatly upon law as a solution, neither did Dolliver accept the view that universal secular education would "solve completely every doubt that relates to the national character and give permanence and efficiency to our institutions." As he observed it, the secular school, ignoring as it often did the Bible and religious instruction, "forgets that infinite spaces may come between what a man knows and what he does, that is to say, between his education and the conduct of his life. It puts out the soul's eye and then graciously holds a candle to the mind's eye." [11] His conclusion was that the ultimate solution to the problem of public virtue lay in the development of individual character, this through the rearing and education of youth in accordance with the Biblical precepts taught in the home, the church, and the Christian college. "The work of the Church from the beginning has been and is now to so deal with individuals as to work in them, in their hearts, the Supreme Miracle which in all generations has been recognized as the sufficient evidence of Christianity," he wrote a friend. "If the Church could succeed in doing that it would put an end to the cheap sociologies which are now threatening to take the place of religion in the modern world." [12]

During the last decade of his life Dolliver devoted much time and energy to the support of his church and of higher education. He came to be regarded as the leading layman of the Methodist Episcopal Church. His areas of service at the national level included membership on the Board of Christian Education of the Methodist Church and on the National Campaign Committee of the Laymen's Missionary Movement. He served as a Fraternal Delegate to the Southern Methodist Church and urged reunion between the Northern and Southern branches of Methodism. He was also a lay member of the General Conference of the Methodist Episcopal Church and sat one term as the Methodist Delegate on the Federal Council of the Churches of Christ in America. [13]

No narrow sectarian, Dolliver thought in terms of the church universal — Protestant, Roman, and Orthodox. Few things disgusted him more than the bigotry of the American Protective Association and the unseemly rivalry and jealousy of various denominations. He once threw an Iowa Methodist Conference into an uproar by asserting that those preachers who slurred and slandered their Roman Catholic brethren were far from being servants of Christ, and he wrote a Methodist preacher who criticized him for supporting a Roman Catholic for a federal judgeship:

> This government of ours is founded upon the law of absolute freedom in religion and I would not for any office in its gift, violate that principle by allowing myself to prescribe a religious test for or against a man aspiring to a place in the public service. If that position is not sound then our inheritance is a fraud. [14]

In a long letter to his Bishop, Dolliver attacked the anti-Catholic attitude of many Methodists of the Middle West. The Methodist Church, he wrote, "can best fulfill its mission by fighting the devil . . . and ought not to waste its energies on the side issues and least of all in fighting other churches."[15]

More important than his work as a churchman was Dolliver's interest in aiding church-related colleges. He served for years as a member of the board of trustees of Morningside College in Sioux City and of other Methodist colleges. Through his wide acquaintance with wealthy men such as Andrew Carnegie and D. K. Pearsons, he helped secure hundreds of thousands of dollars for endowments, building funds, and libraries for several colleges in Iowa and elsewhere.[16] Writing the president of Morningside College of a Pullman car conference with Carnegie, Dolliver reported:

> I told him that having finished his library work he ought to get a list of every one of the little colleges of the United States and put them all on their feet if it took a hundred million dollars. The old man seemed to be pleased to strike a fellow who understood the size of his pile. He told me that that was the very thing that he was now considering, having already started out on that line.[17]

Dolliver thought it sheer nonsense for college trustees to refuse gifts from robber barons. He told a Cornell audience that he believed it wise for colleges to accept money without "too much hemming and hawing over the source . . . for money is like running water — purifying itself." When an official of Wellesley, Mrs. Dolliver's alma mater, sought Dolliver's opinion on the ethics of taking $150,000 from John D. Rockefeller, the Senator suggested that Wellesley's attitude toward "soulless corporations" ought not to stand in the way of getting Rockefeller's money if he would give it.[18]

There is no question but that Dolliver was to some extent a devotee of the gospel of wealth. He believed that hard work was the key to financial success. "Poor people are the only ones who have any chance in the world," he said. "If you have $100,000 and a boy, keep them out of each other's society as much as possible. It will be better for the boy — and also for the $100,000. Let the boys fight the battle of life as their fathers did."[19] He was not alarmed at the great fortunes amassed by the brilliant industrial and financial leaders, although he disapproved of their ruthless methods. In fact, he looked upon the concentrations of wealth as useful to society. "It is not without some design," he wrote, "that the last half century has seen the accumulation of money in the hands of individuals on a scale never before known in the world." He hoped that "thoughtful men" would come to see in this "a large design of Providence for the welfare of mankind," and he thought that it was "more and more evident that wealth honestly come by and intelligently used is a blessing and not a curse to society."[20] The key words are "honestly come by and intelligently used." If it were too late to inquire into the origins of certain great fortunes, Dolliver, at least, felt free to urge their "intelligent use" for the support of higher education.

Believing strongly in education for women, Dolliver supported co-education and asserted that the "opposition to co-education is a relic of barbarism." He told a Methodist Conference:

> Morningside College has a warm place in my heart because it is a co-educational institution. It gives women an equal chance with the men to fit themselves for the duties of life. I believe in the full and complete education of women. . . . Modern society has nothing to fear from granting the largest possible privileges to women, even the ballot.[21]

He always supported equal rights for women and had written his sister, Mollie, as early as 1879: "I expect to live to see a race of educated women — and I hope to see the entire popularization of government." When he wrote that letter he thought that women would and should get "suffrage and complete equality of rights within 50 years." A quarter of a century later he continued to support the suffrage movement, but he told an Iowa feminist leader that he doubted "if the question can be made a pressing one until the matter is seriously taken up by women generally." He had observed that "women in the West and Northwest are interested, but that women, as a general rule, in the older portions of the country take only a slight interest in the subject."[22]

Consistent with his view that an informed and ethical electorate was essential for the maintenance of a sound democracy, Dolliver insisted upon the necessity for providing adequate education for all who were to vote. His opinion as to the most desirable type of education is revealed in the following excerpts from his writings:

> If the world ever solves the problem that confronts it, it will be through Christ, and we want Colleges that are Christian Colleges. Mere ignorance is not what is the matter, mere culture will not touch the problem. . . . I do not mean to disparage educational institutions; I believe most firmly in the schoolhouse, but I am here to say that the system of popular education that deliberately neglects the moral nature of man is a perpetual menace to human welfare. It is because that in the little Colleges the lights of learning and religion are kept burning side by side I feel an interest in them beyond my interest in other schools.[23]

As to curriculum, Dolliver remained all his life a defender of liberal education, placing great emphasis upon history, mathematics, natural science, philosophy, literature, languages, and the fine arts. He believed, too, that "the classics have a place and an honorable place in the course of nearly every College whose scope pretends to be general."[24] He was not unaware, however, of the need for vocational education. As chairman of the Senate Com-

SENATORS JONATHAN P. DOLLIVER AND WILLIAM B. ALLISON

Courtesy, Frances P. Dolliver

THE DOLLIVER FAMILY IN WASHINGTON

Front row, left to right: Margaret Eliza, Senator Dolliver, Mrs. Dolliver holding George P. Dolliver, Margaret
Gay Dolliver

Back row: Agnes Grayson (faithful servant), Victor Dolliver holding Frances P. Dolliver, Robert H. Dolliver

mittee on Education and Labor, he held many hearings and introduced several bills on the subject.[25]

Interest in the Dolliver bill to give federal aid to high schools teaching agriculture, manual training, and domestic science was so great that the committee had to hold hearings in a large hall in the Senate office building. Samuel Gompers testified in support of the bill, as did other labor leaders and spokesmen for education.[26] Although none of these measures sponsored by Dolliver became law in his lifetime, his work in paving the way for such legislation received recognition later as is indicated by the following letter to Mrs. Dolliver from P. P. Claxton of the Bureau of Education in the Department of the Interior in 1917:

> Now that the bill for agricultural extension, generally known as the Smith-Lever Bill, and the bill for vocational education, the Smith-Hughes Bill, have both become laws, I hope you will pardon my presumption in writing to express to you the feeling of obligation and indebtedness which the educational world owes to Senator Dolliver for his great interest in the cause of vocational education and for his continued effort in behalf of this cause. It was largely through the Dolliver Bill and its discussion that sentiment for vocational education was promoted throughout the country, and it was out of this bill that the two bills which have become laws grew.[27]

If, in the early years of the Progressive era, Dolliver emphasized the importance of religious and educational agencies in molding individuals of strong character and high ethical standards, he was getting at the root of the problem. The individual, the good man, in Dolliver's view, was the key. If each citizen fulfilled his obligations in society, if no man bribed another nor sold himself, exploited another nor shunned his own responsibility, then the great problems of the age would become manageable. Hence, Dolliver began with the basic matter of providing the nation with the type of citizen who, as a recent writer has put it, would feel "the necessity of taking up, personally and individually, those civic burdens which the previous generation had forsaken," and follow "the idea that everyone was in some very serious sense responsible for everything." [28]

Dolliver was a man of great humility. Richard T. Ely wrote of him: "The things that impressed me particularly in Senator Dolliver's character were his modesty and generosity. He did not seem to feel so much what he had achieved as what he had to learn . . . another thing that impressed me was his recognition of the metes and bounds of the progressive movement." [29] Furthermore, Dolliver seems to have understood clearly that political controversies are always conflicts between sinners and not between the totally righteous and the hopelessly depraved. Thus, he long had a certain kindly tolerance for both Blythe and Cummins, for both Aldrich and La Follette. If he tended to side with the Progressives (Republican and Democratic) on most issues, it was because they sought ends in which he believed, not because he was altogether convinced that those means would produce the results hoped for.

Although aware that both "the children of light and the children of darkness" were imperfect, that the former as well as the latter were motivated by self-interest and the urge for power, Dolliver could and did discriminate between the greater and the lesser evils. When he reached the conclusion — and he reached it rather belatedly — that the Standpatters stood not only against the means but also against the ends to which the Progressives were dedicated, and that these reactionaries were permitting selfish and dishonest business and political interests to use the Republican party and the United States government for their own enrichment, then Dolliver would rise against them, his religious precepts and his political integrity outraged. For him, democracy in the Great Republic which he loved was the valid form of social and political organization, and he expected it to do justice both to man's spiritual stature and his social character. Once he saw the danger of plutocracy to democracy, Dolliver came to realize his own responsibility in his own time for using the weapons at hand in the defense of democracy.

In the period 1902 to 1905, Dolliver moved quietly, concentrating on religious and educational activities and dealing with certain specific political objectives. His first speech in the Senate, other than memorial addresses, was delivered March 26, 1902, and dealt with the problem of the adulteration of food, which in his "humble judgment" was one of the "pressing and important questions with which we have to deal." He was particularly concerned with the regulation of the manufacture and sale of oleomargarine, a business which he thought had "become fraudulent through and through." It is sometimes forgotten that the effort for government regulation of the processing of foods and drugs began with the agitation over oleomargarine.[30]

Two years later, February, 1904, Dolliver, speaking in behalf of more rigid laws governing the inspection of imported foods, advocated federal legislation to protect the American people "against the sale of adulterated and poisonous and mislabeled and fraudulent food products." To those who objected to granting so much jurisdiction to the central government, Dolliver replied that he was not at all "alarmed about the growth of the power of the Secretary of Agriculture," but that he was deeply concerned about the health of the people of the United States.[31]

The need for the extension of governmental supervision over foods and drugs began to receive general attention in 1905, and in December of that year President Roosevelt specifically recommended congressional action to provide for pure food legislation. The packing interests branded the proposal as "socialistic," a scare word perennially in favor with those wishing to prevent government action in behalf of the people. Nelson Aldrich argued that such a law would "put the liberty of all the people of the United States in jeopardy." Dolliver voted for the Pure Food bill and also for the Beveridge amendment to the agricultural appropriation which provided for rigid inspection of meat packing.[32] Although he did not play a leading role in the enactment of pure food and drug legislation, Dolliver was one of the first Senators to discuss the need for such acts, and he consistently supported efforts to secure effective laws on the subject.

Another matter which early attracted Dolliver's interest was that of flood control in the vast river network between the Alleghenies and the Rocky Mountains. As an Iowan, representing a people living between the Mississippi and the Missouri, he was especially concerned with the waste and damage resulting from the frequent overflow of those rivers. In November, 1903, he said he believed that "the only practical and permanent" solution to the problem would be found in the construction of a system of dams and storage reservoirs along the upper Mississippi and Missouri rivers. Admitting that the expense would be great, he pointed out that the failure to curb these rivers in flood season was far more costly. Furthermore, he advocated use of the dams for the generation of electricity to meet the fuel shortage of the future. "There is power in the Mississippi River going to waste every day in the year," he asserted, "sufficient to turn every wheel in every factory in the United States."[33] That he was ahead of his time on this question is apparent, when a half century afterwards floods and droughts alternate in devastating one of the richest agricultural areas on the face of the earth, while politicians quibble about the "creeping socialism" of an effective solution similar to Dolliver's suggestions.

Dolliver's position on tariff reform was also in advance of that of his party during his first years in the Senate. He took the "Iowa Idea" seriously and felt that the Republicans ought to pursue the policy McKinley had outlined in his Buffalo speech. Having expressed himself clearly on the matter in Iowa in 1901 and 1902, Dolliver found an opportunity to place his views before the Senate in January of 1903, during a debate over a resolution instructing the Committee on Finance to amend the Dingley Act in order to place anthracite coal on the free list. The discussion of free coal was incidental to Dolliver's main purpose of urging Senate action on the Kasson Reciprocity Treaties which were gathering dust in a committee room because of the opposition of Senator Aldrich and the Standpatters.[34]

When Senator Dolliver arose to begin this address, the Senate chamber was practically deserted. Before he had proceeded ten minutes, nearly every Senator had taken his seat to listen. Expressing his disappointment that the Senate had for nearly four years refused to "consider and favorably dispose of the pending reciprocity treaties," Dolliver praised the work of John A. Kasson, a distinguished Iowan, and asserted "that more violence has been done to the protective system of the United States by the quiet and uncommunicative failure of the Senate . . . to take action upon the treaties which were negotiated under the authority of the act of 1897 than by all the noise that has been made on the other side of this Chamber about coal or the other so-called extortions of the law." Dolliver, who had helped write the Dingley bill, asserted that the Ways and Means Committee had raised certain duties "for the express purpose of having them traded down." That is, the intention was that these duties should be lowered through negotiation of reciprocal agreements with other nations.

After telling the Senate that he had a "personal knowledge" of McKinley's purpose and convictions in the matter of readjusting the tariff schedules of the Dingley Act, Dolliver concluded with a challenge to the Senate, and in a sense to Roosevelt, for action:

> I for one have made up my mind that the time has come when somebody whose convictions do not lie along the path of silence and quietude and ease in our political Zion should declare here that the whole future of the protective system in the United States depends upon the wisdom with which the Congress of the United States fulfills the aspirations which found an expression so lofty in the last public utterance of William McKinley.[35]

Following this speech, Senator Aldrich hotly denied Dolliver's statement that Dingley had "deliberately" placed high duties on certain items in his 1897 tariff bill. A rather sharp verbal clash between Dolliver and Aldrich ensued, one which Aldrich, at least, never forgot. Dolliver was right and had the proof; Senator Aldrich had to qualify his statement that "the duties of the Dingley Act were not intended to be reduced by treaties." He agreed that "this was true of only a part of them" — which, of course, is exactly what Dolliver had stated, as he had referred explicitly to "sugar duties."[36]

The newspapers gave much publicity to the speech itself and to the clash with the powerful Aldrich. One Washington columnist, Frank J. Stillman, wrote:

> Everybody recognized it required courage for one of the young Senators to speak out in criticism of the methods of that august body. . . . The prestige of older Senators is enormous, and they have a way of making things uncomfortable for newcomers who are inclined to disturb their plans. Few care to invite their displeasure, and yet one who has ability and courage and the faculty of taking care of himself on his feet is not likely to suffer seriously from a show of independence.[37]

The Old Guard was startled. Some Standpatters blasted Dolliver as an apostate "expressing opinions which are not orthodox." If so, observed George Roberts, who had recently bought the Des Moines *Register*:

> He is tainted with the same heresy as Blaine and McKinley . . . and equally heretical with him must be regarded the many Republican platforms, national and state, whose pledges he simply asks to be redeemed. . . . Is not the advocate of reciprocity entitled to claim for himself that he is more nearly in harmony with the party creed than he who opposes reciprocity? [38]

The Sioux City *Journal's* statement that "however unwelcome Senator Dolliver's suggestions may have been in some quarters they are not being ignored in any quarter" seems to have been true. Nicholas Murray Butler wrote: "I appreciate and approve of the attitude you have taken in the Senate regarding the tariff and reciprocity. You have voiced the sentiments of the very best thought of the party, both East and West." An Iowa friend thought that "the rank and file of the party to a man are in favor of cutting down these high duties." [39]

Dolliver was surprised at the widespread comment his talk aroused and at the scores of letters and telegrams from all over the country, praising his stand. He told a newsman: "If I had stood in my place and advocated a comprehensive revision of the tariff . . . I can see that such observations might have been regarded as somewhat sensational, but when I simply followed the line adopted by President McKinley . . . the same doctrine espoused by James G. Blaine, I am perplexed to understand why such suggestions should be considered sensational and revolutionary." [40]

Among those who opposed Dolliver's stand was the President himself. Roosevelt, having long before 1903 made his peace with the "Big Four" of the Senate — Aldrich, Allison, Platt of Connecticut, and Spooner — on the tariff question, made a personal appeal to Dolliver "not to agitate the tariff." The President likewise talked to his Director of the Mint and urged Roberts to use his influence with Dolliver not to push for action at that time. Dolliver and Roberts agreed to think about the matter. [41]

Roberts' paper in Des Moines, however, continued to advocate the ratification of the reciprocal trade treaties. On the other hand, Secretary Shaw, the Iowa Standpatter in Roosevelt's Cabinet, whose influence on the President's tariff views still awaits investigation, spoke in Peoria on March 31 and bitterly attacked the idea of "tampering with the tariff," emphasizing the dangers of doing so prior to an election. The Des Moines *Register* answered Shaw editorially by pointing out that the former Governor was not in harmony with McKinley's policy. [42] But McKinley was dead. Shaw spoke Roosevelt's sentiments as well as his own.

Even Ret Clarkson, favorable as he was to tariff revision, urged Dolliver to drop the tariff issue:

We will have to stand a little stronger protection than some of us
believe in, for another year, because the election of a Republican
President next year depends on New York, Connecticut, New Jersey,
Delaware, Maryland and Indiana, all of which are strong for protection. Any weakness in the platform on that question would make
these States more doubtful. Iowa can be carried on any platform, and
there will be plenty of time left after 1904 to take up the great problem of revision — a movement which I personally favor, as you long
have known — but first let us make sure that we will have the Republican party in charge to make the revision.[43]

Political expediency, more than anything else, accounts for Roosevelt's cow-
ardly tariff policy and likewise for Dolliver's adherence to the President's
leadership on the issue. Clarkson reflected the view of the professional politician — 1903 was no time to alter the tariff, with elections coming the following year. Speaker Henderson, disgusted with the "Iowa Idea" and the Progressive movement in the Hawkeye State, had already jolted the Old Guard
leaders as well as Roosevelt by retiring from politics in 1902.[44] Uncle Joe
Cannon, Henderson's successor as Speaker, believed that "no matter how much
of an improvement the new tariff may be, it almost always results in the party
in power losing the next election."[45]

The tariff issue also affected Iowa politics. Cummins, desiring renomination
in 1903, journeyed to Chicago for a secret meeting with J. W. Blythe and
Senator Allison on April 3, to work out a compromise state platform containing
a tariff plank similar to an 1896 statement instead of the 1901 "Iowa Idea."
Shortly after this meeting, the Governor wrote Blythe that "everything seems
to be pointing in the direction of a harmonious convention, for which I most
earnestly hope."[46] The Iowa Standpatters did not oppose Cummins' renomination in 1903. Everybody wanted "harmony." Indeed, the allegedly "progressive" Mr. Cummins wrote his close friend Abe Funk that he was irritated
at reports that he was "extremely radical" in his views. "I cannot believe that
this is just," he added. "On the other hand I think I am conservative, at least
I want to be. . . . I agree with you heartily that we should move slowly and
we should keep steadily in our eye the good of the party, which must always
be the equivalent of the good of the country."[47]

Regardless of their differences, real and counterfeit, Blythe and Cummins
found it easy to work out an arrangement under Allison's guidance whereby
Cummins could retain the governorship and Blythe could cease to worry about
tariff agitation. This was possible because Allison knew what Roosevelt intended to do, because Cummins wanted to be Governor, because Shaw hoped
to stay in the Cabinet and to succeed Roosevelt in 1908, and because all breeds
of Republicans desired peace within the party as it entered the 1904 campaign.

A. B. Funk went to Washington to see Roosevelt and Roberts. His report to
Cummins was that the President wanted eventually to "see broader policies

obtained," but that he had to move slowly lest there be a party split which would cost him the 1904 election. Funk explained Roosevelt's attitude as being based on a wish "to hold all we have won and to keep the public sentiment growing." Funk then concluded with the advice that the Cummins people ought not "to provoke irritation in one quarter and over-expectation in another at the eve of a presidential election."[48]

Cummins assessed the situation correctly when he wrote: "Our purpose is to procure harmony. It is universally agreed that whatever Senator Allison will stand for will be accepted by the whole party as an expression of genuine Republicanism." Allison stood for a more liberal tariff than did Aldrich and the Standpatters. The 1903 platform thus endorsed reciprocity and asserted that tariff rates should be "just, fair and impartial, equally opposed to foreign control and domestic monopoly, to sectional discrimination and individual favoritism, and must from time to time be changed to meet the varying conditions incident to the progress of our industries."[49] This statement satisfied both factions, for, while it said something for revision, it meant nothing and pledged nothing.

Roosevelt visited Dolliver in Fort Dodge in May before the convention met. Allison asked Dolliver to ride to Dubuque with the President and told his colleague of trying to "harmonize situations" in the state. "I hope I have made some progress, but would like to talk it over with you."[50] There are no records of Dolliver's conversation with Roosevelt or with the "wise old Senator," but Dolliver agreed to the state platform, and for several years he said very little publicly about tariff reform.

In view of the President's position and that of the leaders of the Senate and House and of the circumstances in Iowa just described, Senator Dolliver's decision to go along with Roosevelt on the tariff is understandable, perhaps defensible. There were, moreover, other powerful factors operating to lead him to proceed with caution. His love of party harmony and his respect for Allison and Roosevelt were important. But Dolliver, too, was a politician faced with the problem of staying in office. He knew that the Standpatters had already started a "well-organized movement" to unseat him. The Burlington and the North Western Railroad people were behind this, not only because of his failure to do their bidding in fighting Cummins in 1901 but also because of his tariff speech and of his vote in favor of an antipooling bill and because he had "an independent way of thinking and voting which makes it impossible for the railroad interests to control him." Standpat newspapers were sniping at him as being a "mere orator," and as one who devoted more time to the lecture business than to the Senate.[51] This worried Dolliver, and the injustice of such criticism hurt him. He did lecture, but never when it required him to be absent from his duties at Washington. Roberts advised him to get into personal contact with the Iowa editors and frankly explain the facts to them, telling them that since he had no other income he had to lecture in order to pay for the home in Washington which he had purchased in 1902 and to meet the living expenses of his wife, daughters, father, and sister.[52]

Dolliver, observing the cooperation between Cummins and Blythe in 1903, also feared that the Standpatters and Cumminsites might combine against him in 1906, should he break with the President on the tariff and upset the harmony movement in Iowa. Thus, Dolliver, seeing no hope of accomplishing anything toward reform, kept in step with the music of the day.

He attended the state convention, received the usual attention, and at the insistence of those present delivered an address. After endorsing the nomination of Cummins, Dolliver told the delegates that he had no fear of party differences over fundamental matters. He thought it was well to air them but always hoped that the "danger that our debate may degenerate into trivialities and into personalities" would be avoided. "Think and let think" was a motto to follow in politics as well as religion, he said. His view of the Allison-Blythe-Cummins platform was that "it is not only strong enough to hold up every one of the 300,000 Republicans in Iowa, but it is wide enough to enable everyone of us to move about on comfortably without having our convictions either jostled or pushed overboard."[53]

Dolliver participated actively in the campaign of 1903, working not only for Cummins but also to insure the victory of state senators favorable to his own election to the Senate in 1906. He spoke every day from October 12 to election day, not only in Iowa but also in Ohio and Massachusetts. In closing the Iowa campaign at Des Moines on October 30, Dolliver addressed a huge crowd, and his reception was regarded as a great tribute to him. He eloquently praised Cummins and defended the policy of protection by ridiculing the Democratic charges that a protective tariff promoted the development of trusts.[54]

During this campaign Dolliver advocated an amendment to the state constitution providing for biennial elections so that all state officers as well as Congressmen would be chosen in the even-numbered years. He looked at this matter from the viewpoint of one "who for twenty years has put in from four to six weeks annually on the stump, an experience worse than service in time of war so far as its burdens and fatigue go."[55] This amendment, which had passed the 1902 legislature and would be passed again, according to the constitutional provisions for amendments, by the 1904 Assembly, was approved by the voters in 1904. As it changed the meetings of the General Assembly from the even-numbered to the odd-numbered years, Dolliver's term was extended until 1907, and as no election was held in 1905, Cummins' second gubernatorial term was three years instead of two.[56]

While Iowans were voting in November, 1903, the famous revolution which liberated Panama occurred. The isthmian canal about which Roosevelt, Dolliver, and other imperialists had talked so much now became a probability. Having recognized the new republic with indecent haste, the Roosevelt administration signed a treaty granting canal rights to the United States. When the treaty came before the Senate for consideration, Dolliver in an extremely long address defended the President and the nation in all that had been done and urged immediate and favorable action in consenting to ratification.[57] This speech, like two he had delivered in 1903 in defense of the American army in the Philippines, received the applause of the imperialists and the partisans, although none of the three speeches was any credit to Dolliver as a scholar or a statesman.[58] The aged John A. Kasson thanked Dolliver for the "admirable speech upon the treaty with Panama" and said, "you have spoken the voice of the majority of our people."[59]

If the President appreciated Dolliver's extravagant defense of his foreign policy, he soon had several reasons to be even more grateful to the Iowa orator in 1904. One matter which worried Roosevelt was his reputation as a "trust buster." On the one hand, there was public pressure for him to continue along the line of his action in prosecuting the Northern Securities Company and in pushing for the establishment of a Department of Commerce and Labor with a Bureau of Corporations empowered to investigate the conduct of interstate business. On the other hand, there was the hostility of certain great interests who had money to contribute to the Republican campaign and who opposed efforts to control trusts and monopolies. At the urging of Ret Clarkson, then one of Roosevelt's professional political agents, Dolliver introduced into the Senate a resolution directing the Secretary of Commrece and Labor to prepare "a statement showing what companies have been incorporated in the United States and what investments of capital made by individuals or copartnerships since the year 1900, outside and independent of the so-called 'trusts,' and the aggregate capital, compared with the total capitalization of trust combinations."[60]

Dolliver's purpose, as his carefully prepared speech on this resolution indicated, was purely political. By showing that far more capital was controlled by individuals in small businesses than by great corporations, he aimed to prove that the trust problem had been greatly exaggerated and that there was no reason for the administration to engage in extensive prosecution of the trusts. Secondly, in denying that the protective tariff fostered the growth of monopoly, he sought to spike the Democratic criticisms of Roosevelt's failure to initiate tariff revision. Thirdly, through emphasizing that some great combinations were socially useful and ought not to be condemned merely because of their size, he hoped to reassure big business that fears of Rooseveltian Republicanism were groundless.

Typical of his arguments were the following:

The oldest law known among men, except the law of the family, is the law of property. It has been comparatively easy to justify that law in all ages, for while it has not always been regarded as certain that what you have earned and saved is yours, it has always been obvious that it is not mine. If it has become harder to defend the law of property, whether individual or corporate, in our own times, it is not because its foundations are any less secure or its rights any less sacred; it is because the inventions of avarice and greed have filled the hearts of millions of people with resentment against the whole tribe of promoters, underwriters, stockjobbers, and cheats at common law.

Dolliver's analysis of the trust problem was not profound. Whether he understood the magnitude of it or not can not be determined from this speech, because of the peculiar purpose for which it was delivered. It is reasonable to believe that he knew more about the question than he cared to reveal and that his suggestion of "natural law'" remedies instead of legislation was a convenient device to minimize the danger of the growing plutocracy to the public so that Roosevelt could trim sail until safely elected. Dolliver's recital of the regulatory legislation sponsored by the Republicans since the Antitrust Act of 1890 and his assertion that if the tariff needed revision it should be done by Republicans are indicative of his convictions that something more than "natural law" was necessary. Like Roosevelt, he distinguished between "good" and "bad" trusts, and in the concluding paragraphs of his address he identified himself with Roosevelt, to whom he paid tribute as "a leader who has enforced the laws of the land without favor and without fear, who has dared to utter the convictions that are in him with absolute reliance upon the integrity of his country and the good will of his countrymen." [61]

So well did Dolliver perform that he received an ovation from the galleries at the end of his two-hour address. Senator Arthur Pue Gorman of Maryland, leader of the reactionary faction in the Democratic party, called the speech "a magnificent effort, delightful and brilliant." Even the unemotional Nelson Aldrich said it was "brilliant" and was so impressed that he invited Dolliver to open the Republican campaign in Rhode Island in the autumn. [62] If Roosevelt wanted the big business element pacified and reassured, his Iowa friend had apparently done a good day's work.

Another service for the President was Dolliver's participation in the Republican National Convention in 1904. At Roosevelt's request both Dolliver and Allison agreed to accept election as delegates-at-large, although it was not usual for Iowa Senators to be members of that state's delegation. [63] The reason for this unusual arrangement was that the harmony of 1903 in Iowa politics had disappeared soon after Governor Cummins won re-election. The fact that Cummins had compromised on the state platform in 1903 had led the Stand-patters to claim that he had "surrendered." The Governor, feeling he had been humiliated by this charge, expressed himself as being henceforth "wholly un-willing to attempt to reconcile the irreconcilable." He realized, correctly, that Blythe was "not for harmony. He simply wants to put me, if he can, in the position of a disturber, so that he can more easily dispose of me." [64] Quite naturally, Cummins forgot that for nearly two decades he had in fact been something of a disturber, motivated, as even his best friends admitted, by his vaunting ambition to be a United States Senator.

Early in 1904 Cummins determined to be a delegate-at-large himself and to win control of the delegation. Blythe, who at this same time was being men-tioned as Hanna's successor as chairman of the Republican National Com-mittee, also intended to be one of the four delegates-at-large. His view was that both he and Cummins ought to go to the convention and that the other members should be divided equally between the two factions. As "the boss" saw it, both he and the Governor were for Roosevelt, "but the difference is that while I am for Roosevelt and for a platform Roosevelt will approve, Cum-mins is for Roosevelt and for a delegation that will force into a platform an idea Roosevelt would not otherwise have there." [65]

Such was the case. Cummins desired again to stand for tariff reform and to get into the national platform a pledge that the party would take up the subject at the next session of Congress. Blythe, fighting Dolliver over patronage mat-ters and angry because the Senator would not speak out for high protection and against reciprocity, wanted nothing about tariff revision in the national platform. Cummins had Senator Funk enter the race for delegate-at-large, and both factions began to maneuver to secure a majority of the district delegates.[66]

It was under these circumstances that Roosevelt had an intimate conference with Blythe, and that Dolliver decided to accept "the personal request of the President several times repeated" to serve as delegate-at-large.[67] George Roberts talked with his friends Cummins and Funk, and the latter agreed to withdraw as a candidate for delegate-at-large, leaving the four positions to Cummins, Blythe, Allison, and Dolliver without opposition. The versatile Governor of Iowa gave up the fight for control, and within a month announced himself as favoring Speaker Joseph G. Cannon, Standpatter-in-Chief of the House, for the vice-presidential nomination. "I don't know any man who better represents the West than Joe Cannon," Cummins told a reporter.[68]

At the first caucus of the Iowa delegation at the national convention in Chicago on June 20, Cummins proposed that the Hawkeye Republicans sponsor a platform plank pledging the party to make necessary changes in the tariff "to preserve for our producers and secure for our consumers adequate protection, no more, no less." Dolliver favored this in principle, but spoke against it on the grounds that "the time has come for Iowa Republicans, and particularly the delegates to the convention, on the threshold of a Presidential campaign, to cease strife and quit quibbling over matters . . . to get together . . . and present the strongest front to the opposition." Cummins' motion was defeated. He said he knew it would be and that he had no hard feelings for Dolliver.[69]

The convention adopted a platform declaring protection to be "a cardinal policy of the Republican party" and that "rates of duty should be readjusted only when conditions have so changed that the public interest demands their alteration." Reciprocity was to be extended "wherever reciprocal arrangements can be effected consistent with the principles of protection and without injury to American agriculture, American labor, or any American industry."[70] With such a platform and with Elihu Root and Joseph G. Cannon presiding over their convention, even the Old Guard Republicans did not fear to permit the unanimous nomination of Theodore Roosevelt.

The President, of course, was in complete control. He arranged for Dolliver to make the speech nominating Charles W. Fairbanks of Indiana for Vice President, and the delegates accepted the Hoosier Senator without a contest. In the course of his address Dolliver said:

> Whatever changes are necessary in our laws ought to be made by the friends or at least the acquaintances of the protective tariff system. . . . We stand at the beginning of a new era, and while the Republican party leans upon the counsel of its old leaders, it has not hesitated to summon to the responsibilities of public life the young men who have been trained under their guidance to take up the burdens which they are ready to lay down and finish the work which comes to them as an inheritance of patriotism and duty.[71]

Dolliver was fairly accurate as regards the "new era," but he was to find that "the old leaders" were not so eager to lay aside their "burdens." In the campaign of 1904 against the arch-conservative Democratic nominees, Alton B. Parker of New York and Henry G. Davis of West Virginia, Dolliver stumped the West with Fairbanks as well as fulfilling his speaking commitments in Iowa, Maine, and other Eastern states.[72] The Republicans won easily. With the benefit of hindsight, one wonders why Roosevelt was so worried.

One thing, at least, is clear. If Dolliver equivocated on the tariff question in the period 1903-1904, he did so because of pressure from Theodore Roosevelt — not at the behest of the Iowa Standpatters — and because Governor Cummins and the so-called Progressive faction in Iowa, who were allegedly behind the movement for tariff reform, disappeared in the direction of "Standpatville" as the 1903 state campaign approached. In 1905 Dolliver wrote his intimate friend, Still Meservey: "I did what I did at the personal request of Roosevelt, who was scared to death for fear that he would lose out in a quarrel in Iowa."[73]

-XVI-

Dolliver's Fight for the Railroad Rate Bill, 1905-1906

Now understand me well: It is provided in the essence of things that from any fruition of success, no matter what, shall come forth something to make a greater struggle necessary.

Walt Whitman

PRESIDENT ROOSEVELT was delighted over the outcome of the 1904 election which returned him to the White House in his own right. He repeatedly took Ret Clarkson's hands into his own and exclaimed with "prodigious force, 'We were elected!'" Teddy also asked Ret to assure Leigh Hunt, Dolliver's 1888 benefactor, "that I still intend to hold him to his promise to take me on a hunt through equatorial Africa after I have retired from the Presidency."[1] The big game hunt lay more than four years in the future; inauguration day was only four months away.

March 4, 1905, was a cool, fair day, and Senator Dolliver took his aged father to the Capitol for the inaugural ceremonies. The old circuit rider was a favorite of the great Rough Rider, as he had been of every President of the United States since Benjamin Harrison. Roosevelt sent for Father Dolliver immediately, greeted him warmly, and said: "I have reserved a seat for you on the speaker's stand next to me; I hope you will be able to be there." James Dolliver accepted the honor and held the President's hat during the proceedings.[2]

A few weeks later, just three days after Louise Dolliver had given birth to a son, Father Dolliver died at the Senator's home in Washington in his eighty-eighth year. He was widely mourned, having become known throughout the capital over a period of fifteen years as a grand old man as well as the father of a distinguished son. His simple piety impressed men of all walks of life. He talked religion by the hour with President McKinley, offered morning prayer each Sunday at the Foundry Methodist Church, frequently officiated at the invocation in the House and Senate, and, according to an ambassador from a

Roman Catholic country, "was the only man in America who ever expressed an interest in my immortal soul." His influence upon Jonathan cannot be overestimated. Editorials and eulogies recognized this. "Senator Dolliver has been Father Dolliver made over for a new era and adjusted to new activities," one editor wrote.[3]

The Senator was forty-seven when his father died and his last child was born. The Dolliver home, a large mansion on a high terrace on Massachusetts Avenue in Washington, was "one of the important ones of the Senatorial set" in the Roosevelt era and was maintained "with due respect to the Senator's position in public life." George Roberts lived only a "stone's throw" away, Secretary Wilson a few houses distant, Senator Shelby Cullom was a next-door neighbor, and most of the Iowa Congressmen resided within a three-minute walk of their junior Senator. Inasmuch as Senator Allison was a widower, Mrs. Dolliver was the "ranking lady" of the Iowa delegation, and she also served as official hostess for the Secretary of Agriculture, after Mrs. Wilson's death. "Tama Jim" Wilson, Allison, Roberts, O'Connell, and other Iowans in Washington frequently gathered at the Dolliver home for social affairs, political talks, or just to enjoy the genial atmosphere and entertaining conversation.[4]

One who knew Dolliver in this period wrote of him:

> His success has the merit of not being measurable in money. After more than two decades of public life, the Senator from Iowa shows up clean. He is comfortable, lives simply, enjoys his home, his library and his forensic battles, and gets along without yachts, automobiles, or millions. . . . In manner he is gracious and attractive, but in dress he is not. His clothes don't seem to fit him and, while he is always clean, he gives the impression of being mussed up. Usually he affects a white vest, and it is a fair gamble that he never had one made to order in his life.[5]

Aside from his Iowa intimates and Ret Clarkson, Dolliver's closest friends during the last years of his life were Senators Albert J. Beveridge of Indiana and William Alden Smith of Michigan; William Allen White, the Kansas editor; and Newell Dwight Hillis, a Brooklyn minister.[6] Dolliver's relations with Roosevelt were good. The two men were almost the same age, Dolliver being some eight months the older — and both had begun their political careers in the early eighties. When their paths first crossed is uncertain, possibly in 1884 at the Blaine convention. The first letter Dolliver received from Roosevelt apparently was that of 1894 complimenting him on the article on Lowell. The two obviously admired each other, but they were never close personal friends.

Few Senators, not excepting Lodge, served Roosevelt as President with greater faithfulness and ability than did Dolliver. He was one of nine Senators who voted on February 11, 1905, to uphold the President in his request that crippling amendments not be made to eight reciprocal trade treaties. Two days thereafter, Roosevelt and Dolliver were the principal guests and speakers at the Lincoln dinner at the New York City Republican Club. The President spoke on the race problem, the Senator on Abraham Lincoln. Dolliver's speech was carefully designed to point to Roosevelt as the spokesman for the equal rights of all men as Jefferson and Lincoln had been — yet he did not once mention Roosevelt. Ret Clarkson wrote Dolliver the next day: "You brought from the hearts of all present to the support of the President and his great purposes the best that is ever in the human heart." [7] Reporters wrote of this address that Dolliver had "reached the high water mark of oratory" and had "again established his right beyond any question to be regarded as one of the very few pre-eminent public speakers of the United States." [8]

Whether by coincidence or pre-arrangement with Roosevelt, on the very day that the Japanese secretly invited the President to act as mediator in the Russo-Japanese War, Dolliver told newspapermen that "the time is opportune for the United States to use its good offices to promote peace between Russia and Japan." He said that America was the only nation of importance which could do so and escape the charge of having a selfish motive, and he predicted that the administration would take this step. Roosevelt, as is now known, had been working secretly for months to bring the war to an end, but until the great Japanese naval victory of May 27, 1905, he had met with no success. Four days later he received the Japanese request that "of his own motion and initiative" he invite Russia and Japan to consider peace. This was May 31, the same date that the Dolliver interview appeared. Possibly the Senator from the isolationist belt was sending up a trial balloon for the interventionist in the White House. At least, their thinking coincided. Nine days later the President sent identical notes to the belligerents, urging them to open direct negotiations for peace. This was the first the public knew of Roosevelt's official interest in the affair.[9]

In September, speaking before a convention of Iowa editors, Dolliver praised Roosevelt for providing America with "leadership of the highest order" and for "that broader guidance of the national purpose which leads [sic. lends] itself with ready sympathy to the freedom of thought and opinions, takes into its councils the wisdom of all and outlines the pathway of the national progress so that the whole people may walk in it with confidence and security." He urged the press to keep the people united and in sympathy with the Roosevelt administration and told the newsmen that "the chief function of newspapers is to inform the public and correctly inform it." Taking note of the continuing demand for tariff reform, Dolliver attempted to defend the President's failure to act by explaining the difficulty involved "because of conflicting opinions within the party." He correctly analyzed the reason for the defeat of the reciprocity treaties as the result of the "combined influence of all the industrial enterprises affected by all of the treaties," and expressed the belief that these same influences would make an effort to nullify all attempts to revise the tariff.[10]

Apparently Dolliver knew Roosevelt's mind on the tariff. The President had not mentioned the subject in his message to Congress on December 6, 1904, after his election. "It is not an issue upon which I should have any business to break with my party," Roosevelt wrote to a friend. Speaker Cannon and the leaders of the Senate wanted no tariff reform, and Roosevelt accepted their views and concentrated on other things.[11] With great accuracy, Dolliver predicted in November, 1905:

> There will be no general tariff legislation prior to the next Presidential election, and I have a very distinct conviction that the Republican party will go into that fight with the fair understanding with the people that the party will take up the tariff question with the view to reduce such duties as are higher than necessary for the protection of domestic industry.[12]

A progressive Fort Dodge doctor, J. W. Kime, wrote Dolliver in 1905 that the people of Iowa were for the Square Deal and wanted a lower tariff and the regulation of railroads and trusts. It was his hope, he maintained, that Dolliver would stand with the President and work for these ends. The doctor thought that Cummins was trying to pose as the Robert La Follette or the Joseph Folk of Iowa, but that the Governor backed and filled too much.[13] This was but one of many similar letters Dolliver received which indicated that Iowans did not understand the President's real position on the tariff. They seemed to feel that Roosevelt wanted action when actually he did not. Dolliver's reply to Dr. Kime stated in part:

> I think that I have done as much as anyone in Iowa to uphold the hands of President Roosevelt throughout his administration. I intend to stand with him in the great work which he has undertaken for the future, and shall rely, as I have in the past, upon the support and good will of our people in Iowa. . . .
>
> Our government, however, is a government of the people, not a government of a few leaders. I do not aspire, therefore, to the role which has been played by eminent citizens of the States you mentioned. . . . What we need just now throughout the United States is the exercise of the best wisdom we have in order that whatever is done may stand the test of truth and right. Our Government is constituted so that nothing can be hurried. Therefore we will have no excuse if what is done does not stand these tests.[14]

Unquestionably, Roosevelt's decision to avoid the tariff issue placed many men like Dolliver in a difficult position. They had gone along with him in 1903-1904 on the grounds that nothing should be done to injure his chances for election. Then, from 1905 on, with that excuse gone, they had to accept the brunt of the criticism from those who did not want to attack the President

SENATOR CUMMINS ENTERTAINS PRESIDENT TAFT, 1909

Left to right: J. A. T. Hull, J. P. Dolliver, President Taft, A. B. Cummins, B. F. Carroll, G. N. Haugen

SENATOR DOLLIVER IN 1906

but did want something done. Dolliver could not well tell the people that the President was afraid to take up the tariff. He merely explained the difficulties of revising the schedules, predicted action in 1909, and with complete honesty said that he would stand with the President and "uphold his hands."

Dolliver's greatest contribution to the success of Roosevelt's administration and the outstanding positive achievement of his own congressional career was his fight for the railroad rate bill generally known, ironically, as the Hepburn Act. "In selecting regulation of the railroads as an issue on which he was willing to fight," observed the President's ablest biographer, "Roosevelt demonstrated his grasp of popular prejudices and popular limitations."[15] The same may be said of Dolliver, albeit he would have fought on the tariff had his chief been willing.

His interest in railroad regulation dated from Dolliver's earliest years in Iowa, and it was strengthened through his long association with Governors Carpenter and Larrabee. Congress had passed the Interstate Commerce Act two years before Dolliver began his first term in the House, and no further legislation dealing with the subject came up during his service as a Representative. A compromise measure when enacted, the Interstate Commerce Act had been weakened by a series of court decisions culminating in the Chattanooga case of 1901 which virtually rendered the Interstate Commerce Commission powerless to act in cases of discriminatory rates between the long and short haul.[16]

The Elkins Act, which Dolliver helped frame in 1903, dealt not with rates but with effective prohibition of rebates. Senator Elkins, chairman of the Interstate Commerce Committee, was a leading "Railroad Senator," and his aim was not merely to protect the shipper from unfair competition resulting from the rebate system, but also to relieve the railroads from the losses of revenue incident to rebating.[17]

The important problem, that of conferring rate-making power upon the Commission and of expediting judicial procedure in cases of appeal, received no congressional action despite increasing public demands for rate regulation. Not only the railroads, but also powerful financial influences concerned with the formation of monopolistic transportation and industrial systems, opposed legislation which might establish effective regulation of freight rates. Railroads, through their power to fix rates, could aid a favored industry and destroy its rival, could ruin the business of a town or section or build it up by favorable rates, depending on the interests of the railroad managers.[18]

Dolliver understood these practices of the roads. Writing in 1904 to a railroad president who was urging the establishment of a pork packing plant in Fort Dodge, the Senator said:

stood that J. P. could not refuse to respond to the idea of doing battle for the
Great Republic against the money power, especially if he saw the fight in terms
of "slavery and emancipation" with his beloved Iowa seeking leadership in a
movement to free herself from railroad domination. The mention of the Cummins threat came at the right moment psychologically, for on February 7, in an
address to the Corn Belt Meat Producers' Association, Cummins had posed as
the champion of railroad regulation and had rapped Iowans in Washington by
saying: "As the Russian and Japanese nations are still at war we could hardly
expect our Iowa delegation in Congress to devote their attention to the troubles
of the Iowa farmer."[26] This infuriated Dolliver, who had been at work in an
effort to get Senate action on a rate bill. "I notice," he wrote Meservey, "that
they passed resolutions of the most stupid character at Des Moines, complimenting Cummins upon his speech and disparaging the Iowa delegation for its
lack of interest on the very day when every member of the Delegation was
casting his vote in the House of Representatives for a measure . . . which fully
expressed President Roosevelt's ideas about rate legislation."[27]

Dolliver also sent a letter to the Des Moines Commercial Club, in which he
observed sarcastically that the "speeches of our friends at home" seemed to be
more entitled to gratitude than the actions of the members of Congress who
were working for the desired legislation. This letter was published on the front
page of the *Register* on February 15, and on the following day that paper
printed a long editorial urging Dolliver to "demand action" and commenting
that Iowans had

> . . . great faith in Senator Dolliver. He has the acquaintance, the
> experience, the talent, and the right inclination. He has shown the
> willingness on more than one occasion to measure up to the Roosevelt
> standard. But Senator Dolliver owes it to himself to take leadership
> in the progressive movements that are scheduled for the coming year.
> . . . Let the young men whose eyes are yet to the front be bold and
> evermore be bold in their support of the new order that is now upon
> them and that cannot be staid [sic] even if forty congresses should
> plant themselves across the track.[28]

Other voices were added to those of Roosevelt, Clarkson, and the *Register* in
encouraging Dolliver to move to the front. One was that of Henry Wallace,
editor of *Wallaces' Farmer*. "Uncle Henry," as Iowans always called Wallace,
felt that Colonel Hepburn, chairman of the House Committee on Interstate
Commerce, was a resolute foe of any effective railroad legislation and that
Hepburn had only advocated passage of the Townsend-Esch bill because it was
politically expedient to do so and because he knew such a bill would not pass
the Senate in any event. Wallace, therefore, prodded Dolliver to be more
active "on the side of the people" in the struggle with the railroads.[29]

The Senator visited Wallace during the summer of 1905 and told him that he was in favor of any legislation needed and wanted by the people and always had been. Wallace, according to his own account, replied that Dolliver had not succeeded in doing anything about rate legislation and informed the Senator of the work of Judge Samuel Cowan, attorney for the National Live Stock Growers' Association, in drawing up amendments to the Interstate Commerce Act. Dolliver agreed to meet Judge Cowan, and Wallace brought them together. Cowan had long represented the Texas Cattle Growers' Association in rate cases before the Interstate Commerce Commission and knew the weaknesses of the law and how it could be strengthened. Dolliver invited Cowan to help him draw up a bill before Congress assembled in December, 1905.[30]

Meanwhile, Dolliver on several occasions publicly defined his position. On April 27, 1905, in a speech prepared for the Grant Club of Des Moines, he expressed his opposition to government ownership of railroads, adding:

> The doctrine of the Square Deal points out a better way. We will say to the railroads of the United States: "You shall charge for your service to the public a just and reasonable rate, and for the same service, the same rate to every man and to every corporation, great or small." We will go further. Whenever a difference of opinion arises between the carrier and the shipper as to what the rate ought to be, we will not leave the individual without an appeal from the error or avarice of the railway. We will provide an effective method of bringing that difference of opinion to a special adjudication and settlement. That is the doctrine of the Square Deal applied to railroads.[31]

In mid-September, sensing trouble in the Senate Committee on Interstate Commerce, which was "packed" with railroad Senators, Dolliver told the press that "a bill framed in accordance with the President's recommendation will be put before the Senate, even if it is necessary for members of the Committee to part company with the majority of their colleagues."[32] By October 11, the Des Moines *Register's* Washington correspondent felt that:

> The only seeming hope for rate legislation of the kind the President wants would be in a coalition of the Democrats and the Republican minority in the Senate of which Senator Dolliver would be the natural leader. But the Democrats are by no means a unit in wanting radical rate legislation, and those that do want it are likely to favor a plan of their own rather than one emanating from the Republican administration.[33]

The Senate Interstate Commerce Committee began holding meetings to study railroad regulation in late October, after having spent much of the summer conducting hearings on the subject in accordance with the plan adopted in February. It immediately became clear that Senators Elkins, Aldrich, Foraker, and the other Old Guard members did not intend to prepare a bill which would be in any degree adequate or satisfactory. Senator Clapp announced on October 23 that he would line up with Dolliver in support of a measure acceptable

to the administration. Three days later Senator Cullom, author of the Interstate Commerce Act of 1887, told reporters that he "would be with Dolliver
and Clapp" when the showdown came. On November 2 Roosevelt called
Dolliver and Cullom to the White House, and following this conference the
newspapers reported that a rate bill would include provisions granting the Interstate Commerce Commission power to replace "unreasonable rates with maximum reasonable rates to go into effect within a reasonable time and without
waiting for action of the Courts."[34]

At about this time Senator Allison, who, although not a member of the Committee, was very close both to Aldrich and to Dolliver and was destined to play
a key role in the drama, wrote privately that he felt a bill could be prepared
which would include all the President asked and "still provide a quick way to
have a review in case real injury falls upon the railroads . . . if they are content to abide by the decision of the courts."[35] The railroads, however, wanted
no rate bill and were using every device of lobbying known to defeat any regulatory law. According to Dolliver, "persistent attempts" were made "to befog
the public mind" into thinking that the President wanted to take "the business
of railroads out of the hands of their managers" and put it into the hands of a
government commission. Sharply denying the nonsense about the socialistic
intentions of the advocates of regulation, Dolliver told the press that the question President Roosevelt wanted answered was simple and easily understood.
"Shall a complaint made by a shipper, that the rate charged is unreasonable,
be decided by the traffic department of the road without appeal; or shall the
government create an impartial public tribunal, to hear and adjudicate such
complaints with fairness and justice to both parties?" To say, he added, that
"such a provision of law takes the business of the railroads out of their hands
and turns it over to the government is an utter confusion of the subject."[36]

The Republican members of the Interstate Commerce Committee met November 21, 1905, to discuss the possibility of agreeing on a bill. Elkins,
Aldrich, Foraker, and Kean of New Jersey opposed "radical legislation" and
asked for harmony. Dolliver and Cullom told them that the only way to have
"harmonious Republican action was for all the Republicans to get in line with
the President and support his recommendations." Two days later, newspapers
stated that seven of the thirteen members of the Committee, four Democrats
and Dolliver, Cullom, and Clapp, would probably unite in reporting a measure
providing the rate legislation the administration wanted. After a long conference with Roosevelt on November 25, Dolliver announced that he, Clapp, and
Cullom would not be stampeded into working with Aldrich and Elkins on the
grounds that failure to do so would "split the party." Dolliver said the party
would "lose nothing by standing for what the public wants and what the head
of the Republican administration is urging." The following week a reporter in
the national capital wrote that Senator Aldrich had "read the riot act to Sena-

tor Dolliver," accusing him of "trying to break up the Republican party" and telling him that he must "get in line." Dolliver, however, refused to budge and told Aldrich that "a bill in line with the President's recommendations would be passed."[37]

Congress convened on December 4, 1905, and on that day Senator Gorman of Maryland, a powerful Democratic leader, told Dolliver that he would support a rate bill. The next day Roosevelt sent his annual message to the Capitol. Having made an agreement with Speaker Cannon not to mention tariff reform if the Speaker would not block railroad legislation, Roosevelt made a strong plea for "the enactment into law of some scheme to secure to . . . the Government such supervision and regulation of the rates charged by the railroads of the country . . . as shall summarily and effectively prevent the imposition of unjust or unreasonable rates." Roosevelt did not propose giving the Interstate Commerce Commission power to "initiate or originate rates generally," but he did recommend granting to some "unequivocally administrative" agency the right "to fix a maximum rate, which rate, after the lapse of a reasonable time, goes into full effect, subject to review by the courts."[38]

For two weeks no member of Congress introduced a measure which responded to the suggestions of the President's message. Rather, Senators Foraker, Elkins, and others proposed bills calculated to side-track the Roosevelt recommendations. In discussing the situation with the President, Dolliver mentioned that he had almost finished a bill upon which he and Judge Cowan had been working for several days. Roosevelt asked Dolliver to bring his proposal to the White House in order that the two of them, together with the Attorney General and the chairman of the Interstate Commerce Commission, could go over it. Aided by Cullom and Clapp, Dolliver hastened to perfect the bill and took it to the White House, where Roosevelt, Elihu Root, and William H. Taft went over it and approved of what Dolliver had done. On the following day, December 19, 1905, Dolliver introduced the bill in the Senate.[39]

The Dolliver bill was immediately "accepted as the most accurate expression of the administration's policy" and was "commonly called the administration bill." Members of the Interstate Commerce Commission, "who for years have led the fight for enlargement of their powers, unhesitatingly declared the Dolliver measure as good as the one the Commission proposed and more likely to stand the test of the courts." Judge Cowan, representing the law department of the Interstate Commerce Law Convention, asserted that the "Dolliver bill is endorsed by practically the unanimous voice of the men who have made the fight of many years which has brought the country nearly in sight of real rate legislation." On December 29, Washington reporters stated that Hepburn, an Iowan for whom Dolliver had done many favors, was "well pleased with the Dolliver measure" and that it had the backing of the White House and of Senator Allison.[40]

Shortly after Congress reassembled following the Christmas recess, Hepburn introduced in the House a bill which "in all the essential features was almost identical" with Dolliver's. It was "almost identical" because it was "framed in the Committee Room of Education and Labor of the Senate . . . and introduced into the Senate before the Holidays and afterwards introduced into the House by the Colonel [Hepburn] in exactly the same form." Hepburn's biographer, admitting in a footnote the origin of this bill, commented that "it is interesting to observe how some newspaper editors who were hostile to Colonel Hepburn but praised the Dolliver bill experienced considerable difficulty in finding defects in the Hepburn measure."[41]

It is obvious that Roosevelt and Dolliver, understanding the problem of getting action on Dolliver's bill in the Senate Committee on Interstate Commerce, must have arranged for Hepburn and Cannon to get the Dolliver measure through the House first. The House was ready to pass a railroad rate law as had been demonstrated in the overwhelming majority secured for the Townsend-Esch bill in the preceding session. Also indicative of the interest of Congressmen was the fact that seventeen rate bills were introduced in the House. On January 10, 1906, the Republican members of the House Committee on Interstate and Foreign Commerce agreed to support the Dolliver-Hepburn bill with a few changes relating to judicial procedure. These changes were approved by Dolliver and were then incorporated in a revised bill introduced by Hepburn on January 11. After this bill had been debated in committee, Hepburn prepared a third version which he introduced on January 24.[42]

At this point the Republican members of the House Committee held a secret caucus to which Dolliver was invited. Those who were not completely satisfied with the bill as it stood apparently wanted to know whether, if they went along with it in the form acceptable to the Democrats, Dolliver expected to get it through the Senate Committee. At that moment Dolliver's Senate bill was exactly the same as the House bill, except that the Elkins Committee had taken no action. Dolliver assured the Congressmen that if they would send the Hepburn bill to the Senate as it was and with the sanction of both the Republicans and Democrats of the House, he would guarantee that it would reach the Senate floor from the Senate Committee as a result of a majority vote obtained through a coalition with the Democrats.[43] Consequently, on January 27, Chairman Hepburn reported the third version of his bill to the House with the recommendation of "every member of the Committee" that it pass. The House passed the measure without amendment on February 8, 1906, with only seven dissenting votes. In its "final form" the Hepburn bill "did not differ materially from the first draft."[44]

In the light of the foregoing it is clear that the real author of the Hepburn bill was Jonathan P. Dolliver. He was aided by Cowan, Cullom, and Clapp and received advice from Roosevelt, Root, Taft, Attorney General William

Moody, Paul Morton of the Santa Fe Railroad, and officials of the Interstate Commerce Commission. Colonel Hepburn and Speaker Cannon had nursed the measure through the House without significant alteration. It then, on February 9, reached the Interstate Commerce Committee of the Senate and awaited the tender mercies of Senators Aldrich, Elkins, and Foraker.

That committee, of course, had had Dolliver's original bill before it since December 19. The genial Senator Elkins had thought "it would be unseemly" for his committee to meet more frequently than once a week, and that other bills ought to be considered prior to Dolliver's. Thus, no action was taken on the Dolliver bill in December or January. Disgusted, but not surprised, at these tactics, Dolliver turned to Senator Benjamin Tillman of South Carolina, ranking Democrat on the committee and a man with whom President Roosevelt was not on speaking terms. On January 5, these two Senators went over the bill to arrange it so that it would receive the support of Democrats on the committee. Hearing of this, Iowa newsmen concluded that "Senator Dolliver is evidently clearing decks for a fight."[45] Dolliver's success in winning the support of the committee Democrats in early January made it possible for him to assure Hepburn's committee that he would get the House bill reported if the House would pass it as it stood in its January 24 version.

Through January great pressure was brought on the President and on Dolliver to agree to some measure which the Old Guard members of the Senate committee would support. Dolliver's decision was not to yield, but to "fight if there was occasion" and to "oppose to the end" any weakening of his bill. Roosevelt invited Dolliver to the White House on January 30 and February 1 to assure him, and the world, that he had "no intention of compromising on rate legislation" and would call an extra session of Congress if necessary to get it enacted. But the President tended to wobble, according to Clarkson. Roosevelt and Dolliver were in "very close consultation" all winter and spring, Clarkson wrote Leigh Hunt.

> Dolliver worked with all his power to accomplish a successful solution to the rate bill problem. . . . He would work nearly all night trying to get a part of the bill into such shape that it would command a majority vote in the Senate; he would get a phrasing of it just right to suit himself and go and see the President, and the President would say it was bully and just the thing. When he went back in the afternoon to see the President again, others who had seen the President — notably Root in my judgment — had changed him into thinking it needed a little modification.[46]

On February 2, the Des Moines *Register* quoted the correspondent "Lincoln" as predicting that the Old Guard in the Senate would perfect a "plan to steal Senator Dolliver's laurels if it becomes apparent that some rate regulation is to pass." Reflecting that it looked as if Dolliver might get enough Democratic support to win, the newsman suggested:

It may turn out that in the "showdown" Senator Dolliver will discover that he . . . has been "lost in the shuffle." It is easy to believe that the older Republican Senators like Aldrich, Elkins, and Foraker and others do not relish the thought that the Junior Senator from
Iowa may get large credit for any effective rate bill the Senate may
pass . . . and it will not be a surprise if the future reveals that the
elder statesmen have some well-considered plans for unhorsing Senator Dolliver as the titular leader among the Republican Senators for
rate legislation such as the Senator desires.[47]

When the Hepburn bill came before the Senate Committee on Interstate
Commerce on February 9, the real fight began. The committee dropped the
other measures and began consideration of the House bill, which was no different from the Dolliver bill they had failed to act on. Senator Dolliver suggested
that the committee ought to get down to business, that he was "heartily tired of
the tendency to delay" and "to talk perpetually over nonessential and trivial
matters." He even ventured the thought that some members did not seem to
want to reach an agreement and charged them with "levity" in dealing with the
rate question. This aroused the usually cool and lordly Aldrich, who objected
to the charge of levity and said he would not have his sincerity questioned, but
would talk in any manner he pleased in discussing proposed legislation without
being called to account by Senator Dolliver. The "War Eagle of Webster
County" replied that he, too, would choose his own language to characterize
as he saw fit the methods resorted to in preventing action. Senator Elkins
rapped for order, and this round ended in a draw.[48]

By February 14 nearly one hundred amendments to the bill had been offered
by members of the committee. The essential features of the bill were these:
Transportation was defined to include private-car line and terminal services.
All "unjust and unreasonable" transportation charges were outlawed, and rate
discrimination "under substantially similar circumstances" was prohibited.
Schedules of rates were not to be changed without thirty days' notice. More
important was the provision giving the Interstate Commerce Commission power
to establish "just and reasonable and fairly remunerative" maximum rates,
which were to take effect thirty days after notice and remain in force until
suspended or modified by the Commission or a court of competent jurisdiction.
Also of significance was the authority granted the Commission to require reports from all common carriers, and to prescribe and publicize their methods
of accounting. The Commission was also empowered to decide reasonable
charges for private cars and to determine the division of rates on through
routes if the carriers could not agree. There were other provisions too numerous to mention. The last three listed here were, in Dolliver's view, "the pillars
of the law." Students of the subject have since agreed with him.[49]

The first aim of the Aldrich forces was to kill the Hepburn bill in committee,
but Dolliver's arrangement with the Democrats made that impossible. The sec-

ond effort of the opponents was to emasculate the bill through amendments, but Dolliver and his allies had the votes to prevent any amendments in committee.[50] On February 23 the committee met at 11 A. M., and the members discussed minor amendments for nearly an hour. Then Dolliver read a telegram from Senator Cullom, ill in Florida, giving instructions to cast his vote to report the Hepburn bill favorably and against any amendments that were not adopted unanimously by the committee. Aldrich, Kean, and Foraker expressed doubt that an absent member's vote could be cast. Chairman Elkins suggested that Dolliver name a specific motion on which he would like to cast Cullom's vote. Aldrich agreed to this. Without further hesitation, Dolliver moved that the Hepburn bill be reported favorably without amendment and asked to have Cullom's vote counted in the affirmative. Elkins then discovered that it was time for lunch, and he recessed the committee until 2 P. M., leaving Dolliver's motion pending for action at that time. The purpose of the recess was not to appease the Senators' appetites but to provide an opportunity for winning the Democrats away from Dolliver and getting them to vote for an amendment giving the courts "broad review" of rate controversies.

When the committee reassembled, Aldrich offered an amendment to Dolliver's motion, reserving the right of every member of the committee to amend the bill on the floor of the Senate. This passed, but it was meaningless, since any Senator could always offer an amendment from the floor if he chose. Then Dolliver's motion to report the Hepburn bill favorably passed. Five Democrats voted with Clapp and Dolliver, with Cullom's vote being counted, for an eight to five victory.[51]

Senator Elkins refused to report the bill to the Senate. Thereupon, in the bitterness of his defeat, Aldrich moved that the measure be reported by Roosevelt's enemy, Senator Tillman, since, as it stood, it was more of a Democratic than a Republican measure. Elkins, a generous and kindly man, suggested that Dolliver ought to report the bill. Dolliver had wanted Cullom to have the honor, but with Cullom ill and absent that could not be. Aldrich demanded a vote. He, Foraker, Kean, Crane, and McLaurin voted for Tillman; Clapp, Elkins, and Newlands voted for Dolliver. The other members abstained.[52] Here was the Aldrich "victory," if such a petty performance is worthy of the term, and here was the fulfillment of correspondent "Lincoln's" prediction.

Many letters and telegrams of congratulation came to Dolliver, and the newspapers headlined his success in getting the bill out of the committee and the Aldrich maneuver to have Tillman make the report. "Senator Aldrich has exposed himself to the country as a defeated man and as a mean man. In fact his meanness is the measure of his defeat," an editor asserted. "Because he was mad and beaten he could not act with either sagacity or decency, and so he advertised what Senator Dolliver could not have established — that a tremendous victory had been won by friends of the bill."[53]

Dolliver approached Aldrich after the adjournment of the committee and said: "That was a trick too shabby for a gentleman to participate in."[54] Later the Iowan told reporters:

> This contemptible proceeding is for three purposes: First, to muddle the situation; secondly, to humiliate the President; and thirdly to humiliate me. But there is one thing to thank God for, and that is that the bill will be reported and taken charge of by an honest man. . . . The action of the Senate Committee . . . places the bill, which the House of Representatives passed with only seven dissenting votes, on the calendar of the Senate, where nothing can happen to it which does not happen in broad day-light after full public discussion. The Senators who favor this legislation care nothing about who reports it; their interest is to get it reported and acted upon in an open and straightforward way.[55]

Getting the bill out of the committee was certainly the major accomplishment. The credit for that achievement must go in large measure to Dolliver, for it was he, aided by Clapp, who secured the Democratic votes and who insisted on reporting the bill without amendment even when Roosevelt had practically given up and was planning to accept a revision.[56] Dolliver was not being stubborn, nor was he trying to force the President's hand as the Aldrich biographer thought. The Senator and the President worked together from the beginning, conferring frequently.[57] Dolliver, however, understood more clearly than Roosevelt that if they ever agreed to allow even one amendment to be made in committee, they were lost. If Roosevelt and Dolliver had permitted the Aldrich forces to alter the bill or had Dolliver and Clapp tried to do so, then the Democrats would have insisted on their right to offer amendments. They would have begun to play for the headlines and the political advantage, and Aldrich and his henchmen would have had the chance they sought so desperately in the two-hour recess on February 23 of splitting all or part of the Democrats away from Dolliver.[58] Had that happened, the bill Roosevelt and Dolliver wanted would probably not have emerged from that Senate committee in 1906.

Dolliver had to work under the most difficult circumstances. He had only two Republicans backing him in the committee fight, and one of them was absent. His January pledge to the Hepburn committee caucus indicates that he had arranged long before February 23 for the Senate committee Democrats to stand with him for the bill as it passed the House. They kept their word, despite all that Aldrich could do in the way of secret politicking with Democratic leaders friendly to him. But their doing so undoubtedly hinged upon Dolliver's success in preventing any alteration of the Hepburn bill.

For the most part, the history of the Hepburn bill after Tillman reported it to the Senate is well known. The long debate on what was regarded as "probably the most important question since the Civil War" was nonpartisan and conducted upon a remarkably high plane.[59] Roosevelt understood perfectly what Aldrich had meant to do by forcing Tillman to report the bill. "The object," wrote the President, "was to create what it was hoped would be an impossible situation in view of the relations between Senator Tillman and myself. I regarded the action as simply childish." Roosevelt avoided the "impossible situation" by working with Tillman through William E. Chandler of New Hampshire. Despite his erratic tendencies, "Pitchfork Ben" Tillman was an able and honest politician sincerely in favor of the rate bill. "I don't propose that this thing shall be turned into a circus with me as the clown," he said as he began the difficult task of piloting through the Senate the measure Roosevelt desired so much.[60]

In the Senate, as in the committee, the aim of Aldrich and the Old Guard was to defeat the Hepburn bill, or, failing that, to render it ineffective through amendment. Tillman reported the bill on February 26, and on February 28 Foraker, the most consistent opponent of railroad rate legislation, opened the debate. He branded the proposed measure as "drastic and revolutionary," one which "would be alarming if its utter unconstitutionality were not as apparent as its unreasonableness."[61]

The following day Dolliver made the first speech in behalf of the bill.[62] He struck at once at Foraker's charges of the revolutionary and unconstitutional aspects of the bill by pointing out that "the chief feature of the pending bill does not differ in substance or purpose" from the Act of 1887. Furthermore, he said that in 1897 Foraker himself had introduced a bill "containing a grant to the Interstate Commerce Commission of many of the powers which he condemned here yesterday as unconstitutional and in violation of sound principles." The same, he added, was true of a measure sponsored by Elkins in 1905, "which conferred upon the Commission the exact powers that are now condemned in this chamber as in violation of the Constitution of the United States."

By this time the floor and the galleries of the Senate were crowded to overflowing.[63] Having hurled back at their author the accusations of unconstitutionality, Dolliver spoke for two hours on the need for and the purposes of the rate bill. He believed "that this question does not involve any of the differences of partisan politics," that it was so far-reaching in its significance that the parties had not and would not divide upon it. Hence, at the outset, he asked "every man without regard to his political party, to unite together in the effort which the American people are now making to bring the Government of the United States to an effective exercise of the power conferred upon the Congress in the wisdom of our fathers for the benefit of the whole community."

This new law would not be needed, Dolliver asserted, if the provisions of the Act of 1887 "had been treated with that reverence and sanctity without which the laws of the land become a mere echo of vain moral aspirations, if

they had been violated only by bad men, indifferent to the disgrace of lawless-
ness." But the old law had not been accepted "by the railway world" or "by
the business community — for both have been parties to its nullification."
Furthermore, the original law was defective in that it did not include private-car
usage within its definition of transportation under the control of the Commission. Thus, the first important provision of the Hepburn bill was necessitated.
The second major aim, according to Dolliver, was "to provide a tribunal for
the prompt and effective settlement" of controversies arising out of alleged vio-
lations of the law. This tribunal should be the Interstate Commerce Commission with its "machinery with which we have been familiar for twenty years."

At this point Dolliver reached the key to the whole dispute between the
opponents and the proponents of the Hepburn bill, and he understood that fact
clearly and stated his position unequivocally when he said that the proposed
bill

> . . . defines and enlarges the power of the Commission by author-
> izing it, where complaint is made that a rate is unreasonable or un-
> duly preferential, to require the carrier to observe as a maximum in
> such a case the rate which, in its judgment, is in conformity with law,
> taking away from the carrier no part of the legal redress in the courts
> which belongs to it under the Constitution of the United States. Here
> is the battle ground of this controversy.

After discussing the third principal reform undertaken by the bill — the
compelling of common carriers to conform their systems of accounting to regulations made by the Commission and to keep their accounts open to reasonable
inspection under public authority — Dolliver returned to the paramount issue
upon which the long battle was beginning. Two major questions were involved
here: Should the Commission have the power to fix rates? To what extent
could the courts review the decision of the Commission?

To the first question Dolliver made this answer: The bill "does not give the
Commission the power to fix the rates," but it does empower the Commission
to determine "the line above which the rate shall not go." It does this, he said,
because the railroads are not merely private property, but "public service corporations under the laws of the land." He went back to the Code of Hammurabi to show that "the supervision of government in the business of transportation" was not an "innovation traceable to recent Presidential messages."
From Hammurabi he moved forward slowly through the constitutional history
of England and of the exercise by Congress of the right to regulate interstate
commerce.

As to the second question, Dolliver's position was that the Hepburn bill
allowed "the carrier, wherever constitutional rights are invaded" by an order
of the Commission in setting a maximum rate, "to secure its vacation by the
courts, *which will exercise in the matter a jurisdiction which it does not lie*

with Congress to take away or in any way abridge." [Italics added.] In short, Dolliver's position was that the bill as it stood left the railroads free to appeal a decision of the Commission to the courts. He opposed a "broad review" in which the court would look into the matter of whether rates were "just and reasonable." He feared that any effort to provide for a "narrow review," whereby the court should merely determine whether the constitutional rights of the carrier were violated by a decision of the Commission, would render the bill unconstitutional. Thus, he preferred to leave the decision as to the type of review to the courts themselves.

For weeks after the opening of this great debate by Foraker and Dolliver, speeches and amendments of all sorts were offered in the Senate. The bill suffered attack by those who thought it ought to grant the Commission more power as well as from those who wanted it to place the real power in the courts. This situation caused Dolliver to lament that the bill "had to stand fire from two directions — from the camp of its opponents and from the scattered tents which shelter its adherents." Aldrich and the railroad Senators wanted a "broad review" by which the courts would in effect take the place of the Commission and empower the judges to retry the case, both as to law and as to facts. If they could not achieve that, then they sought a review so narrow as to render the bill unconstitutional. Some of the friends of the bill, especially Jeffersonian Democrats who distrusted granting too much power to an agency of the executive department, wanted to specify a narrow court review as a check on the Commission.[64]

Dolliver asserted, on March 14, that "while it is true that the bill does not create a court, it is not true that Congress has not heretofore created a court." He cited an act of August 13, 1888, which provided that "the circuit courts of the United States shall have original cognizance, concurrent with the courts of the several states, of all suits of a civil nature, at common law, or in equity, where the matter in dispute exceeds . . . \$2000 and arising under the Constitution or laws of the United States." When a Senator pointed out that a plaintiff could not get a case into a court if the amount of \$2,000 were not involved, Dolliver answered: "I do not desire to allow these great corporations to go into a court of the United States making a false and humbug charge that their property is being confiscated if only \$2000 is involved."[65]

He also stated that he had never objected to "an affirmative statement in this bill giving the circuit court of the United States the jurisdiction which I think it has now. The thing I have objected to is to so framing the provisions as to enlarge the jurisdiction of the circuit court and make it practically an appellate Interstate Commerce Commission." The reason he gave for omitting special mention of the circuit court was that those who framed the bill feared that any attempt "to limit or abridge the equity power of the courts . . . would introduce an uncertain element into the situation."[66]

In his biography of Aldrich, Nathaniel W. Stephenson, dealing with the first month of the debate, stated: "Mr. Dolliver is the centre of the problem. His strategy is not explicit. The one thing certain in it is that he is aiming to seize for the commission the greatest measure of power which by hook or by crook can be got into its hands."[67] Certainly from the point of view of the reactionaries, Dolliver *was* the center of the problem. If his strategy were not clear to them, the reflection is not necessarily upon Dolliver. A general, withstanding a siege, does not inform the enemy of the conditions either of his soldiers or of his services of supply. As to "the one thing certain," it was not that Dolliver sought to "seize for the commission the greatest measure of power," but that he was attempting to prevent the destruction of the Hepburn bill by amendments which would either emasculate it or insure its being declared unconstitutional.

Dolliver, Allison, and Roosevelt were from the beginning of the discussion in 1904 all on record for giving the Commission limited power to initiate rates, not the "greatest measure of power which by hook or by crook can be got into its hands." They were always in favor of limited review by the courts.

By refusing to commit himself on an amendment, Dolliver, in opening the debate, transferred the attention of his enemies to this constitutional question. About this the Senators orated for many days. "During the month of March the Aldrich strategy had one main objective," wrote Stephenson, "to hammer in the challenge — Is the bill, however interpreted, constitutional?" This was exactly what Dolliver wanted the Old Guard to concentrate on. Thus, Dolliver "made his refusal to accept any amendment that would clear up the bill's ambiguity while at the same time admitting that court review of some sort was inescapable." To the great lawyers like Dolliver's old friend of West Virginia University days, Senator Philander C. Knox of Pennsylvania, the Iowan's position was an inexplicable contradiction.[68]

Perhaps the explanation was quite simple and purely political. It appears that Dolliver was engaged in a "holding operation" designed to prevent any significant amendments until Tillman should have an opportunity to rally the Democrats, who were by no means united on any given course, behind the bill to insure its passage with a reasonable compromise statement providing for court review. While the radicals like La Follette and the conservatives like Foraker, Knox, and Lodge talked, and in talking defined the extreme positions, those who really wanted the "three pillars" of Dolliver's measure enacted into law maneuvered behind the scenes, counted noses on both sides of the aisle, and determined the political realities.

By the end of March the President's forces realized that an amendment specifically providing for court review would be necessary to secure the votes for passage of the bill. After a White House conference on March 29, Senator Cullom stated that the rate bill would be passed with a court review amendment. Dolliver still professed hope of seeing the bill enacted as it was, but newsmen reported that he was "outlining a court review amendment" which would allow the courts to inquire whether in fixing the rate the Interstate Commerce Commission had exceeded its authority and whether the rate was confiscatory.[69]

On Saturday, March 31, the President conferred with Dolliver, Allison, Senator Chester Long of Kansas, and others on the question of an amendment, and on April 2, Senator Long introduced the amendment agreed upon. It provided that jurisdiction on appeals should be lodged in the circuit courts which had the power merely "to hear and determine in any such suit whether the order complained of was beyond the authority of the Commission or in violation of the rights of the carrier secured by the Constitution." This was a "narrow review" proposal exactly like that Dolliver was reported to be "outlining" on March 29. In a brilliant address Long defended the constitutionality of his amendment. He was supported by Allison, Dolliver, and others. At this point, the most notable convert to the Hepburn bill with a reasonable provision for court review was Senator Elkins, who, having "taken an inventory" of his affairs, discovered that "my interests as a shipper are ten times as great as my interests in railroads."[70]

Senators Aldrich, Foraker, and Knox insisted that the Long amendment was unconstitutional, and by April 5 reporters suggested that the fight had narrowed to those led by Aldrich versus those led by Allison. Speaking on the Long amendment, Dolliver hinted at the reason for the President's and his own acceptance of the proposal by saying that the Hepburn bill had good friends "on both sides of this chamber. *It has possibly enough to perfect the legislation and put it through in an effective and satisfactory form.* But whether or not it has that number of members of the Senate in favor of it, *its friends do not propose to surrender any principle that is involved in it.*"[71] [Italics added.]

Here was the clue to the April maneuvers of the President when he sought, through his intermediary William E. Chandler, to negotiate with Tillman in an effort to get a "narrow review" amendment acceptable to the Democrats. Dolliver and his Republican allies, aided by the Democrats whom Tillman could muster, lacked the votes to pass the bill with the Long amendment nor could they get the needed support for the Bailey or the Tillman amendments providing for "narrow review."[72] The Old Guard, however, did not have the votes to defeat the bill or to pass crippling amendments. Thus neither side pressed for a showdown vote.

Under these circumstances, Roosevelt decided to retreat slightly on court review in order to gain the victory on the main issue. Therefore, in early May, as a result of the March strategy which some had found "not explicit," the Hepburn bill was still alive; Aldrich had lost Elkins, Spooner, Beveridge, and others, and the President was in a position to turn to Allison to effect the compromise which the passage of time had made possible. Indeed, on May 5, the newspapers reported that the conservatives seemed to be giving up hope of winning and were attacking the managers of the bill by saying that "they have contented themselves with hair-splitting constitutional questions and have ignored the real weakness of the Hepburn bill which is *the new and radical departure it inaugurates.*"[73] [Italics added.] Exactly so. From the opening of the debate in March by Foraker and Dolliver, the constitutional issues had occupied the center of the stage. Two months of brilliant discussion had passed. The "three pillars" of the bill still stood.

They remained unscathed after Aldrich and Roosevelt agreed on the Allison amendment. This provided merely that the orders of the Commission should take effect within a reasonable time and should remain in force not more than two years. Venue on appeals was to lie in the district court where the railroad maintained its principal office. No injunction or restraining order against the Commission's rulings could be issued on less than five days' notice. The Allison amendment made no effort to define the limits of judicial review. It was a victory neither for the proponents of "broad" nor of "narrow" review, but rather left the whole matter in the hands of the courts for future definition. In this respect Allison's amendment left the bill essentially the same as it was when the House passed it.[74] Roosevelt and Dolliver won what they set out to accomplish. Their "retreat" on the court review question was merely a withdrawal from a no man's land they could not and cared not to conquer. Senator Aldrich and his forces did not merely retreat, they were vanquished. They had wanted no effective railroad legislation; they failed to prevent it either in committee or in the Senate.

Dolliver supported and possibly helped shape the Allison amendment. In fact, Senator Allison refused to sponsor it unless it met the approval of his colleague.[75] As amended, the Hepburn bill passed the Senate on May 18, 1906, by a vote of 71 to 3. Senator Aldrich was absent when his battle was finally lost. Senator Foraker, consistent and amiable to the bitter end, was the only Republican voting nay.[76]

The House-Senate Conference Report was adopted, and the bill became law on June 29, 1906. Thus, "the fundamental principle of governmental control over the most powerful corporations in the country had been fully affirmed. It was an historic event — the most important, perhaps, in Theodore Roosevelt's public career — and a not insignificant one in our national history." As John Blum has put it: "The Hepburn Act endowed the Interstate Commerce Commission with power commensurate with its task." Roosevelt, himself, maintained that it represented "the longest step ever taken in the direction of solving the railway rate problem."[77]

When Dolliver returned to Fort Dodge after the adjournment of Congress, the townspeople held a great reception for him at the home of Mayor S. J.

Bennett. During the ceremonies the Mayor read a telegram from President Roosevelt, saying: "Through you permit me to join with the people of Fort Dodge in an expression of hearty good wishes to Senator Dolliver. I particularly and deeply appreciate the admirable work he did in connection with the rate bill and congratulate him and the people of Iowa upon it." [78] Later, Roosevelt, writing of the fight for the Hepburn Act, recorded: "There was one Republican . . . whom Senator Aldrich could not control — Senator Dolliver of Iowa." [79]

Without in any way disparaging the work of Hepburn, Tillman, and Allison, or others who supported this important measure, it is only fair to conclude that no one except Theodore Roosevelt contributed so much to the enactment of the Hepburn Act as did Jonathan P. Dolliver.

- XVII -

Chaos in Iowa Politics, 1906-1808

I have tried to do my duty without fear of consequences, and have never had an opinion on public affairs that I have not freely communicated to my constituents in Iowa. . . . I have tried to repress the growth of factions and personal contentions within the party.
Jonathan P. Dolliver, Grant Club Address, 1905.

IN ADDITION TO HIS prolonged struggle for the Hepburn Act, Dolliver gave attention to several other important measures during the first session of the Fifty-ninth Congress. One of the few Republicans who opposed the Ship Subsidy bill, he was also among the minority who ardently advocated the ill-fated Child Labor bill, and his efforts in behalf of this proposal won him praise from liberals. His votes in favor of the Meat Inspection Act, the Pure Food and Drug Law, and the Employers' Liability bill (which he reported favorably as chairman of the Senate Committee on Education and Labor) were in line with his consistent support of Roosevelt's major policies.[1]

When Congress adjourned on June 30, 1906, Dolliver was physically exhausted. In mid-March he had written a friend: "This has been the hardest working year of my life and I have not been in as good health as I have been in the past." By July he was ill and "in the hands of the doctor," who informed him that he could not fulfill his Chautauqua commitments without risking his life. Actually, Dolliver's health began to fail in the winter of 1904-1905, when he had a severe attack of "La Grippe" followed by a serious infection in his nasal passages and sinuses which required surgical treatment. He also suffered recurrent attacks of malaria and influenza during the last years of his life.[2]

Dolliver was a tireless worker. Although much given to conversation with his friends and seemingly prodigal with his time when anyone wanted his society or his services, he labored unceasingly to perfect his speeches, articles, and lectures, and to master every detail of the public questions with which he had to deal as a statesman. His correspondence was enormous, and he was constantly in demand as an orator for all kinds of occasions. He seldom missed an opportunity to make new friends and always found time to talk in a leisurely way with his constituents, since he never ceased to regard himself as their servant. He knew more Iowans than any other man in the state, and "he could greet and shake hands with several people while other politicians were deciding whom to speak to first."[3] Such activities consumed time and energy but were a part of his daily work. The notion that "Dolliver was by nature somewhat indolent" is utterly without foundation and apparently comes from those who mistook his geniality and gregariousness as indicative of a lack of industriousness.[4] When engaged in an important political campaign or upon some great congressional business such as the Hepburn bill, Dolliver slighted his meals and his sleep and gravely neglected his health.

Lacking a personal fortune and having no financial "angel" to endow him, as some politicians had, Dolliver nevertheless refused to use public life as a means of acquiring wealth through investment or speculation. When offered an opportunity "to get in on the ground floor" by purchasing stock in lucrative business enterprises, he refused, writing in one instance: "I have abstained from taking an interest in industrial corporations in order to keep myself entirely free in the consideration which Congress is bound sooner or later to give to the question involved."[5]

No "conflict of interest" laws, no Senate investigations of campaign contributions were needed to quicken Dolliver's sense of propriety. He had learned from his father's Bible that a man can not serve two masters and that where a man's treasure is, there also is his heart. Thus, year after year, he continued the wearisome lecture grind instead of getting the rest he needed when the Senate was not in session. His records indicate that he earned more than $75,000 from his Chautauqua speeches. Whatever Mrs. Dolliver, who managed the family finances, could save was invested in Iowa farm land, but most of their income was needed for living expenses, for the charitable causes they supported, and for aid to Dolliver's sisters and his older brother.[6]

Although Dolliver undoubtedly needed a complete rest during the summer and autumn of 1906, the exigencies of Iowa politics interfered with his obtaining uninterrupted repose. The factional strife which had been developing for nearly a decade reached a new intensity in the period 1906 to 1908. A. B. Funk had warned Dolliver as early as 1904 that there was little hope of any lasting compromise which would end the disturbances within the Republican party. "Men may cry peace, peace," Funk observed, "but in my judgment there will be no peace until J. W. Blythe is utterly routed and discredited or firmly entrenched as the undisputed leader of Iowa Republicans." The fearless and able Funk clearly discerned that while Blythe's earlier relationship to politics "was the fruit of his desire to shield his corporation from legislative treatment, now his desire is strongly reinforced by the yearnings of personal ambition." Pointing out that Blythe disliked both Cummins and Dolliver, Funk thought it nevertheless possible that the Burlington Roderick would tempt each one with support in hope of splitting the forces naturally opposed to railroad domination of politics. If he could pursue a policy of divide and rule, Blythe might succeed in hanging both Dolliver and Cummins separately. Therefore, Funk urged that the Governor and the Senator reach an understanding. He believed, in short, that Dolliver ought to abandon his traditional independence to join forces with the Cummins machine. "If you are annoyed by doubts, I will do anything I can to aid you in reaching a satisfactory basis of understanding," Funk added, promising to support Dolliver for re-election to the Senate against all comers.[7]

Much as he admired and respected Funk, Dolliver was "annoyed by doubts," and he did not agree to make any arrangement with Cummins. The political relationship of these two great Iowans — Dolliver and Cummins — is fascinating. For a tumultuous decade their paths ran parallel, before Governor and Senator clashed in a dramatic combat. Both were brilliant, both inspired almost fanatical devotion among their followers, and, in general, both believed in the same political principles. Cummins was unquestionably the abler lawyer and administrator, whereas Dolliver excelled as an orator and political strategist. Cummins' great weakness, one which caused him sometimes to temporize and to adopt the methods of those he branded as machine politicians, was his consuming ambition.

Having twice failed to win a senatorship through election and once through appointment, Cummins had accepted the governorship as a steppingstone to the office he desired. He made an excellent Governor. Under his leadership the government of the Hawkeye State was modernized, the railroad domination was further weakened, and Iowa adopted a primary election system including a preferential vote on candidates for United States Senator.[8]

Unquestionably Dolliver and Cummins had a high regard for each other, and on the whole their personal relations were quite friendly. The truth seems to be that Cummins did not understand clearly that Dolliver was not somehow tied up with the Blythe-Shaw faction. The Governor feared that Dolliver would always stand in the way of his becoming a Senator. Such, however, was not Dolliver's intention nor was it the desire of Dolliver's closest friends, Roberts, Hunt, Clarkson, Kenyon, and others.[9] They all looked upon Cummins as Allison's natural successor whenever the "Wise Old Senator" should retire or die. But they looked with suspicion upon what they conceived to be Cummins' intention to supplant Dolliver or to shove Allison aside before he was ready to step down. Again the truth appears to be that Cummins never for long seriously considered an attempt to unseat Dolliver. Very frequently, of course, men are motivated not by what is true but by what they believe to be true.

Hence, as long as Dolliver felt that Cummins' ambition was a threat to himself or to Allison, and as long as Cummins believed that Dolliver would always be against him for Senator, the possibility of their reaching an understanding along the lines Funk proposed was remote.

The suggestion that Dolliver should make a deal with Cummins whereby the Cummins machine would support Dolliver for re-election in 1907 if Dolliver would back Cummins for Allison's seat in 1908 was one that Dolliver indignantly rejected. He had "no stomach for such arrangements." He wrote his friend Meservey in April, 1905: "I have no doubt that I could enter into a compact with the Governor whereby we could amicably divide the Senatorships between us; but I do not intend to do such a thing at the expense of my colleague."[10] Dolliver, distrusting the ambitions of both Cummins and Blythe, determined to continue his independent course. This was possible because Dolliver's personal popularity made it unlikely that either boss could control the legislators on the issue of defeating him for Senator. Likewise, as long as the two machines were fighting one another, each normally preferred to support Dolliver rather than risk the election of the head of the opposite faction. Dolliver intended to stay in the Senate; he would never abandon Allison in his old age. Therefore, unless Cummins were willing to wait for a vacancy to occur, war was inevitable.

The state election of 1906 was of vital concern to Dolliver, since the legislators elected in November would determine the fate of his Senate seat in January, 1907. Likewise for Cummins 1906 was a crucial year. Three choices lay before him. He could retire from office; he could seek Representative Hull's seat in Congress; he could try for a third term as Governor. There is positive evidence that he seriously considered all these alternatives.[11]

While Cummins was pondering his own future and when his friends thought he would not run for the gubernatorial nomination, anti-Blythe politicians persuaded former Congressman George D. Perkins of Sioux City to become a candidate for Governor. Senator Funk, for example, wrote Perkins: "I am perfectly willing to have it understood that I can give you cheerful support, if your candidacy seems wise and timely."[12] Dolliver and Roberts, long-time friends of Perkins, also urged the Sioux City editor to enter the race. Dolliver sent Meservey to see Perkins early in 1905 to talk the matter over with him and to assure him that both the United States Senators felt that Perkins would be acceptable to all factions as Cummins' successor. After his father's funeral in April, Dolliver conferred with Perkins and tried to induce him to enter the race.[13]

This obvious effort to achieve some sort of harmony in the party before the 1906 campaign began failed for a very simple reason. The Cummins machine wanted an absolute assurance that, should Allison die, Perkins would appoint Cummins to the Senate. Perkins was not the type of man to make such a commitment, and had he done so he would have lost the Standpat support, thus in any event blasting the hopes for harmony.[14]

The Blythe people would not have agreed to back Perkins had he been brought out as one acceptable to Cummins. E. H. Hunter, a Blythe spokesman, had said in 1904: "It is practically certain that George D. Perkins will be the candidate of the anti-standpat crowd. He is in favor of tariff revision and reciprocity. We will not . . . support him. He does not represent the standpat views and we cannot stand for him."[15] But when Cummins decided that Perkins was not acceptable, the Blythe forces found it expedient to get behind him, having learned in 1901 that they "could not beat somebody with nobody."

By December, 1905, Funk and other Cummins editors reversed themselves on the Perkins candidacy and began to boom the Governor for a third term. The powerful Des Moines *Register* consistently supported the view that Cummins must run. It was not difficult to persuade Cummins. He had never ruled out the possibility, and he had written one of his closest political allies in July:

> We must win next year, and win in a way that will leave no doubt whatsoever of the meaning of the victory. I do not want to be Governor again, nor do I want to incur the criticisms of those who do not like third terms, but if it is necessary to make the issue sharp and clear, I will make the fight. Please hold this entirely confidential, for the time has not yet come to develop it.

To another confidant, the Governor wrote in August: "I think that next year will see the hottest fight in Iowa that we have had in a long time, and I expect to lead it in some way or other."[16]

Cummins' decision to try for renomination was based upon four closely related factors. In the first place, he believed that his best chance for reaching the Senate lay in keeping control of the statehouse and in staying in the public eye. Secondly, he apparently sincerely believed that if Perkins won, Blythe would get back in the saddle in Iowa and the Cummins forces would be shattered. Thirdly, he felt a certain responsibility for the wider reform movement and believed that anything that might be interpreted as a Standpat victory in Iowa would injure the Progressives nationally. Finally, he had not succeeded in getting all of his program through the legislature, and he still hoped to do that.[17]

Perkins formally announced his candidacy on January 22, 1906. A week later Senator Funk's Spirit Lake *Beacon* denounced Perkins as a Blythe man. While admitting that he liked Perkins and respected his integrity, Funk stated that "to support Perkins would be to join the Blythe machine." George Roberts answered Funk in a widely reprinted *Messenger* editorial endorsing Perkins. Roberts said he could not believe that Perkins had changed since six months

previously when "we all seemed to be for him for Governor" and when the
Beacon had "endorsed him cordially." Professing not to know what Blythe
would do, Roberts asserted that it was "a lame conclusion to be against anyone
because someone else is for him. It is always an attempt to punish one man on
account of another . . . and is never resorted to except in the absence of better reasons."[18]

On February 10, Governor Cummins publicly stated his intention to seek a
third term. He opened his campaign for renomination at Fort Dodge on February 21, 1906, in an auditorium draped with banners emblazoned ROOSEVELT
AND DOLLIVER. Beginning his remarks with a generous reference to Dolliver,
whom he called a "distinguished and eloquent master of public affairs," the
Governor commented on the Senator's fight for the Hepburn bill.

> He is striking a blow for righteous government which will be heard
> throughout the land long after he has gone to his reward upon the
> other shore. . . . Whatever I can do to sustain him in the work he
> has undertaken, and to give him strength for the future will be heart-
> ily done. I intend to make this so explicit that the man who hereafter
> says that there is any conflict between his ambitions and mine, or that
> it is necessary to be my enemy in order to be his friend, will be con-
> victed of a malicious falsehood before any court of conscience or fair
> dealing.[19]

Cummins' aim obviously was to reassure Dolliver's friends that the third-
term bid was not a move to obtain control of the next General Assembly for
the purpose of getting the senatorship. Had the Governor been content in his
address to turn his attention from praise of Dolliver to the larger issues of the
state campaign, all might have been well. Instead, however, Cummins delivered
a blistering attack upon Perkins and the Standpatters and cast thinly veiled
aspersions upon Allison and most of the Congressmen. Furthermore, contemporary correspondence and Cummins' previous tendency to belittle Dolliver's
work for the rate bill indicate that his glowing commendation of the Fort
Dodge statesman was to some extent insincere and was so regarded by the
Senator's intimates.[20]

Dolliver in 1906 was faced with a situation similar to that of 1901. If he
intervened in the gubernatorial race, the result might or might not be the defeat
of Cummins, but it was certain to hurt Dolliver by turning Cummins' friends
against him and identifying him with the anti-Cummins faction. Yet in 1906
Dolliver felt an obligation to Perkins and also believed that to keep silent after
Cummins' Fort Dodge speech would seem to indicate his own endorsement of
Cummins' attack upon Perkins and the Congressmen. A lesser man might have
kept quiet, accepted the Governor's praise, and ignored the other implications.

Dolliver's decision was characteristic. He determined not to enter the campaign but to reject the endorsement of himself made by Cummins and to

explain publicly his own relationship to Perkins. In a press interview in Washington on March 6, Dolliver stated that he had been so busy with the rate bill that he had not had time to read Cummins' speech until, being taken ill on March 4, he had caught up with the Iowa newspapers. "I appreciate the Governor's words of praise," said Dolliver, "but I cannot accept any praise for myself unless I am allowed to share it with Senator Allison . . . and my colleagues in the House of Representatives, especially Colonel Hepburn." Furthermore, he expressed regret at the party division in Iowa and saw no necessity for it since nobody had attacked Cummins' fine record as Governor. Dolliver's view was that all Republicans ought to follow Roosevelt's leadership and "if we do this we will have harmony." As for himself, the Senator asserted: "I do not wish to be the boss of a faction or to be the creature of a machine. I do not intend to be either, nor do I, because of my official position, intend to give up the common right of a Republican in the ranks to have an opinion upon party management." As for Perkins, "nearly a year ago when, of course, I had no expectation that Governor Cummins would be a candidate for a third term, and when others, many of them notably friendly to the Governor as I have always been, had commended the Hon. George D. Perkins as his successor I took occasion to urge upon him that he become a candidate for the Republican nomination." He added that he and Perkins had been friends for nearly thirty years, that they had lived in the same hotel in Washington, and that their families celebrated Christmas, birthdays, and other occasions together as intimates. Thus, Dolliver concluded, "I can not remain silent when silence would seem to give consent to a programme which is made up of words of endorsement and praise to me and condemnation as a corporation tool to him. . . . Whatever endorsement is given to me must be given with the knowledge of my attitude toward [Perkins] and his candidacy. I would prefer to retire from the Senate than have it otherwise." [21]

This interview won Dolliver immediate acclaim from newspapers of each faction. George Roberts wrote that the Perkins people were pleased and that the Cummins faction understood that J. P. acted out of "loyalty to a personal friend." According to Roberts, all that the Cummins group asked was that Dolliver stay out of the fight and "not set the example of a United States Senator making personal efforts to dictate the nomination of state officers." [22] Cummins, recognizing the "old friendship" of Perkins and Dolliver, said publicly that he did not think "it is at all strange or inconsistent that Mr. Dolliver would rather see Perkins nominated, especially as the Senator is somewhat removed from the political eddies which disturb the waters of Iowa." Privately, however, Cummins was angry at Dolliver's blunt statement. [23]

There was unanimity of opinion on both sides that Dolliver's statement was an act of unusual honor. "It certainly shows courage on your part to take what might be your political life in your hands for a friend," wrote W. S. Kenyon.

The Standpat editor, Cyrenus Cole, telegraphed: "Your interview puts a finer stamp on manhood and friendship. . . . It is the noblest word spoken in a decade in Iowa."[24] Even more emphatic was the pro-Cummins *Register's* editorial later in the campaign:

> Senator Dolliver did for George D. Perkins what no other man in the state did, and what no Iowa United States Senator has ever done for a political friend. He risked his popularity in his own county and his own district, did it knowingly, and did it when it was likely to be interpreted as a defiance of Governor Cummins.[25]

Dolliver assured both sides that he had no intention of getting into the fray. As for the interview, he wrote to his friend, H. W. Macomber: "I intend to tell the truth, even to the death, and do the right thing as God gives me to see it, and for the satisfaction of old friends like you, I will say that I do not care whether it drives me out of politics or not."[26]

Within a few weeks the struggle for the gubernatorial nomination had degenerated into one of the bitterest factional fights in Hawkeye history. Cummins, despite all his talk about the issues and principles involved and his professed shock at having been betrayed by the "treachery" of 1903 and 1904, again made a deal with J. A. T. Hull, the ultra-Standpat Congressman, whereby Polk County would elect delegates favorable to Cummins for Governor and others pledged to Hull for Congress.[27]

When the Standpatters accused Cummins of seeking a third term in order to prepare the way to seize Senator Allison's position in 1908, Cummins vigorously denied the charge. In April he wrote a letter, later famous and fatal, to W. H. Torbert of Dubuque in which he said:

> It is true that I would like the good will and esteem of all political parties, but my fight is for a Republican nomination, and what I want is to find some way to the support of the Republicans of your county. I note what you say with respect to Senator Allison. I am not a candidate for Senator Allison's place, nor have I ever suggested such a thing to mortal man. It is simply abominable, the way my enemies lie about me. I am a candidate for governor — nothing else — and it would be just as appropriate for me to deny I was a candidate for President of the United States or for appointment to some vacancy upon the Supreme Court of the United States as to deny a candidacy against Senator Allison. It is unmitigated rot, and should not deceive any man.[28]

This carefully worded letter, designed by the brilliant lawyer, was used to reassure Allison's multitude of friends in 1906 that it was safe to vote for Cummins delegates to the state convention.

Meanwhile, Perkins, who had a reputation for independence, honesty, and sagacity, allowed himself to become a prisoner of the Standpat machine. He acquiesced in bald efforts to steal the nomination from the Governor through the manipulation of county conventions in such a way as to create fake contests over the seating of delegations to the state convention. Having done this, Perkins then appealed to Cummins to join him in asking the Republican National Committee to decide which delegations from the counties having such disputes should be seated. The Governor naturally rejected this foolish suggestion, while Dolliver and Allison both condemned the Standpat scheme to steal the nomination.[29]

The party was in such a muddle by July that it looked as if the convention would produce a crisis fatal to victory in November. Thus it was that moderates prevailed upon the ailing Dolliver to attend the convention. "You come nearer having the confidence of both sides than anybody else," wrote George Roberts, who urged his great friend to try to get some kind of an agreement on the contested county delegations before the convention opened. Dolliver agreed to try, since "our Iowa politics are in such a bad mess — so much so that we can not tell whether our convention will be a deliberative assembly or a riot."[30]

When he arrived at the convention headquarters in Des Moines, Dolliver discovered that Perkins had twelve contested delegations, only three of which were bona fide. Shaw and Hepburn insisted that all twelve contests must be considered seriously. Dolliver called a meeting of the Congressmen, and after investigating the whole matter, the congressional delegation, presided over by the Senator, recommended that all false contests be eliminated and that the usual course be followed by the Central Committee in deciding the others. The convention accepted this honest solution, nominated Cummins for Governor and Warren Garst, a Progressive, for Lieutenant Governor, and adopted a platform endorsing the Governor's program.[31]

Perkins and his Standpat managers turned their fire on Dolliver for his efforts to prevent the success of their scheme. Wiser men thought and wrote, however, that Dolliver had "saved the day" for Republicans and had insured the "Iowa convention against open and unblushing fraud." Clarkson said that "the people of the nation at large fully understand that it was your timely intervention that preserved the party unity."[32]

During the fall Dolliver campaigned strenuously for Cummins and for the state ticket. The threat of the more disgruntled Standpatters to vote Democratic in order to defeat Cummins for Governor and to punish Dolliver for his honesty at the convention as well as for the railroad rate bill was serious. If the Democrats won the legislature, Dolliver would be replaced in 1907 and Allison endangered in 1908. O'Connell and Secretaries Wilson and Shaw returned from Washington to rally the Old Guard behind the state ticket. Secretary Wilson published a letter in Iowa newspapers pointing out that any knifing of Cummins by Standpat Republicans would likely result in retaliation by the Cummins faction at the expense of conservative Congressmen with the result that the party might lose the governorship and congressional seats as well.[33]

Cummins won, and the Republicans carried the legislature. It was estimated that 20,000 Democrats voted the Cummins ticket. Since the Governor's plurality was less than that, he would have been defeated without such support. Some Democratic legislators assured Dolliver that they would vote to re-elect him to the Senate if it became apparent that the Republican factions might succeed in combining against him in January.[34]

There is much evidence that serious efforts were made to work out a plan to supplant Dolliver. As early as April, 1906, Leigh Hunt had heard of a Standpat scheme against the Senator. Hunt wrote that he was trying to make some money because he wanted to help Dolliver win re-election. "Simply because he is honest and independent and poor the C. B. & Q. propose to kill him off. *But they can't do it.*"[35] In November, December, and early January, various papers, especially the Des Moines *Register*, printed stories of plotting between the railroad politicians and the Cummins faction. The reports indicated that some Standpatters were willing either to support Cummins for Dolliver's seat in 1907 in return for Cummins' pledge to back Shaw for Allison's post in 1908, or to promise Cummins the Allison succession if the Progressives would join in electing either Shaw or Lacey to replace Dolliver.[36] Clarkson wrote J. P. that he and Hunt had dined with John S. Runnells who inadvertently "let it out" that he, Blythe, and others hoped to elect either Cummins or Shaw in 1907. Furthermore, Ret had seen a letter from a Cummins man, hinting at similar behind-the-scenes maneuvers.[37]

Governor Cummins was less than candid in word and deed during these weeks. The Democrats rejected proffered deals, and Secretary Shaw wrote Dolliver: "Permit me to say emphatically that I am not a candidate to succeed you to the United States Senate, will not be a candidate, and if in the course of any possible political mix-up in the state I should be elected, I shall promptly and peremptorily decline."[38] Major Lacey stated publicly that he would not seek Dolliver's seat and predicted that the Senator would be re-elected without opposition. Cummins, however, stated in Washington that he felt under "no obligation" to Dolliver since the Perkins interview — this, despite Dolliver's work at the state convention which benefited Cummins more than anyone else, and despite Dolliver's vigorous campaign to help elect him.[39] Privately, Cummins wrote that he could not "overcome a feeling of resentment" toward Dolliver for having rejected the offer of support made at Fort Dodge at the opening of the campaign. While this did not mean that he intended to be a candidate against the Senator, Cummins said, "It does mean that if this improbable event should occur — namely my election to the office without any participation on my part, I would be free to accept it."[40]

Finally, two days before the General Assembly met to elect a Senator, the Governor issued the following statement, which was published in the friendly *Register*:

> I am not a candidate for election to the United States Senate by the
> Thirty-second General Assembly. I shall not be a candidate. I shall
> not do anything, whatever, to further or encourage any proposition
> looking to my election by this General Assembly.
>
> But there is one thing that I shall not say, and that is that I would
> refuse the honor if it were offered to me by the legislature.[41]

The conclusion is inescapable that Cummins privately and publicly invited the
perfection of some scheme to send him to the Senate in place of Dolliver — if
it could be arranged so that Cummins personally would not have to "do anything, whatever, to further or encourage" the proposition. Major Lacey later
wrote Dolliver that "Cummins would have beaten you if he could have found
the combination."[42]

The "combination" could not be found, however, for there were many honorable men in the Iowa General Assembly. Dolliver received every Republican
vote and also that of one Democrat who apparently wanted to run no risk of
the Senator's losing for want of a vote. Thus, in spite of all that his powerful
enemies in Iowa and the East could do, Dolliver won the full term in the Senate that he desired so much. "During the nineteen years of his service Senator
Dolliver has had no political machine, nor organization interested in his political welfare," observed one editor, "but few men in Iowa could today receive
unanimous endorsement [by their party in the legislature] however distinguished their service."[43]

Mrs. Dolliver's first letter to J. P., after he returned to Washington following his appearance before the General Assembly, reveals something of the relief
she felt that the uncertainty was ended:

> I woke up in the morning with great rejoicing in my heart that the
> work of your brain and heart has been rewarded. How I do *rejoice*.
> And you have been so patient there through all your burdens. You
> have won your crown and your laurels. . . . I feel you are now fully
> launched on a very great career — and here is wishing you the very
> *greatest* and best work.[44]

Much of the bitterness, acrimony, and malice of the gubernatorial contest of
1906 was due to the desire of each faction to be in a position to fill the political
shoes of a great man who had not yet passed from the scene. William Boyd
Allison, nearing eighty and suffering from an incurable disease, had already
served in the Senate longer than anyone in the history of the Republic. Undoubtedly one factor prompting Cummins to fight for a third term was his
desire to be Allison's successor should the "Wise Old Senator" die or retire.

One of the first accomplishments of the Governor and the General Assembly
in 1907 was the enactment on April 4 of a primary law which provided for an
expression of popular preference in the choice of United States Senators. Less

than a month after the passage of this act, Cummins wrote to a friend: "I expect to be a candidate for United States Senator, and now that we have a primary law in Iowa which will enable the Republicans to express their preferences, it seems to my friends probable that I will be chosen." On May 28 the Governor replied to a suggestion that he ought to inform Allison through an intermediary of his intention to run for Senator:

> I believe that the best thing to be done is to have it plainly and fairly stated in the *Register and Leader*, before very long, not in the form of a statement from me, but as a newspaper prediction. Our folks will have no doubt about the authenticity of the prediction, and the object sought to be accomplished will I think be attained in that way better than in any other.[45]

Cummins was thus obviously plotting to supplant Allison despite his letter to Torbert and despite his statement during the gubernatorial campaign that "Senator Allison is the beloved nestor of Republicanism, not only in our own commonwealth, but in the nation, and without respect to party, the people are praying for his speedy restoration to perfect health and for his long continuance in the public service."[46] Furthermore, at Christmas time, 1906, Cummins had told Dolliver that he would not oppose Allison's renomination and had asked Dolliver to carry that message to the Senator together with the Governor's best wishes.[47]

Although it is undeniable that Allison ought not to have sought a seventh term and that Dolliver had not expected or desired him to do so, the fact remains that when the venerable Senator decided to run, Cummins by his own admission was pledged not to be a candidate against him.[48] Nevertheless, his commitment overridden by his ambition, the Governor let it be known publicly in May of 1907 that he would oppose Allison in the 1908 primary.

The Governor's change of mind and Allison's determination to die in harness involved Dolliver and Cummins in a gigantic political struggle without precedent in Iowa history. Dolliver, outraged at Cummins' course, felt morally obligated to aid the movement for Allison which Allison himself was too ill to lead. Since this was the first time candidates for the Senate had to appeal directly to the people, the campaign, which began in the winter of 1907-1908 and lasted until midsummer of 1908, was a grass-roots test of the Cummins strength.

Dolliver wrote Allison in June: "I was amazed at announcement of the Governor's intention to run against you for the Senate. . . . The young men of Iowa will fight your battle for you." Later J. P. unburdened himself to his protege, W. S. Kenyon:

> I stumped the state last year for Governor Cummins, assuring the people everywhere that his election was not prejudicial to the continued service in the Senate of my venerable colleague. I did this upon

the Governor's personal assurances made to me and to many others that he was friendly and not hostile to Senator Allison. You may imagine my surprise and indignation to find him with his old favorite methods, organizing and scheming to drive the old Senator out of public life. I do not know who advised him into this, but I am certain that no friend with as much of an appreciation as you have of the amenities of the public service, could have led him to contemplate such a thing. Two months ago I wrote him calling attention to the moral obligation he was under and trying to persuade him instead of harassing Senator Allison's old age to join with me and others in helping the old man to bear his burdens. He replied not a word to my letter.[49]

Allison formally announced in August: "I will be a candidate before the primaries for the Republican nomination. . . . I have invariably so indicated to friends when spoken to on the subject and supposed it was generally understood throughout the state that I was a candidate for re-election."[50]

Leading Republican politicians everywhere became interested in developments in Iowa. William Howard Taft wrote that Iowa's Congressmen ought to get together to support Allison. Ret Clarkson secured Roosevelt's permission to write pro-Allison press releases. "I can't understand," Ret raged, "how any man in Iowa can have an ambition so vaulting as to think he can get the Iowa people to send him to the Senate in your place. I can't understand how an intelligent State would dismiss itself from eminence in the nation and pre-eminence in the Senate saying nothing of what it owes you." Clarkson also suggested that President Roosevelt attempt to persuade Cummins to withdraw, since in doing so the Governor "would simply defer realization of his just ambition."[51] Roosevelt probably did not intervene; if he did so, he failed to convince the Governor that he should not run.

Senator Dolliver, replying to a letter from Cummins in which the latter attempted to explain away his previous promises not to disturb Allison, wrote the Governor in September:

> I have been looking forward to your election to the Senate with pleasure, unalloyed with any feeling of hostility. . . . [But] in the last campaign when we had to stretch every nerve to prevent the party from being swamped in a mire of personal hostility directed against the head of the ticket, assurances were eveywhere given by me and others, and if I am not misinformed by you, that your re-election boded no evil to the venerable Senator but was a bona fide fight for the office of Governor. I think it may be fairly said that, if it had been understood that in the midst of your term your friends would put you forward to harass the old age of the best beloved servant the Commonwealth has ever had, that campaign, full of meanness and bitterness as it was, would have become a nauseous exhibition of recklessness and malice. . . . I took the general spirit of the last campaign and this Christmas interview with you as affording unerring indication of what your course would be.

Cummins had stated: "I know and you know that the desire on the part of most of those who are pressing [Allison] into a candidacy is not to keep him in the office, but to keep me out of the office." Hence, the Governor argued, he was justified in running. This plea did not hold water, of course, since Cummins was Governor, and if Allison died or resigned, he would fill the vacancy. Furthermore, as Dolliver pointed out:

> It is preposterous to suppose that Senator Allison is being used by others to defeat you. I have been in daily intercourse with him for the past year and there never has been an hour when he has not looked forward to his re-election as the crowning event of his public career. Of course, he is an old man and as we know he has been a sick man. All the more ought we who are younger to reverence his years and help him bear his infirmities. In the nature of things this final honor to him cannot long postpone your ambition — an ambition which I in common with your more intimate friends share with and for you.
> The Senator's announcement was made not, as reported by lying tongues, through my influence but against my advice. . . . I think we ought to let the Senator be the judge of whether he is able to meet the responsibilities of his office or lay down its cares. Only those who have worked with him know how he is wedded to it — how fully it occupies his life.[52]

Cummins did not reply to Dolliver's letter but instead foolishly persisted in his quest of Allison's seat. Nor did he avoid the pitfalls which, as Roberts had pointed out, had cost him so dearly in the contest against Senator Gear in 1899-1900 — the attacks upon the age and illness of the incumbent.

Senator Dolliver opened the campaign for Allison in an address at Council Bluffs on November 25, 1907. As anticipated, this brilliant speech set the pace for the months ahead. Having been threatened by the Cummins faction, Dolliver began by accepting their challenge:

> The hint has been conveyed to some of us with more zeal than delicacy, that unless we observe great caution in our behavior towards the candidates in the approaching primaries, the month of June next will decide not only the Allison succession, but also our own; and that the only chance of safety for such wayfaring mortals is to keep their eyes open and their mouths shut. This interpretation of the obligations and immunities of our public life has not heretofore prevented me from participating in political discussions in Iowa; and it is part of my business here to notify all interested persons that it is not likely to influence my conduct hereafter. . . . I intend to support Senator Allison in this campaign and do everything I can to promote the success of his candidacy. . . . I have been notified that having on more than one occasion ignored the jurisdiction of accommodating persons to control either the expression of my opinion or the course of my action, I am therefore left altogether without friends. If that is so, I suppose that I will have to be content. . . . This state expects

her public men to follow their own conscience, to do business in their own name, to answer to their own constituency and to give a wide berth to all bosses, big and little.

Having thus emphasized anew his utter independence of the two machines, Dolliver devoted much of the remainder of his speech to a review of Allison's career. He cited the examples of other states in returning aged Senators to office — notably Cullom of Illinois, Morrill of Vermont, Vest of Missouri, and Morgan and Pettus of Alabama. "Is Iowa morally inferior to Alabama?" he asked. Quoting the words which Cicero, "the great man among the ancient Romans," had placed in the mouth of Marcus Cato, Dolliver applied them to Allison:

> There is, therefore, nothing in the arguments of those who say that old age takes no part in public business. . . . The great affairs of life are not performed by physical strength or activity or nimbleness of body, but by deliberation, character, expression of opinion. Of these old age is not only not deprived, but as a rule has them in a greater degree.

Toward the close of his address Dolliver said of Cummins: "Such was his respect for public opinion in Iowa that in making his campaign for a third nomination as governor, he denounced in scathing terms the report which was in circulation that he sought to supersede Senator Allison as a malicious falsehood, set afloat by his enemies to injure him with the people. He asked the support of Senator Allison's nearest friends upon written assurances over his own signature that he favored the Senator's re-election."[53] This statement produced a sensation for, of course, Cummins' letter to Torbert and his conference with Dolliver in 1906 were then unknown to the public.

Dolliver's address was, as one who heard it commented: "Lofty in its tone, eloquent in its expression and uncompromising in its attitude . . . a speech which read in cold type will have a profound influence throughout the state and yet it loses much when separated from Dolliver's great personality."[54] It was printed in pamphlet form and widely circulated as a campaign document. In a sense most of what was said and published on both sides during the following six months was merely by way of comment upon Dolliver's Council Bluffs address.

The Governor made his own situation worse by his "emphatic denial" that he had given the "written assurance" Dolliver mentioned. Cummins' efforts to weasel and his phony offer of $1,000 to charity if Dolliver or anyone could produce evidence that Cummins had ever indicated that he would not oppose Allison in 1908, amused Dolliver.[55] After two weeks had passed — ample time for the Governor to get well entangled in authoring implications that Dolliver was a liar — the "War Eagle of Webster County" gave the newspapers a copy of the 1906 Cummins letter to Torbert, together with Torbert's own explanation of why he had asked for that letter in order to assure Allison's friends that Cummins had no designs on the Senator's seat.[56]

The frantic efforts of the Governor, the *Register*, and other Cummins supporters to explain away the Torbert letter occupied much of their time and energy. Some more ardent than intelligent Cummins disciples asserted that the Governor never wrote the letter at all. Its author did not disown it, but did repeatedly state that it was not a pledge never to oppose Allison, merely an assertion that in 1906 he was only running for Governor and was not a candidate for the Senate.[57] This lawyer's argument might have had some validity in view of the literal wording of Cummins' letter to Torbert, but it was patently a falsehood in the light of the Governor's verbal statements to Torbert, Dolliver, Benjamin Birdsall, and others, and of his letters to Dolliver and to Cyrenus Cole in which he specifically stated what he intentionally implied in the Torbert letter.

Nevertheless, as the campaign wore on, it became apparent that the Cummins machine was making headway and that if Allison were to have any chance, he would have to have more than the aid of Blythe's rather battered forces. Hepburn, Lacey, Blythe, and John T. Adams, a Dubuque manufacturer, perfected an Allison organization with Adams as state chairman. Even this was obviously inadequate, and by January all sorts of pro-Allison people were writing to Dolliver that unless he could return to Iowa to stump the state for Allison, the cause was lost. "You are the one man who can win out in this fight for Allison," wrote the well-nigh infallible W. S. Kenyon, "but I do not believe without your active efforts that the fight could be won."[58]

Dolliver, of course, agreed to make whatever speeches might be necessary, and he did so in key cities in late April and early May. "You are the only person in the country who is regarded by the people of Iowa as Senator Allison's personal representative," Adams wrote. "The announcement of your coming at this time has been the best thing that has happened to Senator Allison's campaign since your Council Bluffs speech."[59]

In these speeches Dolliver pulled no punches, and for the first time in their long relationship he struck hard at Cummins. At Des Moines, before Dolliver was introduced to the great audience assembled to hear him, a reproduction of the Torbert letter was projected on a screen as was also the Cummins promise to donate $1,000 to charity — then came the question, "Who got that $1000?"[60] Dolliver ridiculed Cummins, "who never paid a cent of railroad fare for twenty-five years," for claiming credit for "all general moral reforms" including the two-cent fare law originated by John Hughes and the primary law sponsored by Senator Crossley of Winterset. As to the Cummins charges that nothing had been done in Washington by Iowa's Senators, Dolliver replied by citing the record, especially in the matter of railroad regulation. Pointing out what he and Allison had done with reference to the Elkins and

Hepburn Acts, Dolliver added: "I wrote the rate bill myself, fought for it, backed by my colleague for days, and had the pleasure of seeing it finally pass."

One of his most effective thrusts was his attack upon Cummins as a factionist. "There was never any reason for dividing the Republicans of Iowa into two classes and stirring up strife between them. . . . We had only to follow the leadership of Theodore Roosevelt to have escaped most of our trouble." Expressing resentment at the Cummins notion that only the Governor's supporters "are the guardians of progressive Republicanism," Dolliver asked the people to remember when Cummins was eager to sit down with J. W. Blythe, "one of the most ominous creations of the progressive imagination," to write a platform broad enough to accommodate the whole party in order that the Governor might escape the "discomforts of unprofitable strife." With telling effect Dolliver exposed Cummins' hypocrisy by quoting Cummins' speech of September 14, 1905, when the Governor had said: "I don't like to hear a man talk of progressive Republicans and standpat Republicans. There is no such thing because every Republican is progressive. . . . And I can't be tempted to divide the old party into any such factions and fanciful names as these." With biting sarcasm the Senator suggested that "whatever crisis there is in Iowa now was here summer before last" and that the "diet of humbug and dissimulation," the "unseemly disparagement" of Allison and all of his supporters as reactionaries ought to stop.

Blasting Cummins and his papers for using Allison's old age against him, Dolliver snapped: "I cannot help feeling that there is a certain intellectual as well as moral debasement in the train of thought which invites men to dwell on the probabilities of other men living or dying as a part of the motive and prospect of their own advancement." Stating frankly that Allison was old and ill, Dolliver asserted that the time had passed when people could discuss whether his candidacy was well or ill advised. "The question for Iowa is: How shall we deal with this man whose name is before us for endorsement or rejection?" Referring to attacks upon his Council Bluffs speech as being "sentimental," Dolliver freely admitted "that is true, and it is because men feel the touch of sentiment that they are called civilized as distinguished from savages, among whom sometimes the old people were put to death in order to avoid inconvenience in moving the camp." He quoted Henry Watterson, Democratic editor of the Louisville *Courier-Journal*, who was publicly advising Cummins to decline any contest which might put him in the Senate "over the dead political body of Senator Allison." Watterson also told Cummins "to bide his time," for "he cannot have very long to wait" and that "it will be better for you, better for Iowa, better for eternal justice and God-given generosity, if you will draw out of a contest where defeat will be ignominy and victory disgrace."

The Fort Dodge orator, revealing again the fire of his youth, concluded by appealing to the people

. . . to help save the history of Iowa from the political barbarism which seeks now through broken covenants, with vainglorious boast and noise, to attach to us a record of perpetual shame. Let us care tenderly for our aged servant who seeks only a parting assurance of our appreciation, and . . . let us when we are called to look for the last time upon his face have the privilege at least of repeating the words of Theodore Parker at the grave of John Quincy Adams: "He died with his harness on; died like a senator in the capital of the nation; died like an American in the service of his country; died like a Christian full of immortality."[61]

Thus spoke Dolliver in city after city to the people of Iowa during April and May, as he fought the last battle for his beloved colleague. On June 2, in their first primary election, Hawkeye voters responded by expressing their desire by a margin of 10,635 that the General Assembly return William Boyd Allison to the United States Senate for a seventh term.[62]

The major credit for Allison's victory was given to Dolliver. Ret Clarkson, who had seen as much of politics as any man of his times, summed up what was frequently expressed in contemporary newspapers and letters:

You, a young man under fifty, risked your whole political career to prove your devotion to a man and a friend nearly eighty. If you had been selfish and like the average man, you would have forgotten the tie of honor and friendship and made terms with younger men for yourself, and could have done so at a mere tithe of the risk, work and sacrifice that you incurred in making yourself the champion of the older man and the pride of the State. In all my years in politics I have never known so generous and noble a deed performed for the sake of friendship as you have performed, and performed so splendidly, for Senator Allison. . . . This is not my view alone; it will be the universal view. Talking with Colonel Hepburn of Iowa on Saturday last, when he was in my office, he fully concurred in my views, and you know that his view is never partial to you.

Clarkson added that many felt that Dolliver's victory for Allison "will increase your standing and power in the nation the same as it will in the State, and will bring what I have always felt would finally come if you shall be spared life and ability — a chance at the Presidency."[63]

Dolliver's victories in the fights for the Hepburn Act and for Allison's renomination placed him foremost among those mentioned as vice-presidential possibilities in 1908. In fact, from 1906 on he was frequently suggested as Roosevelt's successor, but after the President decided to pass his mantle to Secretary Taft the talk of Dolliver centered on the second place.[64] The Dolliver bill providing for the regulation of child labor in the District of Columbia passed the Senate on May 7, 1908, and this again directed the attention of liberals and reformers to the Iowa Senator as a desirable candidate on the national ticket.[65]

The most serious movement to assure Dolliver's nomination came from Roosevelt and Taft. On June 4, two days after Allison's primary triumph, Secretary of Agriculture Wilson wrote to Dolliver:

> So you saved the Senator. . . . Now, there is a heavy current setting in for you for Vice President. . . . I was asked whether you would look favorably on a nomination. I could not give any reply. I was asked to write you and learn anything you cared to say to report to the party most interested after yourself. . . . It is not necessary that you write to me taking position on the matter and, yet if you were in a receptive mood, that much said would set some machinery at work for you. Anything you may say will not go beyond one man, but he is the big one.[66]

On the same date the Washington *Post* stated: "It is no secret that Mr. Dolliver is altogether persona grata to the President and Secretary Taft" and "There was suspicion yesterday that the suggestion of the eloquent gentleman from Iowa for the vice presidential nomination was put out as a feeler from a source very close to the White House."[67]

There were three reasons why Roosevelt and Taft were so eager for Dolliver to accept the nomination in 1908. Foremost among these was their fear of Bryan, the probable Democratic candidate, and their desire to find a man who could equal Bryan as a campaign orator. Secondly, they considered Dolliver of presidential caliber. Thirdly, he had been a consistent supporter of the administration and was regarded as having more appeal to Progressives than did Taft. From early June on, such powerful papers as the Kansas City *Star* and the Des Moines *Register* promoted the Dolliver boom without ceasing, and the New York *Times* devoted much attention to the Roosevelt-Taft support of the Iowan. Stating that Taft's backers were perfecting an organization to push Dolliver's candidacy, the *Times* described Dolliver as

> . . . one of the foremost advocates of the President's policies in the Senate. . . . The presidential contest will be fought out in the West, and Dolliver is the type of man who appeals to Western voters. He is frank and outspoken and strikes from the shoulder. He is an exceptionally able campaigner. He is identified with the progressive faction of the Republican party, which has always stood for the Roosevelt policies and he is not in any sense of the word a trimmer.[68]

By June 10 the *Register* asserted that "the Dolliver choice seems to have been settled" by Roosevelt and Taft, providing Dolliver would accept and the Iowa Standpatters did not try to block the nomination. The same day Borah of Idaho, following a talk with the President, stated: "Senator Dolliver of Iowa is to be the nominee for Vice-President at the Chicago convention" and

QUARANTINED — A VERY BAD CASE

IF THERE ARE ANY OTHER REASONS WHY DOLLIVER SHOULD BE KEPT AT HOME THE STANDPATTERS HAVEN'T THOUGHT OF THEM YET.

Des Moines *Register*, June 13, 1908

CURFEW JUST MUST NOT RING TONIGHT, BY THUNDER.

Des Moines *Register*, June 16, 1908

that if Dolliver would accept "no one else has a chance for the place." [69] The "if," however, was wisely emphasized.

Dolliver did not want the vice-presidency in 1908 any more than he had in 1900, although his chances of nomination in 1908 were even more certain than they had been eight years previously. He told reporters on June 5: "I would not want to belittle the honor of being Vice President, it is a great dignity and honor, but the change does not appeal to me. I want rest and repose this summer and have no desire to plunge into the national campaign in that way." [70] Undoubtedly, he would have accepted if nominated, but he did all he could to prevent being chosen.

The chaos in Iowa politics, however, was the decisive factor in preventing Dolliver's nomination. The Standpatters were in control of the delegation to the national convention. They were determined that Dolliver should not be Vice President for two reasons First, they feared that if he resigned from the Senate, Cummins would get his post or that there would be such a donnybrook that the Democrats would win the legislature and send two Senators to Washington in 1909, thus costing Allison his seat. Secondly, they wanted a Standpat nominee so that if Taft died someone other than J. P. Dolliver would move into the White House. Ex-Secretary Shaw, Colonel Hepburn, and Lafayette Young, Standpat editor of the Des Moines *Capital*, headed the opposition to Dolliver. Shaw urged Lodge to help block the nomination, reportedly saying: "We might vote for Dolliver if he were nominated but we are going to see that he is not nominated, it must not be." The Iowa delegation to the national convention refused to endorse Dolliver, although the Progressive delegates desired to do so as they hoped to make him Vice President and elect Cummins as his successor. [71]

In addition to his own lack of enthusiasm for the office and to the political situation in Iowa, Dolliver's closest friends presented a third argument against his acceptance of the nomination. Clarkson, Roberts, O'Connell, and Allison all believed that Dolliver had a great future in the Senate and that he owed it to himself and to Iowa to remain there. These men were certain that Dolliver would be nominated for Vice President unless he positively refused to allow his name to be presented and refrained from going to the convention himself. The "Wise Old Senator" advised him to "think long & strong before you yield to temptation" to accept. "The forum of the Senate is more attractive and in your case the service will be continuous." Allison felt that if Dolliver went to Chicago, "You may find it difficult to escape." Roberts requested J. P. to authorize him to say that "you desire to retain your seat in the Senate" and urged Dolliver to stay in Fort Dodge in order that a draft movement could be prevented. The same advice came from O'Connell, who said he was telling everyone that "you want to stay where you are, and cannot afford to take the nomination." [72]

From Ret Clarkson came the most eloquent plea, one doubtless echoed by Louise Dolliver. Ret wrote:

> To me a decision in the matter is not difficult, for to me the leadership of a great State clear before you the rest of your life is a much greater prize and more to be preferred than four years of the Vice Presidency. . . . Furthermore, you must think of the Presidency which will one day be within your reach. I believe this is so certain to come that it affects my judgment very much as to any call for you to the Vice Presidency now as being a call at the wrong time and for the wrong place for you.
>
> I am giving you counsel out of forty years experience in actual politics, and giving it to one whom I regard with almost the affection I have for my own son, and with such pride and confidence in your whole career as I have had in my whole life for only one or two men.[73]

Senator Long of Kansas, who had helped Roosevelt and Taft with the Republican platform draft, arrived in Fort Dodge on June 12 to confer with Dolliver. He was regarded as a White House emissary to get Dolliver's acceptance, but he departed without it, and newsmen reported that Dolliver had declined, saying he felt just as Roosevelt had said he did in 1900. Nevertheless, on June 13 the *Register* reprinted a Kansas City *Star* editorial urging that Dolliver be drafted because he was "the best qualified personally, sectionally and politically. He has large capacity, fine training, is in harmony with progressive Republicanism and would give the ticket strength where it will need it most."[74]

Dolliver, however, had made his decision even before Long visited him. On June 11 he authorized George D. Perkins and Lafayette Young to withdraw his name from consideration, "if such consideration is found to be seriously contemplated." On June 14 a telegram from Dolliver to Young appeared in the Chicago papers stating "I have no ambition for the office of Vice President, and I do not think that any exigencies of party require me to sacrifice both my inclination and my interest." All members of the Iowa delegation to the National Convention, and Senator Allison, were asked to telegraph Roosevelt to protest against drafting Dolliver.[75]

Thus, for a variety of reasons, base and noble, selfish and generous, Dolliver's closest friends and bitterest foes joined in reinforcing his expressed preference not to be Vice President. It was a fateful, probably fatal, decision. After trying futilely to nominate Cummins or Beveridge, the administration forces accepted Representative James "Sunny Jim" Sherman of New York to run with Taft. Although Taft had asked Dolliver to make the principal speech seconding his nomination for the presidency, the Senator followed the advice of those who told him to stay at home if he did not want to be drafted.[76]

Dolliver campaigned actively for the election of Taft and Sherman. He repeatedly assured Western audiences that he agreed with Theodore Roosevelt in thinking that "William H. Taft best represents the higher ideals of our politics, that he is better fitted than any other man to carry forward the great task which the government has undertaken." Dolliver also related that McKinley had looked on Taft as his probable successor. "I heard McKinley say to Judge Taft, after he had consented to lay down the ambitions of a lifetime to go to the Philippines, that if he succeeded in his work it would make him President of the United States."[77]

Taft, running on a platform which declared "unequivocally for a revision of the tariff by a special session of the Congress immediately following the inauguration," made clear that he stood for a lowering of duties.[78] Dolliver had predicted exactly such a platform statement in November, 1905, and his support of Taft was all the more enthusiastic because of the nominee's tariff pledges. The Republicans won the election of 1908 with a comfortable margin, retaining control of both houses of Congress.

Before the election, however, William Boyd Allison, who had been in Congress since Lincoln's first administration, died in Dubuque on August 4, 1908. Iowa arranged to hold another primary election to nominate a Senator. Dolliver made it clear that he would not intervene in the selection of Allison's successor and that he was willing to "forgive and forget" so far as Cummins was concerned. The Governor defeated John F. Lacey for the Republican nomination, and at last, on November 24, a special session of the General Assembly elected Albert Baird Cummins to the United States Senate, where he was destined to remain until 1926.[79]

The Standpatters elected B. F. Carroll as Governor of Iowa, and the party division in the Hawkeye State continued after 1908. Jonathan P. Dolliver and Albert B. Cummins, however, finally found themselves at peace with one another and ready to fight as allies for the policies in which they believed, policies to which they fondly hoped William Howard Taft was committed.

- XVIII -

The Leader of Insurgency, 1909

Dolliver brought to the Insurgents not only the largest personality among them, but a quality of amiable bigness and urbanity which at once enabled them to achieve unity among themselves and to make converts.

Mark Sullivan, *Our Times.*

THE DEATH OF Senator Allison grieved Dolliver deeply. In the decade since the passing of Governor Carpenter in 1898, death had repeatedly struck men near and dear to Jonathan — Gear in 1900, McKinley in 1901, George Pearsons in 1904, Father Dolliver in 1905, and Victor, the beloved younger brother and valued political ally, in 1907. Although he was sensitive and sentimental, neither the death of loved ones nor the changed conditions which came with the passage of time could for long dampen the spirits of the irrepressible Dolliver. He loved history and he cherished old friends and old times, but he believed with Jefferson that the earth belonged always to the living.

At fifty he retained his optimism as well as his youthful appearance; his hair and mustache were as dark and his complexion as clear and ruddy as ever. Mark Sullivan, who knew him well, described Dolliver, the senior Senator from Iowa, as follows:

> He was utterly without pose; to a physical figure and a personality so patently big, pose was unnecessary — the most effective pose Dolliver could adopt was merely to be Dolliver. Part of his immense charm lay in his preference, as a rule, to be a spectator upon life, a spectator who ever regarded mankind as interesting, amusing, and on the whole likeable; and who brought to his observation of life rich resources of reading and reflection. By one figure of speech, Dolliver was a mountain of a man — his bulk, as well as his personality, justified that; by another figure he was a deep, quiet lake, restful to the spirits of those fortunate to come in contact with him.[1]

He was indeed a delightful person. As his friend Macomber put it: "He is today a great Senator, but J. P. Dolliver is as cordial in his friendship, as simple, joyous, genial in his conversation as he was a quarter of a century ago.

237

. . . He is the prince of good fellows, the entertaining, fascinating friend and companion." Another acquaintance said of Jonathan that "there emanated from his presence something bright as the flash of a star, yet something sweet and spiritual and of an infinite kindliness, something with an element positively poignant, that sent me from his presence more than once with a smile that was near to tears." [2]

Moderation in all things, nothing to excess seems to have been the rule of Dolliver's life — except in the matter of overworking himself. He cared little for exotic food or for luxurious furnishings or clothing. One mild cigar a day usually sufficed. A Kentucky friend kept him well supplied with the finest whisky. Dolliver enjoyed "the cup that cheers," but apparently never indulged himself sufficiently to give offense to his Methodist constituents. When asked if he drank, J. P. replied with his usual wit that he was "abstinent, but not totally so." [3]

Although his fraternal affiliations included the Masons and the Elks, Dolliver was not much of a joiner. What free time he had he preferred to spend with his wife and children whom he adored or with a few close friends casting for bass, rather than attending lodge meetings. From 1905 on, however, he had little time for rest and recreation. At the beginning of Taft's administration, Dolliver wrote his wife of his regret that "the years have been almost too full of cares to give us our own personal share in the joy of living with and for each other, yet I am truly grateful to God for the happiness, repose and usefulness which have come to us two since we became one." [4]

On the whole, the Roosevelt years had been years of achievement and happiness for Dolliver. As he watched the inauguration of Taft on the cold, snowy March 4, 1909, Dolliver may have mused that but for a quirk of fate, he, instead of Roosevelt, might have been the retiring President. After the death of McKinley, J. P. had often told friends he "thanked God that in His wisdom He saved me from this awful Presidential responsibility." [5] To his protege, W. S. Kenyon, who had hoped Dolliver would be Roosevelt's successor, he had written in 1907: "I may have carried to extremes the injunction of the apostle that a man should not think more highly of himself than he ought to think, but I have never been able to warm up over the notion that I am fit for the presidency of the United States." [6] Here, again, one sees that amazing humility which is the hallmark of the truly great and which doubtless caused Mark Sullivan to say that "Dolliver was utterly without the egotism that his ability would have abundantly justified." Nevertheless, it is difficult to believe that despite his sincere modesty, Dolliver did not to some degree share the hope of his wife and many friends that sometime he would attain that supreme political distinction which belongs only to the President of the United States. [7]

As he sat in the Senate chamber, listening to Taft read his inaugural address, which included an account of the accomplishments of the Roosevelt era, Dolliver undoubtedly thought of the part he had played in support of the Rough Rider. Few Senators had spoken more frequently and none more eloquently for Roosevelt's policies than Dolliver. But on March 4, 1909, the great fights for the railroad rate bill, pure food and drug and meat inspection legislation, conservation and national forests, child labor restriction in the District of Columbia, employers' liability, shorter hours for railway employees, physical evaluation of railroads, government supervision of railway security issues, reorganization of the Washington school system, better pay for postal employees, and enlarging the navy — all these were but memories.

But all that was past. Roosevelt was through as President and was soon to leave for the long-planned hunting trip to Africa. The future lay in the hands of Taft who was speaking and who included in his inaugural message some remarks concerning the years ahead. Dolliver heard him say again, as he had during the campaign, that the tariff must be revised downward. Indeed, the new President declared that in "the making of a tariff bill the prime motive is taxation and the securing of revenue." The nation's forests and other natural resources must be preserved, Taft continued, and additional protection against the abuses of industrial life should be provided for labor.[8] This all sounded fine to Dolliver. Tariff reform at last — it had been a long time since the birth of the "Iowa Idea" and the clash with Aldrich over the Kasson Treaties.

Dolliver thought well of Taft and had traveled 12,000 miles campaigning tirelessly "from one ocean to the other" to help put him in the White House. He looked upon the new President as one who "might be endued with power from on high to grapple with the corrupt influences that stood ready to recapture the strongholds of this Government."[9] Dolliver was not the only politician to misjudge Taft. Roosevelt had handpicked his successor to carry on his work, and Beveridge believed that Taft would continue the policies of his predecessor. Archie Butt, military aide to both Roosevelt and Taft, seems to have evaluated the new President more accurately than did the Rooseveltian politicians. He thought Taft well intentioned but feared that his amiability and his "doctrine of expediency" would allow control of the government to drift into the hands of the reactionaries. "I don't think he realizes yet," Butt wrote, "that for seven years he has been living on the steam of Theodore Roosevelt and that the latter has been his motive power. . . . With Roosevelt out of the country, the President will find . . . that his steam has been cut off. He will have to find his own fuel now, and, like a child, will have to learn to walk alone."[10]

Unfortunately for his political reputation and for his party, Taft not only failed to "learn to walk alone," but was most indiscreet in choosing those with whom to walk. Those Republicans who had expected Taft to lead them forward — toward the completion of reform begun, or postponed, during the Roosevelt regime — were already being called "insurgents" against the leadership of Speaker Cannon and Senator Aldrich when Taft's administration began.[11] Whether Taft could have accomplished more — and much was accomplished during his term — had he chosen to support the Insurgents instead of joining the Old Guard is problematical. It is a fact, however, that the course he did follow wrecked his party.

Having called the Congress into extraordinary session on March 14, 1909, for the purpose of revising the Dingley Tariff, Taft sent a brief message — it required two minutes for the clerks to read it — which made no mention of *downward* revision. The Insurgents were amazed that the President had not made the most of his opportunity to present an historic appeal for tariff reform in fulfillment of campaign promises. Some wondered if Taft were already in retreat before the battle started. Had they been able to compare his private statements in November and January, when he was storming at Cannon, Payne, and Aldrich, and threatening to veto any bill that was not a "genuine revision," with his spineless message, they would have had even greater cause to ponder.[12] Already many were disappointed that the President had given no aid to the movement to block Cannon's re-election as Speaker of the House, although, of course, Taft was on solid ground in refusing to intervene in that matter. The tariff was quite a different thing; he had given his word to the American people on that question, and his aim, like that of the Insurgents, could have been expected to be to get the Congress to make good on the Republican "contract" with the voters.

The dreary story of the Payne-Aldrich Tariff bill began, of course, in the House, where the Ways and Means Committee, following the precedent of 1896, had begun holding hearings the preceding November and had a bill practically ready for presentation when the Congress convened. Prepared in the time-honored way, the bill, introduced by Sereno E. Payne, provided for some increases, maintained some rates as in the Dingley Act, and made some "significant reductions, none of revolutionary character, or likely to have serious economic effects, yet indicative of a disposition to bring about some 'real' revision."[13] As it passed the House after less than three weeks of debate, the Payne measure was a far cry from an adequate tariff reform, and the President indicated that he might veto it unless the bill were improved in the Senate.[14]

While the leadership of the House pushed the Payne bill toward passage without significant alteration, Nelson Aldrich and his Senate Finance Committee began rewriting the measure to satisfy the interests they represented. Thus, when the House bill came to the Senate and was referred to the Finance Committee, only forty-eight hours were needed for Aldrich and his cohorts to make 847 changes, increasing the rates on more than 600 items in the Payne bill and raising some even higher than the existing schedule of the Dingley Act. This cynical disregard of the campaign promises to reduce tariff duties outraged those Republicans who favored reform and who believed that the party ought to make good on pledges rendered. Thus, when the Payne-Aldrich bill was introduced in the Senate, it precipitated a debate which deserves to rank with any conducted in that body.[15]

No man played a greater or more effective role in that debate than Jonathan Dolliver. "He was the great popular figure, the favored orator, the Mirabeau of the insurgent movement," wrote a contemporary.[16] Mark Sullivan's evaluation, written years after the great fight had ended, bears repeating here:

> Dolliver was, moderately, of the newer Western type. . . . A phlegmatic good nature that went with his bulk, a personal philosophy which taught him that things didn't matter much, and an intellectual tolerance that arose from his wide reading as well as his contact with men, led him to have distaste for the harsh hates, the increasing suspicion, the shrill stridency, of most of the Insurgents. . . . Dolliver brought to the Insurgents not only the largest personality among them, but a quality of amiable bigness and urbanity which at once enabled them to achieve unity among themselves and to make converts.
> Dolliver was persuasive. La Follette and the other Insurgents could say things that pleased themselves and pleased those who already felt as they did; no one among them until Dolliver had the gift of saying the same thing in a manner that would please also the public and the rank and file of Congress, and thereby make their cause popular.[17]

Some historians, apparently unacquainted with the work of Dolliver, since so little has been written about him, have called Senator Robert La Follette "the leader" of the Senate Insurgents in 1909-1910. La Follette, as well as Albert Beveridge of Indiana, was certainly a leader of Insurgency, and since La Follette continued in public life long after the death of Dolliver and the defeat of Beveridge it is understandable that the assumption that the Wisconsin Senator was the generalissimo of the Insurgents has come to be widely accepted. There is much evidence, however, that the Insurgents themselves as well as many of their contemporaries among publicists would have seriously disputed that assumption. Unquestionably, many of them looked upon Dolliver, informally at least, as "the leader" of the Insurgents in the Senate. This was true for three rather obvious reasons.

In the first place, Dolliver was a tariff expert, having spent years in both the House and Senate mastering that subject. Indeed, since Aldrich had turned to the study of finance in his later years, probably no man in the Senate knew as much about the tariff question as did Dolliver at the time of this debate. Secondly, Dolliver was widely regarded, as Beveridge phrased it, as "beyond any possible doubt the greatest orator in the contemporaneous English-speaking world." Thirdly, his national reputation, his seniority in Congress, and his standing in the party as a Rooseveltian spokesman identified neither with the Old Guard nor the extreme Progressives made Dolliver, rather than La Follette, the Senator around whom all anti-Standpat factions could rally.[18]

Most writers have misjudged the reason for Dolliver's Insurgency and have unwittingly done him an injustice. The explanation which has gained wide acceptance is that Dolliver was an unswerving regular who suddenly turned to Insurgency after Aldrich had excluded him from the Finance Committee in 1909.[19] This is remote from the truth. In the first place, of course, Dolliver had clashed with Aldrich over the tariff in almost his first speech in the Senate and had broken with him and defeated him in the greatest legislative battle of the Roosevelt administration. Dolliver had never been a Standpatter either in Iowa or in Washington. His 1908 fight for Allison's renomination may have confused some writers and led them to believe that Dolliver was allied with the Standpatters, but his motives for aiding Allison had nothing to do with the old Senator's relations either with Aldrich or with the Old Guard in Iowa. For the sake of harmony and out of reverence for Allison, he had sometimes "gone along" with the Senate organization when he would have preferred a different course, but never on a question involving great principles, as his record on the rate bill, employers' liability, pure food, and other measures indicates.

The facts concerning the committee assignment in 1909 are these: When the special session of the Sixty-first Congress met, Senator Aldrich, the majority leader, was named chairman of the Committee to Select Committees in the Senate. Inasmuch as Cummins was a new Senator and as his special interest was in railroad legislation, Dolliver undertook to help him secure appointment to the Interstate Commerce Committee. Since two men of the same party from the same state could not be on the same committee, Dolliver wrote Aldrich requesting that Cummins be named and stating that "as an act of friendly interest in the promotion and success of my colleague in the work of the Senate, I desire to withdraw from the Committee on Interstate Commerce, in case the Committee appoints Mr. Cummins to that position. I hope this can be done."[20]

Aldrich had at about this time sent to each Senator a formal inquiry asking what committee assignments each desired. Dolliver replied that in addition to his other committees, he expected to receive Allison's place on the Finance Committee. There were five vacancies on that important committee, and Dolliver felt entitled, on the basis of precedent, on geographical grounds, and by his personal status, to the opening created by Allison's death. Furthermore, in conversation with Aldrich concerning the withdrawal from the Interstate Commerce Committee, Dolliver gained the impression that Aldrich promised to assign him to the Finance Committee. Whether such a promise was made or not can not be determined and is of little consequence. As Senator Clapp phrased it, "in view of what Dolliver had previously demonstrated . . . he merited the position under the unwritten law of the Senate."[21] Nevertheless, Senator Aldrich did not appoint Dolliver to the Finance Committee, but did place two Standpat Senators serving their first terms, Reed Smoot of Utah and Frank P. Flint of California, on this committee.

Although, according to La Follette, Cummins "came within a hair's breadth of losing the appointment to the Committee on Interstate Commerce," Aldrich did keep his word on that part of the understanding with Dolliver. Aldrich told both Cummins and James E. Watson that he would not appoint Dolliver to the Finance Committee, because he and Dolliver could not work together in preparing a new tariff.[22]

Inasmuch as Dolliver took the lead of the Insurgents against the Payne-Aldrich Tariff shortly after this episode, several writers have assumed that he was motivated by his anger at Aldrich. La Follette, who seems to have believed that he had "converted" Dolliver to Insurgency, is partly responsible for this error. He recorded several years later his recollection of having talked with Dolliver "after the appointments were announced" and gave the impression that Dolliver agreed to "break away" from Aldrich because of the committee squabble. La Follette's statement, however, reveals that they discussed Dolliver's whole past relationship with the "masters of legislation in the House and in the Senate" and that Dolliver had talked with Allison about unhorsing the Old Guard as early as 1906. According to La Follette, Allison had asked Dolliver to "wait until I am gone."[23]

On the basis of the record and in all fairness to Senator Dolliver, it must be said that his exclusion from the Finance Committee had very little to do with his position on the tariff bill. There is no evidence that he was ever motivated by anger, spite, or a desire for revenge. The testimony of friend and foe is unanimous that "he had no bitterness in his soul, no animosities, no hates."[24] Doubtless he felt a bit disappointed, for as he said to Roberts, "You know that I have been carrying water to the elephant for a long time."[25] There is no question, however, but that Senator Dolliver would have taken exactly the same course in Insurgency even if he had been named to the Finance Committee. Aldrich must be given credit for intelligence and for being one of the ablest politicians ever to lead the Senate. He knew perfectly well that putting Dolliver on the committee would not bind him to support an Aldrich tariff. He knew Dolliver and his tariff views. He remembered 1901, 1902, 1903, and 1906. He knew what apparently La Follette did not know, namely that Dolliver had never belonged to the "Old Guard" circle in the Senate and that, therefore, there was no question of his "breaking away" because of disgruntlement over a committee assignment. Aldrich, by denying Dolliver's request, merely prevented Dolliver from fighting him in the committee as had happened in the Interstate Commerce Committee over the rate bill. That is clear from his statements to Cummins and Watson — statements which also reveal Aldrich's intentions to ignore President Taft's campaign promises on tariff reform.

The talk of Dolliver's being "suddenly converted" to Insurgency is meaningless and misleading. As Hechler has shown, the term "Insurgency" as applied to American politics "was little used before 1908, and did not come into common practice until after Taft became President."[26] If the word has any meaning before that time, it is with reference to opposing the Old Guard leadership in the Republican party in the first decade of the twentieth century. Dolliver's long record of independence in relation to the Blythe-Shaw machine in Iowa from 1900 on and his clashes with the Senate leaders over various legislative measures during the Roosevelt era indicate that he was in no sense a "sudden convert" to Insurgency. As has been explained heretofore, Dolliver's silence on the tariff from 1903 to 1908 was due to his acquiescence in Roosevelt's request and not to any lack of willingness on his part to fight the Old Guard. In Roosevelt's time the national party did not promise tariff revision. In 1908 the reduction of the tariff *was* an important issue in the campaign, and Dolliver, as well as Taft and others, had specifically promised to work for a genuine revision. Until the leadership demonstrated its intention to renege on the pledge, neither Dolliver nor anybody else became Insurgent on that question.

Judson Welliver, one of the four journalists who share the honor of making the term "Insurgency" an accepted word in the political vocabulary, wrote in 1912:

> It was not the passion of a moment that made Dolliver defy and flaunt the ruling powers of the party. He had been slow to believe that influences of the most reprehensible sort had secured a grip upon it that menaced the very spirit of popular institutions. . . . He was strong with party men, because he had always been the most loyal of them all. They knew he would go as far as any to save the party; but they knew, too, that he wanted to save it for service to the nation, not as a monument of longevity in senility.[27]

The basic reasons for Dolliver's outspoken support of the Insurgents in 1909-1910 were simply that he felt morally bound to keep his word and to preserve the honor of his party in the tariff pledges, and that he had realized from 1906 on that the "money power," working through the Old Guard, was threatening the democracy in which he believed as well as the economic well-being of the American people. It was in the last analysis Dolliver's loyalty to the people and to his own ethical and political standards that counted most — more even than his loyalty to the party he had loved so well and served so long. He was like that Mark Twain character in *A Connecticut Yankee*, who said:

> You see my kind of loyalty was loyalty to one's country, not to its institutions or its office holders. The country is the real thing, the substantial thing, the eternal thing; it is the thing to watch over, and care for, and be loyal to; institutions are extraneous, they are its

clothing, and clothing can wear out, become ragged, cease to be comfortable, cease to protect the body from winter, disease, death.

From the Insurgent viewpoint the policy of high protection was mere "clothing," and by 1909 that "clothing" had turned to "rags" which were incapable of protecting the nation from "winter, disease, death." Dolliver, who throughout his life had believed that all free governments are founded upon the authority of the people and exist for the benefit of the people, realized as did Mark Twain that "the citizen who thinks he sees that the Commonwealth's political clothes are worn out, and yet holds his peace and does not agitate for a new suit is disloyal, he is a traitor." [28]

Two or three weeks before the debate in the Senate began, the Insurgent Senators started planning their attack. Dolliver spent several days during late March and early April listening to the discussion of the Payne bill in the House.[29] His long experience in that body and his service on the Ways and Means Committee enabled him to estimate the strategy of the Standpatters, and he soon saw through their subterfuge of seeming to lower rates while in reality raising them. Their plan was clever, and they had perfected it right after the 1908 election in the hope that when the special session convened they could fool the President and the people into believing that they were keeping the pledge to reduce the tariff. Briefly, the Old Guard scheme was this: They would actually reduce the *rate* of duty on an import, but at the same time so change the *classification* of the merchandise as to increase the total amount of duty to be paid. A Standpat Congressman confidentially explained it with the following example.

> You take a set of dishes for instance that under the present law pays sixty per cent duty, and is so classed under the administrative clauses as to be valued at ten dollars. That would be six dollar duty. We will reduce the rate to forty per cent, and if the classification were not changed that would make the duty only four dollars. But we'll fix that so it will be valued at from fifteen to twenty dollars. Then with a forty per cent duty, it will pay at least as much as it does now, and perhaps a couple of dollars more.[30]

Of course, in a tariff bill three hundred pages long, it could be expected that few would discover such carefully concealed jokers. Dolliver and his little band of Insurgents understood full well why Aldrich was in such haste to have the bill passed in the Senate without full discussion and were not fooled by his plea that quick action was necessary in order that business should not become "unsettled" because of the uncertainty over tariff legislation.

Even Taft was worried about the trend of developments in early April. He urged the Insurgents in the Senate to "criticize the bill, amend it, cut down the

duties — go after it hard," and promised that unless the bill "complies with
the platform, I will veto it." [31] The President also called Dolliver to the White
House and personally requested that he and Beveridge, then ill in the hospital,
get other Senators "to fight for a downward revision of the tariff." [32] It appears that Taft assured everybody he met that he was not afraid to veto the bill
if it did not suit him. His shrewd and observant aide commented, however:
"I think he is giving it out this way so as to frighten the high tariff people,
but the feeling is pretty well abroad that he will not dare to veto any bill. I
doubt myself whether he would have the grit to hand a veto to Congress."
Vice President Sherman, who had served long in the House, warned Taft to cut
off all patronage "so that the innocent can get to work on the guilty" to force
the passage of the reform bill to which the party had committed itself. The
President replied that he hated "to use patronage as a club" unless he had to.[33]

It is bootless to discuss Taft's ineptness or to rehash the question as to
whether he meant what Dolliver, La Follette, and Beveridge understood him to
mean when he asked them to fight to lower the rates proposed and implied his
willingness to use the veto if necessary. These men, as well as Clapp, Cummins,
and Bristow, would undoubtedly have pursued the course they did even had
they known from the outset that the President lacked the courage to keep his
pledges and would desert them. Indeed, Dolliver had already told La Follette
and others: "I am going to judgment in the next twenty years, and I am going
so that I can look my Maker in the face. I do not have to stay in public life.
I can take my books, my wife and children, and if I am dismissed from the
service for following my convictions, I will go out to my farm and stay there
until the call comes." [34]

When Aldrich introduced the tariff measure in mid-April, he did not submit
the customary written report explaining the amendments to the House bill made
by his committee. He hoped these would be accepted without question, and he
demanded prompt action by the Senate. Dolliver immediately requested that
certain items be passed over during the first reading in order that further consideration could be given to them. Aldrich benignly replied: "I am perfectly
certain that the Senator from Iowa, when he gets the facts before him, will
accept the action of the Committee." [35] If the Rhode Islander could have been
"perfectly certain" of anything at that moment, it was that Dolliver positively
intended to get "the facts before him" — and the people. Of the 733 paragraphs of the bill covered in its first reading, 217 were passed over for further
consideration at the demand of Insurgents and Democrats.[36]

There were three main objections to the bill, as Hechler has clearly shown.
These were: "Use of the protective principle to guarantee excessive profits on
manufactured goods, raising of the tariff upon raw materials that were also
natural resources, and lowering of the tariff upon raw materials that aided
trusts in gaining greater profits." Aldrich frankly preferred a tariff designed

primarily to benefit the manufacturers of the East who desired high duties on finished products and low rates on raw materials. His "system was to fashion a tariff" which would benefit the manufacturers of New England, the owners of timber lands, the mineowners and cattle herders of the West, the fruitgrowers, lumber and sugar interests of the South, and the steel, iron, and coal magnates of Pennsylvania, Ohio, and West Virginia. He cared nothing for the consuming masses. "I ask who are the consumers? Is there any class except a very limited one that consumes and does not produce? And why are they entitled to greater consideration?" A Senator capable of asking such a question was naturally unable to understand the Insurgents who were trying to defend the consumer and were not asking for "greater consideration for any one group, but for a better balance in the entire protective system, an ending of the excessive favors to specific classes, and a guarantee that prices of finished products would be within the reach of more people."[37] It need hardly be stated that Dolliver and his Insurgents were protectionists, not free-traders. Their aim was a fair deal for the masses without injustice to any industry having a legitimate need for protection against destructive competition from imports.

In order to hasten passage and to make adequate study of the measure as difficult as possible, Aldrich arranged for the Senate to hold sessions lasting from 10 A. M. until 11 P. M. The Insurgents divided among themselves the work of mastering the various schedules of the bill. Dolliver specialized on cotton, "Schedule I," and also mastered the wool schedule, "K," which was assigned to La Follette. Bristow took the lead and sugar duties; Cummins was responsible for metals and glass. Beveridge, still recuperating, and Clapp had no special assignments, but helped wherever needed.[38]

The debate began in earnest on April 22, with a blasting attack upon the whole bill by La Follette and a scathing general denunciation of the textile schedules by Dolliver, who also made biting comments about the principles which had dictated the writing of the measure. Aldrich, apparently taken by surprise, could only make the lame reply that Dolliver was indulging in Democratic propaganda and was departing from the course always set for true Republicans by the late Senator Allison. With incredible impudence the majority leader asked: "Where did we ever make the statement that we would revise the tariff downward?"[39] This slip of the tongue exposed the hypocrisy of those Standpatters who had been arguing and were later to argue that the Payne-Aldrich bill was a revision downward instead of upward.

The opening attack led by La Follette and Dolliver and supported by Beveridge, Knute Nelson of Minnesota, and Coe Crawford of South Dakota, made a profound impression upon the country. Dolliver received a flood of correspondence commending his stand and urging him to fight on. Aldrich's implication that no statement pledging lower rates existed precipitated an argument, in and outside of the Senate, only slightly less important than the main debate.

The Insurgents and their journalist allies resurrected Taft's speech accepting the Republican nomination, wherein he used the words "a revision which shall reduce excessive rates." The President's inaugural address was quoted also, as were his campaign speeches in which he said "the tariff . . . should be reduced" and pledged "that if the party is given the mandate of power in November, it will perform its promises in good faith."[40] Dolliver and Beveridge, having done more than any men in the Senate in campaigning for Taft, reviewed their own speeches. Frank B. Kellogg provided Dolliver useful evidence on the intention of the platform committee in 1908:

> I was on the sub-committee which drew the platform, and all this talk about the party does not stand pledged to revision downward is absurd. No apostle of protection thought of claiming there should be revision upwards. Everyone admitted that the time had come when there must be a reasonable reduction in many of the rates. . . . Unless we keep the pledges we have made the country we might as well fold up our political tent.[41]

Dolliver made one of the briefest and most devastating answers to the Old Guard when he observed that "Congress was not called into session to increase the tariff — there was not a voice raised on that proposition. It certainly was not called . . . to let the tariff stand exactly as it did, for an extraordinary session was not necessary for that purpose!" This facet of the great debate was pointless, of course, except that it exposed such Senators as Henry Cabot Lodge, Nelson Aldrich, Eugene Hale, and Weldon B. Heyburn as politicians willing to win votes with party promises they had no intention of honoring.[42] Taft's failure to speak out on this subject led many to suppose that he was of the same stripe and helped convince the voters that the Republican party could not be trusted to reform the tariff.

From late April through July the Insurgents waged a spectacular battle for reduction. These Republican Senators made "a more thorough attack on the high tariff than Democrats had ever made" — with very little aid from the Democrats.[43] Senator Beveridge later described the magnitude of the task:

> I sometimes wonder if the people know just what it meant to men like Dolliver and those others who fought the good fight to engage in that struggle. The tariff fight lasted for months. The great majority of both parties in the Senate did little work. The progressive Republican Senators had to do all the fighting. This meant from the physical viewpoint, that we had to sit in the stifling heat of the Senate chamber for long hours every day watching, debating, fighting. The watchful few who wanted the bill put through right or wrong always were on hand and relieved each other. . . . At night, while most of the others took their amusements and their rest, Dolliver and the men who stood with him had to go to their offices or to their homes to study until two or three o'clock in the morning to be ready for the conflict they

had planned out. . . . The strain told on Dolliver more than anyone else.

From the other viewpoint it meant ostracism, contempt, sneers, insults, and every form of abuse. . . . Our political and personal friends told us that we were making terrible political and personal mistakes. The leaders of the opposition party assailed us. All this had its physical effect as well as mental and moral effect. But the fight went on, and in the fight no man was braver, no man so effective as Senator Dolliver.[44]

After his April 22 speech a veiled threat was sent Dolliver, hinting that if he persisted in attacking the textile schedules, the Finance Committee would overwhelm him with a flood of statistics and make a fool of him in the eyes of the public. Dolliver secured the aid of H. D. Tichenor of the New York Produce Exchange, who, like his father, Colonel George Tichenor, an adviser of the Ways and Means Committee in 1896-1897, was a tariff expert. With the help of Tichenor and other specialists employed at his expense, Dolliver worked day and night to master every paragraph and to search out every joker in Schedules I and K which would result in increasing the duties on cotton and woolen imports. Ida Tarbell wrote that "the wool schedule is one of the most difficult in our tariff laws to understand and to explain" and "Schedule I, as the cotton schedule is known, is one of first importance." Nevertheless, within two weeks Dolliver was prepared to launch the first of his three major speeches on the textile schedules. By May 2 the New York *Tribune* was speculating with awe as to what would happen "when Dolliver opened fire."[45]

What has been aptly called "Dolliver's intellectual sledgehammer" descended on the tariff bill in a brilliant analytical address, some seven or eight hours long, delivered on May 4 and 5.[46] He began by replying to the Aldrich claim that he was yielding to pressure in Iowa to stand for more moderate duties. "The fact is, Mr. President, that I am no recent convert to moderate duties for any reason, of any sort." Dolliver recalled his 1902 remarks to the Iowa General Assembly when accepting his first election to the Senate, quoted those remarks in full, pointed out that he was fighting in 1909, "at the first opportunity," for exactly what he stood for in 1902. "I am here . . . not for the purpose of winning the favor of the men and women of Iowa, for I enjoy that now, but for the purpose of fulfilling my agreement made on the occasion of my election to the Senate." Turning to Aldrich, Dolliver spoke pointedly of feeling a duty

> . . . to the public and especially to the party which has honored me with its good will for nearly a quarter of a century. . . .
> If in times past I took, without disturbing the peace, every act of the party, it was because I loved it; because the young men of that day found it a good deal easier to idealize it than they sometimes find it now. . . . If it is a reproach that I have felt it incumbent upon me

to re-examine, with a judgment, I trust, somewhat more mature, the
tariff act of 1890, for which I voted, or the act of seven years later,
which bears the name of dear old Governor Dingley, under whom I
served on the Committee on Ways and Means of the House, I shall
try to carry the reproach as cheerfully as possible. . . . If the Senator from Rhode Island intended to humiliate me by the intimation
that my course in these matters is dictated by political conditions at
home, he unintentionally pays me a compliment which I sincerely appreciate, because this Nation has entered upon a new era of direct
responsibility on the part of Presidents and Congresses alike to that
enlightened public opinion which ought to be the real Government of
the United States.[47]

Aldrich was growing restless. He was not accustomed to such remarks being directed at him by anyone. His fury increased as Dolliver recalled that
"the duty of this Congress is to reduce the margin of protection provided in the
Dingley rates." As for the cotton schedule, the Iowan asserted that in 1897
Governor Dingley himself had deprecated "any increase in the cotton schedule
because in his judgment the tendency of the rates ought to be down instead of
up," and he quoted a letter from Dingley to prove his point. As Dolliver began
his analysis of the textile schedules, he stated that he could comment adversely
upon them without impeaching the abilities of the Senator from Rhode Island,
since Aldrich had already told the Senate that the amendments offered were
not the work of the Finance Committee but of customs experts from New York,
men who, as Dolliver observed, had never been elected to the United States
Senate. Dolliver thought it a "very curious proceedings" to discover that

. . . this schedule was not the product of the genius of the man who
has been reputed in the mythology of our public life as the greatest
living expert on the technicalities of cotton manufacture, but that
when the Senator from Rhode Island was confronted by the task set
before him by his constituents of raising the table of these rates, without touching them, he turned the matter over to the general appraiser's office in New York.

Dolliver somewhat overstated the case as to what Aldrich had said but not
as to what had been done. Aldrich was so incensed that he interrupted to object to "a statement which has no foundation in fact whatsoever." Senator
Elmer J. Burkett of Nebraska handed Dolliver the *Congressional Record*, and
the "War Eagle" read to the Senate quotations from statements by Aldrich and
Senator Frank P. Flint proving that there was adequate "foundation in fact"
for his own remark just denied by the majority leader. When Aldrich repeated
a former charge that Dolliver was "simply reiterating to-day the Democratic
claims which have been current in this country for a generation," Dolliver replied, "If they tell the truth, why should they not be current?" There being no
answer to this, Aldrich sat down and Senator Smoot, the Utah Mormon, entered
the fray for the Standpatters.

Smoot desired to know whether Dolliver was aware of the origin of Schedule K. Naturally, Dolliver knew that in the beginning, half a century before, the manufacturers and woolgrowers had joined in getting Eastern and Western members of Congress to give them the protection they wanted. Hence, he amused the Senate and the people by answering that "the shepherd's crook and the weaver's distaff were joined together in the joyous wedlock which no man has been able to put asunder. . . . There was a wedding feast and I do not think people ought to blame the Democratic party so much about it." Senator Smoot retired from the combat for the moment. Senator Francis E. Warren, a sheepraiser from Wyoming, next attempted to squelch Dolliver by entangling him in a technical discussion. Having prepared himself for such eventuality, Dolliver quoted exact definitions and statistics and remarked, amid the laughter of his audience, "I hope the Senator will not become elementary with me. I have spent weeks in studying every subject relating to the production of wool, from the birth of lambs to the manufacture of cloth, and I will not ask anybody to instruct me on details."

For hours Aldrich, Smoot, and Warren constantly attempted by repeated interruptions to confuse Dolliver. He seemed to be speaking extemporaneously, and they thought he would founder in the welter of fractions, technicalities, "tops and noils" of the textile schedules. But to no avail did they harass the Iowa statesman. He pursued his course unperturbed and rested his argument on the coldly factual data which he had mastered by poring over statistics and technical treatises, visiting mills, importing houses, and retail shops, and listening to his own expert aides. Dolliver's aim was to show that the wool schedule should be lowered from the existing rates and that the cotton schedule, which the new bill increased, should be kept as it was under the Dingley Act, but simplified to apply only to cotton. Moreover, he desired to reveal how absurd and unfair many provisions of the tariff were. Furniture, for example, made largely of heavy wood but with a covering of silk containing a few threads of wool would be appraised under the excessive rates of the wool schedule. Since "the rate of the wool duty depends upon the value per pound" the appraiser must charge the wool duty on a 200-pound sofa containing a few threads of wool — forty-four cents a pound plus 55 per cent of the invoice value. Dolliver demonstrated that rubber boots with woolen linings were assessed not at the 30 per cent rate for manufactured rubber, but at the rate of "44 cents a pound and 60 per cent of ad valorem as wearing apparel composed in whole or in part of wool."

The nonplussed Aldrich interrupted again:

> Mr. Aldrich: Mr. President, rubber boots are cheaper in the United States than in any other country in the world.
> Mr. Dolliver: Then why is there an increase from 30 to 35 per cent on manufactures of rubber. . . . If they are cheaper in the

United States than anywhere else, I intend to move to put them on the free list.

Mr. Aldrich: There are many other manufactures of rubber besides rubber boots.

Mr. Dolliver: I will single out boots and move to put them on the free list. I am on the side of the citizens who sometimes have to walk in the mud to the polls to vote the Republican ticket in Iowa.

Mr. Aldrich: We have automobile tires made of rubber — a great quantity of them.

Mr. Dolliver: It would not require very much sagacity to separate an automobile tire from an ordinary gum boot. Besides automobile tires seem to be down in this bill in the metal schedule at 45 per cent.

. . .

Mr. Aldrich: The Senate committee on the woolen schedule followed precisely the act of 1897 in every word; they have not changed it.

Mr. Dolliver: This is exactly what I am complaining about.

So it went, hour after hour. At one point Dolliver asked Aldrich: "Do you dispute the truth of what I say about these things?" Aldrich, battered and weary, replied: "I do not." "Then," observed Dolliver, "you ought not to attack men of character who have been sitting up nights with me." When Aldrich accused Dolliver of wishing to destroy the tariff system, Dolliver denied it. He proposed that the Senate adopt the woolen schedule of 1888 written by Aldrich and Allison, one which "commanded every Republican vote in the Senate, and won the presidential campaign of 1888." That 1888 bill, said Dolliver, "reduced the woolen schedule more radically than I propose to do now."

When he turned to the cotton schedule, Dolliver asked why the Senate Finance Committee had increased the rates when the cotton manufacturers of the nation had advised the House Ways and Means Committee not to advance them. "Do I speak the truth?" he prodded Aldrich. That gentleman replied: "Mr. President, I have no knowledge whatever of anything that transpired before the Committee on Ways and Means. I have never read the hearing before that body. I have no knowledge or idea about any statement that was made before that committee." This amazing statement was certainly a self-damning admission from the man largely responsible for framing the measure before the Senate. Dolliver merely commented that if such were the case, Aldrich was in no position "to belittle the honest efforts that I have made to get at the truth of these matters, for I have thought it my duty to read these hearings."

Then, as the day wore on, and during the following day, Dolliver proceeded to show how by changing the classifications of grades of cotton goods, the Payne-Aldrich bill had effected hidden increases in the tariff in almost every category. He brought in samples of cloth which he had taken to the custom house to have appraised under both the new and old schedules and quoted the

THE GENTLEMAN FROM IOWA RISES TO REMARK

Des Moines *Register*, February 23, 1910

Des Moines *Register*, June 3, 1909

rates assessed to prove his contention as to raises. He had the provisions of certain paragraphs printed in parallel columns, showing what lobbyists had requested, what the Ways and Means Committee had recommended, what the House bill contained, and what the Senate committee had presented to the Senate. He did this to indicate how certain interested parties had undertaken "in a covert way" to raise the existing duties "substantially above the Dingley rates of 1897."

On the second day of his speech, considered by some the greatest ever delivered in the Senate, the "scholar in politics," Lodge of Massachusetts, undertook to cross swords with Dolliver. Lodge, one of those who said that the party was not committed to downward revision, had joined Aldrich in supporting the fiction that the cotton rates had not been increased. The exchange between Dolliver and Lodge on May 5 merits quotation in brief. Dolliver, speaking of Lodge's contentions, said:

> After my honored friend from Rhode Island gets the Senate thoroughly satisfied that no raises have been made in these rates, I want him to explain and have his colleague explain how it happens that one of our wisest men, who mixes in one character all the graces of the student and the scholar and all the skill of the American statesman— that the first thing he did was to send for the reporter of the Boston Herald to tell the people of New England . . . what great victories had been won and what a splendid showing had been made for the cotton manufacturers [by the Finance Committee]. . . . Said the Senator from Massachusetts: "The cotton schedule, as amended by the Senate committee is of great value to Massachusetts industries."
>
> How did it get to be of great value to Massachusetts? It certainly did not get that great value by being left as Dingley left it, because it had that value to start with. . . . [Lodge] said: "the ad valorem rate on cotton has been increased. . . . The Senate committee has increased the number of classes carrying specific duties, and there can be no doubt that if this arrangement is accepted by the House it will be of enormous value to our great textile industries."

Lodge arose to state that he had been misquoted by the newspapers.

> Mr. Lodge: I said the average ad valorem rate had not been increased.
> Mr. Dolliver: Then you were mistaken in stating that, as I have just demonstrated to the Senate?
> Mr. Lodge: I think not.
> Mr. Dolliver: The ad valorems had only hit Governor Dingley's ad valorems in two cases, and outside of those two cases . . . every ad valorem has been increased. If the Senator did not state that to the Boston newspapers, he omitted a very important part of his duty. [Laughter.]

After pointing out many instances in the cotton schedule which provided for the assessing of cumulative duties greatly increasing the rates on certain cloths,

Dolliver concluded by proposing that a tariff commission be established to deal with future revisions. "I want an end to the scandals that have already corrupted American politics incident to the management of great industrial and financial questions as a mere adjunct of political agitation in the United States," he thundered.

> The protective tariff doctrine is sound. It fails only through the inequality with which it is applied to our affairs. It fails only when avarice and greed, anxious to make more money, have such influence with Congress as to rewrite our tariff laws, not in the interest of the unnumbered millions of our people, but in the narrow, naked, personal interest of a few men scattered here and there in various sections of our beloved country.

By the end of Dolliver's speech the Old Guard realized that there would be no quick passage of the bill. Aldrich and his henchmen had been unable to defend the action of the Finance Committee. The leader of the Senate had fumbled. Having admitted the truth of Dolliver's charges, Aldrich, by accusing the Iowan of peddling Democratic propaganda, revealed that he had no specific answer to the criticism and the best he could do was to say that the attack on the cotton and woolen schedules was an assault upon the "very citadel of protection."

The Chicago *Tribune* commented:

> Senator Dolliver's effort is recognized as much the strongest speech delivered during the present debate and it seems to have more influence because it comes from an avowed protectionist, who sat with Governor Dingley in the Ways and Means Committee when the present tariff law was framed and whose acquaintance with the technicalities of the subject is not surpassed by that of any other man, not excepting even the great Senator Aldrich.[48]

An Iowa Standpat paper stated:

> Senator Dolliver's speech on the new tariff bill . . . has been the surprise of the extra session. . . . No other man has said so much, said it so well, or to such an effect. The speech is referred to by those who heard it as the most eloquent delivered in either house of Congress in many years and is the most striking speech ever delivered by the Iowa Senator. . . . Dolliver has placed himself before the country as the indomitable representative of the people themselves.[49]

An Ohio correspondent recorded his observations of the scene in the Senate chamber on May 4 and 5:

> There was no sparring for openings. Dolliver waded right in. . . . He did what no man had dared to do; he shook his fist full in the face of the Rhode Islander. That face went white with anger and indignation and the muscles of the jaw stood out hard and tightly set, as Dolliver drove home his blows. . . .

It was a battle between two great champions: Dolliver the matchless orator, Aldrich the statistician. It was not a David and Goliath
affair, for each was a Goliath in his way. But Dolliver had this advantage — he had mastered the statistics as well as Aldrich, but Aldrich could not meet him on a similar basis in Dolliver's own realm of
oratory.[50]

The next day, May 6, Cummins delivered his first major speech in the Senate. He arraigned the steel trust, and demanded that iron ore be placed on the
free list. The same Ohio newsman wrote an interesting comparison of the
Dolliver and Cummins speeches:

> There was this difference between Dolliver and Cummins — the
> former was always prepared to go into details and the latter confined
> himself to glittering generalities. . . . The amusing side of things
> stuck out prominently in Dolliver's view and he hung his retorts
> thereon whenever opportunity offered. . . . Those who interrupted
> him with obviously hostile intent withdrew quickly to apply hartshorn
> to their smarts. Cummins was not so caustic. Neither was he as effec-
> tive as Dolliver proved himself to be. Dolliver fortified himself
> against every emergency. He knew that the minds of men of deep
> and analytical turn would busy themselves to destroy the fabric of
> his argument. . . . Those who endeavored, early in the debate to
> confound him soon gave up the effort. Cummins showed his weak-
> ness in his failure to learn the facts before he ventured forth on the
> steel trust and the schedules which he denounced as excessive. When
> Aldrich, Smoot, Scott, and Depew pressed him for facts and figures
> on the costs, he could not answer . . . and thus his position was
> greatly weakened.[51]

Dolliver spoke briefly on May 11, this time advocating the retention of duties
on earthenware and stoneware and emphasizing that he was a protectionist
wherever a tariff was needed to preserve an American industry.[52] Thus, "with
the aid of Dolliver, the Republican Party became reunited for a day" as only
three Insurgents voted against amendments relating to glass and china. For
almost a week it looked as if the Insurgents had succeeded in their aim, for
Aldrich began to offer reductions on several items such as window glass, scrap
iron, iron ore, hides, and lumber. These were not imports of major importance,
and most Westerners, including Dolliver, were opposed to lower duties on hides
and lumber on the grounds that only the shoe manufacturers and the lumber
trust would benefit.[53]

The harmony did not last. The Old Guard had no intention of yielding on
any matter of importance such as the textile schedules, and the Insurgents
could not be induced to abandon their principles for such sops as lowered
duties on Christmas tree decorations and knitting needles. Furthermore, by the
end of May the Insurgents were losing faith in Taft. According to Beveridge,
Dolliver came to him one day, "his face as white as that of a dead man," to

report that Taft had turned against the Insurgents and had said he "would not have anything to do with such an irresponsible set of fellows." To test this rumor, Beveridge made a speech on May 25, in which he quoted Taft's campaign speeches interpreting the platform as a pledge to revise the tariff downward. The following day the Hoosier orator called at the White House, where the President received him "in the coldest atmosphere" he had ever "encountered in politics." On May 27 Bristow wrote: "Confidentially, we have received no support whatever in this tremendous fight we have made from the White House. We can't understand it." [54]

By the beginning of June all thoughts of conciliation were cast aside. On the 2nd, 3rd, and 4th, La Follette delivered a great address during which he showed that increases in duties on cotton affected $10,000,000 in imports and the decreases only $45,000. His figures were based on a report furnished him on the orders of Taft. Aldrich attempted an answer on the night of June 4, defending the Finance Committee's amendments and demanding an immediate vote on the bill.

Dolliver, "working like a galley slave day and night . . . was now prepared for a smashing attack upon the cotton schedule." When he faced the Senate on June 5, in the "most magnificent oration of his life," he had mastered every detail of his subject, and his speech was in the nature of a reply to Aldrich's of the preceding evening.[55]

As was the case just one month previously, Dolliver had hardly begun to speak before Aldrich interrupted him. After a sharp exchange of remarks, Aldrich arose and began to walk out of the chamber. Noticing this, Dolliver said: "I hope the Senator from Rhode Island will remain here for a few minutes." Aldrich replied: "I am engaged elsewhere." Raising his voice, Dolliver retorted:

> I want to engage you here, or make it understood that you propose to assault the criticisms made here by me and a few associated with me without giving me the opportunity to which I am entitled in debate. The Senator will not turn his back upon what I have to say here without taking the moral consequences which would naturally arise in the mind of a man anxious to get the facts in this case.

The majority leader returned to his seat.

There were a few interruptions, most of them by Smoot, or by the friendly Beveridge and Tillman. Dolliver shattered the Standpat argument that the cotton schedule had not been increased, citing importers, merchants, textile manufacturers, general appraisers, and even the conflicting statements of Senators like Lodge and Smoot to prove his contention that the opposite was true. Aldrich sneaked out while Dolliver's back was turned, and in time only one member of the Finance Committee remained on the floor. Otherwise, the chamber and galleries were crowded. Beveridge arose to suggest that some of the committee ought to be present, inasmuch as Dolliver was specifically and with brutal frankness exposing what they had done. Dolliver's reply became famous: "I have intimated several times my desire to have the committee here . . . and I will now say publicly I do not give 2 cents a square yard and 5 per cent cumulative ad valorem whether the committee is here or not."

As he pleaded for the Senate to vote against the amendments offered by the Finance Committee, Dolliver told his colleagues:

> Our controversy, then, has descended to this — not whether the tariff ought to be raised, not whether it ought to be lowered, but what has actually been done to this bill. . . . I want to tell you gentlemen, however, it will be a great deal better for you to go to your constituents and tell them that you voted to increase these duties than for you to go to your constituents and tell them that these duties have not been increased. A man can defend himself for increasing a duty, but he will not be able to defend himself against the charge of not knowing what he was about. . . . There is one thing the American people do not like. They often submit with patience to being robbed, but no American community is willing to be flimflammed, and it is a good deal easier to defend a vote increasing a duty than it is to defend a proposition which claims that a rate has not been increased, when, in point of fact it has been.

There was humor mingled with the undercurrent of righteous wrath of this unusual address. Perhaps nothing provoked more laughter than Dolliver's description of Lodge and Smoot juggling statistics and

> . . . so jumbling their figures and mystifying themselves and everybody who tried to listen to them. . . . Curious companions these — the great statesman of Massachusetts and the great theologian of the Rocky Mountains, friends and partners in this curious business, juggling the tables, manipulating the figures, and at length blowing out the gas and going to bed together.

In response to an observation by Senator Tillman that there seemed to be two different Dingley laws, Dolliver quipped: "We have two Dingley laws, one existing on the statute books and one in the imagination of the Senator from Rhode Island."

Still loyal to the doctrine of protection, Dolliver concluded:

> I am trying to preserve the tariff laws of the United States. . . . I say to you gentlemen you can not do a thing so harmful to the protective system, so injurious to this industry, as to make it the storm center of an agitation which will not cease when you have incorporated these amendments in the bill notwithstanding the showing of facts that has been made on the floor of the Senate.[56]

Senator Cummins described Dolliver's June 5 speech in the words of Daniel Webster: "I only had to reach out my hand and grasp the thunderbolts as they went smoking by." Ida Tarbell called it "an analysis which must stand as a model of the kind of criticism which every schedule in the tariff bill needs from *Protectionists*." According to another writer, when Dolliver "had finished, there was not a senator or a correspondent in the gallery who did not know that he had heard one of the most memorable orations ever heard in the American Senate; and the cotton schedule was a stench in the nostrils of a nation."[57]

After a brilliant speech by Beveridge on June 7, Aldrich attempted to read the Insurgents out of the party. "I have heard remarks of that kind before," said the majority leader, "rarely from Republicans, never from protectionists." Cummins, who had had much experience with Iowa Standpatters' attempts to put him beyond the pale, told the Senate that no man could read him out of the party and that party loyalty consisted of loyalty to principles rather than to the whim of certain leaders.[58]

Dolliver then came forward with his promised amendment to remove rubber boots and other rubber goods from the textile schedule. To the Insurgents' surprise, Aldrich arose to announce his acceptance of the amendment.[59] He apparently realized that he needed to give Schedule I "a little better window-dressing before the party had to go to its defense at the polls."[60] If Aldrich thought to appease Dolliver, he was to be sorely disappointed, for on the following day the Iowan began a five-hour arraignment of the woolen schedule. Aldrich regarded this as "the crucial schedule in this bill" and said that "if by insidious or any other means [Dolliver] can induce the Senate to break down this schedule, that is the end of protection, for the present anyway in this country." This was nonsense, of course, indicating merely the incapacity of the Old Guard to present a respectable intellectual defense of this "very citadel of protection."

Ida Tarbell said of Dolliver's speech on the woolen schedule:

> He went onto the floor of the senate without a manuscript and literally played with Schedule K, and incidentally also with Senator Aldrich and several other stand-patters whose long experience in juggling with untruths had destroyed their agility in handling truths. When he had finished his clean, competent dissection, Schedule K lay before the Senate a law without principles or morals.[61]

Senator Warren of Wyoming was Dolliver's chief antagonist on this occasion. At one point they carried on a colloquy for more than an hour, standing two feet apart, facing each other, and frequently gesticulating with vigor. It was during this exchange that Dolliver called public attention to Warren's immense holdings of sheep in a phrase which, "bringing smiles to millions of lips, did more to damn the tariff than tons of statistics." According to Dolliver, Warren was "the greatest shepherd since Abraham."[62]

Gradually the tariff battle dragged to its close. The last extensive analysis of a single schedule was a speech of four and a half hours by Beveridge on June 24, exposing the tobacco trust and its influence on the tariff.[63] The Standpatters did not bother to reply. They no longer needed to waste energy answering Insurgent oratory in the heat of the summer, for they had the votes to pass their bill and apparently feared no presidential veto.

How did they get the votes? They had discovered that the Democrats and about fifteen Republican allies of the Insurgents were going to vote to restore an income tax provision struck out of the House bill. Aldrich and his followers were bitterly opposed to the income tax but did not have the votes to kill it. They appealed to Taft to help them break up the alliance worked out by Cummins and the Democratic leader, Joe Bailey, to attach an income tax amendment to the tariff bill. Taft proposed a tax on the earnings of corporations. Aldrich and the reactionaries naturally opposed this, since it would "give a degree of publicity to the business of all corporations." However, they realized that unless something were done the Insurgent-Democratic combination would beat them. Aldrich, therefore, agreed to support the corporation tax and a joint resolution proposing a constitutional amendment providing for an income tax.

Taft sent a message requesting the corporation tax as an amendment to the tariff bill and pointing out the danger of enacting an income tax law which the Supreme Court had already once voided. Then he began to work on the Republicans who had allied themselves with the Insurgents — men who were more interested in the tax than in the tariff — to get them to abandon the arrangement with the Democrats. Doubtless he and Aldrich both had some pleasant chats with their friend Bailey, a Texas conservative, whose relations with Aldrich had long been good and whom Taft had offered to appoint to the Supreme Court. The Senate voted to include the corporation tax in the tariff bill and in so doing made that bill acceptable to several Republicans. Aldrich and his men voted for the corporation tax as a means of defeating the income tax and of winning votes for their tariff bill, because they knew that the corporation tax could easily be passed on to the consumer. All Senators voted for the joint resolution for the income tax amendment to the Constitution — the Democrats and Insurgents because they believed in it as the fairest form of taxation, the Standpatters because it was a part of the "deal" Aldrich had agreed to and because they hoped to defeat ratification in the future.[64]

The Insurgents deserved notice for forcing the Old Guard into a position which made possible the resolution for the income tax amendment, but they claimed little credit for it inasmuch as they knew that this had been achieved only through a maneuver which cost them vitally needed votes to reform the tariff. Dolliver favored the income tax and voted for the joint resolution. He, as well as Borah, Bristow, Clapp, Cummins, and La Follette voted against the corporation tax, however, as a matter of principle. They believed it was discriminatory since it left individual businesses and copartnerships untaxed, taxed stockholders but not bondholders, and because, as Senator Bristow phrased it, they "could not consent to be switched about to please Mr. Aldrich, even by the President."[65]

Beveridge and Dolliver both insisted that a tariff commission should be provided in order that in the future the tariff could be revised "scientifically" instead of through the log-rolling process. But, as H. D. Tichenor predicted in a letter to Dolliver, Aldrich "and the clique he represents will never permit the creation of any real tariff commission, if they can prevent it as they know that a careful investigation of our textile industries of New England will prove that they are being excessively protected." Subsequent events proved the truth of this, for even the weak commission which the Insurgents provided for in the bill was emasculated by the conference committee.[66]

The vote in the Senate on the Payne-Aldrich bill came on July 8. The majority leader, in a final plea, attempted to make the vote a test of party regularity with the plain implication that if any Republican voted against it, he would be read out of the party. Since May there had been little question but that Dolliver, La Follette, and Bristow would vote against the bill. At the end, the bill passed 45 to 34, but ten Insurgents stuck by their colors and voted nay: Beveridge of Indiana, Bristow of Kansas, Brown and Burkett of Nebraska, Clapp of Minnesota, Crawford of South Dakota, Cummins and Dolliver of Iowa, La Follette of Wisconsin, and Nelson of Minnesota.[67]

Speaker Cannon and Senator Aldrich packed the conference committee with Standpatters. For four weeks the conferees attempted to agree upon the final report on the bill — actually the House and Senate versions were so different that these gentlemen in reality had to combine two "totally different bills" into their final version. When the conference report was submitted to the House, Dolliver and five of his Senate colleagues appeared on the floor of the House and pointed out to numerous Representatives that the report was full of "jokers" and did not fulfill party promises for downward revision. Nevertheless, the Cannon machine, aided by President Taft, forced the House to accept the report — although by the uncomfortably close vote of 191 to 186.[68]

Meanwhile, Taft tried to win the Insurgents to support the conference report in the Senate. He invited some of them to breakfast and attempted to sell them the party line that the bill as it came from the conference committee was a redemption of the party pledges. Dolliver was both disgusted and amused at the bungling President. This was the Taft who had wanted Dolliver to be his running mate, the Taft who had asked him to second his nomination for the presidency, the Taft for whom he had stumped the nation, the Taft who had appealed to him in March to fight for downward revision and at the same time had written "I have better use for my time than spending it with such a blatant demagogue as either Dolliver or Cummins," the Taft who talked of using the veto but rode "in the cool of the evening" with Aldrich and Payne to plot the passage of the bill, the Taft who hated to use patronage against the Old Guard to get a decent bill but who used it against Insurgents to force passage of the conference report in the House, the Taft who after Dolliver's attack on Schedule K had written that Aldrich was "quite willing" to have the woolen duties reduced (despite Aldrich's repeated statements that that schedule was the very citadel of protection and must not be touched).[69] Yes, Dolliver went to breakfast and listened. He then stopped in to see La Follette. "Bob," he said, "I was invited up to the White House to a tariff breakfast." And then, as La Follette recalled, Dolliver paused and with a twinkle in his eye added, "The muskmelon he served was not very good."[70]

On August 1 the President wrote that the Senate Insurgents "will vote against the bill probably but I don't think they will make bitter speeches on the subject."[71] But he seems to have been worried about his own course of action. He talked with the ever-present Butt on the south portico of the White House late at night: "There is something about the atmosphere of this South Portico which challenges your thoughts for the past and brings to your mind the fact that every President, since Monroe at least, has come here when worried and from this spot has renewed his courage," Taft remarked. Then he and Butt went at midnight for a quiet ride. "We got into the motor and never spoke, and we rode for nearly an hour without a word," Butt recorded, "and stranger than all he never slept, and when I glanced at him to see if he were asleep, he was looking hard into the fleeting darkness ahead."[72]

Taft did not see the light, nor was his courage renewed. In the days immediately following, between August 1 and 5, seven Insurgent Senators arose in the Senate chamber to offer again unimpassioned statistical proof that the party pledges were not being fulfilled. The Standpatters kept quiet. Aldrich, reconciled that some Insurgents would vote against the report, attempted to make it appear that there was no split in the party and had arranged the list of speakers so that La Follette could not make an emotional speech just before the roll call.[73]

Dolliver upset the majority leader's strategy, however. He had written his wife on August 2: "This is Monday night, and we are in the midst of the final struggle on the tariff. I cannot on my conscience vote for it." She telegraphed him to "Vote against the report if you are the only one."[74] Tichenor advised him that "the Conference has agreed to a compromise of *most* of the *worst features* of the House and Senate Bills — instead of accepting the *best* of both bills. If this suits the President, they have him hypnotized. . . . You were right when you said 'It would be better to tell the people the truth than to flimflam them.' " Kenyon and Meservey both urged the Senator to oppose the report; only George Roberts, among Dolliver's intimates, felt that it would be better for him to stand by the President.[75]

Dolliver had never faltered in his determination not only to vote against but to make one more massive attack on the bill. His opportunity for a final effort to prevent party perfidy came on August 5. He denounced not merely the conference compromises but the methods by which the bill had been prepared and forced through both houses. Speaking of the sneers, ridicule, accusation, and disparagement with which the Old Guard Senators had met every suggestion that he, "a consistent protectionist," had offered, he asked: "What has been the sum of my offence? I asked the Senate to retain the Dingley law upon the cotton schedule and to reject an underhand attempt to raise it without anybody knowing it. I asked the Senate to open Schedule K . . . not to destroy its protective efficiency, but to equalize its burdens and to distribute its benefits fairly."

Again he provided tables of statistics prepared by experts of the customs service to show the effects of hidden increases. He printed in parallel columns the words of the bill in various stages to show that one increase of duties was rejected unanimously by the House, re-inserted by the Finance Committee, rejected by the Senate, and then re-inserted by the conference committee. "I can not support this measure, because I am opposed to the methods by which it was prepared," Dolliver asserted.

> What fills my mind with indignation is that we are duped with humbug and misrepresentation, whereas the American people are entitled to know the truth and to take whatever steps may be necessary to protect themselves against these excesses. . . . The figures which I presented were never disputed; the facts which I put into the *Record* can not be challenged; and the conclusion which I have reached is a conclusion shared by unnumbered millions of people who are just as indifferent as I am to the voice of the Majority of the Senate as now constituted. . . .
>
> Mr. President, the Republican party, if I understand its history, is a great deal larger than the schedules of a tariff law . . . it is ridiculous to . . . fix the party standing of its members by calling the roll upon the report of a conference committee. The Republican party is face to face, as in the days of its youth, with the elementary questions which concern justice and liberty.[76]

The historian of Insurgency wrote that "When Dolliver sat down, everyone realized that Insurgency was a living and a vital movement." The weary and aging Aldrich, displaying no longer the haughty superiority which had formerly characterized his actions, expressed regret that the important measure was not to receive the unanimous approval of Republicans and stated again that he regarded the issue as a test of party fealty.[77] The Senate then voted 47 to 31 to pass the Payne-Aldrich Act, and the special session came at last to an end. Among the 31 who voted "nay" were seven Insurgent Republicans — Dolliver, La Follette, Bristow, Beveridge, Clapp, Cummins, and Nelson.

On August 5, 1909, William Howard Taft affixed his signature to the bill, thereby sealing the doom of his party for some years to come. "President Taft," said Dolliver, "is an amiable man, completely surrounded by men who know exactly what they want." Mark Sullivan thought this "the most damaging sentence ever uttered by any of Taft's critics, a sentence whose aptness did more than anything else to crystallize the public impression about Taft."[78]

George Roberts had already expressed what has come to be history's verdict as to Dolliver: "I think your fight on this bill has been the greatest public service of your life."[79]

-XIX-

Broken Party, Broken Heart, 1910

Great men are plentiful in this country, but not as great as Dolliver.
Benjamin R. Tillman, 1910.

WHEN DOLLIVER returned to Fort Dodge after the final vote enacting the
Payne-Aldrich Tariff, fifteen thousand people assembled to do him homage and
to parade down Central Avenue, which was "ablaze with incandescent and arc
lights, the national colors displayed from every business house and home along
the route."[1] Never had quite such a demonstration been accorded him on a
previous homecoming, although he must have remembered fondly that first one,
just twenty-five years before, when he reached Fort Dodge after stumping the
East for Blaine. Fort Dodge had welcomed him home many times between 1884
and 1909, but there is something special about these two great outpourings of
affection and admiration. Each occasion signalled a magnificent personal triumph for the city's favorite son, but preceded a well-merited defeat for the
party he loved.

The Senator was badly in need of rest. He had overtaxed his strength during
the special session. In fact, his long and vigorous address of June 5 had caused
a lesion of the heart, a condition which was worsened by the constant strain of
the subsequent two months during which he ignored his physician's advice to
limit his speaking and to "slow down."[2] Thus for several weeks after reaching
his Iowa home, Dolliver relaxed and attempted to recuperate. In mid-September he wrote a delightful letter to Beveridge, also recovering from physical
exhaustion:

> Don't you worry about what is going on in the country. If we had
> had a direct line from the skies we could not have "done a better job"
> for ourselves than we did when we stood for our convictions against
> all comers including the big chief. The penalty for doing right exists
> only in the imagination of grafters and time servers. If we never see
> the inside of the senate chamber again, the last three months of your
> labors there will make your life notable and famous when biographies
> are written. . . . It is an incredible thing that as sensible a man as
> Taft should start out by tying the Aldrich millstone about his neck

265

and traveling like a peddler of damaged goods. "Leader of the Senate" — we will jar that myth in the next three years. Wait for results, my boy. We will see how the public will take to a tariff revision made by its intimate friend and certified by a total stranger.
. . .

> *We have got to fight.* They can't beat you in Indiana without beating *the party.* . . . We will all go in with the common weapons of truth and good sense and make a new era in national life. With Pinchot knocked out and Aldrich put in command I think you can hear a *lion* roar in East Africa. . . . I never saw so clearly my duty and yours, and our opportunity. I am in a happy frame of mind. I would give more for one more session in the old senate with the right to think for myself, speak my own thoughts and hit the big heads, than to have a guaranteed term of twenty years more *as a servant* of a syndicate of played out New England politicians.[3]

The letter was typical of the joyful, independent, battling Dolliver. It was filled with prophetic import — the assessment of the value history would place upon their Insurgency, the prediction that if the Old Guard defeated Beveridge (as they were to do in 1910), they would beat the party, the belief that Aldrich's leadership would soon be at an end (as it was by 1911), the insight into Roosevelt's reaction to the Pinchot affair, even the prayer for just "one more session in the old senate." The "new era in American life" was to come, too, but, while the Insurgents unquestionably helped pave the way, it was to be guided by Woodrow Wilson and later by a Roosevelt greater than Theodore.

Meanwhile, as Dolliver slowly regained his strength and the year moved down hill into autumn, the people began to react to the tariff revision in just the way the Insurgents had anticipated. It is merely of academic interest to argue whether the Payne-Aldrich Tariff increased or decreased rates. The point is that the people thought the rates were increased. The impartial judgment of Taussig, an expert on the subject, was that the new law "brought no essential change in our tariff system. It still left an extremely high scheme of rates. . . . The one change of appreciable importance was the abolition of the duty on hides." If Taussig's view had been universally known and accepted, the reaction of the people could scarcely have been any different from what it was. The Republican promise had been to revise the tariff downward; "no essential change" was hardly a satisfactory substitute. Furthermore, the abolition of the duty on hides was something the Insurgents of the West opposed. Far from appeasing Westerners, this item on the free list enraged them. It was an example of the very thing the West objected to — free raw materials desired by the Eastern manufacturers at the expense of the American farmer and cattle raiser. During the fight on the bill, for example, Dolliver's closest political advisers informed him that "no man from the Middle West can afford to vote for any bill that provides free hides let alone the other bad features."[4]

The Insurgents and many journalists did not agree that "no essential change" was made. From New York, H. D. Tichenor wrote Dolliver: "I note with increasing delight how nearly all the papers and periodicals uphold and commend your position in regard to the tariff . . . and there can be no doubt how most of the people feel about it."[5] Beveridge in New Hampshire heard and read similar expressions indicating that "the sentiment of the country" was with the Insurgents. Clapp in Minnesota, Bristow in Kansas, Cummins in Iowa, Borah in Idaho, and others discovered that the West was aroused.[6] Ret Clarkson, old and wise, put his finger on the causes of discontent when he wrote that the tariff not only was not lowered but was made "largely for New England and Pennsylvania interests, the people and the states who constitute a real majority in the nation were largely ignored."[7]

In the midst of this political turmoil the President, hearing that Insurgency was aflame in the West, decided to "get out and see the people and jolly them." Starting from Boston, where he publicly lavished praise on Aldrich, the President posed with his arm about the shoulders of Uncle Joe Cannon in Illinois, and allowed himself to be surrounded with Standpatters in every state he visited. If this were not enough, Taft proceeded to go to Winona, Minnesota, to make a speech in behalf of the reactionary Congressman James Tawney on September 17, 1909. In this unfortunate and ill-prepared address Taft challenged the Insurgents to stay in line or leave the party and spoke rather disparagingly of tariff reformers. The President adopted the Aldrich-Lodge line, with modifications in the direction of the literal truth, in stating: "Now the promise of the Republican platform was not to revise everything downward." He attempted, without success, to defend the cotton and other schedules, but he did admit that the wool rates were too high. The fatal words, perhaps, as his biographer thought, "the most damaging twenty-five words" ever uttered by a President, were: "On the whole, however, I am bound to say that I think the Payne bill is the best bill that the Republican party ever passed."[8]

H. D. Tichenor wrote Dolliver:

> I read the President's defense of the Payne-Aldrich Bill with a mingled feeling of disgust and delight. . . . He certainly made it a "cinch" for you to answer. While attempting to politically paddle the Progressives who voted against the Bill, he found *you* were right regarding the woolen schedule and also acknowledged (after all the denials of Aldrich and others) that the cotton schedule was "*revised upward.*" . . . So on the whole he sustained *your* views regarding those two most important schedules, covering more articles of wearing apparel and other necessities in which the majority of the people are interested than any other of the tariff schedules.[9]

When asked if he considered that Taft's comments on the Insurgent Senators were meant to read them out of the party, Dolliver replied: "It all depends on what you call the Republican party. It depends on whether the

Republican party consists of the People or a subcommittee of the Senate. If it is the latter, we can't be read out of the party for we were never in it."[10] The Winona address contributed greatly to the further alienation of the Insurgent Republicans, and Progressives generally (whether nominal Republicans or liberal Democrats), from the administration. During the tariff fight, Insurgency had been directed primarily against the leadership of the party in Congress. Henceforth, it was more and more evident that the Insurgents must also count the President as the ally of their enemies in Congress. Beveridge wrote Dolliver that Taft's speech in Minnesota had "raised a storm of dissent in the East." In the Midwest there was open talk of Roosevelt for 1912.[11]

On September 20 the President and his party, together with Senator Dolliver, Governor Carroll, and Iowa's Representatives in Congress, were breakfast guests of Senator and Mrs. Cummins in Des Moines. Afterwards Taft delivered a major address at the soldiers' monument south of the Capitol building. He praised the work of Dolliver in connection with the Hepburn Act of 1906 and the efforts of Cummins to secure railroad legislation in Iowa. Virtually ignoring the tariff dispute, Taft devoted his speech largely to the necessity for improving the Interstate Commerce and Antitrust Acts. He proposed the creation of a special court to hear appeals from the Commission in order to expedite litigation.[12]

Taft continued his junket to the Pacific coast and back through the South. He was properly received everywhere, but Archie Butt recorded that "there was some coldness discernible in the Middle West . . . due to the unpopularity of the tariff bill in that section." More picturesque, if less accurate, was a newsman's comments that Taft's trip in the Midwest was "a polar dash through a world of ice." Only the blindly unrealistic failed to understand that the split within the Republican party and the popular dissatisfaction with the administration were deepening as Taft's journey ended. Speaker Cannon had declared open war on the Insurgents, and in making up the committee assignments for the House, he demoted three Progressive-minded Congressmen from their posts as committee chairmen.[13]

When the Sixty-first Congress convened at noon on December 5, 1909, the prospects were for a long and tumultuous session. In both houses, Insurgency was growing and opponents of the old order were active and energetic. At the same time, the Standpat leaders were in a fighting mood, determined to give the rebels no quarter and to eliminate them if possible.[14]

The day Congress assembled, Ret Clarkson wrote Dolliver that he had been notified to terminate his duties as Surveyor of the Port of New York on January 1, 1910, although his term did not expire until April 18. Clarkson had been active in exposing the frauds in connection with weighing sugar imports and had made an exceptionally fine record in office. It was well known, however, that he was Dolliver's friend, and as the New York *Press* put it, "a rash young man rocks the boat — and some elderly conservative three miles away falls into the water."[15] Clarkson had not expected to be reappointed in April, nor did he need the position, but he and his friends were irritated that he should be pushed aside a few months before his term expired. Whether his dismissal resulted, as he thought, so that the Collector of the Port, William Loeb, would get the credit for completing the exposure of the sugar frauds, or, as some suggested, to appease the sugar trust, or merely as a petty slap at Dolliver is an unresolved question. Probably all were contributing factors, but Clarkson's treatment did not endear the Taft regime to the Iowa Insurgents.

On December 7 the Senate ordered Taft's Winona speech, as well as one by Speaker Cannon at Kansas City attacking the Insurgents, printed as Senate documents. One reason for this was that the Standpat faction in Iowa desired to flood the state with these addresses as a part of a campaign to gain control of the Republican convention in 1910 in order to endorse Taft, repudiate Dolliver and Cummins, and nominate an Old Guard candidate for Governor. The Hawkeye Senators and Insurgent Congressmen were already aware that the administration had decided to ignore their recommendations in matters of patronage. Dolliver called at the White House on the tenth to discuss various problems with the President but was informed by Fred Carpenter, Taft's secretary, that the President was too busy to see him. This tactless treatment was unfortunate, but worse followed a few days later. Taft agreed to see the Iowa delegation to discuss the proposal that he appoint Judge H. E. Deemer of Iowa to the Supreme Court. Before the Iowans arrived for the interview, however, the President let it be known that he would appoint Judge Horace H. Lurton to the post. By early January the Republican Congressional Campaign Committee publicly admitted that it was fighting "the principle of insurgency" and that it believed it to be within its province "to criticize and condemn those who oppose the administration and the acts of the party and those who aid and give comfort to such opponents."[16]

All of these incidents contributed to the conviction of the Insurgents of Iowa that Taft had joined forces with Aldrich and Cannon to punish those Republicans who had fought for the redemption of the party pledges of 1908 relative to tariff revision. This view was valid and was shared by one of Taft's closest associates, who wrote: "I feel that the Rhode Islander is the most sinister influence around the President. The President thinks he has captured Aldrich and can make him do anything he wants of him, but I fear it is the case of the wolf in sheep's clothing."[17]

The episode which most clearly dramatized the break between Taft and the

Rooseveltian Republicans was the famous Pinchot-Ballinger affair of 1909-1910. This controversy had begun during the early months of the new administration, when Chief Forester Gifford Pinchot, a close friend of Roosevelt, had accused Taft's Secretary of the Interior, Richard A. Ballinger, of failing to protect public water power sites and coal lands from "greedy" private exploitation. Taft, tending to support Ballinger, whom he had appointed to replace Secretary James R. Garfield, was giving the impression that Roosevelt's conservation program might be reversed.[18] This program was very dear to Dolliver, who had consistently supported it and had been especially active in behalf of the Forestry Service in the Roosevelt era.

The Pinchot-Ballinger affair came to a climax after Pinchot had encouraged Louis R. Glavis, an investigator in the Interior Department, to present a written report to the President accusing Ballinger of illegally aiding the delivery of rich coal lands in Alaska to the Guggenheim-Morgan interests. The insubordination of Glavis was soon followed by a public address by Pinchot charging Ballinger with being a virtual traitor to Roosevelt's conservation doctrines. The President authorized Ballinger to dismiss Glavis, and at the same time wrote Pinchot expressing appreciation for his services and hoping that he would not make Glavis' cause his own. Glavis published his version of the situation in *Collier's Weekly*, strongly implying that Ballinger was corrupt. Thus, the newspapers took up the case and stirred up the public. By the time Congress met there was widespread demand for a congressional investigation.[19]

On December 21 there was talk in Washington of a resolution to appoint a special committee composed of members of both houses to investigate the Pinchot-Ballinger controversy. It was predicted that Dolliver would be on the committee. The Des Moines *Register* reported that since "Senator Dolliver believed in conservation and in Pinchot" the latter would get "a square deal in the investigation" if the Iowa Senator were a member of the committee. The following day the President expressed approval of a congressional investigation, although he had previously been opposed to it.[20]

Inasmuch as the Old Guard Vice President was to appoint the Senate members of the committee, Dolliver had no illusion that he would be named. He, Pinchot, and others apparently thought that the investigation would turn into a routine suppression of opposition criticism, since they anticipated that Standpatters would dominate the committee. Dolliver, however, was the chairman of the Senate Committee on Agriculture and Forestry and in that capacity he suggested that Pinchot write a letter to him explaining the affairs of the Forestry Bureau. Pinchot conferred with his superior officer, "Tama Jim" Wilson, the perennial Secretary of Agriculture, and said he obtained Wilson's permission to write to the Senator. Wilson later admitted talking to Pinchot regarding the letter but denied he knew what it contained.[21] Dolliver received the letter on January 5, 1910, and the following day he read it to the Senate and had it printed in the *Congressional Record*. It was a thinly veiled attack upon the administration and a defense of Glavis.[22]

The primary intent of Pinchot's letter was to defend his own subordinates who had provided Glavis with information with which to attack Ballinger. The Forester desired this defense to be read in the Senate at the time that Taft's message transmitting the record of the Glavis case reached there, and he informed Wilson that he believed he could induce Dolliver to read the letter.[23] Whether, in the beginning, Dolliver or Pinchot took the initiative in the discussion of getting the letter before the Senate is not clear. In view of Dolliver's close personal relations with Wilson, it is probable that the Senator acted only after carefully considering a hint from Pinchot that a request from the chairman of the Committee on Agriculture and Forestry for information would provide the opportunity Pinchot wanted to get his case before the Senate without embarrassing the Secretary of Agriculture. In presenting the letter to the Senate, Dolliver defended Pinchot's right to write to him and pointed out that Ballinger had written to another Senator. Whatever the origin of the letter, it proved to be a sensation. Dolliver was immediately hailed as Pinchot's champion in the Senate. The President, "sick at soul," ordered Wilson to dismiss Pinchot, an action which was not unanticipated by the Forester and which was everywhere interpreted as presaging a break between Roosevelt and Taft.[24] "What will Roosevelt think?" That question, according to Archie Butt, was uppermost in Taft's mind, although the President pretended to be unperturbed by rumors that the "Pinchot-Garfield-Dolliver" people were plotting a "Back from Elba" movement in behalf of the African lion hunter.[25]

Insurgents and journalists voiced enthusiastic support of Pinchot and praised Dolliver for aiding him. Henry Wallace wrote to the Senator: "I am very glad that you read the Pinchot letter. It was a political stroke on his part quite equal to anything that Roosevelt could have done. . . . The President has made a blunder from which he will never recover."[26]

In mid-January, Dolliver told the press that he had read the Pinchot letter because he thought it might throw some light on the Ballinger-Pinchot affair which the Senate was discussing. "I have been an interested spectator, observing some differences of opinion between these two men. It developed to the point where it became evident they were both fighting for their lives." He alluded to a presidential order of November 26, 1909, forbidding bureau chiefs and subordinates to apply to Congress for action of any kind or to respond to any request for information from either house of Congress, congressional committees, or members of Congress except as authorized by the head of the department. This order undoubtedly accounted for Pinchot's consultation with Secretary Wilson, and it assuredly had some bearing on the attitude of the Insurgents in the Pinchot affair. Congress has never taken kindly to efforts of the executive branch to deny it information. As Dolliver put it, the November

26 directive "struck me as a good deal like putting two men into a ring to fight and then tying the legs of one of them."[27]

Probably Pinchot's position as the "underdog" fighting for Rooseveltian ideals against a Cabinet officer backed by the President and aided by an order which hindered the Forester from making his case had much appeal for Dolliver. Unquestionably Dolliver's interest in maintaining the conservation program was sincere, as were his doubts concerning Ballinger. It is likely, however, that he was also interested in getting Theodore Roosevelt back into political action, and on the side of the Insurgents, before the 1910 congressional elections. Dolliver understood political warfare as well as any man in the nation. He knew the value of Roosevelt's name and that if the Rough Rider would take the stump for the Insurgents, they might avoid the defeat the Old Guard plotted for them. Perhaps Dolliver thought Roosevelt could play the role for the Congressmen fighting for their lives in 1910 that the "War Eagle of Webster County" had played in 1908 for Allison. If so, Pinchot's dismissal might be the very thing to bring Theodore charging into the fray.

Taft had no alternative but to dismiss Pinchot, as the latter and his supporters knew. The President had mishandled the affair from the beginning. He might, in the end, have salvaged something had he ousted Ballinger as well as Pinchot. The congressional investigation began on January 28 and lasted until June. Dolliver was not a member of the committee, but Louis D. Brandeis, attorney for Pinchot and Glavis, brought out much damaging evidence against Ballinger, and although the Secretary was upheld by the committee report, he was not completely whitewashed.[28]

Meanwhile, Pinchot departed for Europe to meet Theodore Roosevelt. On March 25 Dolliver dispatched a six-page letter to the ex-Forester, in care of the British Embassy at Copenhagen. This letter was obviously written for Roosevelt's eyes. Dolliver began by telling Pinchot that it was of "very great importance for [Roosevelt] to know the exact state of things here as respects the administration which he left behind him a year ago." Referring to Roosevelt's "aggressive activities, all looking to the restoration of this Government to the millions of people which it represents," the Senator continued:

> I had hoped and believed that Mr. Taft, having been closely associated with the former administration, would sympathize with its purposes and cooperate with those who aided in carrying them forward. I have had no differences of any sort with the President of a merely personal character, and am conscious of no sentiment in connection with our situation except one of disappointment and sorrow that he has lost the opportunity and wasted the prestige which his predecessor passed over to him. . . .
> The moment the extraordinary session of Congress came together and it became evident that a fight was on hand between the public and the trust managers, Mr. Taft discovered that the only way to

give the people what he promised in his campaign speeches to give
them meant a battle lasting all summer, he dismissed the advisers who
were ready to help him and willing to go down to defeat with him,
and tied up with Aldrich and Cannon, giving to these two ancient
worthies carte blanche to revise the tariff exactly as they pleased.

. . .

After Congress adjourned the President went to Boston and began
a long public journey with a eulogy of Mr. Aldrich, and followed it
up at Winona by reading out of the Republican party all the Members of Congress who had sense enough to know what that amiable
brother was doing while he was at it and courage enough to state the
facts to the public after he was through. In other words, the President took the certificate of character which Mr. Roosevelt had given
him and turned it over to the Senator from Rhode Island.

If you see the former President and happen to think of it, I wish
you would tell him for me that the next certificate of character he
issues ought, for the sake of caution, to be marked "Not Transfer-
able."

After detailing Taft's shortcomings in the matter of leadership for Progressive
legislation in the current session, Dolliver concluded:

In all these things the President seems to be helplessly following
the very men who took the field in the effort to crush Mr. Roosevelt
in 1906. . . .

I do not know that I ought to say anything else. I would not on
any account draw Mr. Roosevelt into our unfortunate controversies.
He is about to receive in the United States a popular welcome un-
paralleled in our history. There is a little group of us in both houses
of Congress who are fighting for public rights, under the inspiration
which we gained in other years from serving in the ranks under his
leadership. His affirmative approbation of the things that went on
here last summer and the things that are going on here now, would,
from my point of view, make the battle which we are waging so desperate and uncertain as to postpone for generations the triumph which
is bound to come to the plain citizens, acting within the ranks of a
political party, over the beneficiaries of bad laws and rotten methods
of political organizations.[29]

If anything were needed to disenchant Roosevelt with his successor, Pinchot's
visit, armed with "a sheaf of letters" from Progressives and with Dolliver's
skillful arraignment of Taft and his oblique plea for Roosevelt to resume leadership of the party, must have provided it. Probably nothing was needed, as
the former President had written a series of letters to Lodge indicating that the
"tariff issue was not met as it was necessary to meet it," that Taft had not
carried out "my work unbroken," that the party leaders were "cynically indifferent and contemptuously hostile" to the things "I have promised."[30]

————————

While the Pinchot investigation continued in the headlines and Roosevelt visited the crowned heads of Europe, the Insurgents in Congress fought for Progressive legislation. In the House they finally succeeded in curbing the power of the Speaker but failed to gain control either of the chair or of the Rules Committee. Taft's defense of Cannon in this fight meant he had to share the humiliation of the Speaker's defeat and caused the people to think that the President was definitely allied with the Old Guard.[31]

The major bills under consideration during the 1909-1910 session were the Mann-Elkins proposal for amending the Interstate Commerce Act and a plan for establishing postal savings banks. On his Western tour Taft had proposed changes in the Interstate Commerce law which would provide that a special Court of Commerce be created to facilitate the disposal of cases arising from rate regulations, that railroads be prohibited from owning stock in competing lines, and that the Interstate Commerce Commission be given full power to regulate the issuance of railroad securities.[32]

During the fall Attorney-General George W. Wickersham and others attempted to draw up a bill embodying the President's views on amending the existing interstate commerce legislation. On the whole, the Wickersham measure strengthened the Commission, but the Insurgents and others objected to provisions permitting railroads to make rate agreements and mergers without the approval of the Commission and giving the new Court of Commerce original jurisdiction in entertaining appeals on both law and fact from the decisions of the Commission. Objections were also made to the omission from the proposed bill for the physical evaluation of carriers as a basis for scientific rate-making and for a stronger long and short haul clause. La Follette and Dolliver had already attempted to get legislation for physical evaluation. The developments which caused the Progressives the greatest concern, however, were that Taft conferred repeatedly with the railroad magnates in connection with the Wickersham measure before having it redrafted to submit to Congress and that the railroad presidents, as well as Nelson Aldrich, would support the bill.[33]

As introduced in the House in January, the bill was completely unacceptable to the Insurgents. It permitted the railroads, but not the shippers, to get injunctions in the Court of Commerce against the Interstate Commerce Commission and permitted a judge of the court to enjoin temporarily the enforcement of the Commission's orders reducing rates without notification to the Commission. Furthermore, the court was to have the right to set aside the findings of the Commission on grounds other than those of jurisdiction or of a constitutional nature — a revival in disguise of the old "broad review" scheme of the 1906 fight. Moreover, the bill legalized agreements among railroads as to rates and classifications, thus repealing the Sherman Antitrust Act as it applied to railroads. It also deprived the Commission of its existing right to appear in appeal cases and made the Attorney General responsible for representing the Commission in appeals.[34]

When the bill reached the Senate Committee on Interstate Commerce, Senators Cummins and Clapp had already prepared more than a hundred amendments. The Standpatters, following Dolliver's 1906 example, refused to permit any amendments at all and reported the bill without any changes. To the Insurgents, especially to Dolliver, the author of the Hepburn Act, the so-called Mann-Elkins bill was an administration measure dictated by the railroads and a step backward in rate regulation. Nevertheless, Taft, Aldrich, and Cannon determined that the bill should be passed as drawn up and that anyone who opposed it should be treated as an enemy of the party.[35]

Since Dolliver was suffering from a painful nasal infection and was no longer a member of the Interstate Commerce Committee, Senators Cummins and La Follette led the fight to force revisions in the Mann-Elkins bill. They were aided constantly, on and off the Senate floor, by Dolliver, Beveridge, Bristow, and Clapp — the same group who had worked so valiantly against the Payne-Aldrich Tariff in the preceding session. In the middle of March, Cummins made a four-day speech in which he "ripped and tore the railroad bill to shreds."[36] So effective was the opposition that Aldrich withdrew the bill from the Senate. In conference with Wickersham, the Old Guard leaders revised the bill in an effort to meet some of the criticism. The Insurgents, aided by Democrats, were making some progress.

Just as the Senate resumed consideration of the bill as resubmitted, Wickersham delivered an address in Chicago during which he demanded that "everyone must choose whether or not he is for the President and the Republican party." He warned that Republicans in Congress must prove their Republicanism "by their actions on bills in Congress" — or read themselves out of the party.[37] This, of course, infuriated the Insurgents. Beveridge wrote that:

> Wickersham's speech, which voices the real sentiment of the administration, has made things much worse than ever, and I haven't the slightest doubt Dolliver is going after him horse, foot, dragoons, mounted batteries, and heavy artillery. The unfortunate thing about it is that Wickersham's speech was carefully prepared, read over and O. K.'d by the President, and yet on the very night of its delivery, the President pats us on the head — at the same time Wickersham, for the President, is knocking our heads off.[38]

Dolliver planned to do just what Beveridge predicted. Before he had a chance, however, La Follette not only replied to Wickersham but in so doing attacked the provisions of the Mann-Elkins bill which gave the Attorney General the power to prosecute railroad cases for the Interstate Commerce Commission. La Follette so completely demolished that scheme and discredited Wickersham as having already demonstrated his subservience to the railroads by withdrawing a government suit against a proposed merger when he had every prospect of winning the case, that the Senate voted to give the Commission power to have its own counsel represent it in cases before the commerce court.[39]

The next attack was on the proposal to permit the railroads to make traffic and rate agreements with each other despite the antitrust laws. The debate now reached an intensity comparable to that of the preceding June on the tariff. Borah began the assault on April 23, and two days later Dolliver delivered his major speech on the bill.

Dolliver had three purposes in view. First, he desired to chastise Wickersham for his presumption in telling the Congress it must pass a bill the admintration had written and that those Republicans who opposed the measure were reading themselves out of the party. "I have always had certain old-fashioned views about the Congress of the United States," the Iowan began. "I do not hesitate to confess a certain resentment, not personal in nature, which arises in my mind on finding the work of Congress so elaborately mapped out by other departments of the Government as it has been during the present session." Furthermore, he pointed out that all legislation on the railroad question from 1887 to 1906 had been nonpartisan in character and that those who were really interested in effective action on the subject "ought to put away all impertinent prejudices in respect to politics." He also blasted the "constant appeal to the authority of individuals" on the question and suggested that he knew of nothing in Taft's "history, his studies, his experience in the world of great affairs, which gives him authority that should be accepted without debate in either House of the Congress . . . on the amendment of our railway code." After pointing out that he and other Iowans had been concerned with the railroad problem for many years, he informed the administration spokesmen and the Senate that he intended to speak and vote as he pleased on the bill under discussion. "If it ever comes to the time when I can not do that, there will be a back seat in the Senate vacant and no inventions of the imagination brought forward to explain my absence."

Secondly, Dolliver desired to force adoption of an amendment which should give the Interstate Commerce Commission the power to "inspect everything that is done and every step that is taken" with regard to rate agreements and railroad consolidation.

Thirdly, he opposed giving to the Court of Commerce the power "to exercise an appellate jurisdiction over the discretion which the law confides to the Interstate Commerce Commission."

He dealt extensively with the Wickersham scheme of exempting the railroads from the antitrust acts and expressed alarm that the Attorney General demanded that Congress "declare legal what is now criminal," and his parting thrust at Wickersham was squelching. "The good legal brother who feels warranted by a little brief authority to purge the Republican party of unworthy members, when this bill was written either did not know what the Republican platform was or felt at liberty to treat it with that silent inattention which is characteristic of really great minds."[40]

Dolliver's efforts, and some able parliamentary work by Cummins and other Insurgents, contributed to a revision of the bill which eliminated all sections contrary to the antitrust laws.[41]

In mid-May the Insurgents began their final effort to enact an amendment revising the long and short haul clauses in order to prevent discriminatory rates. Dolliver spoke on this question on May 13, urging careful regulation of such schedules and blasting Senator Elkins for suggesting that if the people of the Western towns were not satisfied with the rates charged they should move out of the Rocky Mountain area. After much frantic dickering to prevent an effective amendment of this sort, Aldrich and the Old Guard had to capitulate.[42] On the whole, the Insurgents were "eminently successful" in their fight on the objectionable features of the original bill, and "the Mann-Elkins Act was a real advance in railroad regulation."[43]

The administration bill to establish a system of postal savings banks precipitated a less spectacular fight in the Senate. Dolliver favored the creation of postal savings banks as promised during the 1908 campaign. In his view, the party pledge, as interpreted by Taft in his acceptance speech, was that the law would be so framed that the money deposited at a post office should be placed by the government in the banks of the community. In accordance with the wishes of Aldrich, however, Taft supported a bill which allowed the postal savings money to be invested in the 2 per cent bonds held by the national banks.[44]

The administration bill was unacceptable to the Senate Insurgents. They desired that the money deposited be kept in the local banks instead of being siphoned off into the Eastern financial centers for investment in low-interest bonds. Dolliver, a member of the Post Office Committee, served on a subcommittee designated to revamp the bill. When debate began, the line was drawn again between Insurgents and Standpatters. Senator Elihu Root offered an amendment stipulating that the funds be invested in government securities which could be sold for cash in times of panic. The President supported this. To counter the Root move, Dolliver and La Follette prepared an amendment which would enable the government to withdraw the funds from local communities only in time of war or extreme emergency. At this point Dolliver had to be hospitalized for a nasal operation, but when he returned in early March he made a speech denouncing the attempts to get the postal savings funds away from the local banks and criticizing the President rather sharply for abandoning the campaign pledges.[45]

This speech helped pave the way for the passage of a significant amendment offered by Borah on March 5. Borah's plan prohibited the investment of the postal savings funds in bonds bearing a rate of interest less than $2\frac{1}{4}$ per cent

— obviously wrecking Aldrich's scheme for using the funds for the benefit of the national banks' 2 per cent bonds. The majority leader was absent in Florida, and his less skillful lieutenants accepted the Borah amendment; it passed, 49 to 11. The Insurgents then voted for the bill as amended.[46]

The President intervened and brought sufficient pressure to cause the House to reject the Borah amendment. As finally passed, over the opposition of Dolliver, Cummins, and several other Senate Insurgents, the conference report permitted the investment of 30 per cent of the postal funds in 2 per cent bonds. Dolliver explained his opposition on the grounds that the Old Guard had designed the law not to afford a place of deposit for the masses of the people, but to get the people's money where the government could use it "to take up government bonds and thus pave the way for a central bank." While it was true, the Senator added, that only a part of the deposits could be invested in bonds, he felt that this was a limitation which a succeeding Congress could easily remove. This reasoning is not convincing, and the conclusion is inescapable that the Insurgent Senators refused to support the bill largely because it was not left the way they passed it and because they resented the President's tactics in whipping it through the House and the conference committee.[47]

The battles over the dismissal of Pinchot, the Mann-Elkins bill, and the postal savings bank system dramatized the depth of the schism within the Republican party. By March it was an open secret that Taft was plotting the defeat of every Progressive Republican seeking renomination and the humiliation of others not up for re-election in 1910. Thus, as the session drew to a close, Dolliver arose on June 13 to defend the course he and his supporters in the Senate had followed during the preceding fifteen months.[48] This address was in fact a declaration of war on Taft and the Old Guard and upon the time-honored methods of tariff making.

Dolliver had, he said, "always been a disciple of party peace, party harmony, of party good-will," and he expressed wonder at having been so bitterly assailed for voting against the same wool tariff in 1909 which Charles Sumner and Henry Wilson of Massachusetts had voted against four decades before "when it was fresh and for the first time presented to the Congress." Was there no longer freedom of conscience and judgment and opinion in the Republican party? "When it is said that I betray my party . . . I deny it. I fight for the Republican party and propose, with millions of other people, to do what I can to make it more than ever the servant of the great constituency which it has represented for so many years."

Turning to the root of the party troubles, the tariff debacle, Dolliver said he proposed to tell the American people "exactly what went on here last summer and exactly what is going on here now." That "disagreeable duty" could have

been avoided, he said, if the President had felt content to leave members of
Congress to settle with their own constituencies the question of their party
relations without having interposed "the weight of the greatest political office
in the world to humiliate and disparage" them.

Challenging Taft and the party leadership to read him out of the party,
Dolliver thundered:

> I notify all interested persons that I have no intention of leaving
> the Republican party, even to oblige old and valued friends. . . . I
> was born in the Republican party — down among the loyal mountains
> of Virginia. I think I know what the articles of its faith are. . . .
> The President is in error. It is not necessary for men to swallow
> down every tariff law that is set before them or "in conscience aban-
> don the party."

For hours the matchless orator discussed the Payne-Aldrich Tariff — its
origin, its defects, its injustices to the consuming public. He described the act
as "brutal and sordid" and Taft's defense of it and of Aldrich as "grotesque."
With a thrust at the President's gullibility which delighted the Senate and the
nation, Dolliver noted that "the past year witnessed two events of unusual interest — the discovery of the North Pole by Doctor Cook and the revision of
the tariff downward by the Senator from Rhode Island — each in its way a
unique hoax, and both promptly presented to the favorable notice of the public
by the highest official congratulations." As he recalled Aldrich's telling him
before the Senate that the cotton schedules had been changed on the advice of
government experts, Dolliver inspired the cartoonists by depicting the majority
leader as "gathering the spring chickens of his committee under a motherly
wing and retreating to the protection of the New York Custom House" while
Senator Flint, "one of the most lusty of the brood . . . stuck his head out of
the feathers, even while the storm was raging, with the reassuring remark that
the same thing was true of the other schedules."

To make clear that it was not the Insurgents alone who deplored the "scan-
dalous abuses" in tariff making, Dolliver quoted two Old Guard leaders of
impeccable party standing on the subject. First, Taft's Secretary of the Treasury, who said: "The opinion is practically universal that . . . hereafter such
legislation must be based on facts and knowledge and scientific investigation,
and not on mere bartering between sections and different interests." Secondly,
he alluded to the disillusionment of Stephen Benton Elkins with Aldrich, and
quoted Elkins as explaining his tariff votes as follows:

> I voted for nearly everything that was prepared by the Senator
> from Rhode Island to get what I did for my state. . . . I could not
> get off the reservation during the consideration of the tariff. I was
> afraid to try. The distinguished Senator from Rhode Island knows
> why. The Senate knows why. . . . I was on the reservation. I do

not have to stay there always. The tariff is considered only once in about six or seven years. Some Senators have freedom the balance of the time.

Thus, Dolliver observed, it seemed strange to criticize the Insurgents, whom he had once defined as people who insisted upon reading a bill before voting on it. "You would hardly believe it," he added, "but there are a lot of good people who have not spent as much time as I have in studying the principles of civil liberty, who are trying to put me off and down and out because I hunger for freedom as the representative of the people all the time, while my friend from West Virginia seems to be satisfied if he can get it six years out of seven."

As he concluded his last speech in the Senate, Dolliver warned his party that it must put an end to the domination of its leadership by selfish corporate wealth. How long, he asked, would the Senate of the United States allow important legislative matters, "affecting every man, woman, and child, to be managed with a brutal tyranny, without debate and without knowledge and without explanation, by the very people that are engaged in monopolizing the great industries of the world?" This must stop, he cried.

> So far as I am concerned, I am through with it . . . but I intend to fight it as a Republican and as an American citizen. I intend to fight without fear — I do not care what may be my political fate. . . . For the day is coming — it is a good deal nearer than many think — when a new sense of justice, new inspirations, new volunteer enthusiasms for good government shall take possession of the hearts of all our people. The time is at hand when the laws will be respected by great and small alike. . . . A thousand forces are making for it. It is the fruitage of these Christian centuries, the fulfillment of the prayers and dreams of the men and women who have laid the foundations of their Commonwealth, and with infinite sacrifice maintained these institutions.

It is no wonder that Mark Sullivan called Dolliver "the principal weapon of the Insurgents."[49] When the Senator sat down at the end of his peroration, the galleries burst into applause and cheers, and the Vice President had to bang his gavel for order and warn against violation of the rules of the Senate as to manifestations of "approval or disapproval."[50] The speech had lasted three hours and had very nearly exhausted Dolliver. He spoke to a Senate in which every seat was filled, the galleries were packed, and members of the House of Representatives stood in the aisles and against the walls. Insurgent and Standpatter alike surrounded him at the end to congratulate him and shake his hand. The Old Guard Washington *Herald*, which had never lost an opportunity to criticize Dolliver, commented: "It has been many a day since Senators have listened to a speech such as was delivered yesterday by Senator Dolliver. From any viewpoint it was a classic and will go in the annals of the Senate as one of the greatest addresses before that body."[51]

The speech made a profound impression throughout the country, for Dolliver was widely known and very popular, having spoken in one capacity or another in practically every state in the Union.[52] Uncle Henry Wallace sat on his porch steps reading the text printed in the morning paper until he was late for church. "I think it is the greatest speech of your life," he wrote J. P., "and it is so regarded by everyone with whom I have talked. . . . Your real work in Congress has just commenced; the previous quarter century has simply been preparatory to the work you are to do in the future."[53]

In a sense Wallace was right. All of Dolliver's life had really been a preparation for these tense later years. His ancestry, his religious convictions, his education, his conception of citizenship and of duty, his political and legislative experience, his belief in democracy, his love of the Great Republic, and all the moral forces within him had gathered for the supreme test of his life. He who had had so much help in the early years, he who had been the fair-haired boy pushed forward by Carpenter, Clarkson, Blaine, Hobart, and Allison, he who had had the favor even of McKinley and of Taft was nonetheless able to stand unflinchingly and lead the minority against the powerful presidential and senatorial machine in the greatest crisis in the history of the Republican party.

The "future" of which Wallace wrote was already at hand, the "work" was already begun. As soon as Congress adjourned, less than two weeks after Dolliver's last speech in the Senate, Senators and Representatives rushed homeward to engage in party battles in connection with the 1910 elections. The Republican schism was widening. No Insurgent called to bid Taft good-bye when the session ended. The President's days of running with the hare and hunting with the hounds were over so far as the Insurgents were concerned. Yet, strange to say, Taft felt hurt.[54] He had not learned that while a man may with sincerity fight on one side or the other of any issue, he can never with honor pretend to fight on both sides.

As early as January, 1910, the President had ordered that all appointments for postmasters recommended by Insurgents should be held up.[55] In February, Colonel W. P. Hepburn had gone to Washington to confer with Taft and others as to "the best manner of securing organized and aggressive action" against Dolliver and the other Iowa Insurgents. The President wrote Hepburn to bring a group of Iowa Standpatters to the White House "to dine with me" and go over the Iowa situation. Twelve Iowans attended the dinner on February 20. Taft informed these gentlemen that he had deprived the Insurgents of patronage and would cooperate in efforts to defeat them in Iowa. The President asked Hepburn to handle patronage in his district just as he had done prior to his defeat for re-election in 1908 — thus depriving the Senators of the usual control of appointments in a district represented by a Democrat.[56]

During this White House meeting Hepburn and his cohorts informed Taft that they thought they could help him unseat four Hawkeye Congressmen and repudiate Dolliver and Cummins at the state convention if "some outside help in the way of money" were forthcoming. The President shortly thereafter took Senator Aldrich for a cold, windy ride and explained the Iowa situation to him. The majority leader agreed to see what funds could be raised to aid Hepburn's plot and promised to contribute personally to "aid the cause." Taft said he also would give money. By mid-March the "funds from the East" began to reach Iowa, where ex-Governor Frank D. Jackson received them and used the money in the organization of Taft Republican Clubs and a press bureau.[57]

The Old Guard crowd was so desperate that some of their actions were ludicrous. Some Iowa and Eastern men went so far as to offer a half million dollars to Ret Clarkson to establish a Standpat newspaper in Des Moines. Ret declined, of course, but another group promised to try to purchase the *Register* if Clarkson would return to it. Naturally he refused, much as he wanted to go back to journalism. He would not think of fighting Dolliver, whom, as he wrote General Dodge, "he considered as a son." Clarkson wanted a Midwestern paper to use in helping make Dolliver President — but, of course, the Taft faction had no knowledge of Ret's plans in 1910. They were grasping at straws and appeared to believe money could buy them support and safety.[58]

Henry Wallace wrote Dolliver of a Standpat meeting in Des Moines in early March and told the Senator that the real aim of the Old Guard was to get control of the state convention and of the committees which would control the naming of delegates to the national convention of 1912.[59] Speaker Cannon interested himself in Iowa politics, and the Standpatters attempted to arrange for him to give a series of free Chautauqua lectures in the state, financed by the Republican Campaign Committee. In April, Cannon and other Standpatters of national reputation announced plans to stump Iowa for the Old Guard.[60]

Governor Carroll, who reportedly had his eye on Dolliver's Senate seat in 1913, sought renomination as a Standpatter. Against him the Insurgents supported Warren Garst and organized Garst-Dolliver-Cummins committees throughout the state.[61] On May 10 a "Progressive Rally" met in Des Moines with both the Hawkeye Senators present. Dolliver spoke at length, explaining the Insurgent opposition to the tariff act, the Mann-Elkins bill, and the Postal Savings bill. He told the audience that "the future of the Republican party lies in the success of the movement, now nationwide, to disown and put aside a leadership which has betrayed the welfare of the party and the country."[62]

Dolliver was enthusiastically received, and although he attended contrary to the doctor's orders, his address was in no way disappointing. A Nebraska friend who heard it wrote: "I did not anticipate such a treat as I enjoyed when I sat in the vast audience. . . . As you proceeded in your address I became profoundly impressed with the strange folly of Taft in allowing himself to

make the issues any test of party fealty or personal friendship."[63] Senator
Cummins, speaking just after Dolliver concluded, told the crowd: "You have
heard tonight, from the man who knows more about the tariff law than any
other man in the United States, more truth than ever before fell upon your
ears."[64]

The Senators were so engaged in Washington that they were unable to aid
Garst in person during the pre-primary campaign. That, plus the long tradition of giving an incumbent Governor renomination, made possible Carroll's
defeat of Garst. Otherwise, however, the Progressives won, beating Captain
Hull and other Old Guard Congressmen for renomination. Wallace, English,
and other Progressive leaders considered the primary results a victory for Dolliver and Cummins. Meservey thought Garst would have won had the Progressives fought harder to get out the vote and if many pro-Dolliver people had
not thought Carroll deserved a second term.[65]

The June primary was not a clear-cut victory, but it was indicative of the
degree to which the party was broken. The state convention in August, on the
other hand, provided the Insurgents an unquestionable triumph and left no
doubt that many Standpatters would vote for Democratic congressional nominees rather than support Progressive Republicans.

This convention named Dolliver permanent chairman and Cummins temporary chairman and passed resolutions endorsing their Insurgent stand and ap-
proving "only such efforts as President Taft and his advisers have made to
fulfill the promise of the national platform." Hepburn, Lacey, Perkins, and
other Old Guard bitter-enders had led movements from the floor to prevent the
election of Dolliver and Cummins and to adopt a substitute platform condemning their action in Washington. These efforts were defeated, of course, but
they hurt Dolliver, who had already pledged himself to support Carroll for
Governor and had voiced the hope that the convention would "express in a
tolerant way the prevailing sentiment and judgment of the party as it is represented in the state convention."[66]

When Dolliver took the gavel to preside over this faction-ridden party meeting, he must have remembered that just twenty-six years before he had been
named chairman of a similar convention in order to bring harmony to his party
and that his keynote speech on that occasion had led him quickly to national
fame. Then he had been an unknown boy with nothing but dreams to sustain
him. In 1910 he was one of the ablest Senators in the nation, one of the finest
orators in the world, but he could not do for the Iowa Republicans what he had
done in 1884. His final address to a Republican convention was short, philosophical, beautiful:

> I suppose, I have suffered as much as anybody from the antago-
> nisms of old friends, but there are not rewards enough in public life
> to justify any man in allowing personal bitterness to degrade the dif-

ferences of opinion which ought to be held in neighborly good will. The finest tribute ever paid to the freedom and independence which is the birthright of all students and thinkers, was paid by Herbert Spencer to one whose doctrines he had assailed with savage criticism. In his eulogy upon the memory of John Stuart Mill he attributed to him "This fine trait — that ability to bear with unruffled temper and without any diminution of kindly feeling, the publicly expressed antagonism of a friend."

While some think that we are going to harm the Republican party by publicly admitting our differences, the fact is, popular government depends on discussion. Without that, it never could have come into existence. Without that, it cannot last very long. The truth is found in controversy. It usually lies between the extremes of opinion, and the most important truth which the world cherishes has come down to us through the greatest trial and tribulation.

The fleeting distinctions of politics do not attract me as they once did. I have but one ambition left, and that is to keep on the firing line in defense of public rights against the sordid private interests which are seeking to usurp the government of the United States.

Reminding the delegates that he had not sought nor desired to serve as chairman of the convention, he concluded by thanking "both those who voted for me and those who voted against me for this honor — the former for pressing their own feeling toward me and the latter for sharing my own personal feeling on the subject."[67]

The success of the Iowa Insurgents in controlling the state convention gave renewed hope to Progressives throughout the nation. Dolliver sent campaign materials to Bristow to aid in his fight in Kansas, where Aldrich and other outside speakers were attempting to defeat all Insurgents.[68] In August the Fort Dodge orator spoke in Ohio in support of James R. Garfield's gubernatorial candidacy. From there he went to Wisconsin to speak for La Follette who had taken ill in the midst of a bitter primary campaign against a candidate backed by the White House.[69]

Before returning home from Wisconsin, Dolliver met Theodore Roosevelt in Omaha for a breakfast reunion. Roosevelt had written Dolliver in July, expressing a desire to see him "and go over matters in full. . . . You are one of the men whom I especially value and believe in, and I shall always retain a very lively remembrance of the invaluable support you gave me while I was President."[70] Dolliver was well briefed by Clarkson on Roosevelt's attitude toward the Insurgents, for Clarkson had seen the Colonel before the Western trip began and had written J. P. on August 21 that Roosevelt knew who his friends in Iowa were. "I have heard no one who so highly praises or more highly *rates* your work in the Senate on the tariff bill," Clarkson wrote Dolliver of the former President. "He ranks your speeches in that debate as worthy to rank among the greatest ever made in the Senate. His personal friendship for you amounts to affection, and to unshaken and unshakeable confidence." As to Roosevelt and his successor, Clarkson wrote with his old-time insight: "I consider the breach between him and Taft practically impossible of being closed, and more likely to be widened than narrowed or closed." Ret added that he thought Roosevelt had "*no personal wish* to be President again, but I am also sure that no man can or will refuse to become President if the people desire that he shall." Clarkson hinted at the possibility that Roosevelt might help Dolliver secure the presidential nomination in 1912.[71]

The details of the Omaha conference between the Rough Rider and the War Eagle were not recorded. The following day, however, the Progressive Republicans of Nebraska began to organize a movement for the nomination of Theodore Roosevelt for President and J. P. Dolliver for Vice President in 1912, declaring openly that if Roosevelt would not run, the Nebraska delegates would be instructed to nominate Dolliver for President.[72]

Such rumors and the continuing victory of the Insurgents in primaries and conventions may have made some impression on Taft. On September 6 reports from Washington indicated that the "powers that be" had decided to place Dolliver on the Senate Finance Committee in the new Congress. A few days later the President appointed George E. Roberts Director of the Mint, a post he had held in the McKinley and Roosevelt administrations. In mid-September, Taft's secretary, Charles D. Norton, informed Iowa Republicans that the administration had decided to return to the usual methods of handling patronage and would "treat all Republican Congressmen and Senators alike, without distinction."[73]

If by these belated tactics the President hoped to appease the leader of the Insurgents and prevent a Roosevelt-Dolliver combination in 1912, he had hardly assessed properly either Dolliver or the movement he headed. This is not to say that Dolliver would not have sought to work for harmony in the party had the President been willing to cut loose from the Old Guard and honestly seek to implement the pledges of 1908. Dolliver constantly insisted on making his fight within the Republican party, and he undoubtedly would have made every honorable effort to unite the party in order to prevent Insurgency from blundering into the futility and frustration of a third-party blind alley. Whether Taft would have turned toward Dolliver after the 1910 elections seems doubtful. The President had had his opportunity in 1909. He had wasted it. Time was running out as summer turned to autumn in 1910.

On October 7 Dolliver dispatched a letter to his friend Beveridge, who was fighting for his political life in Indiana and whom Dolliver had planned to aid:

> It is with deep regret that I dictate this to you. I find it impossible
> to tell what I can do in the way of campaign work, as, for the first

time in my life, I am entirely disabled and unable to do anything. For three weeks I have been confined to my house, unable to eat my meals, and just barely able to get my breath. . . . The probability is that it will be a long time before I am able to make a speech of any sort. I regret the situation, but I am up against the real thing.[74]

Ten days later the Fort Dodge *Messenger*, which for thirty years had faithfully chronicled Dolliver's victories and reverses, recorded with deepest mourning his final defeat. The great heart, which he had strained in the tariff speeches in 1909, had broken down at last. It stopped beating suddenly at 7:30 P. M., Saturday, October 15, as the Senator sat in his Fort Dodge home talking with his physician. Valvular leakage and enlargement of the heart aggravated by prolonged overexertion caused his death.[75]

The nation was shocked at the unexpected news. Expressions of genuine grief poured forth in hundreds of newspapers throughout the country and in countless letters and telegrams from people in all walks of life. Many advanced the view that Dolliver had given his life in the battle to preserve democracy, that he was the first martyr of the Progressive cause. Even more numerous were those who voiced the sentiment best phrased by a Southern Democrat, Senator Benjamin Tillman, who said: "Great men are plentiful in this country, but not as great as Dolliver." President Taft commented that "the Senate has lost one of its ablest and most brilliant statesmen, the country has lost a faithful public servant."[76] A Negro leader said that the word of the Senator's death was "the saddest news which telegraph and press have flashed to the colored citizens of this great state and country for many years. Few men in his day have so endeared themselves to all classes and especially to the common masses of my people. . . . Everything of merit that tended to uplift and aid our oppressed people could count with confidence on Senator Dolliver's aid and influence."[77]

Aside from his family and personal friends, the Insurgents felt most deeply the loss of Dolliver. La Follette refused to believe the first "heart-breaking rumor" of Dolliver's death.[78] Senator Cummins hastened to Fort Dodge to call on Mrs. Dolliver and then telegraphed Beveridge not to leave the Indiana campaign to attend the funeral because "it would be an irretrievable disaster if, after losing Dolliver by death, we should lose you by defeat." Beveridge, stricken with unconcealed sorrow, complied with Cummins' suggestion, but on the day of the funeral the Hoosier orator devoted his speeches to eulogies of Dolliver who, he said, "died for his country as literally as any soldier who ever expired on a battlefield." Dolliver was, wrote Beveridge, "our best, our most gifted man, our only genius."[79]

Iowans crowded into Fort Dodge by the train-load to pay their last homage to their beloved servant. The Democratic State Committee ordered all political meetings and campaign speeches cancelled on the day of the Senator's funeral.

ENATOR JONATHAN P. DOLLIVER DIED SATURDAY EVENING

ation of Heart Direct Cause of Death of Distinguished Iowa Statesman

ND COMES WITHOUT PAIN

tation Takes Place as Physician Is ecting Heart Action of Patient, Who Had Been Out for Walk During Afternoon

IOWA'S BEREAVEMENT

BY HARVEY INGHAM.

HIS PUBLIC SERVICE AND HONORS

Thousands stood in the rain outside the "jam-packed armory building" to listen to Senator Moses E. Clapp eulogize Dolliver "as one who stands as the incarnation of great purposes."[80]

When due allowance is made for obituary fervor in the 1910 estimates of Jonathan Dolliver, the fact remains that he made a tremendous impression on his contemporaries. In truth, he was one guided by great principles, one who stood for great purposes. Neither love of money nor lust for power tempted him to veer from the course his conscience set. He believed in liberty, in democracy, and in the common man. He sought, through his work as a churchman, as an advocate of universal education, and as a statesman, to preserve the freedom of individuals, to make possible opportunities for all to have "a fair chance in the race of life," and to undergird politics with a morality which should make the Great Republic worthy of her heritage and of the destiny which he believed God intended for her.

Though always basically a Jeffersonian, Dolliver is notable as a man who began his congressional career as a rather conservative youth and grew increasingly liberal the older and more powerful he became. In this respect he differs from most historic figures who either began and ended as liberals or conservatives, or, more frequently perhaps, began as liberals and ended as conservatives.

Dolliver's career merits study because of his pre-eminence as an unselfish professional politician, independent of pressure groups, and wholeheartedly devoted to the public good — a rare type, indispensable to the preservation of the Republic. His character, his principles, his achievements, and his services go far to justify those who agree with Mark Sullivan in calling Jonathan Prentiss Dolliver "the greatest Senator of his time."[81]

Dolliver deserves to be remembered as an eloquent spokesman of that conservative liberalism which is so typically American. He was just as concerned with preventing capitalists and reactionaries from destroying capitalism and democracy as he was in preventing socialists and radicals from doing so. He was not complacent about American social evils. He detested the reactionary position which holds that nothing should be attempted to remedy injustices, but he perceived that there are metes and bounds to political reform, that there are some problems which yield more readily to the "conservative influences which belong to time" than to the frantic application of radical panaceas. In the last speech of his campaign for La Follette in 1910, Dolliver summarized his own political viewpoint by identifying himself with "the school of the Apostle who, in a single sentence pointed out a plain road well-suited to the program of society, 'Prove all things and hold fast to that which is good.' "

Bibliography

THE JONATHAN PRENTISS DOLLIVER PAPERS, indispensable source material for this book, are in the possession of the State Historical Society of Iowa in Iowa City. These manuscripts include family letters dating from the 1850's to 1910, genealogical data, autobiographical statements, scrapbooks, account books, lectures, articles, drafts of bills, speeches, campaign literature, and thousands of political and business letters. In addition to this collection, there are some personal and family papers of importance which have been preserved by Mr. J. M. Guy Brown of Morgantown, West Virginia, and by Miss Frances P. Dolliver of Des Moines. Miss Dolliver also has several letters from George E. Roberts which contain useful information.

Other manuscript collections of great value in a study of Dolliver and his era are the William Boyd Allison Papers, the Albert Baird Cummins Papers, the James S. Clarkson Papers, the Grenville M. Dodge Papers, the John A. T. Hull Papers, the John Fletcher Lacey Papers, and the George Douglas Perkins Papers, all of which are in the care of the Iowa State Department of History and Archives at Des Moines. In addition to the Clarkson collection in Des Moines, there are numerous Clarkson papers in the Library of Congress.

Though a relatively small collection, the Cyrus Clay Carpenter Papers at the State Historical Society of Iowa are of significance because of Carpenter's close relationship to Dolliver's early career. The Cyrenus Cole Papers and the Albert F. Dawson Scrapbooks, at the same place, contain items of interest.

Several manuscript collections which provide much background information, but which do not include extensive Dolliver correspondence, are: the John A. Kasson and Samuel J. Kirkwood Papers, Iowa State Department of History and Archives, Des Moines; the Stephen Benton Elkins Papers, West Virginia University, Morgantown; the unrestricted items in the Nelson W. Aldrich Papers, the papers of Andrew Carnegie, Benjamin Harrison, William McKinley, and Theodore Roosevelt in the Library of Congress.

As the footnote citations indicate, newspapers, magazines, and secondary works, biographical and monographic, have been widely consulted. The following publishers have kindly granted permission to reprint illustrative passages from works in which they hold the copyright:

Appleton-Century-Crofts, Inc.:
    Thomas A. Bailey, *A Diplomatic History of the American People* (1950)
Columbia University Press:
    Kenneth W. Hechler, *Insurgency* (1940)
Dodd, Mead & Company:
    David S. Muzzey, *James G. Blaine* (1934)
    Allan Nevins, *Grover Cleveland* (1948)
Doubleday & Company, Inc.:
    Archie Butt, *Taft and Roosevelt: The Intimate Letters* (1930)
Harcourt, Brace and Company, Inc.:
    Matthew Josephson, *The Politicos* (1938)
    Matthew Josephson, *The President Makers* (1940)
    Vernon L. Parrington, *Main Currents in American Thought* (1930)
    H. F. Pringle, *Theodore Roosevelt* (1931)
Harper & Brothers:
    Merle Curti, *The Growth of American Thought* (1951)
Harvard University Press:
    John Blum, *The Republican Roosevelt* (1954)
Henry Holt and Company, Inc.:
    Samuel F. Bemis, *A Diplomatic History of the United States* (1942)
    L. W. Busbey, *Uncle Joe Cannon* (1927)
Houghton Mifflin Company:
    Henry Adams, *Education of Henry Adams* (1918)
    Claude G. Bowers, *Beveridge and the Progressive Era* (1932)
    W. C. Ford (ed.), *Letters of Henry Adams* (1930)
    Oscar King Davis, *Released for Publication* (1925)
    Russell Lord, *The Wallaces of Iowa* (1947)
Alfred A. Knopf, Inc.:
    John A. Garraty, *Henry Cabot Lodge: A Biography* (1953)
    Richard Hofstadter, *The Age of Reform* (1955)
    Arthur S. Link, *The American Epoch* (1955)
Longmans, Green & Company, Inc.:
    William Z. Ripley, *Railroads: Rates and Regulations* (1924)
Louisiana State University Press:
    F. B. Simkins, *Pitchfork Ben Tillman, South Carolinian* (1944)
The Macmillan Company:
    Ida Tarbell, *The Tariff in Our Times* (1911)
Michigan State College Press:
    Russel B. Nye, *Midwestern Progressive Politics* (1951)
The Progressive Magazine:
    Robert M. La Follette, *Autobiography* (1913)
G. P. Putnam's Sons:
    F. W. Taussig, *The Tariff History of the United States* (1923)
Rutgers University Press:
    Festus P. Summers, *William L. Wilson and Tariff Reform* (1953)
Charles Scribner's Sons:
    H. C. Lodge (ed.), *Selections from the Correspondence of Theodore Roosevelt
        and Henry Cabot Lodge* (1925)
    Nathaniel W. Stephenson, *Nelson W. Aldrich: A Leader in American Politics*
        (1930)
    Mark Sullivan, *Our Times* (1926-1937)
The University of Wisconsin Press:
    George E. Mowry, *Theodore Roosevelt and the Progressive Movement* (1947)

Footnotes

CHAPTER I — IN THE BEGINNING

[1] *Congressional Globe*, 35 Cong., 1 sess., 603; New York *Tribune*, Feb. 6, 1858; *Harper's Weekly*, 2:90, 98, 102 (February 6, 13, 1858).

[2] J. H. Hammond, speech in the Senate, Mar. 4, 1858, *Cong. Globe*, 35 Cong., 1 sess., Appendix, 69-71; John G. Nicolay and John Hay, *Abraham Lincoln: A History* (10 vols., New York, 1890), 2:136-7.

[3] James M. Callahan, *History of West Virginia* (3 vols., Chicago, 1923), 1:330-35; William P. Willey, *The Formation of West Virginia* (Wheeling, 1901), 5-15; Roy Franklin Nichols, *The Disruption of American Democracy* (New York, 1948), 251-2.

[4] Bernard Lee Butcher (ed.), *Genealogical and Personal History of the Upper Monongahela Valley, West Virginia* (3 vols., New York, 1912), 1:108.

[5] W. Scott Garner, *The Press of Preston* (Kingwood, W. Va., 1885), 8. In similar vein, the Kingwood *Chronicle* regularly boasted: "The Union right or wrong — we'll defend her when right, when wrong, we'll right her."

[6] Mrs. J. J. Dolliver to Jonathan P. Dolliver, Feb. 6, 1880, *Jonathan Prentiss Dolliver Papers* (State Hist. Society of Iowa, Iowa City). Hereafter cited as *Dolliver Papers*. Jonathan P. Dolliver will be cited hereafter in footnotes as JPD.

[7] William H. Dolliver, *Some Notes on the Dolliver, Dolliber, Dollaber, Doliber, Dolover, Dolever, Originally Dalyber, Families* (Gloucester, Mass., c. 1898), 1. This pamphlet, together with several letters from its author, is in the *Dolliver Papers*. William H. Dolliver was a distant cousin of JPD.

[8] William H. Dolliver, "Some Notes on the Dolliver . . . Families," *Putnam's Monthly Historical Magazine and Magazine of New England History*, 6:158, 159, 161 (June-July, 1896).

[9] Deed recorded Apr. 1, 1710, Book 22, 1, 63, Salem Essex Register, So. District; Dolliver, *Some Notes on the Dolliver . . . Families*, 6. Peter and Abigail were married Jan. 25, 1722; he died Apr. 1, 1752. William H. Dolliver to JPD, Jan. 15, 1890, *Dolliver Papers*; "Pepperell Papers," *Collections of the Massachusetts Historical Society* (Ser. 6), 10:202-203 (Cambridge, 1899).

[10] William H. Dolliver to J. J. Dolliver, Feb. 20, 1899; Robert Goldthwaite Carter to JPD, Feb. 14, 1904, *Dolliver Papers*. Robert G. Carter was also a great-great-grandson of Col. Goldthwaite.

11 William H. Dolliver to Mrs. JPD, Mar. 5, 1899, *ibid.*

12 Robert G. Carter to JPD, Feb. 14, 1904; William H. Dolliver to J. J. Dolliver, Mar. 7, 1890, *ibid.*

13 John J. Bergen, manuscript statement concerning the life of Bergen's father's cousin, Mrs. Henry Dolliver, dated June 28, 1906, in *ibid.* JPD, in an address at the Clinton Avenue Reformed Church, Newark, N. J., Feb. 22, 1905, stated that his grandparents had lived on the banks of the Raritan River.

14 Fort Dodge *Messenger*, Apr. 29, 1905. James J. Dolliver, manuscript autobiographical statement, 3, *Dolliver Papers.* Other children of Henry and Maria Dolliver were Victor Monroe, Henry, Maria, Margaret, and Ann Jane.

15 J. J. Dolliver, autobiographical statement, 5, *Dolliver Papers.*

16 *Ibid.,* 4, 5.

17 *Ibid.,* 6; Fort Dodge *Messenger*, Apr. 29, 1905. For data as to conference areas and the procedure for admitting preachers "on trial," see Wallace G. Smeltzer, *Methodism on the Headwaters of the Ohio* (Nashville, Tenn., 1951), 132-59, 204-205. See also *Sixtieth Anniversary of Father Dolliver's Service in the Ministry* (Richwood, Ohio, 1903), 6.

18 Fort Dodge *Messenger*, Apr. 29, 1905; James M. Callahan, professor emeritus, West Virginia University, interview with T. R. Ross, Oct. 26, 1951, Morgantown, W. Va. Professor Callahan, an authority on West Virginia history, was personally acquainted with James J. Dolliver and with many older people who had heard him preach when in his prime.

19 Fort Dodge *Messenger*, Apr. 29, 1905; Smeltzer, *Methodism on the . . . Ohio*, 161; S. T. Wiley, *History of Preston County* (Kingwood, W. Va., 1882), 472; John C. McEldowney, Jr., *History of Wetzel County, West Virginia* (n. p., 1901), 61.

20 Fort Dodge *Messenger*, Apr. 29, 1905.

21 Charles H. Ambler, F. H. Atwood, W. B. Matthews (eds.), *Debates and Proceedings of the First Constitutional Convention of West Virginia* (3 vols., Huntington, W. Va., c. 1940), 1:Intro., 15, 16.

22 Smeltzer, *Methodism on the . . . Ohio*, 162.

23 Fort Dodge *Messenger*, Apr. 29, 1905; Frank K. Stillman, Washington Correspondence in Sioux City *Journal*, May 3, 1905; Callahan-Ross interview, Oct. 26, 1951.

24 JPD, "Address on the Occasion of the Presentation of the Statue of Governor Francis H. Pierpont to the Hall of Fame," *Cong. Record*, 61 Cong., 2 sess. (Apr. 30, 1910), 5603-5608.

25 William G. Brown represented his Virginia district in Congress from 1845 to 1849 as a Democrat, and from 1861 to 1863 as a Unionist, and was the first to represent his district in West Virginia in Congress, Dec., 1863 to Mar., 1865. *Biographical Directory of the American Congress, 1774-1949* (Washington, D. C., 1950), 902.

26 Much information concerning the Brown family has been made available by Mr. J. M. Guy Brown of Morgantown, W. Va., who kindly granted the author a half-day interview on Aug. 12, 1955, and permitted examination of the carefully preserved family records in his possession. Mr. Brown is a grandson of Robert Brown and a first cousin of Jonathan P. Dolliver. See also Butcher (ed.), *Genealogical and Personal History . . . West Virginia*, 1:384.

[27] *Ibid.*, 1:384; Annie R. Heavener to Mrs. JPD, Mar. 7, 1899, *Dolliver Papers*. Mrs. Heavener was a cousin of JPD.

[28] Ethel P. Beerbower, *Through the Years; A History of Methodism in Kingwood, West Virginia* (Parkersburg, W. Va., 1951), 13. See also, Wiley, *Hist. of Preston County*, 50.

[29] Annie R. Heavener to Mrs. JPD, Mar. 7, 1899; William G. Brown to Mrs. Robert Brown, Jan. 18, 1864, *Dolliver Papers*; Brown-Ross interview, Aug. 12, 1955; Butcher (ed.), *Genealogical and Personal History . . . West Virginia*, 1:385.

[30] Ambler, *et al.* (eds.), *Debates and Proceedings*, 1:63-4.

[31] Anna Lee Reger to Mrs. Robert Brown, Dec. 31, 1865, *Dolliver Papers*; Brown-Ross interview, Aug. 12, 1955.

[32] Beerbower, *Through the Years*, 17. The authority for the statement that James J. Dolliver was in Wetzel County in the years immediately before 1855 is in McEldowney, Jr., *Hist. of Wetzel County*, 61, 78. When in Wetzel County, J. J. Dolliver spent much time in the home of John M. Lacey, later an Iowa Congressman, friend and rival of JPD.

[33] Fort Dodge *Messenger*, Aug. 23, 1900; Brown-Ross interview, Aug. 12, 1955; Frances P. Dolliver interview with author, Oct. 29, 1955. The letters between James and Eliza are in Miss Dolliver's possession. Frances P. Dolliver, the younger daughter of Jonathan P. Dolliver, has taught for thirty years in the common schools of Iowa and is now on the faculty at Warren Harding Junior High School, Des Moines.

[34] Fort Dodge *Messenger*, Aug. 23, 1900; Wiley, *Hist. of Preston County*, 472.

[35] Butcher (ed.), *Genealogical and Personal History . . . West Virginia*, 1:386-8; Ambler, *et al.* (eds.), *Debates and Proceedings*, 1:63.

[36] Wiley, *Hist. of Preston County*, 154; Butcher (ed.), *Genealogical and Personal History . . . West Virginia*, 1:114; Ambler, *et al.* (eds.), *Debates and Proceedings*, 1:63-4; Virgil A. Lewis, *How West Virginia Was Made: Proceedings of the First Convention . . . at Wheeling . . . and the Journal of the Second Convention . . . Wheeling* (Charleston, 1909).

[37] Victor B. Dolliver, letter to Fort Dodge *Messenger*, Aug. 31, 1905; JPD, newspaper interview, *ibid.*, Oct. 17, 1910.

[38] Wiley, *Hist. of Preston County*, 119; Butcher (ed.), *Genealogical and Personal History . . . West Virginia*, 1:105.

CHAPTER II — BOYHOOD AND EDUCATION

[1] The nicknames appear repeatedly in the family correspondence in the *Dolliver Papers*. Madge Stoetzer to Frances P. Dolliver, Oct. 5, 1945. (This letter was made available through the courtesy of Miss Dolliver.) Mrs. Stoetzer was a first cousin of JPD.

[2] Annie R. Heavener to Mrs. JPD, Mar. 7, 1899; Mrs. J. J. Dolliver to JPD, July 28, 1880; Rebecca Reger to Mollie Dolliver, Sept. 4, 1881, *Dolliver Papers*.

[3] JPD, Autobiographical statement, given to James B. Morrow, Washington, D. C., Aug. 7, 1909, and reprinted in Fort Dodge *Messenger*, Oct. 17, 1910. (Hereafter cited as JPD Autobiographical Statement.) A typewritten copy upon which various newspaper articles were based is in the *Dolliver Papers*.

[4] JPD, *Cong. Record*, 57 Cong., 1 sess. (Mar. 26, 1902), 3277.

[5] Mrs. J. J. Dolliver to JPD, Feb. 6, 1880; JPD to parents, Dec. 9, 1877, *Dolliver Papers*.

6 JPD Autobiographical Statement. There are many references in his personal correspondence to his love of fishing.

7 William G. Brown to Mrs. Robert Brown, Jan. 18, 1864, *Dolliver Papers*. In this letter, Brown comments on "Prent's" interest in farming.

8 JPD, "Ex-Governor Cyrus C. Carpenter," *Midland Monthly*, 10:76 (July, 1898).

9 JPD to parents, Dec. 9, 1877; Nov. 28, 1880; R. H. Dolliver to JPD, Sept. 5, 1884, *Dolliver Papers*; Robert M. La Follette, *La Follette's Autobiography: A Personal Narrative of Political Experiences* (Madison, Wisc., 1913), 435.

10 JPD, interview with Frank J. Stillman, Fort Dodge *Messenger*, May 3, 1905.

11 George C. Fort, "James J. Dolliver," Fort Dodge *Messenger*, May 3, 1905; Frank J. Stillman, Washington Correspondence, Sioux City *Journal*, May 1, 1905.

12 JPD to parents, Sept. 20, 1880; J. J. Dolliver to JPD and R. H. Dolliver, Oct. 20, 1878; Nov. 5, 1879; Mrs. J. J. Dolliver to JPD and R. H. Dolliver, Dec. 2, 1878, *Dolliver Papers*.

13 JPD, *Cong. Record*, 61 Cong., 2 sess. (Apr. 30, 1910), 5604; Fort Dodge *Messenger*, Oct. 17, 1910; Butcher (ed.), *Genealogical and Personal Hist. . . . West Virginia*, 1:387.

14 J. J. Dolliver to JPD and R. H. Dolliver, Mar. 17, 1878, *Dolliver Papers*.

15 Mollie Dolliver to JPD, June 9, 1880, *ibid.*

16 JPD, "Memorial Day Address," Metropolitan Opera House, New York City, in Des Moines *Register*, May 30, 1890.

17 Fort Dodge *Messenger*, Mar. 10, 1904; J. J. Dolliver to JPD, Apr. 28, June 9, Nov. 3, 1880, *Dolliver Papers*.

18 Fort Dodge *Messenger*, Aug. 23, 1900; J. A. Bowen to JPD, Sept. 10, 1900, *Dolliver Papers*; A. R. Whitehill, *History of Education in West Virginia* (Washington, 1902), 13-21.

19 Mark Sullivan, *Our Times* (6 vols., New York, 1926-1937), 2:7; in Callahan-Ross interview, Oct. 26, 1951, Callahan stated that the McGuffey *Readers* were widely used in West Virginia and that Dolliver had undoubtedly studied them for three or four years. Miss Frances P. Dolliver is quite sure that her father read McGuffey. Positive proof is not available. Cf. Gordon F. Hostettler, "Jonathan Prentiss Dolliver: The Formative Years," *Iowa Journal of History*, 49:26-8 (January, 1951).

20 Sullivan, *Our Times*, 2:23, 52. See also Sullivan's excellent analysis of the *Readers* in *ibid.*, 24-48.

21 Frank R. Warden, M. D., to JPD, Nov. 28, 1908; JPD to Victor Dolliver, Nov. 1, 1879, *Dolliver Papers*. Warden was a boyhood playmate in Granville. "Uncle Billy" was ex-Congressman William G. Brown of Morgantown.

22 *Catalog of West Virginia University, 1869-1870*, 7; *1868-1869*, 25, 257; *1870-1871*, 33.

23 Preparatory Dept., West Virginia University, Report Cards for J. Prentiss Dolliver for the years ending June 16, 1869, June 15, 1871, *Dolliver Papers*; Registrar's Files, West Virginia University, Morgantown.

24 *Catalog of West Virginia University, 1869-1870*, 23.

25 JPD to parents, Dec. 9, 1877; Mrs. J. J. Dolliver to Mrs. J. W. Reger, Dec. 2, 1878, *Dolliver Papers*; Brown-Ross interview, Aug. 12, 1955.

26 Charles H. Ambler, *A History of Education in West Virginia* (Huntington, W. Va., 1951), 186-190; Whitehill, *Hist. of Education in West Virginia*, 56; Callahan, *Hist. of West Virginia*, 1:654. The name of the institution was changed to West Virginia University by an act of the legislature, Dec. 4, 1868.

27 JPD, MS and printed copy of address on Abraham Lincoln to Chamber of Commerce of Pittsburgh, Feb. 12, 1908; Philander C. Knox to Mrs. JPD, Oct. 16, 1910, *Dolliver Papers;* Ambler, *Hist. of Education in West Virginia*, 192.

28 *Catalog of West Virginia University, 1871-1872*, 5; *1872-1873*, 4; *1873-1874*, 5; *1875-1876*, 7; *Register of West Virginia University, 1871-1872*, 33; *1872-1873*, 60. JPD's over-all average was 9.50, with the lowest grade 9.44 in Latin. *Ibid., 1873-1874*, 74; *1874-1875*, 86.

29 *Laws of the University of West Virginia* (1871-1875), 8. A leaflet setting forth these rules is bound with the University catalogs each year from 1867 to 1875.

30 Minutes of the Columbian Literary Society (West Virginia Univ. Library), Apr. 13, 20, 1871. JPD was evidently admitted to membership even before he entered the University proper as a freshman. Ledger of the Columbian Literary Society (West Virginia Univ. Library), 6, 79, *passim.*

31 Morgantown *Post*, Mar. 23, 1872; Minutes of the Columbian Literary Society, Nov. 13, 1874; Mar. 19, 1875; W. L. Steele to JPD, Aug. 23, 1900, *Dolliver Papers.* Steele, who was a student at the University in 1873-1874, wrote that he remembered how he used to visit the Columbian Society to hear Dolliver speak.

32 The MSS of the orations and speeches mentioned hereafter in this chapter are all preserved in the *Dolliver Papers.*

33 Minutes of the Columbian Literary Society, 1872-1875, *passim.*

34 JPD to Mollie Dolliver, Sept. 22, 1878, *Dolliver Papers.*

35 James E. Downey, "A Poor Boy's Country," Humboldt (Iowa) *Humboldt County Independent*, Apr. 26, 1900; Callahan-Ross interview, Oct. 26, 1951.

36 Claude G. Bowers, *Beveridge and the Progressive Era* (New York, 1932), 13.

37 JPD, "Grant Club Address," Des Moines, Apr. 27, 1905, in Des Moines *Register and Leader*, Apr. 28, 1905; Ambler, *Hist. of Education in West Virginia*, 195.

38 Whitehill, *Hist. of Education in West Virginia*, 57; Ambler, *Hist. of Education in West Virginia*, 194.

39 Harold T. Ross, "The Education of an Orator," *Quarterly Journal of Speech*, 18:77 (February, 1932).

40 *Register of West Virginia University, 1874-1875*, 86. F. W. Wood, Professor of Languages and Literature, West Virginia Univ., Morgantown, letter of recommendation for JPD, June 21, 1875, *Dolliver Papers.*

41 Alexander Martin, letter of recommendation for JPD, June 22, 1875, *Dolliver Papers.*

CHAPTER III — CHOOSING A CAREER

1 JPD Autobiographical Statement; J. J. Dolliver to JPD, Apr. 20, 1881, *Dolliver Papers;* M. L. Temple in Manson (Iowa) *Journal*, Mar. 10, 1898; Brown-Ross interview, Aug. 12, 1955.

2 JPD Autobiographical Statement, *Dolliver Papers.*

[3] Morgantown *Post*, June 23, 1875.

[4] Manson *Journal*, Mar. 10, 1898; Morgantown *Post*, Oct. 2, 1875.

[5] JPD Autobiographical Statement, *Dolliver Papers*.

[6] Sandwich (Ill.) *Gazette*, 1875. Clipping, without day or month, in Dolliver Scrapbook, *Dolliver Papers*.

[7] Frank O. Lowden, quoted in Sullivan, *Our Times*, 2:198-9.

[8] *Dolliver Papers*.

[9] JPD Autobiographical Statement, *ibid.*; Brown-Ross interview, Aug. 12, 1955.

[10] JPD Autobiographical Statement; John James Brown letters to Mrs. J. J. Dolliver, Mar. 11, 1878; to R. H. Dolliver, Mar. 16, 1878, and letter of reference for JPD, Jan. 1, 1878, *Dolliver Papers*.

[11] JPD Autobiographical Statement, *ibid.*

[12] George F. Hoar, *Autobiography of Seventy Years* (2 vols., New York, 1903), 1:378-81; Arthur M. Schlesinger, *The Rise of Modern America* (New York, 1951), 61; Matthew Josephson, *The Politicos, 1865-1896* (New York, 1938), 213, 214-15; James G. Blaine, *Twenty Years in Congress* (2 vols., Norwich, Conn., 1886), 2:567-72; David S. Muzzey, *James G. Blaine: A Political Idol of Other Days* (New York, 1934), 101-127.

[13] Muzzey, *Blaine*, 112; Hoar, *Autobiography*, 1:381-2.

[14] JPD Autobiographical Statement, *Dolliver Papers*.

[15] The MS is in *ibid.*, and quotation from it appears in the Morgantown *Post*, Sept. 2, 1876, which also printed an article describing the meeting.

[16] Morgantown *Post*, Sept. 2, 1876.

[17] *Ibid.*, Oct. 7, 1876.

[18] Brown-Ross interview, Aug. 12, 1955; JPD, "The Opportunities of Young Men in the Republic," an address at Plymouth Church, Brooklyn, N. Y., Feb. 28, 1904; John James Brown to Mrs. J. J. Dolliver, Mar. 11, 1878, *Dolliver Papers*.

[19] JPD to C. E. Manderville, Apr. 24, 1877, *Dolliver Papers*; this letter and letters of reference supporting his application were returned to Dolliver.

[20] James J. Dolliver, property listed as personal and exempted from execution and other process, July 4, 1877, *ibid.*

[21] Richard Van Fleet to Rev. and Mrs. J. J. Dolliver, Oct. 17, 1877; R. H. Dolliver to Mollie Dolliver, Jan. 2, 1878, and to Victor Dolliver, Mar. 17, 1878, *ibid.*

[22] Richard Van Fleet to Rev. and Mrs. J. J. Dolliver, Oct. 17, 1877, *ibid.*

[23] JPD to mother, Jan. 19, 1878, *ibid.*

[24] R. H. Dolliver to Victor Dolliver, Mar. 17, 1878, *ibid.*

[25] JPD to Victor Dolliver, Nov. 3, 1878; Charles F. Sedgwick to JPD, Aug. 23, 1900, *ibid.*

[26] JPD to father, Dec. 9, 1877, *ibid.*

[27] JPD, "Opportunities of Young Men in the Republic."

28 JPD to father, Dec. 9, 1877, *Dolliver Papers.*

29 George C. Sturgis to JPD, Jan. 10, 1878, *ibid.*

30 John James Brown, certificate for JPD, Jan. 1, 1878, *ibid.*

31 JPD to mother, Jan. 19, 1878, *ibid.*

32 John James Brown to R. H. Dolliver, Mar. 16, 1878, *ibid.*

33 John James Brown to Mrs. J. J. Dolliver, Mar. 11, 1878, *ibid.*

CHAPTER IV — NEOPHYTE LAWYER IN FORT DODGE

1 JPD Autobiographical Statement, *Dolliver Papers;* JPD, first speech in Iowa, so indicated in the MS in *ibid.* Although no date is given, internal evidence indicates it was delivered in Fort Dodge a few weeks after his arrival in 1878.

2 JPD Autobiographical Statement, *ibid.*

3 H. M. Pratt, *History of Fort Dodge and Webster County* (2 vols., Chicago, 1913), 1:69-83, 85.

4 Mildred Throne (comp.), "Iowans in Congress, 1847-1953," *Iowa Journal of History*, 51:333-6 (October, 1953). Webster County had been in various congressional districts: the 9th, 1872-1882; the 10th, 1882-1932; the 8th, 1932-1942. The county is now in the 6th district, which was represented by James I. Dolliver of Fort Dodge, a nephew of Jonathan P. Dolliver, from 1945 to 1956, when Dolliver was defeated by a Democrat.

5 JPD realized the advantages, for him, of a smaller town with less competition. He wrote his mother, June 30, 1878, "If we had money we would go to Dubuque — but as it is Ft. Dodge is our best hold." *Dolliver Papers.* The population of Fort Dodge was 3,537 in 1875 and 3,586 in 1880.

6 The original of the certificate is in *ibid.*

7 R. H. Dolliver to father, Apr. 22, 1878; JPD to mother, June 30, 1878, describing their first week in Fort Dodge, *ibid.*

8 Mildred Throne, "Electing an Iowa Governor, 1871: Cyrus Clay Carpenter," *Iowa Journal of History*, 48:336 (October, 1950).

9 Cyrus Clay Carpenter Diary, Sunday, Apr. 7, 1878, *Cyrus Clay Carpenter Papers* (State Hist. Society of Iowa, Iowa City). Hereafter cited as *Carpenter Papers.* This diary was brought to my attention by Dr. Mildred Throne, associate editor of the State Historical Society of Iowa, who is preparing a biography of C. C. Carpenter.

10 Johnson Brigham, *Iowa, Its History and Its Foremost Citizens* (3 vols., Chicago, 1915), 1:601.

11 JPD, "Ex-Governor Cyrus C. Carpenter," 77.

12 Throne, "Electing an Iowa Governor," 345-50.

13 Carpenter to J. J. Dolliver, Oct. 21, 1879; JPD to father, Sept. 1, 1878, and to Mollie Dolliver, Oct. 7, 1878; R. H. Dolliver to father, Oct. 27, 1878, *Dolliver Papers;* Carpenter Diary, Apr. 25, Oct. 7, Nov. 19, 28, 1878, and various other entries, *Carpenter Papers;* JPD, "Ex-Governor Cyrus C. Carpenter," 75-81.

14 R. H. Dolliver to father, Apr. 22, 1878, JPD to mother, June 30, 1878, *Dolliver Papers.*

[15] JPD to Gay Dolliver, Oct. 20, 1878; and to Mollie Dolliver, Sept. 22, 1878; JPD's account book, *ibid.*

[16] R. H. Dolliver to father, Oct. 27, 1878; JPD to mother, June 30, 1878, *ibid.* JPD later wrote to his father, Feb. 24, 1879: "Bob and I owe it to you to invest in a *home* out here to which we may all come in a few years and make an unbroken family."

[17] JPD to mother, June 30, 1878, *ibid.* The Methodist Church had never paid J. J. Dolliver more than $500 a year. Often what was pledged him was never paid. Mollie Dolliver to JPD, Nov. 25, 1879, *ibid.*

[18] Gay Dolliver to JPD and R. H. Dolliver, July 29, 1878, and to R. H. Dolliver, June 19, 1878; R. T. Taylor, president of Beaver College, to Mollie Dolliver, July 5, 1878; J. J. Dolliver to JPD and R. H. Dolliver, May 21, 1879, *ibid.* The father said he could not go to Mollie's graduation for lack of money.

[19] JPD to father, Sept. 1, 1878, *ibid.*

[20] JPD to Mollie and Gay Dolliver, Oct. 7, 20, 1878; and to Mollie, Sept. 22, 1878, *ibid.*

[21] JPD to Mollie and Gay Dolliver, Oct. 7, 1878, *ibid.*

[22] JPD to father, Sept. 1, 1878, *ibid.*

[23] JPD to Victor Dolliver, Nov. 3, 1878; to father, Sept. 1, 1878, *ibid.*

[24] JPD to Victor Dolliver, Nov. 3, 1878; to Mollie Dolliver, Jan. 13, 1879; to mother, Nov. 13, 1880, *ibid.*

[25] JPD to mother, Nov. 13, 1880, *ibid.*; Erik M. Eriksson, "A Tribune of the People," *The Palimpsest*, 5:37 (February, 1924).

[26] *Catalog of West Virginia University*, 1878-1879, p. 8.

[27] JPD to Victor Dolliver, May 13, 1879, *Dolliver Papers*.

[28] JPD to father, Sept. 1, 1878, *ibid.*

[29] Fred E. Haynes, *Third Party Movements Since the Civil War With Special Reference to Iowa* (Iowa City, 1916), Chap. XII; Charles Roll, "Political Trends in Iowa History," *Iowa Journal of History and Politics*, 26:508 (October, 1928); Brigham, *Iowa*, 1:609.

[30] Brigham, *Iowa*, 1:601; Fort Dodge *Webster County Gazette*, Sept. 20, 1878; Carpenter Diary, Oct. 7, 1878, *Carpenter Papers*; MS of Dolliver's set speech, *Dolliver Papers*. Much of this MS is now illegible.

[31] JPD to Mollie and Gay Dolliver, Oct. 7, 1878, *Dolliver Papers*; Brigham, *Iowa*, 2: 624-5. Although Carpenter was elected, his Greenback opponent carried Webster County by 686 votes.

[32] JPD to father, Feb. 24, 1879, *Dolliver Papers*.

[33] The MS is in *ibid.* Robert Burns's mother was a cousin of James Brown, Dolliver's great-grandfather.

[34] Fort Dodge *Webster County Gazette*, Feb. 14, 1879, quoting the Algona *Republican*.

[35] Jefferson *Bee*, July 7, 1879; Mollie Dolliver to JPD, July 28, 1879, *Dolliver Papers*.

[36] Charles T. Mindling, "The Grand Army of the Republic in Iowa" (unpublished thesis, State University of Iowa, 1949), 27, 30, 62ff.; Iowa Dept., Grand Army of the Republic, *Journal of the Proceedings, 1883,* 11, 13, 17, 129; *ibid., 1948,* 106-107; Des Moines *Iowa State Register,* 1882-1890, *passim.* This paper will hereafter be cited simply as Des Moines *Register* to save confusion in several changes of name.

[37] JPD to Carpenter, June 3, 1879, *Carpenter Papers.*

[38] W. S. Schemmerhorn to JPD, Sept. 22, 1879, *Dolliver Papers.*

[39] H. C. Laud to JPD, Sept. 29, 1879, *ibid.*

[40] Carpenter Diary, Sept. 17, 18, 1879, *Carpenter Papers;* Carpenter to J. J. Dolliver, Oct. 21, 1879, *Dolliver Papers.*

[41] Fort Dodge *Webster County Gazette,* Sept. 26, 1879; Des Moines *Register,* Sept. 2, 1879; Maple Valley *Era,* Sept. 8, 1879 (clipping in *Dolliver Papers*).

[42] Fort Dodge *Webster County Gazette,* Oct. 15, 1879.

[43] JPD to mother, Sept. 1, 1879, *Dolliver Papers.*

[44] Carpenter to J. J. Dolliver, Oct. 21, 1879, *ibid.*

[45] JPD to Mollie Dolliver, Nov. 11, 1879, *ibid.*

CHAPTER V — GAINING A FIRM FOOTHOLD IN IOWA

[1] The facts upon which these remarks descriptive of Dolliver in the 1880's are based have been gleaned from a careful study of innumerable personal letters written by Dolliver, his parents, brothers and sisters, and intimate friends, in the *Dolliver Papers;* from the Carpenter Diary, *Carpenter Papers;* from newspaper sketches in the Des Moines *Register,* Des Moines *Register and Leader,* Fort Dodge *Messenger,* Fort Dodge *Webster County Gazette,* Morgantown *Post,* and items about Dolliver from various other newspapers clipped and pasted in the Dolliver Scrapbooks; from Cyrenus Cole, *I Remember, I Remember* (Iowa City, 1936), 113-17, 327ff. Cole, editor, historian, and Congressman, knew Dolliver for over twenty-five years. Information also came from personal interviews with J. M. Guy Brown, Dolliver's cousin, and from Emory H. English of Des Moines, former editor and member of the Iowa General Assembly, who knew Dolliver.

[2] Cyrenus Cole, *A History of the People of Iowa* (Cedar Rapids, 1921), 452.

[3] Denison (Iowa) *Review,* Oct. 9, 1880; JPD to his wife, Oct. 26, 1898; and to V. B. Dolliver, Feb. 6, 1889, *Dolliver Papers;* Brown-Ross interview, Aug. 12, 1955; E. H. Hubbard, *Cong. Record,* 61 Cong., 3 sess. (Feb. 26, 1911), 3621; JPD interview with Sam Clark, Algona (Iowa) *Upper Des Moines,* May 13, 1896; Fort Dodge *Messenger,* Nov. 5, 1885; Cole, *I Remember,* 116.

[4] JPD, "The Orators and Oratory of the Stump," *Saturday Evening Post* (May 5, 1901), 6. Harvey Ingham, "Dolliver's Start in Politics," Des Moines *Register,* Nov. 5, 1936, quoted Dolliver as saying he could memorize a speech by reading it through twice.

[5] Shelby M. Cullom, in *Memorial Addresses in Honor of Jonathan Prentiss Dolliver,* Senate Doc. 872, 61 Cong., 3 sess. (1911), 18-19.

[6] Fort Dodge *Messenger,* Apr. 1, 1886; JPD, notation on a MS of Victor Dolliver's, sent him for comment, 1885, *Dolliver Papers.*

[7] Senator Albert B. Cummins, "Dolliver — A Tribune of the People," *Review of Reviews,* 42:682 (December, 1910).

[8] C. G. F. Wilcox (comp.), *Illustrated Fort Dodge* (Des Moines, 1896), 91.

[9] Emory H. English, "Capable in Public Service," *Annals of Iowa* (3rd ser.), 29:425-33 (October, 1948); Wm. R. Boyd, "George E. Roberts," *ibid.*, 29:413-24 (October, 1948). Roberts' career was highlighted by his services as Director of the Mint under Presidents McKinley, T. Roosevelt, and Taft; membership on the Finance Committee of the League of Nations, 1930-1932; and his famous 1895 booklet, *Coin at School in Finance*, used to combat W. H. Harvey's *Coin's Financial School*.

[10] Wilcox (comp.), *Illustrated Fort Dodge*, 173. There are numerous letters from Meservey to Dolliver in the *Dolliver Papers*. They, and the newspaper articles of the period 1880-1910, show conclusively that Meservey was Dolliver's close ally and, after 1890, his "political lieutenant" in Fort Dodge.

[11] Frank Luther Mott, "Master of Oratory," *The Palimpsest*, 5:72 (February, 1924).

[12] JPD, "A Glance at the Early Life of James Russell Lowell," *Midland Monthly*, 2:357 (November, 1894); Dolliver's love of history was expressed explicitly and implicitly in hundreds of his speeches and letters.

[13] Fort Dodge *Gazette-Messenger*, Feb. 27, Mar. 5, 1880.

[14] R. H. Dolliver to father, Feb. 20, 1880, *Dolliver Papers*.

[15] Deposition by Charles Andrews, Feb. 28, 1880, *ibid.*

[16] Fort Dodge *Gazette-Messenger*, Feb. 27, Mar. 5, 1880; Dolliver's certificate of election, dated Mar. 6, 1880, indicates that the election was Mar. 1, 1880, and that he was to take office for the two-year term on the third Monday of March, 1880, *Dolliver Papers*.

[17] Fort Dodge *Messenger*, Apr. 17, 1884.

[18] JPD, "Early Life of James Russell Lowell," 360.

[19] R. H. Dolliver to father, Feb. 20, 1880; J. J. Dolliver to JPD, Apr. 20, 1881, *Dolliver Papers*. Congressman James I. Dolliver to T. R. Ross, Dec. 14, 1955, states that his father, Robert H. Dolliver, was influenced to enter the ministry by James J. Dolliver and probably to some extent also because the law business in Fort Dodge was very skimpy in 1878-1880. Maude Lauderdale, "The Webster County Bar," *Annals of Iowa* (3rd ser.), 31:116 (October, 1951), quotes Dolliver as saying they cut their hair, etc.

[20] J. J. Dolliver to JPD, Nov. 5, 1879; Apr. 20, 1881; to R. H. Dolliver, Jan. 19, 1880, *Dolliver Papers*.

[21] R. H. Dolliver to Victor Dolliver, Dec. 13, 1880, *ibid.* R. H. was ordained Sept. 20, 1880, Carpenter Diary, Sept. 20, 1880, *Carpenter Papers*; Fort Dodge *Messenger*, Sept. 22, 1880.

[22] R. H. Dolliver to JPD, Dec. 12, 1880, *Dolliver Papers*.

[23] JPD to Mollie Dolliver, Aug. 1, 1880, *ibid.*

[24] R. H. Dolliver to mother, June 7, 1880; to JPD, May 17, 1880; JPD to Gay Dolliver, May 18, 1880, *ibid.*

[25] Hoar, *Autobiography*, 1:384-98; Josephson, *Politicos*, 276-87; Schlesinger, *Rise of Modern America*, 65-6; Blaine, *Twenty Years in Congress*, 2:657-67; Muzzey, *Blaine*, 158-83.

[26] JPD to father, Oct. 14, 1880, *Dolliver Papers*.

[27] JPD, MS speech, 1884; JPD to father, Mar. 7, 1881, *ibid.*

[28] Victor Dolliver to mother, July 7, 1880, *ibid.*

²⁹ Carpenter Diary, July 8, 1880, *Carpenter Papers.*

³⁰ JPD to Mollie Dolliver, Aug. 1, 1880, *Dolliver Papers;* Fort Dodge *Messenger,* July 23, 1880.

³¹ JPD to Mollie Dolliver, Aug. 1, 1880, *Dolliver Papers.*

³² Carpenter Diary, Aug. 5, 17, 28, 1880, *Carpenter Papers.*

³³ JPD to Mollie Dolliver, Sept. 22, 1880, *Dolliver Papers;* Fort Dodge *Messenger,* Oct. 8, 1880.

³⁴ Des Moines *Register,* Oct. 18, 1880.

³⁵ Jefferson *Bee,* Oct. 19, 1880.

³⁶ JPD to father and mother, Nov. 28, 1880; to father, Oct. 14, 1880, *Dolliver Papers.*

³⁷ Carpenter Diary, Nov. 2, 1880, *Carpenter Papers.*

³⁸ Al Swalm to JPD, Nov. 6, 1880, *Dolliver Papers.*

³⁹ JPD to mother, Nov. 13, 1880, *ibid.*

⁴⁰ *Idem;* JPD to father, Mar. 7, 1881, *ibid.;* Dayton (Iowa) *Review,* Nov. 20, 1880.

⁴¹ JPD to mother, Nov. 28, 1880; R. H. Dolliver to JPD, Jan. 30, 1881, *Dolliver Papers.*

⁴² J. J. Dolliver to JPD, Apr. 20, 1881, *ibid.*

⁴³ JPD to Mollie Dolliver, Aug. 7, 1881; to mother, Aug. 29, 1881; R. H. Dolliver to JPD, July 11, Aug. 22, 1881, *ibid.;* Fort Dodge *Messenger,* Oct. 21, 1881. The letters between JPD and R. H. reveal the cheerful willingness with which both accepted the duty of providing for their parents and the younger children.

⁴⁴ JPD to Gay Dolliver, Dec. 6, 1880, *Dolliver Papers;* Fort Dodge *Messenger,* Apr. 1, 1881; Rosa S. Jennings, "The Country Teacher," *Annals of Iowa* (3rd ser.), 31:58 (July, 1951).

⁴⁵ Fort Dodge *Messenger,* Dec. 10, 1880; Jan. 28, Feb. 20, Oct. 14, 1881; Mar. 24, 1882; Dec. 6, 1883. The MSS of many of these are in the *Dolliver Papers.* JPD read an essay on Carlyle before the Lyceum.

⁴⁶ Fort Dodge *Messenger,* Mar. 24, 1882.

⁴⁷ Gear (May 9), Larrabee (Mar. 1), and Wilson (Mar. 25, Apr. 5), 1881, to JPD, *Dolliver Papers;* Dan E. Clark, *History of Senatorial Elections in Iowa* (Iowa City, 1912), 190-92.

⁴⁸ Wilson to JPD, Mar. 25, Apr. 5, 1881, *Dolliver Papers;* Clark, *Senatorial Elections,* 199; Wilson to Allison, Mar. 18, 1881, *William Boyd Allison Collection* (Iowa State Dept. of Hist. and Archives, Des Moines). Hereafter cited as *Allison Papers.*

⁴⁹ Gear to JPD, May 9, 1881; JPD to Gear, May 11, 1881, *Dolliver Papers.* As to Carpenter's position in 1880, Carpenter Diary, July 6, 1880, *Carpenter Papers,* shows that Gear went to Fort Dodge to ask Carpenter's support and that Carpenter stated he already had commitments to Kirkwood — much to Gear's disappointment.

⁵⁰ Carpenter Diary, May 16, 1881, *Carpenter Papers;* JPD to R. H. Dolliver, May 20, 1881; Wilson to JPD, June 4, 1881; R. H. Dolliver to JPD, June 4, 1881, *Dolliver Papers.* R. H. advised JPD not to run unless Wilson would pay all the costs.

[51] Larrabee (Mar. 1, June 7), Henderson (June 7), 1881, to JPD (thanking him for supporting Larrabee), *Dolliver Papers.*

[52] Wilson (Dec. 19, 1881), and Carpenter (Jan. 12, 1882), to JPD, *ibid.;* Clark, *Senatorial Elections,* 199.

[53] Buren R. Sherman to JPD, Jan. 24, 1882, *Dolliver Papers.*

[54] Mollie Dolliver to Gay Dolliver, Aug. 30, 1881, *ibid.*

[55] Fort Dodge *Messenger,* Feb. 9, 1882. For election returns, *ibid.,* Mar. 10, 1882.

[56] JPD to R. H. Dolliver, Apr. 3, 1882, *Dolliver Papers.*

[57] R. H. Dolliver to JPD, Aug. 22, 1881, *ibid.*

[58] Benjamin F. Gue, *History of Iowa . . .* (4 vols., New York, 1903), 3:113-14.

[59] *Iowa State Prohibitionist,* November, 1880.

[60] JPD, speech at Dayton, Iowa, June 26, 1882. MS in *Dolliver Papers.*

[61] Dayton *Review,* June 30, 1882. Clipping in *Dolliver Papers.*

[62] Fort Dodge *Messenger,* June 30, 1882; Gue, *Hist. of Iowa,* 3:115-16; Dan E. Clark, "History of Liquor Legislation in Iowa," *Iowa Journal of History and Politics,* 6:525 (October, 1908).

[63] Paul S. Peirce, "Congressional Districting in Iowa," *Iowa Journal of History and Politics,* 1:347-51 (July, 1903); Gue, *Hist. of Iowa,* 3:114.

[64] Carpenter to JPD, July 25, 1882, *Dolliver Papers.*

[65] Brigham, *Iowa,* 1:602. Pray had heard Dolliver speak at a soldiers' reunion and had agreed to become a candidate only if JPD would make his nominating speech.

[66] *Idem;* Webster City *Hamilton Freeman,* Aug. 9, 1882. The Fort Dodge *Messenger* reprinted many similar comments from papers in all sections of Iowa.

[67] A. E. Shipley to JPD, Sept. 12, 1882, *Dolliver Papers.*

[68] Shipley to JPD, Nov. 21, 1882; Cutts to JPD, Nov. 17, 1882, *ibid.;* Throne (comp.), "Iowans in Congress," 342-3.

[69] Brooklyn (Iowa) *Chronicle,* quoted in Fort Dodge *Messenger,* Nov. 2, 1882.

[70] Carpenter Diary, Sept. 8, 1882, *Carpenter Papers.*

[71] JPD, "Senator William B. Allison, His Life and Public Service," speech at Council Bluffs, Iowa, Nov. 25, 1907. Copy in *Dolliver Papers.* Leland L. Sage, *William Boyd Allison: A Study in Practical Politics* (Iowa City, 1956), 177-82.

[72] Gue, *Hist. of Iowa,* 3:125-6; Edward Younger, *John A. Kasson, Politics and Diplomacy from Lincoln to McKinley* (Iowa City, 1955), 318.

[73] Pratt, *Hist. of Fort Dodge,* 1:90; Gue, *Hist. of Iowa,* 3:127; Mrs. J. J. Dolliver to Mollie and Gay Dolliver, Nov. 8, 1883, *Dolliver Papers.*

[74] Mrs. J. J. Dolliver to Mollie and Gay Dolliver, Nov. 23, 1883, *Dolliver Papers.* Mollie was teaching at Cincinnati Wesleyan; Gay was a student there.

CHAPTER VI — NATIONAL FAME FOR THE FORT DODGE ORATOR

[1] Cole, *Hist. of People of Jowa*, 455.

[2] Younger, *Kasson*, 318; Cyrenus Cole, *Jowa Through the Years* (Iowa City, 1940), 362.

[3] Clark, *Senatorial Elections*, 209.

[4] Cole, *Hist. of People of Jowa*, 456-7; Iowa City *Republican*, July 21, 1884.

[5] Fort Dodge *Messenger*, Mar. 6, 1884; Des Moines *Register*, May 2, 1884.

[6] Clarkson to JPD, Nov. 22, 1878, *Dolliver Papers*; J. S. Clarkson, "Farewell Tribute to Dolliver," Des Moines *Register and Leader*, Oct. 23, 1910. Cole, in the histories cited above, and other historians and publicists accept 1884 as the date of the beginning of the Dolliver-Clarkson relationship. However, evidence in the *Dolliver Papers* and in the Des Moines *Register* shows that it began much earlier. In his autobiographical statement, previously cited, JPD recalled that he "once worked on the public road for $1.50 a day" but when elected city solicitor in 1880 "right there I ceased to be an intermittent day laborer on the streets."

[7] George Mills, "The Fighting Clarksons," *The Palimpsest*, 30:283-9 (September, 1949); Cole, *J Remember*, 143.

[8] Des Moines *Register*, May 2, 1884; Younger, *Kasson*, 319.

[9] New York *Times*, June 6, 1884; Henry F. Pringle, *Theodore Roosevelt: A Biography* (New York, 1931), 79-85; Hoar, *Autobiography*, 1:406-408; Ellis P. Oberholtzer, *A History of the United States Since the Civil War* (5 vols., New York, 1917-1937), 4:171-4; Muzzey, *Blaine*, 272-3; Gail Hamilton, *Biography of James G. Blaine* (Norwich, Conn., 1895), 622-4; George F. Dawson, *Life and Services of Gen. John A. Logan* (Chicago, 1887), 313-15.

[10] Fort Dodge *Messenger*, June 5, 1884.

[11] New York *Times*, June 7, 14, 19, 1884; New York *Nation*, June 12, 1884; Schlesinger, *Rise of Modern America*, 70.

[12] Allan Nevins, *Grover Cleveland: A Study in Courage* (New York, 1932), 146; Schlesinger, *Rise of Modern America*, 70.

[13] Cole, *Jowa Through the Years*, 365.

[14] Cole, *J Remember*, 114. There are three manuscript drafts of the address in the *Dolliver Papers*. Brigham, *Jowa*, 1:602; Des Moines *Register*, Aug. 21, 1884.

[15] Cole, *Hist. of People of Jowa*, 460; Des Moines *Register*, Aug. 21, 1884.

[16] J. B. Weaver, "Address at Dolliver Park," June 28, 1925, Fort Dodge *Messenger and Chronicle*, June 29, 1925.

[17] Schlesinger, *Rise of Modern America*, 70.

[18] JPD, "Address to the State Republican Convention," Des Moines, Aug. 20, 1884, in Des Moines *Register*, Aug. 21, 1884. All quotations are from the text as printed in the *Register*.

[19] Albert J. Beveridge, in *Memorial Addresses in Honor of Jonathan Prentiss Dolliver*, 24; Bowers, *Beveridge*, 21, 22; Des Moines *Register*, Aug. 21, 1884.

[20] Fort Dodge *Messenger*, Aug. 28, 1884.

[21] R. H. Dolliver to JPD, Sept. 5, 1884, *Dolliver Papers*. The clipping is still pinned to this letter.

[22] Oberholtzer, *Hist. of U. S.*, 4:194n, 194-5; Josephson, *Politicos*, 360-65; Muzzey, *Blaine*, 295-8. Nevins, *Cleveland*, 181, states that the Democrats were hampered for lack of funds.

[23] Josephson, *Politicos*, 360-65; Nevins, *Cleveland*, 158, 169-75; Oberholtzer, *Hist. of U. S.*, 4:195, 202-204.

[24] Fort Dodge *Messenger*, Sept. 4, 1884; JPD to Mollie Dolliver, Oct. 25, Nov. 11, 1884, *Dolliver Papers*.

[25] Henry Adams to C. M. Gaskell, Sept. 21, 1884, in W. C. Ford (ed.), *Letters of Henry Adams* (2 vols., Boston, 1930), 1:360.

[26] Nevins, *Cleveland*, 164, 178; Thomas Nast's cartoons in *Harper's Weekly*, August-November, 1884, depicted Blaine as "Boodle" Blaine; Beecher's alleged sexual irregularities had been the subject of countless headlines; Conkling's distaste for Blaine was not due to any allergy on "Lord Roscoe's" part to corruption in office.

[27] Josephson, *Politicos*, 365.

[28] JPD to Gay Dolliver, Sept. 16, 1884, *Dolliver Papers*; *Harper's Weekly*, Sept. 13, 1884.

[29] JPD to Gay Dolliver, Sept. 16, 1884; Garret A. Hobart to JPD, Dec. 4, 1884, *Dolliver Papers*; Des Moines *Register*, Sept. 25, 1884; Des Moines *Register and Leader*, Oct. 23, 1910.

[30] Fort Dodge *Messenger*, Sept. 25, 1884.

[31] Philadelphia *Press*, Oct. 26, 1884, quoted in Fort Dodge *Messenger*, Oct. 30, 1884; JPD to Gay Dolliver, Sept. 16, 1884; to Mollie Dolliver, Nov. 11, 1884; and to mother, Oct. 23, 1884, *Dolliver Papers*. Muzzey, *Blaine*, 312-13, does not list Dolliver among the "prominent" men who spoke with Blaine. Dolliver, of course, was not "prominent" in that period in the sense that Muzzey used the term.

[32] Utica *Tribune*, Oct. 19, 1884.

[33] JPD, 1884 Campaign MS, *Dolliver Papers*; Norwich (Conn.) *Daily Bulletin*, Oct. 25, 1884, praised this speech as being "eloquent, vivid, epigrammatic" and said that it was received "amid enthusiastic cheering."

[34] JPD to Mollie Dolliver, Oct. 27, 1884, *Dolliver Papers*.

[35] Clarkson dispatch from New York to Fort Dodge *Messenger*, Oct. 30, 1884.

[36] Gay Dolliver to Mollie Dolliver, Oct. 31, 1884, *Dolliver Papers*.

[37] Fort Dodge *Messenger*, Nov. 6, 1884.

[38] JPD to Mollie Dolliver, Nov. 11, 1884, *Dolliver Papers*.

[39] *Idem*. The Prohibition party nominee, John P. St. John of Kansas, received 25,016 votes in New York, most of them from voters usually Republican. Cleveland's plurality in New York was less than 1,200; Nevins, *Cleveland*, 187; cf. Oberholtzer, *Hist. of U. S.*, 4:211.

[40] JPD, "Address at Des Moines," Sept. 25, 1885, in Des Moines *Register*, Oct. 2, 1885.

41 JPD to Mollie Dolliver, Nov. 11, 1884, *Dolliver Papers.*

42 The phrase "Young War Eagle of Webster County" was apparently first used by the Humboldt *Kosmos* in October and November, 1884. Clippings from it and other papers are in the Dolliver Scrapbook, 1884, *Dolliver Papers.*

43 Garret A. Hobart to JPD, Dec. 4, 1884, *Dolliver Papers.*

CHAPTER VII — HAT IN THE RING

1 Throne (comp.), "Iowans in Congress," 332-42; Pocahontas *Record,* Apr. 29, 1886.

2 Des Moines *Register,* Aug. 22, 1884.

3 JPD to Victor Dolliver, Jan. 23, 1885, *Dolliver Papers.*

4 JPD to Mollie Dolliver, Feb. 23, 1885; letterheads, O'Connell and Dolliver Law Firm, 1882-1885, *ibid.*

5 Lauderdale, "Webster County Bar," 124-5.

6 JPD to Mollie Dolliver, Feb. 23, 1885, *Dolliver Papers.*

7 R. H. Dolliver to JPD, Mar. 8, 1885, *ibid.*

8 Cole, *Iowa Through the Years,* 369.

9 Larrabee to JPD, Apr. 20, 1885, *Dolliver Papers.* Russel B. Nye's statement in his *Midwestern Progressive Politics* (East Lansing, Mich., 1951), 224, that Larrabee was a Democrat is an error.

10 Cole, *I Remember,* 115; Clarkson to JPD, May 8, 1885, *Dolliver Papers.*

11 The MS of the address is in the *Dolliver Papers;* Gue, *Hist. of Iowa,* 3:127.

12 Des Moines *Register,* Aug. 29, 1885.

13 Cole, *I Remember,* 116.

14 JPD speech at Des Moines in Des Moines *Register,* Oct. 2, 1885.

15 Gue, *Hist. of Iowa,* 3:127, 135; Mindling, "The Grand Army of the Republic in Iowa," 59-62; Pratt, *Hist. of Fort Dodge,* 1:90; David C. Mott, "Iowa Political Conventions and Platforms," *Annals of Iowa* (3rd ser.), 14:109 (October, 1923).

16 Des Moines *Leader,* Dec. 30, 1885.

17 MS in *Dolliver Papers.*

18 Cole, *Hist. of People of Iowa,* 419ff.; Henry Wallace, *Uncle Henry's Own Story* (3 vols., Des Moines, 1917-1919), 3:34ff.; Emory H. English, "Evolution in Iowa Voting Practices," *Annals of Iowa* (3rd ser.), 29:249-62 (April, 1948).

19 Wallace, *Uncle Henry's Own Story,* 3:35; cf. Earle D. Ross, *Iowa Agriculture, An Historical Survey* (Iowa City, 1951), 65.

20 Cole, *I Remember,* 161.

21 JPD to Mollie Dolliver, May 17, 1885, *Dolliver Papers.* JPD's correspondence indi-

cates that he used free passes for himself and family from June, 1880, when he traveled on one to the Republican National Convention, until 1905, when he began to refuse passes. It is interesting to note that N. M. Hubbard furnished Dolliver a pass to the Republican National Convention in 1884, but that in 1885 Hubbard refused Dolliver's request for a pass. Hubbard to JPD, May 17, 1884; Jan. 8, 1885, *ibid.*

22 Thomas J. Bray, "Memoir of Iowa Politics in the Blythe-Hubbard-Cummins Era," typescript in the Iowa State Dept. of Hist. and Archives, Des Moines; Emory H. English, Des Moines, interview with T. R. Ross, Oct. 27, 1955.

23 J. J. Dolliver to Mollie Dolliver, Feb. 2, 1886; R. H. Dolliver to Mollie and Gay Dolliver, Feb. 13, May 10, 1886; and to Gay Dolliver, Mar. 8, 1886, *Dolliver Papers.*

24 Fort Dodge *Messenger*, Mar. 4, 1886.

25 Des Moines *Register*, Mar. 5, 17, 30, 1886; Francis O. Wilcox, "Congressional Redistricting in Iowa," *Iowa Journal of History and Politics*, 29:463 (October, 1931).

26 Peirce, "Congressional Districting in Iowa," 353-5.

27 John A. Lindberg to JPD, Apr. 9, 1886, *Dolliver Papers*; JPD to Lindberg, Apr. 12, 1886, in Dayton *Review*. Clipping in *Dolliver Papers.*

28 R. H. Dolliver to Mollie and Gay Dolliver, Feb. 13, Mar. 8, 1886, *Dolliver Papers.* Fort Dodge *Messenger*, Apr. 22, 1886.

29 Rolfe *Reporter*, May 1, 1886. The Fort Dodge *Messenger*, May 13, 1886, reprinted many editorials from Iowa newspapers favoring Dolliver.

30 Pocahontas *Record*, Apr. 29, 1886.

31 Carpenter to A. D. Bicknell, May 4, 1886, in Fort Dodge *Messenger*, May 13, 1886.

32 Huitt Ross (July 7), A. K. Knowles (May 3), and H. C. Laub (July 7), 1886, to Carpenter, *Carpenter Papers.*

33 Allison to JPD, June 20, 1886, *Dolliver Papers.*

34 Fort Dodge *Messenger*, Aug. 12, 1886.

35 *Ibid.*, Aug. 26, 1886.

36 *Idem.* Jacob Van Ek, "Two District Conventions," *The Palimpsest*, 5:50, 51, 54 (February, 1924).

37 Fort Dodge *Messenger*, Aug. 26, 1886. The MSS of both speeches are in the *Dolliver Papers.*

38 Webster City *Freeman*, Aug. 25, 1886.

39 Des Moines *Register*, Aug. 26, 1886.

40 JPD, "Address at the Republican State Convention," Des Moines, Aug. 25, 1886, in Des Moines *Register*, Aug. 26, 1886.

41 Des Moines *Register*, Aug. 26, 1886; Mott, "Iowa Political Conventions and Platforms," 115.

42 Holmes to JPD, Sept. 30, 1886, *Dolliver Papers;* Des Moines *Register*, Oct. 2, 13, 15, 16, 1886.

43 *Iowa Official Register, 1887* (Des Moines, 1887), 162-4.

⁴⁴ Detroit *Tribune*, Feb. 24, 1887; J. H. Stone to JPD, Feb. 7, 1887; JPD to Victor Dolliver, Feb. 15, 1887, *Dolliver Papers.*

⁴⁵ Detroit *Tribune*, Feb. 24, 1887.

⁴⁶ R. H. Dolliver to JPD, Feb. 28, 1887, *Dolliver Papers.*

⁴⁷ Henderson (Jan. 22, 29, Feb. 1, 4, Apr. 8), Ernest Hofer (June 7), J. O. McVay (Aug. 29), 1887, to Dolliver, *ibid.*

⁴⁸ Des Moines *Register*, Aug. 26, 1887; Mott, "Iowa Conventions and Platforms," 127-30.

⁴⁹ Des Moines *Register*, Sept. 30, 1887, listed Dolliver's October schedule; Charles Beardsley to JPD, Nov. 14, 1887, *Dolliver Papers.*

⁵⁰ Clarkson to JPD, Dec. 25, 1887, *Dolliver Papers.* Clarkson wrote: "Everything is moving to Blaine. He will be nominated."

⁵¹ John McCleave to JPD, Dec. 16, 1886, *ibid.*

CHAPTER VIII — TWOFOLD VICTORY

¹ James D. Richardson (ed.), *Messages and Papers of the Presidents* (10 vols., Washington, 1909), 8:580-91; Nevins, *Cleveland*, 370-82.

² F. W. Taussig, *The Tariff History of the United States* (7th ed., New York, 1923), 253.

³ *Ibid.*, 254ff.; Nevins, *Cleveland*, 388-94.

⁴ Oberholtzer, *Hist. of U. S.*, 5:53-6; Josephson, *Politicos*, 404; Nathaniel W. Stephenson, *Nelson W. Aldrich, A Leader in American Politics* (New York, 1930), 70-74; Sage, *Allison*, 231-3.

⁵ Cole, *Hist. of People of Iowa*, 465-8; Gue, *Hist. of Iowa*, 3:142-51; Brigham, *Iowa*, 1:484; Cole, *Iowa Through the Years*, 373.

⁶ Clarkson to Allison, Jan. 13, 1888, *Allison Papers.*

⁷ Cole, *I Remember*, 164; Cole, *Hist. of People of Iowa*, 469; Des Moines *Register*, Jan.-Mar., 1888, *passim.*

⁸ Secretary to Gov. Wm. Larrabee to Carpenter, Apr. 18, 1888, *Carpenter Papers.*

⁹ Cole, *Hist. of People of Iowa*, 469.

¹⁰ Typescript in *Dolliver Papers*; text in Des Moines *Register*, Mar. 22, 1888.

¹¹ Brigham, *Iowa*, 1:605.

¹² Henderson to JPD, Mar. 24, 1888, *Dolliver Papers.*

¹³ Cole, *Hist. of People of Iowa*, 470; Fort Dodge *Messenger*, Mar. 22, 1888.

¹⁴ Cole, *Hist. of People of Iowa*, 470.

¹⁵ James C. Young to Clarkson, Mar. 31, 1888, *James S. Clarkson Collection* (Iowa State Dept. of Hist. and Archives, Des Moines). Hereafter cited as *Clarkson Papers* (Des Moines).

¹⁶ JPD to Allison, Feb. 19, 1888, *Allison Papers.*

17 Henderson to Carpenter, Feb. 4, 1888, *Carpenter Papers,* cf. Clarkson (Apr. 1, 1887), Sam M. Clark (Jan. 11), Charles E. Perkins (Feb. 17), Jacob Rich (Feb. 21), 1888, to Allison, *Allison Papers.*

18 Rich to JPD, Mar. 27, May 5, 14, June 7, 1888, *Dolliver Papers; Des Moines Register,* May 3, 1888.

19 Muzzey, *Blaine,* 376-80; Hamilton, *Blaine,* 604-607; Sage, *Allison,* 204-229.

20 Clarkson to Allison, June 8, 1888, *Allison Papers.*

21 Robert M. La Follette, in *Memorial Addresses in Honor of Jonathan Prentiss Dolliver,* 36.

22 Clark, *Senatorial Elections,* 214; John E. Briggs, *William Peters Hepburn* (Iowa City, 1919), 140-44. Josephson's statement in *The Politicos,* 412, that Clarkson "ruled unchallenged" in Iowa needs qualification. Clarkson was not able to prevent Larrabee's railroad legislation, and he was badly beaten when he and the *Register* attempted to defeat Senator Wilson's renomination by booming Col. Hepburn in 1887-1888.

23 Hoar, *Autobiography,* 1:413. Aaron Burr in 1800, Samuel Tilden in 1876, and many other men who actually received a presidential nomination came nearer the presidency than Allison. See Sage, *Allison,* Chap. 14, for the latest account of this convention.

24 Des Moines *Register,* June 28, 1888; Oberholtzer, *Hist. of U. S.,* 5:30.

25 Alexander McDowell (comp.), *Platforms of the Two Great Political Parties, 1865-1908* (Washington, 1908), 71-2.

26 Clarkson to Allison, July 9, 1888, *Allison Papers;* Ida M. Tarbell, *The Tariff in Our Times* (New York, 1911), 175.

27 McDowell (comp.), *Platforms,* 66-70; Oberholtzer, *Hist. of U. S.,* 5:43-5.

28 Cole, *Hist. of People of Iowa,* 472.

29 Fort Dodge *Messenger,* Apr. 12, May 10, 1888.

30 Barkley to JPD, Apr. 19, 1888, *Dolliver Papers.*

31 Clarkson to JPD, Apr. 19, 1888, *ibid.* Later Clarkson wrote: "I do not believe that it is a good thing for you, but I would hate to see you defeated, after you have started for the race." Clarkson to JPD, July 19, 1888, *ibid.*

32 Donald L. McMurry, "The Soldier Vote in Iowa," *Iowa Journal of History and Politics,* 18:352 (July, 1920); Des Moines *Register,* 1887-1888, *passim,* especially June 17, 1887.

33 JPD Autobiographical Statement; S. C. Higbee to JPD, Aug. 13, 1888, *Dolliver Papers.*

34 Barkley to JPD, June 5, 1888, *ibid.;* Roberts to Carpenter, July 25, 1888, *Carpenter Papers.*

35 Fort Dodge *Messenger,* Aug. 16, 1888; R. E. Carpenter to Carpenter, Aug. 26, 1888, *Carpenter Papers.*

36 Fort Dodge *Messenger,* Aug. 23, 1888.

37 *Idem;* Des Moines *Register,* Aug. 22, 1888.

38 Des Moines *Register,* Aug. 22, 1888.

39 Conner to JPD, Feb. 9, 1892, *Dolliver Papers.*

[40] Des Moines *Register*, Aug. 23, 1888.

[41] *Ibid.*, Aug. 22, 1888; clippings in Dolliver Scrapbook, 1888, *Dolliver Papers*; Boone *Republican*, Aug. 22, 1888.

[42] R. H. Dolliver to JPD, Aug. 21, 1888, *Dolliver Papers*; Fort Dodge *Messenger*, Aug. 23, 1888.

[43] Des Moines *Register*, Aug. 23, 1888.

[44] Clarkson (July 19), and Joseph H. Manley (July 12, 21), 1888, to JPD, *Dolliver Papers*; Des Moines *Register*, Aug. 23, 1888.

[45] "Captain Joseph A. O. Yeoman," *Annals of Iowa* (3rd ser.), 4:637-8 (January, 1901); Lauderdale, "Webster County Bar," 108-109; Des Moines *Register*, Nov. 2, 1888; Fort Dodge *Messenger*, Oct., 1888, *passim*.

[46] Des Moines *Register*, Oct. 7, 1888.

[47] Fort Dodge *Messenger*, Oct. 11, 1888; Des Moines *Register*, Oct. 13, 16, 23, 1888; A. Welliver to Victor Dolliver, Oct. 3, 1888, *Dolliver Papers*.

[48] Yeoman to JPD, Mar. 14, 1893, *Dolliver Papers*.

[49] Josephson, *Politicos*, 423-5, 430; Nevins, *Cleveland*, 437-9; Oberholtzer, *Hist. of U. S.*, 5:72-3; Clarkson to John F. Lacey, Oct. 12, 1888, *John Fletcher Lacey Collection* (Iowa State Dept. of Hist. and Archives, Des Moines). Hereafter cited as *Lacey Papers*.

[50] "Leigh S. J. Hunt," *Annals of Iowa* (3rd ser.), 19:314-15 (April, 1934).

[51] JPD to Hunt, June 2, 1905, *Dolliver Papers*.

[52] Des Moines *Register*, Nov. 10, 1888.

[53] Oberholtzer, *Hist. of U. S.*, 5:69.

[54] JPD to Benjamin Harrison, Dec. 22, 1888, *Dolliver Papers*; Benjamin Harrison (Nov. 13, 1888), and Clarkson (Feb. 26, 1892), to Allison, *Allison Papers*; Josephson, *Politicos*, 438, 440.

[55] JPD (Dec. 28), M. D. O'Connell (Dec. 9), and J. Fred Meyers (Dec. 8), 1888, to Allison, *Allison Papers*.

[56] Gen G. M. Dodge (Jan. 31), and J. K. Graves (Feb. 2), 1889, to Clarkson, *Clarkson Papers* (Des Moines). See Sage, *Allison*, 235-9.

[57] Henderson to JPD, Dec. 11, 1888, *Dolliver Papers*.

[58] Joseph G. Cannon to Carpenter, Dec. 27, 1888, *Carpenter Papers*.

[59] JPD to editor of New York *Herald*, Dec. 26, 1888, *Dolliver Papers*.

CHAPTER IX — ADVOCATE OF PENSIONS AND PROTECTION

[1] JPD to father, Nov. 25, 1889, *Dolliver Papers*.

[2] JPD, campaign speech, 1884, *ibid.*

[3] *The Methodist Review*, 68:453 (May, 1888), quoted in Merle Curti, *The Growth of American Thought* (2nd ed., New York, 1951), 608.

[4] JPD, "The Basis of Equal Rights Among Men," and "Public Virtue as a Question of Politics," lectures written in the 1880's and delivered repeatedly in the decade 1888-

1898, *Dolliver Papers.* Curti, *American Thought,* 607-612, discusses the formulas of protest and reform typical of Dolliver's approach to the problems of the era.

⁵ Curti, *American Thought,* 610.

⁶ JPD, "Basis of Equal Rights," *Dolliver Papers.*

⁷ *Idem.*

⁸ JPD, "Public Virtue as a Question of Politics" (delivered at West Virginia University in 1889), typescript in *ibid.*

⁹ Meservey to JPD, Feb. 18, 1905, *ibid.*

¹⁰ JPD, "Public Virtue as a Question of Politics," *ibid.* He often expressed this view in other speeches.

¹¹ Vernon L. Parrington, *Main Currents in American Thought* (3 vols., New York, 1930), 3:137; cf. Nye, *Midwestern Progressive Politics,* 11-27.

¹² Bowers, *Beveridge,* 328.

¹³ Arthur M. Schlesinger, *Paths to the Present* (New York, 1949), 82-3.

¹⁴ Gay Dolliver to Victor Dolliver, Feb. 10, 1889, *Dolliver Papers.*

¹⁵ JPD to Gay Dolliver, Feb. 14, 1889, *ibid.*

¹⁶ JPD to Mrs. C. C. Carpenter, Feb. 28, 1889, *Carpenter Papers.*

¹⁷ Oberholtzer, *Hist. of U. S.,* 5:90.

¹⁸ Carpenter to JPD, Feb. 19, Mar. 23, 1889, *Dolliver Papers.*

¹⁹ JPD to F. E. Bean (Mar. 20); and Carpenter (Mar. 23), Clarkson (May 27), 1889, to JPD, *ibid.* Between March and August, 1889, Clarkson removed 13,000 Democratic postmasters, Oberholtzer, *Hist. of U. S.,* 5:92.

²⁰ O'Connell to JPD, Mar. 7, 11, 1889, *Dolliver Papers.*

²¹ JPD to father, Mar. 30, 1889; July 14, 1890, *ibid;* H. C. Lodge to Theodore Roosevelt, Mar. 29, 1889, in *Selections from the Correspondence of Theodore Roosevelt and Henry Cabot Lodge, 1884-1918* (2 vols., New York, 1925), 1:76.

²² Gue, *Hist. of Iowa,* 3:154, 155; Cole, *Hist. of People of Iowa,* 476.

²³ Gue, *Hist. of Iowa,* 3:156; Cole, *Hist. of People of Iowa,* 477; Clark, *Senatorial Elections,* 221; Sage, *Allison,* 240-41.

²⁴ JPD to father, Nov. 25, 1889, *Dolliver Papers.* JPD used the expression "stepping on a corkscrew" when explaining the cause of the Republican defeat to the fourth annual dinner of the Republican Club of New York City, Feb. 12, 1890, *ibid.* When Representative Charles H. Mansur, a Missouri Democrat, intimated in the House that Iowa went Democratic because of dissatisfaction with the tariff, JPD replied that anyone who thought that "does not know the difference between the tariff and a corkscrew." *Cong. Record,* 51 Cong., 1 sess. (May 16, 1890), 4794.

²⁵ JPD to father, Nov. 25, 1889; receipt dated Dec. 18, 1889, for the month Nov. 25-Dec. 25, signed William A. Woods, *Dolliver Papers.*

²⁶ JPD to father, Dec. 1, 1889, *ibid.* Iowa politicians and newspapers habitually used "The Delegation" when speaking of the Iowa members of the House of Representatives.

²⁷ Richardson (ed.), *Messages and Papers,* 9:32-58.

28 JPD to father, Dec. 14, 1889, *Dolliver Papers.*

29 Mrs. C. C. Carpenter to JPD, Dec. 28, 1889, *ibid.*

30 JPD to father, Dec. 21, 1889, *ibid.; Cong. Record*, 51 Cong., 1 sess. (Apr. 8, 1890), 3167.

31 *Cong. Record*, 51 Cong., 1 sess., 949-60, 979-95; New York *Times*, Feb. 1, 2, 7, 15, 1890; William A. Robinson, *Thomas B. Reed: Parliamentarian* (New York, 1930), 217-34; O. O. Stealey, *Twenty Years in the Press Gallery* (New York, 1906), 68-100.

32 JPD, "Address at the Fourth Annual Dinner of the Republican Club at New York City," Feb. 12, 1890; JPD to Gay Dolliver, Feb. 1, 1890, *Dolliver Papers. Cong. Record*, 51 Cong., 1 sess. (Sept. 27, 1890), 10594.

33 *Cong. Record*, 51 Cong., 1 sess., *passim*, especially Sept. 27, 1890, pp. 10594ff.

34 JPD to father, Feb. 23, 1890, *Dolliver Papers.*

35 Mott, "Master of Oratory," 68; *Cong. Record*, 51 Cong., 1 sess. (Apr. 4, 1890), 3018-3020.

36 *Cong. Record*, 51 Cong., 1 sess. (Apr. 4, 1890), 3019-3020.

37 *Ibid.*, 51 Cong., 1 sess. (1889-1890), through 61 Cong., 2 sess. (1909-1910).

38 Mrs. JPD's diary, *passim, Dolliver Papers.*

39 JPD, "Address . . . Republican Club of New York City," *ibid.*

40 The speech was printed in full in the New York *Mail and Express*, Feb. 13, 1890, and in the Des Moines *Register*, Feb. 16, 1890, and received much favorable comment in Iowa Republican papers. Gay Dolliver to JPD, Feb. 16, 1890, *Dolliver Papers.*

41 JPD to Victor Dolliver, Apr. 10, 1890, and to father, May 4, 1890, *Dolliver Papers.*

42 JPD, "Address at Memorial Day Exercises, Metropolitan Opera House, New York, May 30, 1890," Des Moines *Register*, May 31, 1890.

43 Paul Buck, *The Road to Reunion, 1865-1900* (Boston, 1947), 278-82, 298-307.

44 JPD to father, June 2, 1890, *Dolliver Papers.*

45 W. R. Boyd, "Dolliver Possessed Rare Oratorical Ability," *Annals of Iowa* (3rd ser.), 29:340 (July, 1948); George E. Roberts to Frances P. Dolliver, Aug. 5, 1946, gives a similar account. This letter used through the courtesy of Miss Dolliver.

46 Taussig, *Tariff Hist. of U. S.*, 255-83; Oberholtzer, *Hist. of U. S.*, 5:111, 160ff.; Schlesinger, *Rise of Modern America*, 77; Festus P. Summers, *William L. Wilson and Tariff Reform* (New Brunswick, 1953), 107.

47 Muzzey, *Blaine*, 442-51; Taussig, *Tariff Hist. of U. S.*, 279-82; Benjamin Harrison to the Senate and House of Representatives, June 19, 1890, Richardson (ed.), *Messages and Papers*, 9:74.

48 *Cong. Record*, 51 Cong., 1 sess. (May 16, 1890), 4790, 4791.

49 *Ibid.* (Sept. 27, 1890), 10594; Hamilton, *Blaine*, 688.

50 J. C. Kerr to JPD, Apr. 2, 1890, *Dolliver Papers.*

51 Oberholtzer, *Hist. of U. S.*, 5:112; Josephson, *Politicos*, 458-60.

52 *Cong. Record*, 51 Cong., 1 sess. (Sept. 27, 1890), 10595.

53 *Ibid.*, 10594-5; Summers, *Wilson and Tariff Reform*, 115; Josephson, *Politicos*, 455-7; Oberholtzer, *Hist. of U. S.*, 5:113-16; Fred W. Wellborn, "The Influence of the Silver Republican Senators, 1889-1891," *Mississippi Valley Historical Review*, 14:462-80 (March, 1928).

54 *Cong. Record*, 51 Cong., 1 sess. (Sept. 27, 1890), 10595, 10641; (Sept. 30, 1890), 10725; (Oct. 1, 1890), 10799.

55 Victor Dolliver (June 20), and JPD (June 23), 1890, to father, *Dolliver Papers*.

56 Oberholtzer, *Hist. of U. S.*, 5:126-9; Josephson, *Politicos*, 441-3, 463; Pringle, *Roosevelt*, 123ff.

57 Clarkson to JPD, Dec. 7, 1892, *Dolliver Papers*.

58 Pringle, *Roosevelt*, 124ff.

59 Haynes, *Third Party Movements*, 221-31; Solon J. Buck, *The Agrarian Crusade* (New Haven, 1920), 102-123.

60 H. C. Nixon, "The Populist Movement in Iowa," *Iowa Journal of History and Politics*, 24:40, 42 (January, 1926); Des Moines *Register*, Apr. 5, Aug. 10, 1890.

61 Des Moines *Register*, Nov. 7, 1890; Throne (comp.), "Iowans in Congress," 346-8.

62 Oberholtzer, *Hist. of U. S.*, 5:132, 135.

63 Fort Dodge *Messenger*, Jan. 21, 1891; R. H. Dolliver to JPD, Feb. 4, 1891, *Dolliver Papers*.

64 *Cong. Record*, 51 Cong., 1 sess. (July 1, 1890), 6861.

65 John A. Garraty, *Henry Cabot Lodge: A Biography* (New York, 1953), 190-91; Oberholtzer, *Hist. of U. S.*, 5:137-8; Hoar, *Autobiography*, 2:150-65; Wellborn, "Influence of the Silver Republican Senators," 462-80.

66 JPD to father, Dec. 11, 1891, *Dolliver Papers*.

67 *Cong. Record*, 52 Cong., 1 sess. (Feb. 15, 1892), 1152.

68 Walter E. Nydegger, "The Election of 1892 in Iowa," *Iowa Journal of History and Politics*, 25:374-6, 377 (July, 1927); H. C. Nixon, "The Economic Basis of the Populist Movement in Iowa," *ibid.*, 21:391 (July, 1923); *Annual Report of the Secretary of Agriculture, 1889* (Washington, 1889), 262-3; *Yearbook of the U. S. Dept. of Agriculture, 1894* (Washington, 1895), 545.

69 *Cong. Record*, 52 Cong., 1 sess. (Mar. 29, 1892), 2666-75; also printed as pamphlet entitled "The Tariff Act of 1890," several copies of which are in the *Dolliver Papers*, as are numerous letters from Iowans asking for it, commenting on it, and thanking him for it.

70 Muzzey, *Blaine*, 470, quoting Clarkson's letter to Blaine, Jan. 15, 1892; Des Moines *Register*, Feb. 28, 1892; Oberholtzer, *Hist. of U. S.*, 5:181-4.

71 Des Moines *Register*, Feb. 22, 1892; Clarkson to Allison, Feb. 26, 1892, *Allison Papers*.

72 Des Moines *Register*, Mar. 6, 13, 1892. For complete story of this, see Sage, *Allison*, 250-52.

73 Des Moines *Register*, Mar. 6, 1892.

74 JPD to Clarkson, June 9, 1892, *James S. Clarkson Papers* (Library of Congress). Hereafter cited as *Clarkson Papers* (L. C.). Cf. Oberholtzer, *Hist. of U. S.*, 5:184-6.

75 Muzzey, *Blaine*, 475ff.; James Ford Rhodes, *From Hayes to McKinley* (New York, 1919), 380ff.; William Allen White, *Masks in a Pageant* (New York, 1928), 101n.; Nydegger, "Election of 1892 in Iowa," 381, 426ff., 437.

76 George H. Knoles, *The Presidential Campaign and Election of 1892* (Stanford, Calif., 1942), 211ff.

77 *Ibid.*, 424-5.

78 Roberts to JPD, Apr. 11, 1892, *Dolliver Papers*. See also J. B. Hungerford (May 5), re Head; Roberts (May 25), re Holmes, Head, and Kamrar; J. D. McVay (Mar. 18), re Holmes and Kamrar; A. J. Barkley (June 17), re Holmes's withdrawal, 1892, to JPD, *ibid.*

79 Clarkson to JPD, Sept. 2, 1892; Mollie Dolliver to Gay Dolliver, Sept. 19, 1892, *ibid.*

80 Nydegger, "Election of 1892 in Iowa," 436-7, 439; *Iowa Official Register* (Des Moines, 1893), 193ff.; Fort Dodge *Messenger*, Nov. 17, 1892.

CHAPTER X — POLITICS AND ROMANCE

1 Nevins, *Cleveland*, 441-2, 523-5; Summers, *Wilson and Tariff Reform*, 156-8; Stephenson, *Aldrich*, 106-107; Josephson, *Politicos*, 526-31; Davis R. Dewey, *Financial History of the United States* (11th ed., New York, 1931), 444-6.

2 Joseph A. Schumpeter, *Business Cycles* (2 vols., New York, 1939), 1:381-3; Nevins, *Cleveland*, 524-7; F. P. Weberg, *Background of the Panic of 1893* (Washington, 1929), *passim*. Cf. Alvin H. Hansen, *Fiscal Policy and Business Cycles* (New York, 1941), 22-4, for the suggestion that curtailment in building construction was a cause of depression.

3 Richardson (ed.), *Messages and Papers*, 9:396, 401-405.

4 Dewey, *Financial Hist. of U. S.*, 444-5; Nevins, *Cleveland*, 534-6; Briggs, *Hepburn*, 170-71. Clarkson and the *Register* opposed repeal of the Sherman Act.

5 *Cong. Record*, 51 Cong., 1 sess. (Sept. 27, 1890), 10594-5.

6 JPD to father, Aug. 1, 1893, *Dolliver Papers*.

7 J. Fred Meyers (Aug. 7), Earl Billings (Aug. 15), J. B. Romans (Aug. 12), J. M. Linn (Aug. 15), 1893, to JPD, *ibid.*

8 S. A. Wolcott to JPD, Aug. 8, 1893, *ibid.*

9 S. J. Bennett to JPD, Aug. 18, 1893, *ibid.* Cf. Briggs, *Hepburn*, 170-72, for Hepburn's similar view of tariff revision. Hepburn refused to vote to repeal the Silver Bill.

10 Edward O. Leech to JPD, Aug. 19, 1893, *Dolliver Papers*. Cf. Dewey, *Financial Hist. of U. S.*, 445ff.

11 J. H. Weimer to JPD, Aug. 16, 1893, *Dolliver Papers*.

12 JPD to Victor Dolliver, Aug. 20, 1893, *ibid.*

13 *Cong. Record*, 53 Cong., 1 sess. (Aug. 25, 1893), 920.

14 Josephson, *Politicos*, 537; Nevins, *Cleveland*, 541ff.; Stephenson, *Aldrich*, 104-110; Sage, *Allison*, 257.

[15] *Cong. Record,* 53 Cong., 1 sess. (Aug. 25, 1893), 921, 922.

[16] *Ibid.* (Aug. 28, 1893), 1008; (Oct. 30, 1893), 2958.

[17] J. H. Prichard to JPD, Oct. 22, 1893, *Dolliver Papers.*

[18] Denison *Review,* Sept. 15, 1893, clipping with letter of same date from Meyers, *Dolliver Papers.*

[19] JPD to Meyers, Oct. 10, 1893, quoted in Nixon, "Populist Movement in Iowa," 74.

[20] Carpenter to JPD, Sept. 2, 1893, *Dolliver Papers.*

[21] *Cong. Record,* 53 Cong., 1 sess. (Aug. 25, 1893), 922.

[22] Dewey, *Financial Hist. of U. S.,* 448-50, 458-60; Nevins, *Cleveland,* 594-6, 600-603, 655-7; Richardson (ed.), *Messages and Papers,* 9:485-9, 553-5, 561-5; James A. Barnes, *John G. Carlisle: Financial Statesman* (New York, 1931), 287-360; *Cong. Record,* 53 Cong., 2 and 3 sess. (Dec., 1893-Mar., 1895), *passim.*

[23] JPD to Victor Dolliver, Aug. 20, 1893, *Dolliver Papers.*

[24] Cole, *Iowa Through the Years,* 403-405; Nixon, "Populist Movement in Iowa," 71-2.

[25] Des Moines *Register,* Jan. 13, 1893; Clarkson to Cyrenus Cole, Feb. 4, 1893, *Cyrenus Cole Papers* (State Hist. Society of Iowa, Iowa City). Hereafter cited as *Cole Papers.* Clarkson to JPD, Feb. 7, 1893, *Dolliver Papers.*

[26] Clarkson to JPD, Dec. 7, 1892; Feb. 7, 1893, *Dolliver Papers.*

[27] Carpenter (Feb. 1), S. T. Meservey (Feb. 12), M. D. O'Connell (Feb. 12), L. R. Train (Jan. 31), 1893, to JPD, *ibid.*

[28] Carpenter to JPD, Feb. 10, 1893, *ibid.*

[29] Cummins to JPD, Aug. 21, 1893, *Dolliver Papers;* Cummins to Allison, Aug. 21, 1893, *Allison Papers;* Thomas J. Bray, "The Cummins Leadership," *Annals of Iowa* (3rd ser.), 32:241ff. (April, 1954). Ralph M. Sayre of the College of Idaho is preparing a biography of Albert B. Cummins. He has kindly made his notes available to this writer.

[30] Perkins (Nov. 24), and John F. Lacey (Nov. 18), 1893, to JPD, *Dolliver Papers.*

[31] Cummins to JPD, Sept. 15, 1893, *ibid.*

[32] L. S. Coffin to JPD, Dec. 22, 1893, *ibid.*

[33] Clark, *Senatorial Elections,* 233-4.

[34] Richardson (ed.), *Messages and Papers,* 9:459, 460.

[35] *Cong. Record,* 53 Cong., 2 sess. (Jan. 9, 1894), 573; William L. Wilson, "The Principle and Method of the New Tariff Bill," *The Forum,* 16:574 (January, 1894).

[36] Summers, *Wilson and Tariff Reform,* 174-5; Taussig, *Tariff Hist. of U. S.,* 289ff.; Nevins, *Cleveland,* 565.

[37] Nevins, *Cleveland,* 565 (quoting New York *Journal of Commerce*), 667-8; Summers, *Wilson and Tariff Reform,* 168-75, 176; New York *Nation,* Jan. 11, Feb. 1, 1894; Taussig, *Tariff Hist. of U. S.,* 289.

[38] *Cong. Record,* 53 Cong., 2 sess. (Jan. 11, 1894), 733-9; (Feb. 1, 1894), Appendix, 203.

[39] Summers, *Wilson and Tariff Reform*, 187-222; Nevins, *Cleveland*, 567-87 (especially 583 and 587), 650-52; Stephenson, *Aldrich*, 112-20.

[40] *Cong. Record*, 53 Cong., 2 sess., 2529, 4550, 4557-8.

[41] JPD to father, July 31, 1894, *Dolliver Papers*. For Des Moines River Land appropriations, see Sundry Civil Expenses Act, 28 *U. S. Statutes at Large*, Chap. 301, pp. 396-7.

[42] M. D. O'Connell (Mar. 31), and S. J. Bennett (July 10), 1894, to JPD, *Dolliver Papers*; Fort Dodge *Messenger*, July 11, 1894.

[43] Des Moines *Register*, Nov. 8, 9, 11, 1894; Nixon, "Populist Movement in Iowa," 76-8; Cole, *Iowa Through the Years*, 405-406. For party platforms, see *Iowa Official Register, 1895.*

[44] Oberholtzer, *Hist. of U. S.*, 5:304; *Iowa Official Register, 1895*, 188-91. The Populist state ticket in Iowa received its maximum vote in 1894, but it cost the Democrats more votes than the Republicans. See Nixon, "Populist Movement in Iowa," 74-5.

[45] Nevins, *Cleveland*, 651; Summers, *Wilson and Tariff Reform*, 222.

[46] Oberholtzer, *Hist. of U. S.*, 5:303-304; cf. Summers, *Wilson and Tariff Reform*, 209ff.; Nevins, *Cleveland*, 650-51; Josephson, *Politicos*, 592.

[47] Thomas B. Reed to JPD, Nov. 18, 1894, *Dolliver Papers*.

[48] Theodore Roosevelt to JPD, Nov. 19, 1894, *ibid.*

[49] JPD, "A Glance at the Early Life of James Russell Lowell," 356, 360-61.

[50] JPD to mother, n. d., 1878, *Dolliver Papers*.

[51] JPD to Mollie Dolliver, Jan. 13, 1879, *ibid.*

[52] JPD to Jennie Berry, Aug. 20, 1881; Jennie Berry to JPD, July 25, 27, Aug. 5, 23, 24, 1881, *ibid.*

[53] Letters from Mrs. William Larrabee, Mrs. C. A. Boutelle, Mrs. Philip S. Post, Augusta Larrabee, and Harriette Post, 1885-1894, *ibid.*

[54] Gay Dolliver to JPD, Aug. 14, Sept. 5, 1893, *ibid.*; "George R. Pearsons," *Annals of Iowa* (3rd ser.), 6:560 (October, 1904).

[55] Mollie Dolliver Graham to Gay Dolliver, Aug. 27, 1894; R. H. Dolliver (Sept. 17), Louise Pearsons (Dec. 31), 1894, to JPD, *Dolliver Papers*.

[56] Gay Dolliver to Louise Pearsons, July 20, 1895; R. H. Dolliver (Aug. 29), George Perkins (Sept. 4), and A. B. Funk (Sept. 13), 1895, to JPD, *ibid.*

[57] Fort Dodge *Messenger*, Nov. 21, 1895; Fort Dodge *Messenger and Chronicle*, Oct. 29, 1932.

[58] JPD to Louise Pearsons, Oct. 30, 1895, *Dolliver Papers*.

[59] Champ Clark to JPD, Sept. 21, 1895, *ibid.*

[60] JPD to wife, Nov. 19, 1900, July 2, 1902, *ibid.*

[61] Louise Pearsons to JPD, Oct. 14, 1895, *ibid.*

CHAPTER XI — THE BATTLE OF SILVER AND GOLD

[1] Mrs. JPD to J. J. Dolliver, Dec. 10, 31, 1895, *Dolliver Papers*.

[2] Richardson (ed.), *Messages and Papers*, 9:626, 640ff., 643-5; Nevins, *Cleveland*, 597-603, 649-76; Dewey, *Financial Hist. of U. S.*, 453.

[3] Oberholtzer, *Hist. of U. S.*, 5:381ff.; Nevins, *Cleveland*, 597-627, 685; Mrs. JPD to J. J. Dolliver, Dec. 31, 1895, *Dolliver Papers*.

[4] *Cong. Record*, 54 Cong., 1 sess. (Dec. 26, 1895), 325ff.; Oberholtzer, *Hist. of U. S.*, 5:381; Nevins, *Cleveland*, 685-8.

[5] Garraty, *Lodge*, 168-72; Joseph B. Foraker, *Notes of a Busy Life* (Cincinnati, 1916), 465-80; Charles S. Olcott, *The Life of William McKinley* (2 vols., Boston, 1916), 1:310-11; Josephson, *Politicos*, 654-60; Oberholtzer, *Hist. of U. S.*, 5:385-8.

[6] Wm. R. Boyd, "George E. Roberts," *Annals of Iowa* (3rd ser.), 29:416 (October, 1948); Oberholtzer, *Hist. of U. S.*, 5:364-6.

[7] Champ Clark to JPD, Sept. 21, 1895, *Dolliver Papers*; Boyd, "George E. Roberts," 416; Cole, *Iowa Through the Years*, 412; Des Moines *Register*, Sept., 1895-Oct., 1896, *passim*.

[8] J. B. Romans to JPD, Feb. 1, 1896, *Dolliver Papers*.

[9] *Cong. Record*, 54 Cong., 1 sess. (Feb. 12, 1896), Appendix, 161-70.

[10] *Ibid.*, 166; Des Moines *Register*, Feb. 13, 1896; New York *Nation*, May 14, 1896; Brigham, *Iowa*, 1:609; Oberholtzer, *Hist. of U. S.*, 5:382-4. The Fort Dodge *Messenger*, July 21, 1896, reprinted the whole speech.

[11] Des Moines *Register*, Mar. 11, 12, 1896.

[12] Clarkson to Allison, Oct. 15, 1894, *Allison Papers*.

[13] Cummins to Allison, Apr. 5, 1894, *ibid.*

[14] Allison to Cummins, Apr. 25, 1894, *Albert Baird Cummins Collection* (Iowa State Dept. of Hist. and Archives, Des Moines). Hereafter cited as *Cummins Papers*.

[15] Clarkson to Cole, Dec. 9, 20, 23, 1895, *Cole Papers*.

[16] Olcott, *McKinley*, 1:304ff.; Oberholtzer, *Hist. of U. S.*, 5:383-90; Josephson, *Politicos*, 645-8; Garraty, *Lodge*, 166-7.

[17] Chicago *Tribune*, Mar. 9, 11, 12, 1896; Des Moines *Register*, Mar. 8, 12, 1896.

[18] All quotations from the text of Dolliver's address printed in Des Moines *Register*, Mar. 12, 1896.

[19] Chicago *Tribune*, Mar. 12, 1896; Des Moines *Register*, Mar. 12, 1896.

[20] H. H. Kohlsaat (June 26, 1896), Clarkson (June 1, 1897), to JPD, *Dolliver Papers*; Olcott, *McKinley*, 1:298n.

[21] JPD to wife, June 16, 1896; Clarkson to JPD, May 26, 1896, *Dolliver Papers*; Oberholtzer, *Hist. of U. S.*, 5:384; Garraty, *Lodge*, 166-8; Sage, *Allison*, 262-6.

[22] C. F. Kuehnle (Mar. 21), A. J. Barkley (June 25), 1896, to JPD, *Dolliver Papers*; Jefferson *Bee*, July 30, 1896; Fort Dodge *Messenger*, Mar.-July, 1896, *passim*.

[23] Bryan's fame as an orator is well established. Many contemporaries who knew them both rate Dolliver at least as great an orator as Bryan. Beveridge asserted that Dolliver was "beyond any possible doubt the greatest orator in the contemporaneous English-speaking world." Bowers, *Beveridge*, 328. Cummins said that "no one approached him in the art of expression." *Review of Reviews*, 42:682 (December, 1910). Cordell Hull

wrote: "Jonathan Dolliver [was] the greatest combined orator and debater." *The Memoirs of Cordell Hull* (2 vols., New York, 1938), 1:108. La Follette recorded that Dolliver's "command of language and facility of expression equaled that of any man I ever knew." La Follette, *Autobiography*, 428. Blaine, who may never have heard Bryan, called Dolliver "the most eloquent orator I have ever heard." Sioux City *Tribune*, Oct. 17, 1910. Lew Sarett, authority on the teaching of public speaking, who knew Dolliver and heard him, Bryan, Beveridge, La Follette, and others, stated, "Dolliver, in my opinion, was twice the speaker that Beveridge was. . . . He was so strong that I have been amazed down through the years at the colossal ignorance of Dolliver's power manifested by Americans." Lew Sarett to Gordon Hostettler, June 19, 1945. Quoted through the courtesy of Professor Hostettler, whose doctoral dissertation at the State University of Iowa (1947) was "The Oratorical Career of Jonathan Prentiss Dolliver."

[24] J. B. Hungerford to JPD, June 25, 1896, *Dolliver Papers.*

[25] JPD to Hungerford, June 26, 1896, *ibid.*

[26] Jefferson *Bee*, July 30, 1896.

[27] Letters from J. Fred Meyers, C. F. Kuehnle, J. J. McWilliams, A. J. Barkley, J. B. Hungerford, J. D. Hunter, G. C. Call, and others, to JPD, June-July, 1896, *Dolliver Papers.*

[28] Clarkson to JPD, July 11, 1896, *ibid.*; Herbert Croly, *Marcus Alonzo Hanna* (New York, 1923), 217; Josephson, *Politicos*, 701; Des Moines *Register*, July 31, Aug. 25, Sept. 4, 1896.

[29] Jefferson *Bee*, July 30, 1896; typescripts of JPD's 1896 campaign speeches, *Dolliver Papers*; Des Moines *Register*, Aug.-Nov., 1896, *passim.*

[30] JPD to wife, Aug. 30, 1896; H. G. McMillan (Oct. 27), John F. Lacey (Nov. 5), J. M. Treynor (Nov. 6), 1896, to JPD, *Dolliver Papers*; Cole, *Iowa Through the Years*, 417-18; Roll, "Political Trends in Iowa History," 513.

[31] Cummins (Oct. 26), John McCarthy (Aug. 28), 1896, to JPD, *Dolliver Papers*; Des Moines *Register*, July 24, 1896; Fort Dodge *Messenger*, Apr. 24, May 15, 1896.

[32] Jesse Macy, letter in *American Review of Reviews*, 14:526 (November, 1896).

[33] Fred A. Shannon, *The Farmer's Last Frontier* (New York, 1945), 327. Cf. John D. Hicks, *The Populist Revolt* (Minneapolis, 1931), 405ff.

[34] *Cong. Record*, 54 Cong., 1 sess. (Feb. 12, 1896), Appendix, 170.

[35] Nye, *Midwestern Progressive Politics*, 115.

[36] Josephson, *Politicos*, 684ff.; Nye, *Midwestern Progressive Politics*, 116ff.; *Harper's Weekly*, Aug.-Nov., 1896, *passim*; Ida M. Tarbell, *The Nationalizing of Business, 1878-1898* (New York, 1936), 256ff.; William Allen White, *The Autobiography of William Allen White* (New York, 1946), 278-9.

[37] JPD, speech at Jefferson, Jefferson *Bee*, July 30, 1896.

[38] Josephson, *Politicos*, 702n.; H. T. Peck, *Twenty Years of the Republic* (New York, 1906), 511; M. R. Werner, *Bryan* (New York, 1929), 102.

[39] Cummins (Nov. 6), H. G. McMillan (Nov. 6), J. M. Treynor (Nov. 9), John F. Lacey (Nov. 5), Lafayette Young (n. d.), Clarkson (Nov. 25), 1896, and numerous others to JPD, *Dolliver Papers.*

[40] H. G. McMillan to JPD, Oct. 27, 1896, *ibid.*

[41] Copies of such campaign material are in *ibid*. Schlesinger, *Rise of Modern America*, 185, states that McKinley was pictured on billboards throughout the country as "The Advance Agent of Prosperity." Cf. Olcott, *McKinley*, 1:298, 324. McKinley to JPD, July 1, 1896, *Dolliver Papers*. McKinley requested JPD to send a copy of the speech to the National Committee.

[42] McKinley to JPD, Nov. 18, 1896, *Dolliver Papers*.

[43] Cole, *Iowa Through the Years*, 415; M. D. O'Connell to JPD, Feb. 7, Apr. 30, 1897, *Dolliver Papers*. George E. Roberts to Frances P. Dolliver, Aug. 5, 1946. (This letter used through the courtesy of Miss Dolliver.) "My friendship for your father," wrote Roberts, "was the most intimate and valued of my life. He was the soul of honor."

CHAPTER XII — MAKING A TARIFF AND A GOVERNOR

[1] Ford (ed.), *Letters of Henry Adams*, 2:96.

[2] Allan Nevins (ed.), *The Letters of Grover Cleveland* (Boston, 1933), 461.

[3] JPD, "A Poor Man's Government and a Poor Boy's Country," Chautauqua address delivered in Greeley, Denver, Pueblo, and several lesser cities in November, 1896, *Dolliver Papers*.

[4] Oberholtzer, *Hist. of U. S.*, 5:471-3; Olcott, *McKinley*, 1:348-9; Dewey, *Financial Hist. of U. S.*, 463-4.

[5] Taussig, *Tariff Hist. of U. S.*, 326.

[6] JPD to wife, Dec. 8, 13, 1896, *Dolliver Papers*; JPD, speech in Des Moines, Oct. 30, 1903, *Des Moines Register*, Oct. 31, 1903; *Cong. Record*, 55 Cong., 1 sess. (Mar. 22, 1897), 127.

[7] JPD to F. W. Bicknell, Oct. 2, 1906, *Dolliver Papers*.

[8] *Tariff Hearings*, 54 Cong., 2 sess., House Doc. 328, pp. 173-2082.

[9] *Cong. Record*, 55 Cong., 1 sess. (Mar. 4, 15, 1897), 3, 4, 19.

[10] *Ibid*. (Mar. 19, 1897), 71; (Mar. 22, 1897), 120.

[11] Taussig, *Tariff Hist. of U. S.*, 123ff. Cf. Dewey, *Financial Hist. of U. S.*, 464, who shows that the Treasury deficit steadily *declined* from 1893-1894 to 1896-1897.

[12] *Cong. Record*, 55 Cong., 1 sess. (Mar. 23, 1897), 191, 194.

[13] Boston *Globe*, Mar. 24, 1897; Des Moines *Capital*, Mar. 24, 1897.

[14] *Cong. Record*, 55 Cong., 1 sess. (Mar. 31, 1897), 557; (Apr. 1, 1897), 559; Taussig, *Tariff Hist. of U. S.*, 326-7; Stephenson, *Aldrich*, 140-43; Oberholtzer, *Hist. of U. S.*, 5:469-71; Olcott, *McKinley*, 1:353-7.

[15] *Cong. Record*, 55 Cong., 1 sess. (May 25, 1897), 1227.

[16] Taussig, *Tariff Hist. of U. S.*, 328-33, 351; Stephenson, *Aldrich*, 149.

[17] Taussig, *Tariff Hist. of U. S.*, 328; Stephenson, *Aldrich*, 148; Oberholtzer, *Hist. of U. S.*, 5:466-71.

[18] H. D. Tichenor to JPD, Nov. 22, 1909, *Dolliver Papers*. Tichenor, a tariff expert, was the son of Col. George C. Tichenor of Iowa. Col. Tichenor had been one of the chief advisors on tariff revision in 1897 and had aided both the House and Senate.

¹⁹ Stephenson, *Aldrich*, 144-5, 149; cf. Taussig, *Tariff Hist. of U. S.*, 333, 351-2. When duties were restored on raw wool to satisfy the Western producers, high compensating duties were levied on woolens to protect the Eastern manufacturers.

²⁰ Taussig, *Tariff Hist. of U. S.*, 328; JPD, "The Dingley Tariff," *Home Market Bulletin*, 9:7-9 (December, 1897).

²¹ Taussig, *Tariff Hist. of U. S.*, 358.

²² Cummins to Henry C. Payne, Nov. 27, 1896, *Cummins Papers*.

²³ Cummins to Charles G. Dawes, Dec. 3, 1896, and to W. T. Durbin, Dec. 10, 1896, *ibid*.

²⁴ Cummins to W. L. Roach, Feb. 27, 1897, *ibid*.

²⁵ O'Connell to JPD, Jan. 29, 1897, *Dolliver Papers*.

²⁶ Cummins to S. D. Cook, July 30, 1897, *Cummins Papers*; Gue, *Hist. of Iowa*, 3:190; Des Moines *Register*, May-Aug., 1897, *passim*; Cole, *Iowa Through the Years*, 416-17; Des Moines *Register*, editorial, Mar. 23, 1906; Shaw to JPD, Aug. 6, 1897, *Dolliver Papers*.

²⁷ Shaw to JPD, July 26, Aug. 3, 1897; JPD to Shaw, July 31, 1897, *Dolliver Papers*.

²⁸ Carl F. Kuehnle to JPD, Aug. 5, 1897, *ibid*.; Fort Dodge *Messenger*, Aug. 4, 5, 1897.

²⁹ Shaw to JPD, Aug. 6, 1897, *Dolliver Papers*.

³⁰ Cummins to S. D. Cook, July 30, 1897, *Cummins Papers*; Gue, *Hist. of Iowa*, 3:190.

³¹ JPD to Shaw, Aug. 6, 1897; Shaw to JPD, Aug. 7, 13, 1897, *Dolliver Papers*.

³² Des Moines *Register*, Aug. 20, 1897; Gue, *Hist. of Iowa*, 3:190.

³³ Cole, *Iowa Through the Years*, 417.

³⁴ Politicians, in Iowa at least, did not put in writing specific accounts of how these matters were arranged. This analysis is an "educated guess" based upon a comprehensive study of the correspondence between JPD and Shaw in this period in 1897 and again in 1900-1901, and of the correspondence bearing on the Shaw nomination found in the Dolliver, Cummins, Perkins, and Cole collections; on a general knowledge of Iowa politics in the period 1890-1910; and on whatever insight into Dolliver's mental and political habits is afforded by several years of careful study of everything available written by or about him.

³⁵ Cummins to H. W. Macomber, Aug. 20, 1897, *Cummins Papers*. Cf. A. B. Funk to George D. Perkins, June 18, 1899; Harvey Ingham to Perkins, Feb. 13, 1900, *George D. Perkins Collection* (Iowa State Dept. of Hist. and Archives, Des Moines). Hereafter cited as *Perkins Papers*.

CHAPTER XIII — DEFENDER OF IMPERIALISM

¹ Samuel Flagg Bemis, *A Diplomatic History of the United States* (rev. ed., New York, 1942), 437-8; Nevins, *Cleveland*, 716-19.

² Julius W. Pratt, *Expansionists of 1898* (Baltimore, 1936), 3ff.

³ Julius W. Pratt, "The 'Large Policy' of 1898," *Mississippi Valley Historical Review*, 19:219-42 (September, 1932); Pringle, *Roosevelt*, 165-75.

⁴ McDowell (comp.), *Platforms*, 101.

[5] *Cong. Record*, 54 Cong., 1 sess. (Apr. 6, 1896), 3627.

[6] JPD to wife, Dec. 13, 1896, *Dolliver Papers*.

[7] Nevins, *Cleveland*, 716-19; Walter Millis, *The Martial Spirit: A Study of Our War with Spain* (Boston, 1931), 65; Garraty, *Lodge*, 184-5; Oberholtzer, *Hist. of U. S.*, 5:491.

[8] Olcott, *McKinley*, 1:396-400; Millis, *Martial Spirit*, 71-90.

[9] Cf. Millis, *Martial Spirit*, 94, who states that the so-called Havana riot was simply an attack by Spanish army officers in revenge for editorial criticism of the army.

[10] J. F. Rhodes, *The McKinley and Roosevelt Administrations* (New York, 1927), 47-8; Oberholtzer, *Hist. of U. S.*, 5:500; Millis, *Martial Spirit*, 93-7.

[11] *Cong. Record*, 55 Cong., 2 sess. (Jan. 27, 1898), 1113.

[12] *Ibid.*, 1113-14. On March 8, Dolliver spoke briefly in the House in behalf of a peaceful settlement, *ibid.*, 2162.

[13] JPD, address at Vanderbilt University, Nashville *Banner*, June 20, 1899; JPD, address before the Massachusetts Republican convention, Apr. 27, 1900, Boston *Herald*, Apr. 28, 1900.

[14] Bemis, *Diplomatic Hist.*, 450.

[15] Olcott, *McKinley*, 2:26-30; Garraty, *Lodge*, 185-9; Millis, *Martial Spirit*, 131-45; Pratt, *Expansionists of 1898*, 280ff.

[16] J. C. Spooner to C. W. Porter, May 2, 1898, quoted in Thomas A. Bailey, *A Diplomatic History of the American People* (4th ed., New York, 1950), 508n.

[17] London *Times*, Apr. 14, 1898, quoted in Bailey, *Diplomatic Hist.*, 509. Cf. Millis, *Martial Spirit*, 142-3; *Cong. Record*, 55 Cong. 2 sess. (Apr. 11-18, 1898), *passim*.

[18] *Cong. Record*, 55 Cong., 2 sess. (Apr. 18, 1898), 4062-4.

[19] Robinson, *Reed*, 354-72; Garraty, *Lodge*, 184-8; Pratt, *Expansionists of 1898*, 232-52; Rhodes, *McKinley and Roosevelt Administrations*, 55; *Cong. Record*, 55 Cong., 2 sess. (Apr. 16, 1898), 3993.

[20] *Cong. Record*, 55 Cong., 2 sess. (Apr. 25, 1898), 4244, 4252.

[21] Mrs. JPD's diary, Apr. 4, 1898, *Dolliver Papers*.

[22] Earley V. Wilcox, *Tama Jim* (Boston, 1930), 91.

[23] *Cong. Record*, 55 Cong., 2 sess. (Apr. 27, 1898), 4297-4337.

[24] New York *Times*, editorial, Apr. 29, 1898; Washington *Post*, May 16, 1898. Similar praise came from the Kansas City *Times*, Atlanta *Constitution*, and, of course, from the Des Moines *Register* and other Iowa papers. Clippings in *Dolliver Papers*.

[25] Clark Howell (May 4), and W. C. Michaels (Apr. 28), 1898, to JPD, *Dolliver Papers*.

[26] Buck, *Road to Reunion*, 306-307.

[27] Nevins, *Cleveland*, 550-62.

[28] Bailey, *Diplomatic Hist.*, 474-5.

[29] JPD to wife, June 16, 1898, *Dolliver Papers*.

[30] *Cong. Record,* 55 Cong., 2 sess. (June 15, 1898), 6002-6004; Pittsburgh *Press,* June 15, 1898; New York *Tribune,* June 15, 1898.

[31] *Cong. Record,* 55 Cong., 2 sess. (June 15, 1898), 6018-19.

[32] JPD to wife, June 17, 1898, *Dolliver Papers.*

[33] Copy of address in *ibid.* Pratt, *Expansionists of 1898,* 3ff.; and Richard Hofstadter, *Social Darwinism in American Thought, 1860-1915* (Philadelphia, 1944), *passim,* develop in detail the influence of the sociological popularizers of "survival of the fittest" and "struggle for existence" in providing an intellectual undergirding for advocacy of imperialism.

[34] JPD to Mrs. C. C. Carpenter, May 31, June 6, 1898, *Carpenter Papers.*

[35] John Pearsons to Mrs. JPD, May 31, 1898; J. A. O. Yeoman to JPD, June 2, 1898; JPD to wife, June 5, 1898, *Dolliver Papers.*

[36] Fort Dodge *Messenger,* July 1, 1898; Webster City *Tribune,* Apr. 22, 1898; Fort Dodge *Post,* July 15, 1898.

[37] Fort Dodge *Messenger,* July 1, 2, 1898; Webster City *Tribune,* July 2, 1898.

[38] Webster City *Tribune,* July 2, 1898; Fort Dodge *Messenger,* July 5, 1898; Des Moines *Register,* July 2, 1898.

[39] Shaw to JPD, July 9, 1898, *Dolliver Papers.*

[40] Algona *Upper Des Moines,* Apr. 27, 1898.

[41] Fort Dodge *Messenger,* July 5, 1898.

[42] New York *Journal,* Aug. 9, 1898.

[43] Oberholtzer, *Hist. of U. S.,* 5:523-8, 552-70, 587; Pringle, *Roosevelt,* 203-204; Millis, *Martial Spirit,* 152-60, 196-228; Olcott, *McKinley,* 2:76-92.

[44] [Finley Peter Dunne], *Mr. Dooley in Peace and in War* (Boston, 1899), 9.

[45] F. H. Harrington, "The Anti-Imperialist Movement in the United States, 1898-1900," *Mississippi Valley Historical Review,* 22:211-30 (September, 1935); Bailey, *Diplomatic Hist.,* 521-2; Hoar, *Autobiography,* 2:304-326.

[46] *Cong. Record,* 55 Cong., 3 sess. (Jan. 25, 1899), 1030-34. Cf. Chicago *Tribune,* May 8, 1899, for similar views expressed by Dolliver in a May 7 address in Chicago.

[47] JPD, address at Monona, Wisconsin, July 20, 1899. *Wisconsin State Journal,* July 21, 1899.

[48] JPD, "The Nation's Duty," text printed in University of Michigan *Daily,* Oct. 28, 1899.

[49] *Cong. Record,* 56 Cong., 1 sess. (Feb. 27, 1900), 2343, 2347, 2349, 2351. The Supreme Court's decision in the Insular Cases, May, 1901, upheld Dolliver's views. Cf. Carl B. Swisher, *American Constitutional Development* (Boston, 1943), 475ff.

CHAPTER XIV — THE HINGE OF FATE

[1] Roberts to Frances P. Dolliver, Aug. 5, 1946 (courtesy of Miss Dolliver). Roberts wrote of Dolliver's state of mind in 1900: "He disliked the factional strife in the party which was growing bitter, and detested the post office squabbles." Dolliver's letters to

his wife in this period indicate his worry over finances and his determination to earn more by increasing his lecture schedules.

2 Cummins to Robert Mather, Aug. 23, 1897, *Cummins Papers.*

3 See biography of Cummins in *Dictionary of American Biography,* 4:597-9. See also Funk to Perkins, June 18, 1899, and Harvey Ingham to Perkins, Feb. 13, 1900, *Perkins Papers,* for letters illuminating the Funk-Cummins relationship.

4 J. W. Blythe to JPD, Aug. 23, 1900; JPD to J. W. Blythe, Apr. 12, 1901; R. Root to Shaw, Aug. 19, 1900, *Dolliver Papers.*

5 Des Moines *Daily News,* May-June, 1899, *passim;* Fort Dodge *Times,* Jan. 20, 1899.

6 Des Moines *Leader,* July 7, 1899; Fort Dodge *Messenger,* Jan.-July, 1899, *passim;* Des Moines *Register,* Jan.-July, 1899, *passim.* The Jefferson *Bee,* Sept. 14, 1899, explained Dolliver's great popularity as being due to the fact that he never refused to speak for the party in all campaigns "year in and year out." He met the people, learned and remembered their names, kissed their babies, told them jokes, listened to their problems, and complimented their towns and cities.

7 Iowa City *Republican,* quoted in Des Moines *Register,* July 28, 1899.

8 Cummins to Harvey Ingham, Sept. 7, 1898, *Cummins Papers.*

9 Dolliver had campaigned for Gear's re-election as Governor in 1879, and they served together in the House from 1889 to 1893, and 1895 to 1897, when Gear entered the Senate. Throne (comp.), "Iowans in Congress," 346-9.

10 Des Moines *Leader,* July 7, 1899; Fort Dodge *Times,* Jan. 20, 1899; Fort Dodge *Messenger,* June-Aug., 1899, *passim;* Des Moines *Register,* June-Sept., 1899, *passim.* Even Cyrenus Cole, editor of the Cedar Rapids *Republican,* sought to be "independent" of the Blythe-Hubbard influence, as his personal relations with Cummins were good in 1899. Cole to Allison, Sept. 25, 1899, *Allison Papers.*

11 Clark, *Senatorial Elections,* 243-5; Des Moines *Register,* Jan. 19, 1900.

12 Fort Dodge *Messenger,* Oct. 3, 1899.

13 Clark, *Senatorial Elections,* 245.

14 Ingham to Perkins, Feb. 13, 1900, *Perkins Papers;* JPD to Cummins (Aug. 27), to Col. J. W. Sweney (Aug. 25), to J. M. Junkin (Aug. 25), to Thomas Kendall (Aug. 27), 1900, *Dolliver Papers;* Fort Dodge *Messenger,* Jan.-Feb., 1900, *passim.*

15 Fort Dodge *Messenger,* Oct. 3, 1899.

16 Des Moines *Register,* Apr. 18, 21, 28, May 31, June 6, 14, 1900; Washington *Star,* June 1, 1900; Washington *Times-Herald,* June 3, 1900; Roberts to Frances P. Dolliver, Aug. 5, 1946; J. S. Clarkson, "American Presidents and Iowa Men," Des Moines *Register,* Dec. 29, 1901; Fort Dodge *Messenger,* Apr. 16, June 7, 1900; St. Louis *Globe-Democrat,* Apr. 14, 1900; Boston *Herald,* Apr. 28, 1900. Olcott's statement, in his *McKinley,* 2:269, that Dolliver was not strong enough to rally a following outside his own state is a generalization completely unsupported by the facts and is explicitly contradicted by Olcott himself in *ibid.,* 2:278-82.

17 Pringle, *Roosevelt,* 218; Olcott, *McKinley,* 2:267-8; Oberholtzer, *Hist. of U. S.,* 5:630-31.

18 St. Louis *Globe-Democrat,* Apr. 13, 1900; Fort Dodge *Messenger,* Apr. 16, 1900; Garraty, *Lodge,* 213; Pringle, *Roosevelt,* 216-18.

19 Boston *Herald*, Apr. 28, 1900.

20 Des Moines *Register*, Apr. 18, 1900. This same view was later advanced in the *Register*, May 31, June 6, 1900; and in Washington *Star*, June 1, 1900; New York *Press*, June 4, 1900. Charles G. Dawes of Illinois, McKinley's Comptroller of the Currency, backed Dolliver behind the scenes.

21 Smith McPherson to Perkins, June 2, 5, 1900, *Perkins Papers*; Des Moines *Register*, June 14, 1900; Charles G. Dawes, *A Journal of the McKinley Years* (Chicago, 1950), 231; Bascom N. Timmons, *Portrait of an American: Charles G. Dawes* (New York, 1953), 88.

22 Fort Dodge *Messenger*, June 7, 1900.

23 Cole, *Iowa Through the Years*, 431; Brigham, *Iowa*, 1:610.

24 R. H. Dolliver to Allison, June 11, 1900, *Allison Papers*; Pringle's statement, in his *Roosevelt*, 219, that Roosevelt's friends felt that his acceptance of the vice-presidency "meant the end of presidential dreams; no Vice-President had ever been elected to the Presidency" is incredible. Lodge, for example, believed the vice-presidency offered Roosevelt the best chance at the presidency. Pringle, *Roosevelt*, 217; Garraty, *Lodge*, 213; H. H. Kohlsaat, *From McKinley to Harding* (New York, 1923), 86. Furthermore, of course, Vice Presidents John Adams, Jefferson, and Van Buren had been elected to the presidency.

25 "How Dolliver Missed the Presidency," Minneapolis *Sunday Tribune*, June 14, 1908. Material in this article was based on an exclusive interview with Dolliver at Fort Dodge.

26 Clarkson, "American Presidents and Iowa Men." Clarkson also wrote that McKinley, early in April, had privately requested three newspapermen to write articles suggesting Dolliver as a possible nominee. When these appeared, then the Congressmen took up the idea and started a "serious, sincere, and spontaneous movement" for Dolliver.

27 "How Dolliver Missed the Presidency"; cf. Croly, *Hanna*, 310-11. Croly says Hanna favored the nomination of Cornelius N. Bliss, but Bliss refused to be a candidate. Kohlsaat, *From McKinley to Harding*, 87, states that Hanna favored Dolliver, Long, "or anybody rather than Roosevelt." Cf. Thomas Beer, *Hanna* (New York, 1929), 309-311.

28 Washington *Times-Herald*, June 3, 1900. Cf. Des Moines *Register*, May-June, 1900, *passim*, for almost daily front-page articles on the Dolliver boom.

29 "How Dolliver Missed the Presidency"; cf. Pringle, *Roosevelt*, 220-22; Oberholtzer, *Hist. of U. S.*, 5:630-31; G. Wallace Chessman, "Theodore Roosevelt Campaigns Against the Vice-Presidency," *The Historian*, 14:173-90 (Spring, 1952). Olcott, *McKinley*, 2:269-83; John W. Bennett, *Roosevelt and the Republic* (New York, 1908), 136.

30 Dawes, *McKinley Years*, 231; Timmons, *Dawes*, 88; Des Moines *Register*, June 14, 1900.

31 Timmons, *Dawes*, 88: Olcott, *McKinley*, 2:271-8, 280-81; Clarkson, "American Presidents and Iowa Men"; Chicago *Times-Herald*, June 21, 1900.

32 Roberts to Miss Frances P. Dolliver, Aug. 5, 1946; "How Dolliver Missed the Presidency"; Dawes, *McKinley Years*, 233, gives the impression that Dolliver would have accepted if Roosevelt had declined, and it is difficult to believe that Dolliver could have refused the nomination, regardless of his wishes, after having remained silent until the convention met.

33 Dawes, *McKinley Years*, 232; Pringle, *Roosevelt*, 222-3; Walter Davenport and

Robert B. Vale, "Power and Glory," *Collier's Weekly*, 87:25ff. (Feb. 27, 1931); Croly, *Hanna*, 316; Thomas C. Platt, *Autobiography of Thomas Collier Platt* (New York, 1910), 383-94; Clarkson, "American Presidents and Iowa Men."

[34] "How Dolliver Missed the Presidency"; Olcott, *McKinley*, 2:282-3; Pringle, *Roosevelt*, 221; Brigham, *Iowa*, 1:610; address by Lafayette Young at Memorial Services for J. P. Dolliver, *Cong. Record*, 61 Cong., 3 sess. (Feb. 18, 1911), 3464; Croly, *Hanna*, 317; cf. Walter Wellman, "Dolliver is Chosen to Act as Sacrifice?" Chicago *Record-Herald*, June 6, 1908.

[35] James Wilson to JPD, June 23, 1900, *Dolliver Papers*. In addition to his enthusiastic Iowa support, Dolliver had the backing of the Michigan and Connecticut delegations and of many delegates from other states. Olcott, *McKinley*, 2:278; Thomas F. Tracy to JPD, July 6, 1900, *Dolliver Papers*.

[36] Des Moines *Register*, July 15, 1900; Fort Dodge *Messenger*, July 15, Aug. 23, 1900.

[37] Des Moines *Register*, July-Aug., 1900, *passim*.

[38] Richard Root to Shaw, Aug. 18, 1900; James E. Blythe to JPD, Aug. 6, 23, 1900, and to Shaw, Aug. 6, 1900, *Dolliver Papers*; Cedar Rapids *Republican*, Aug. 23, 1900.

[39] JPD, "The Forward Movement of the Republican Party," *Outlook*, 96:167 (Sept. 24, 1910).

[40] James E. Blythe to Shaw, Aug. 6, 1900, copy in *Dolliver Papers*. J. E. Blythe to JPD, Aug. 6, 1900, *ibid.* Blythe advised Dolliver to say nothing to Hubbard about Dolliver's relationship with the Blythes. Whether this indicated a temporary rift between J. W. Blythe and Hubbard over Hepburn and Hull, or a desire on J. E. Blythe's part to protect himself and his brother from the charge of dealing with an outsider (Dolliver) before consulting Hubbard is not clear. Neither J. W. Blythe nor Hubbard wanted Dolliver, and it is likely that J. E. Blythe was attempting to pose as pro-Dolliver in order to win Dolliver's favor should he finally get the senatorship.

[41] Richard Root to Shaw, Aug. 19, 1900, copy in *Dolliver Papers*.

[42] Shaw to JPD, Aug. 22, 1900, *ibid.*

[43] Fort Dodge *Messenger*, Aug. 23, 1900.

[44] *Idem*.

[45] Many letters expressed the belief that Dolliver would be the presidential nominee in 1904. Champ Clark wired: "May you rival Benton in length of service." McKinley wrote a note of congratulations. A second lieutenant hoped "you continue your deserving advance until you are my 'commander-in-chief.'" Stephen Elkins wired: "W. Va. rejoices with Iowa on this event and is equally proud of you." *Dolliver Papers*. Cf. Briggs, *Hepburn*, 224.

[46] JPD to Clarkson, July 6, 1901; to Allison, Aug. 25, 1900 ("I am also aware how much your good will had to do with my selection as your colleague"); to Thomas Kimball, Aug. 27, 1900 (Shaw knew "that I have not been identified with the controversy of last winter in such a way as to make my appointment disagreeable to either side. I have, as everybody knows, pulled steadily in the party traces."); James E. Blythe to Shaw, Aug. 6, 1900, *Dolliver Papers*. Cedar Rapids *Republican*, Aug. 23, 1900 (editorial by Cyrenus Cole); Des Moines *Leader*, Aug. 23, 1900; Des Moines *Register*, Aug. 23, 1900; Washington *Post*, Aug. 23, 1900.

[47] Des Moines *Leader*, Aug. 23, 1900.

[48] JPD to Clarkson, July 6, 1901, *Dolliver Papers*.

[49] JPD to J. M. Junkin, Aug. 25, 1900; and to A. F. McCall, Aug. 25, 1900, *ibid.*

[50] JPD to Allison, Aug. 25, 1900, *ibid.*

[51] JPD to Cummins, Aug. 27, 1900, *ibid.*

[52] Paul E. Stillman to JPD, Sept. 19, 1900, *ibid.*; Roberts to Cummins, Feb. 28, 1901, *Cummins Papers.*

[53] J. W. Blythe (Aug. 28), N. M. Hubbard (Aug. 24), Allison (Aug. 24), 1900, to JPD; JPD to Hubbard, Aug. 27, 1900, and same answer to Blythe and Allison, *Dolliver Papers.*

[54] J. W. Blythe to JPD, Sept. 5, 1900; JPD to J. W. Blythe, Sept. 7, 1900, *ibid.*

[55] Fort Dodge *Messenger*, Sept. 25, 26, 1900; Thomas A. Way to Cummins, Sept. 28, 1900, *Cummins Papers*, explains the outcome of the convention.

[56] Cummins announced his candidacy on Feb. 10, 1901. Fort Dodge *Messenger*, Feb. 11, 1901.

[57] J. W. Blythe (Feb. 12, 22, 23, 25, Apr. 8, 26), Shaw (Feb. 16), F. W. Bicknell (Feb. 16), Meservey (Feb. 2), 1901, to JPD; Shaw to J. W. Blythe, Apr. 6, 1901, *Dolliver Papers*; J. W. Blythe to Lacey, Apr. 3, 5, 8, June 1, 1901, *Lacey Papers*. There was also much comment in the anti-Cummins press as to a "plot" to get Cummins in control of the legislature so that he could take Dolliver's Senate seat. Clippings in Dolliver Scrapbook, 1901, *Dolliver Papers*. C. D. Hellins wrote JPD, Feb. 11, 1901, that "Gov. Shaw regards the pledge of Cummins not to be a candidate as the sheerest buncombe, and so do I." There are many letters expressing similar views in the *Dolliver Papers.*

[58] F. W. Bicknell to JPD, Feb. 16, 1901, *Dolliver Papers*. Bicknell wrote that a Cummins leader offered "to bet a hat that you would never be elected United States Senator."

[59] In announcing his candidacy for Governor, Cummins pledged to support Dolliver for Senator. Fort Dodge *Messenger*, Feb. 11, 1901. See also: JPD to Meservey, Feb. 16, 1901; A. B. Funk to Roberts, Apr. 2, 1901; A. J. Barkley (Feb. 11), and Marion Bruce (Apr. 11), 1901, to JPD, *Dolliver Papers*; Cummins to Roberts, Feb. 20, 1901, and to JPD, Feb. 20, 1901; Roberts to Cummins, Feb. 28, 1901; JPD to Cummins, Mar. 11, 1901, *Cummins Papers.*

[60] The correspondence in the *Dolliver Papers* on this subject between Dolliver and his supporters is extensive from Feb. to July, 1901.

[61] A. B. Funk to Roberts, Apr. 21, 1901; and JPD to J. W. Blythe (Apr. 12, July 29), to J. H. Trewin (May 8), and to Cyrenus Cole (May 22), 1901, *ibid.*

[62] JPD to J. W. Blythe, Feb. 20, 1901, *ibid.* Funk, Roberts, and others agreed that Cummins could never injure Dolliver because the very people who wanted Cummins for Governor wanted Dolliver for Senator. Cf. Funk to Roberts, Apr. 21, 1901, *ibid.*

[63] JPD to Clarkson, July 6, 1901, *ibid.*

[64] JPD to J. W. Blythe, Apr. 12, 1901, *ibid.*

[65] JPD to Cummins, Sept. 19, 1907, *ibid.*, and *Cummins Papers.*

[66] Geo. E. Roberts, "The Origin and History of the Iowa Idea," *Iowa Journal of History and Politics*, 2:69-70 (January, 1904).

[67] Arthur S. Link, *American Epoch* (New York, 1955), 105. Cf. Haynes, *Third Party Movements*, 452-3.

[68] Des Moines *Register*, Jan. 22, 1902; Roberts, "Origin and History of the Iowa Idea," 73; *Cong. Record*, 57 Cong. 2 sess. (Jan. 13, 1903), 714; Roberts to Miss Frances P. Dolliver, May 15, 1946.

[69] New York *Times*, Sept. 6, 7, 1901; Pringle, *Roosevelt*, 342, 414-15.

[70] Roberts, "Origin and History of the Iowa Idea," 75; Des Moines *Register and Leader*, 1903-1905, *passim*.

[71] Shaw to Perkins, Aug. 27, 1902, *Perkins Papers*.

[72] JPD, campaign address, Davenport *Republican*, Oct. 17, 1901.

[73] JPD, "Remarks to the Republican Caucus," Jan. 14, 1902, Des Moines *Daily Capital*, Jan. 15, 1902.

[74] *Iowa Senate Journal, 1902*, 80.

[75] Des Moines *Register*, Jan. 23, 1902.

[76] Minneapolis *Journal*, Jan. 23, 1900; Chicago *Tribune*, Jan. 24, 1900.

CHAPTER XV — PRELUDE TO GREATNESS

[1] Stephenson, *Aldrich*, 163. The words describing Aldrich and Allison are Beveridge's: Bowers, *Beveridge*, 138.

[2] *Cong. Record*, 56 Cong., 2 sess. (Jan. 19, 1901), 1217ff.

[3] Schlesinger, *Rise of Modern America*, 202; Nye, *Midwestern Progressive Politics*, 240-42; C. C. Regier, *The Era of the Muckrakers* (Chapel Hill, N. C., 1932), 111-19; William Allen White, *The Old Order Changeth* (New York, 1912), 21-31; George E. Mowry, *Theodore Roosevelt and the Progressive Movement* (Madison, Wisc., 1947), 16-17. Cf. Stephenson, *Aldrich*, 162-215.

[4] For the Progressive position, see: Mowry, *Roosevelt*, *passim*; Nye, *Midwestern Progressive Politics*, *passim*; Schlesinger, *Rise of Modern America*, 200-220; Richard Hofstadter, *The Age of Reform from Bryan to F. D. R.* (New York, 1955), 131-269; Harold U. Faulkner, *The Quest for Social Justice, 1898-1914* (New York, 1931), 81-103; Bowers, *Beveridge*, 193-283.

[5] Cummins used railroad, telegraph, and railway express courtesy passes until 1905. See especially, Cummins to J. S. Runnels, A. G. Briggs, Wells Blodgett, and ten other railroad attorneys, Feb. 1, 1905, *Cummins Papers*.

[6] Des Moines *Register*, Aug. 2, 1907; Aug. 29, 1908; correspondence in *Dolliver Papers*, 1904-1907. Emory H. English, pro-Cummins editor and Progressive politician who supported the primary election law in Iowa, recalls discussing this question frequently with Dolliver. English, after nearly fifty years of observing Iowa politics under the primary system, unequivocally stated (1955) that Dolliver was right and that the primary has not only failed to produce any better candidates (if as good) than the convention system, but also has weakened party discipline and party responsibility. English-Ross interview, Oct. 22, 1955. Cf. Hofstadter, *Age of Reform*, 265. Dolliver may have modified his view on the primary in the last months of his life. Cf. JPD, "The Forward Movement of the Republican Party," 163.

[7] JPD to Richard T. Ely, Sept. 28, 1901, *Dolliver Papers*.

[8] Hofstadter, *Age of Reform*, 202.

[9] Niebuhr's views on this subject are fully developed in Reinhold Niebuhr, *Christianity*

and Power Politics (New York, 1940), 1-4; and in his *The Nature and Destiny of Man* (New York, 1941), *passim*, especially 320-21.

10 Text printed in *Bible Society Record* (April, 1904), 53-6.

11 *Ibid.*, 54.

12 JPD to Rev. F. L. Loveland, Apr. 2, 1904, *Dolliver Papers.*

13 Fort Dodge *Messenger*, Oct. 17, 19, 20, 1910; *Central Christian Advocate* (Kansas City), October, 1910; Joseph F. Berry (Nov. 10, 1897), E. G. Andrews (Dec. 8, 1897), Thomas Nicholson (Nov. 30, 1908), J. O. Dobson (Mar. 7, 1908), C. A. R. Janvier (Oct. 29, 1908), to JPD; also numerous letters to and from R. H. Dolliver and Bishop W. S. Lewis deal with JPD's services on various boards and councils, *Dolliver Papers.*

14 JPD to Rev. Robert Smylie, Nov. 2, 1903, *Dolliver Papers.*

15 JPD to Bishop R. McCabe, Oct. 31, 1903, *ibid.*

16 Dolliver got Carnegie to give $50,000 to Morningside College in 1905-1906. Ida B. Lewis, *Bishop William S. Lewis* (Sioux City, 1929), 79-81; W. S. Lewis to JPD, Apr. 10, 1905, May 9, 1906, *Dolliver Papers.* JPD also got $10,000 from Carnegie for Simpson College at Indianola. Charles E. Shelton to JPD, Feb. 20, 1905, *ibid.*

17 JPD to Dr. W. S. Lewis, Feb. 20, 1905, *Dolliver Papers.*

18 JPD, commencement address, Cornell College (Iowa), June 16, 1903, Cedar Rapids *Republican*, June 17, 1903.

19 JPD, address at Northwestern University, Evanston, Ill., Chicago *Inter-Ocean*, Sept. 20, 1902. Cf. Dolliver's memorial address on Garret Hobart, *Cong. Record*, 56 Cong., 1 sess. (Jan. 26, 1900), 1223ff. for similar expressions.

20 JPD, "A Poor Man's Government and a Poor Boy's Country," 653.

21 *Idem*; JPD, address to Northwestern Iowa Methodist Episcopal Conference, Sioux City *Journal*, Sept. 23, 1899.

22 JPD to Mollie Dolliver, Jan. 13, 1879, and to Mrs. A. M. Williams, Nov. 11, 1904, *Dolliver Papers.* His lecture, "The Basis of Equal Rights Among Men," cited *supra*, which he delivered for years on the Chautauqua circuit contained similar statements. His wife was an ardent feminist.

23 JPD, address to Northwestern Iowa Methodist Conference, Sioux City *Journal*, Sept. 23, 1899. Cf. similar views in his speech at American University, *The University Courier*, 9:2 (Washington, June, 1902).

24 Fort Dodge *Messenger*, Nov. 24, 1882.

25 *Cong. Record*, 61 Cong., 2 sess. (1910). See especially bills P4675 and P4676; Des Moines *Register*, Apr. 12, June 22, 1910.

26 Des Moines *Register*, Apr. 12, 1910.

27 P. P. Claxton to Mrs. JPD, Mar. 9, 1917, *Dolliver Papers.*

28 Hofstadter, *Age of Reform*, 204-205.

29 Richard T. Ely, "Dolliver — A Tribune of the People," *Review of Reviews*, 42:682-3 (December, 1910).

30 *Cong. Record*, 57 Cong., 1 sess. (Mar. 26, 1902), 3272-8; Sullivan, *Our Times*, 2:516-18.

31 *Cong. Record,* 58 Cong., 2 sess. (Feb. 24, 1904), 2303-2304.

32 Pringle, *Roosevelt,* 428-9; Sullivan, *Our Times,* 2:471-550; Stephenson, *Aldrich,* 234; Bowers, *Beveridge,* 229-33; *Cong. Record,* 59 Cong., 1 sess., 9025.

33 JPD, speech of Nov. 21, 1903, in Des Moines *Register,* Nov. 23, 1903.

34 *Cong. Record,* 57 Cong., 2 sess. (Jan. 13, 1903), 710-14; Des Moines *Register,* Jan. 14, 1903; Younger, *Kasson,* 377-9; Stephenson, *Aldrich,* 168, 176-9.

35 *Cong. Record,* 57 Cong., 2 sess. (Jan. 13, 1903), 711-12.

36 *Ibid.,* 713-14; Des Moines *Register,* Jan. 14, 15, 16, 1903. Henry H. Smith, Journal clerk of the House in 1896-1897, had a letter proving beyond a doubt that Dolliver's statement was literally true. Cf. Des Moines *Register,* Jan. 16, 1903.

37 Des Moines *Register,* Jan. 14, 15, 1903.

38 *Ibid.,* Jan. 17, 1903. Roberts had bought the *Register* from R. P. Clarkson and purchased the Des Moines *Leader,* both in 1902, combining them into the Des Moines *Register and Leader* (hereinafter always referred to as Des Moines *Register*). One reason for this was the hope of J. S. Clarkson, Roberts, and others of maintaining a strong pro-Dolliver paper in the state capital. Cummins and Funk tried to buy the *Register* and so did Blythe and Shaw. Ret Clarkson persuaded his brother not to sell to either faction. Ret thought that J. W. Blythe intended to try for Dolliver's Senate seat in 1906. Everyone knew Cummins would not rest until he reached the Senate. Leigh Hunt, Dolliver, and Allison helped Roberts raise the capital for the purchase. Roberts soon decided he could not manage the paper and the Mint both, and as he did not wish to leave Washington, he sold the paper to Gardner Cowles, Sr., of Algona, a friend of Dolliver, who kept Roberts' editor, Harvey Ingham, in charge. The *Register and Leader* soon became a Progressive organ supporting both Dolliver and Cummins. The correspondence dealing with Roberts' purchase and sale of this powerful paper is extensive. The facts stated in this summary are in the following: J. S. Clarkson (Nov. 12, Dec. 1, 28, 1901; Mar. 13, May 1, 19, 1902), Roberts (May 11, 1902), to JPD; and JPD to Clarkson, Apr. 12, 1902, *Dolliver Papers;* Roberts to Perkins, Apr. 9, 1902, *Perkins Papers;* Thomas A. Way to Cummins, July 6, 1903, *Cummins Papers.* See also George Mills, "The Des Moines *Register,*" *The Palimpsest,* 30:290-94 (September, 1949).

39 Sioux City *Journal,* Jan. 20, 1903; Nicholas Murray Butler (Jan. 15), and H. W. Macomber (Jan. 15), 1903, to JPD, *Dolliver Papers.*

40 Des Moines *Register,* Jan. 21, 1903.

41 The account of the Roosevelt conferences with Dolliver and Roberts was not published until 1910, when it appeared in the Des Moines *Register,* May 30, 1910. Ingham, a close personal friend of Dolliver and Roberts, and a man of the utmost honesty and accuracy, still edited the paper at that time. For Roosevelt's 1901 agreement with "The Four" and his fear of tariff reform, see Stephenson, *Aldrich,* 174-83; Pringle, *Roosevelt,* 342ff., 414-15; Sage, *Allison,* 294-6.

42 Des Moines *Register,* Feb. 13, Apr. 3, 10, 1903.

43 Clarkson to JPD, May 27, 1903, *Dolliver Papers.* Clarkson had informed Perkins in 1902 that the tariff needed revision and that the "Iowa Idea" had "struck a responsive chord among the great mass of the people." Clarkson to Perkins, Aug. 13, 1902, *Perkins Papers.*

44 Henderson sent a telegram to Allison, who was at Oyster Bay with Roosevelt, Aldrich, Hanna, Spooner, and Lodge, informing the leaders that "Being satisfied that I am not in harmony with many of our party who believe that free trade in whole or in part

will remedy the trust evil have withdrawn from the Congressional race." Henderson to Allison, Sept. 16, 1902, *Allison Papers*. Henderson felt mistreated by the Cummins faction in his district, and despite efforts of Allison, Roosevelt, Aldrich, Spooner, Lodge, and others to get him to reconsider, Henderson refused. Cf. Stephenson, *Aldrich*, 193-5, 454; Cole, *I Remember*, 329-30; Sage, *Allison*, 285-8; and Willard L. Hoing, "David B. Henderson: Speaker of the House," *Iowa Journal of History*, 55:1-34 (January, 1957), a study of this episode published since this book was written.

[45] L. W. Busbey, *Uncle Joe Cannon* (New York, 1927), 211.

[46] Cummins to Perkins, Apr. 7, 16, 1903, *Cummins Papers*. Cummins told Perkins of the meeting and stated that the draft of the platform "was expressly agreed to by Senator Allison, Mr. Blythe, and myself." Cf. Cummins to J. W. Blythe (Apr. 14), to E. N. Foss (July 3), and to Thomas C. Dawson (Aug. 3), 1903; and Perkins (Apr. 8, 13), Funk (Apr. 8), Allison (Apr. 16), 1903, to Cummins, *ibid.*; Allison to J. W. Blythe, Mar. 21, 1903; J. W. Blythe to Allison, Mar. 15, 18, 25, 1903, *Allison Papers*; Shaw to Clarkson, Apr. 13, July 21, 1903, *Clarkson Papers* (Des Moines). Cf. Elbert W. Harrington, "A Survey of the Political Ideas of Albert Baird Cummins," *Iowa Journal of History and Politics*, 39:348n (October, 1941).

[47] Cummins to Funk, Jan. 29, 1903, *Cummins Papers*.

[48] Funk to Cummins, Jan. 26, 1903, *ibid*. Roberts had discovered in late August, 1902, when he visited Roosevelt at Oyster Bay, that the President had no heart for tariff reform. Roosevelt said then that it was his "personal desire" that some action be taken on tariff before the 1904 campaign but that it was impossible for him to advocate it "publicly without knowing what he was going to get." Roberts felt that Roosevelt wanted "to get the French reciprocity treaty and one or two of the small treaties confirmed if possible, and then he would like to have the metal schedule and possibly others modified." But Roberts concluded that the President "would not publicly urge these things." Shaw, according to Roberts, was "looking to 1908" and opposed any tariff action, as he "wants to have the favor of the dominant interest of the party." Roberts to Perkins, Aug. 23, 1902, *Perkins Papers*. Cf. Shaw to Perkins, Aug. 27, Sept. 6, 1902, *ibid*.

[49] Cummins to Perkins, Apr. 16, 1903, *Cummins Papers*; Des Moines *Register*, July 3, 1903.

[50] Allison to JPD, May 14, 1903, *Dolliver Papers*. Roosevelt was returning from his trip to the West Coast. He stopped in Fort Dodge and then spent the night with Allison at Dubuque. Cf. Pringle, *Roosevelt*, 339; Stephenson, *Aldrich*, 220.

[51] Minneapolis *Journal*, June 10, 1903; Gardner Cowles, Sr. (May 20), and Roberts (May 23), 1903, to JPD, *Dolliver Papers*.

[52] Roberts to JPD, May 23, 1903, *Dolliver Papers*. JPD earned more than $4,000 in 1903 from lecturing. JPD to wife, June 1, 1903, *ibid*. The Dollivers purchased a fine house at 1415 Massachusetts Ave. in the summer of 1902, at a cost of about $19,000. JPD to wife, June 22, 1902, *ibid*. Their second daughter, Frances Pearsons Dolliver, was born in 1901.

[53] Des Moines *Register*, July 3, 1903.

[54] *Ibid.*, Oct. 31, 1903.

[55] JPD to J. W. Blythe, Aug. 1, 1903, *Dolliver Papers*. Cf. George M. Titus, "The Battle for Biennial Elections," *Annals of Iowa* (3rd ser.), 29:163-75 (January, 1948), who states that a Dolliver letter supporting the amendment was used effectively in helping win the popular endorsement needed in 1904.

[56] Clark, *Senatorial Elections*, 248ff.; Benjamin F. Shambaugh, *The Constitutions of Iowa* (Iowa City, 1934), 291.

[57] *Cong. Record*, 58 Cong., 2 sess. (Jan. 22, 1904), 1023-32; Pringle, *Roosevelt*, 327ff.; Tyler Dennett, *John Hay: From Poetry to Politics* (New York, 1923), 364-83.

[58] For the Philippine speeches, see *Cong. Record*, 57 Cong., 1 sess. (May 8, 1902), 5167-71, and (May 19, 1902), 5620-28. Of Dolliver's May 19, 1902, speech on the Philippine question, Lodge wrote: "Dolliver made a fine speech today. The best I ever heard him make. It was a very powerful argument, admirably put. When you see him say a word about it." Lodge to Roosevelt, May 19, 1902, in Lodge (ed.), *Correspondence of Theodore Roosevelt and Henry Cabot Lodge*, 1:515.

[59] John A. Kasson to JPD, Feb. 19, 1904, *Dolliver Papers*.

[60] *Cong. Record*, 58 Cong., 2 sess. (Apr. 20, 1904), 5161; Clarkson to JPD, May 12, 1904, *Dolliver Papers*; Pringle, *Roosevelt*, 251-78, 339-42; Stephenson, *Aldrich*, 217-19; John M. Blum, *The Republican Roosevelt* (Cambridge, 1954), 118-20.

[61] *Cong. Record*, 58 Cong., 2 sess., 5161-70, especially 5163, 5169.

[62] *Des Moines Register*, Apr. 21, May 28, 1904. This pro-Cummins paper, by then owned by Cowles, praised Dolliver and commented that "the public should realize that the trusts do not yet bestride our industrial world like a colossus, and that a tariff that protects American industry is not primarily or even secondarily a shelter for trust production." *Ibid.*, Apr. 23, 1904. The statement that this paper was pro-Cummins is based upon the paper's editorial policy and on a letter from Cummins to Harvey Ingham, Jan. 30, 1904, *Cummins Papers*.

[63] Thomas C. Geary, "The Presidential Campaign and Election of 1904" (unpublished Ph.D. dissertation, State Univ. of Iowa, 1937), 225ff.; JPD to H. W. Byers, Feb. 9, 1904, *Dolliver Papers*.

[64] Cummins to Perkins, Jan. 30, 1904, *Cummins Papers*. Cf. Harrington, "Political Ideas of . . . Cummins," 348-9.

[65] Cummins to Wm. E. Hamilton (Feb. 1), and to W. N. Foss (Mar. 14), 1904, *Cummins Papers*; J. W. Blythe to Perkins, Jan. 19, 1904, *Perkins Papers*; Geary, "Presidential Campaign . . . 1904," 43.

[66] Harvey Ingham to J. W. Blythe, Feb. 9, 1904; J. W. Blythe to Ingham, Feb. 10, 1904, and to JPD, Feb. 9, 1904; Meservey to JPD, Mar. 12, 17, 1904, *Dolliver Papers*; Cummins to Wm. E. Hamilton (Feb. 1), and to Funk (Mar. 17), 1904, *Cummins Papers*; *Des Moines Register*, June 21, 1904.

[67] Geary, "Presidential Campaign . . . 1904," 43; JPD to H. W. Byers, Feb. 9, 1904, *Dolliver Papers*.

[68] Roberts to Perkins, Mar. 19, 25, 1904, *Perkins Papers*; Meservey to JPD, Mar. 17, 1904, *Dolliver Papers*; Cummins to Funk, Mar. 17, 1904, *Cummins Papers*; *Des Moines Register*, Apr. 27, May 17, 19, 1904.

[69] *Des Moines Register*, June 21, 25, 1904; JPD to Meservey, Feb. 11, 1904, *Dolliver Papers*.

[70] McDowell (comp.), *Platforms*, 135.

[71] *Des Moines Register*, June 24, 25, 1904; JPD to Meservey, Feb. 11, 1905, *Dolliver Papers*; JPD, address nominating Fairbanks for Vice President, June 23, 1904, in *Des Moines Register*, June 24, 1904.

[72] Geary, "Presidential Campaign . . . 1904," 229.

[73] JPD to Meservey, Feb. 11, 1905, *Dolliver Papers.*

CHAPTER XVI — THE RAILROAD RATE BILL

[1] Clarkson to Leigh Hunt, Dec. 1, 1904, *Clarkson Papers* (Des Moines). Hunt had written Clarkson in 1903 of his intention of getting Roosevelt to go to Africa to hunt big game whenever he left the White House. Hunt to Clarkson, Dec. 11, 1903, *ibid.*

[2] Pringle, *Roosevelt*, 362; Fort Dodge *Messenger*, Mar. 5, Apr. 28, May 3, 1905; Frank Stillman, Washington correspondent, in Sioux City *Journal*, May 2, 1905.

[3] Des Moines *Register*, Apr. 29, 1905; Fort Dodge *Messenger*, Apr. 25, 29, May 1, 3, 1905. Father Dolliver died Apr. 28, 1905; Senator and Mrs. Dolliver's son was born April 25. The boy was named George Prentiss Dolliver, but after the Senator's untimely death the name was legally changed to Jonathan Prentiss Dolliver. He now lives on the old Carpenter farm near Fort Dodge.

[4] Philadelphia *Record*, May 2, 1909; Washington *Post*, Feb. 26, 1908; Des Moines *Register*, July 3, 1904; Oct. 31, 1909; Wilcox, *Tama Jim*, 133; *The Independent*, 59:65 (July 12, 1906).

[5] Sloane Gordon, "J. P. Dolliver, Wordmaster," *Pearson's Magazine*, 22:195 (August, 1909).

[6] Letters from these men in the *Dolliver Papers* indicate his relationship with them to have been especially close. Beveridge loved him as a brother and wrote Mrs. Dolliver, "I am so thankful that I was privileged to become one of his closest friends." Beveridge to Mrs. JPD, Nov. 16, 1910, *ibid.* Smith said Dolliver "was the dearest friend I ever had in public life." Grand Rapids (Mich.) *Herald*, Oct. 21, 1910. Cf. William Allen White to Frances P. Dolliver, May 7, 1935; and Mrs. W. A. White to Miss Dolliver, Mar. 9, 1944. Courtesy of Miss Dolliver.

[7] Clarkson to JPD, Feb. 14, 1905, *Dolliver Papers*; Des Moines *Register*, Feb. 12, 16, 1905.

[8] New York *Times*, Feb. 14, 1905; Des Moines *Register*, Feb. 15, 1905.

[9] Des Moines *Register*, May 31, 1905; Pringle, *Roosevelt*, 379-85; cf. Tyler Dennett, *Roosevelt and the Russo-Japanese War* (Garden City, 1925), *passim.*

[10] Des Moines *Register*, Sept. 15, 1905.

[11] Roosevelt to James Ford Rhodes, Nov. 29, 1904, quoted in Pringle, *Roosevelt*, 414, 415; cf. Bowers, *Beveridge*, 218-20; Busbey, *Uncle Joe Cannon*, 212-13. Dolliver was said to have been among the congressional leaders present in Roosevelt's office in November, 1904, when Roosevelt sided with T. C. Platt and Cannon in deciding not to press for tariff revision during his second term.

[12] Des Moines *Register*, Nov. 21, 1905; Fort Dodge *Messenger*, Nov. 20, 1905.

[13] Dr. J. W. Kime to JPD, Jan. 12, 1905, *Dolliver Papers*. For Roosevelt's view of La Follette, see Pringle, *Roosevelt*, 418.

[14] JPD to Kime, Jan. 24, 1905, *Dolliver Papers.*

[15] Pringle, *Roosevelt*, 415.

[16] William Z. Ripley, *Railroads: Rates and Regulation* (New York, 1924), 451-86; Shelby M. Cullom, *Fifty Years of Public Service* (Chicago, 1911), 305-332.

[17] Ripley, *Railroads*, 492; Pringle, *Roosevelt*, 417; Ray Stannard Baker, "Railroad Rebates," *McClure's Magazine*, 26:179-94 (December, 1905).

[18] Sullivan, *Our Times*, 3:266-7. Cf. Ripley, *Railroads*, 215-63; Ray Stannard Baker, "The Railroad Rate: A Story in Commercial Autocracy," *McClure's Magazine*, 26:47-59 (November, 1905).

[19] JPD to A. B. Stickney, Sept. 22, 1904, *Dolliver Papers*.

[20] Ripley, *Railroads*, 487-92.

[21] JPD to Allison, Nov. 12, 1904, *Allison Papers*.

[22] Theodore Roosevelt, Fourth Annual Message, in *The Works of Theodore Roosevelt* (National ed., 20 vols., New York, 1926), 15:226.

[23] Ripley, *Railroads*, 496; Pringle, *Roosevelt*, 419; Briggs, *Hepburn*, 251-5; *Cong. Record*, 58 Cong., 3 sess., 2194, 2205-2206.

[24] JPD to Meservey, Feb. 11, 1905, *Dolliver Papers*; Cullom, *Fifty Years of Public Service*, 330; Des Moines *Register*, Feb. 15, 16, 21, 22, 25, 1905; Briggs, *Hepburn*, 261.

[25] Clarkson to Leigh Hunt, Mar. 1, 1906, *Clarkson Papers* (Des Moines).

[26] Des Moines *Register*, Feb. 8, 1905.

[27] JPD to Meservey, Feb. 11, 1905, *Dolliver Papers*.

[28] Des Moines *Register*, Feb. 15, 16, 1905.

[29] *Wallaces' Farmer*, Jan. 20, Feb. 3, 1905; Des Moines *Register*, Feb. 26, 1906; Wallace, *Uncle Henry's Own Story*, 3:34; Briggs, *Hepburn*, 252-9, 405n., 407; Russell Lord, *The Wallaces of Iowa* (Boston, 1947), 103. Lord states that "Tama Jim" Wilson always thought and Uncle Henry Wallace "flatly stated that establishment of the Interstate Commerce Commission was a direct result of the defeat of Colonel Hepburn" in 1886.

[30] Des Moines *Register*, May 14, 1905; Henry Wallace to JPD, July 17, 1906; JPD to S. H. Cowan, Nov. 20, 1906; Newell Dwight Hillis to JPD, June 9, 1905, *Dolliver Papers*.

[31] JPD, address to Grant Club of Des Moines, Apr. 27, 1905, in Des Moines *Register*, Apr. 28, 1905. This address was read by Harvey Ingham as Dolliver could not leave Washington because of the birth of his son and the fatal illness of his father the last week of April.

[32] Des Moines *Register*, Sept. 15, 1905. Cf. Cullom, *Fifty Years of Public Service*, 330; Sullivan, *Our Times*, 3:226ff., for views of the committee members.

[33] Des Moines *Register*, Oct. 15, 1905.

[34] *Ibid.*, Oct. 24, 27, Nov. 3, 1905; C. H. Livingstone to JPD, Sept. 15, 1905, *Dolliver Papers*.

[35] Allison to Perkins, Nov. 12, 1905, *Perkins Papers*.

[36] Fort Dodge *Messenger*, Nov. 20, 1905; Ripley, *Railroads*, 497-8; Des Moines *Register*, Nov. 15, 1905-Feb. 10, 1906, *passim*; Pringle, *Roosevelt*, 420.

[37] Des Moines *Register*, Nov. 22, 24, 26, Dec. 2, 1905.

38 *Ibid.*, Dec. 5, 6, 16, 1905; Pringle, *Roosevelt*, 419; *Cong. Record*, 59 Cong., 1 sess. (Dec. 5, 1905), 92-3; Stephenson, *Aldrich*, 279, states that Roosevelt dropped tariff revision because of Aldrich and Allison.

39 Des Moines *Register*, Dec. 20, 21, 1905; *Cong. Record*, 59 Cong., 1 sess. (Dec. 19, 1905), 577; (Mar. 14, 1906), 3779; (May 12, 1906), 6778; Des Moines *Mail and Times*, Oct. 13, 1906; Briggs, *Hepburn*, 408n.; JPD to F. W. Bicknell, Oct. 2, 1906, and to S. H. Cowan, Nov. 20, 1906, *Dolliver Papers*. S. H. Cowan to Henry Wallace, July, 1906, in Des Moines *Register*, May 14, 1908. Stephenson, *Aldrich*, 283, 285, obviously did not know of Dolliver's relationship to Roosevelt and to the rate bill prior to January, 1906.

40 Des Moines *Register*, Dec. 29, 1905; *The Independent*, 60:242 (Feb. 1, 1906).

41 Briggs, *Hepburn*, 408n.; JPD to Cowan, Nov. 20, 1906, *Dolliver Papers*; Des Moines *Register*, Jan. 5, 6, 1906; Des Moines *Mail and Times*, Oct. 13, 1906; *Cong. Record*, 59 Cong., 1 sess. (Jan. 5, 1906), 712. Cf. Senate Bill S2261 and House Bill HR10099. In Cowan's letter to Henry Wallace, July, 1906, quoted in Des Moines *Register*, May 14, 1908, he stated that "the life and kernel" of the Hepburn Act "lies in that part of it which was prepared by Senator Dolliver and me, and which was copied by Mr. Hepburn." Dolliver was chairman of the Senate Committee on Education and Labor.

42 Briggs, *Hepburn*, 265-6; Des Moines *Register*, Jan. 11, 26, 1906; *Cong. Record*, 59 Cong., 1 sess., 981, 1520; JPD to Bicknell, Oct. 2, 1906, *Dolliver Papers*. Cf. John Sharp Williams, "The Democratic Party and the Railroad Question," *The Independent*, 60:485-8 (Mar. 1, 1906).

43 Des Moines *Register*, Jan. 26, 31, 1906, quoting the Washington correspondent of the Chicago *Evening Post*; JPD to Bicknell, Oct. 2, 1906, *Dolliver Papers*.

44 Briggs, *Hepburn*, 266; Des Moines *Register*, Jan. 28, Feb. 9, 1906; *Cong. Record*, 59 Cong., 1 sess., 1765, 2255, 2257-63, 2265, 2269, 2303, 7432.

45 Des Moines *Register*, Jan. 8, 1906; Pringle, *Roosevelt*, 422; Sullivan, *Our Times*, 3:231-2.

46 Clarkson to Leigh Hunt, Mar. 1, 1906, *Clarkson Papers* (Des Moines): "The people who have tried to mislead the President are Crane and Lodge of Massachusetts." Clarkson blamed Root most of all for Roosevelt's wavering. Root "has been the attorney of more capital in this country and more syndicates of money and more trusts ten times over than any other lawyer." See also Des Moines *Register*, Jan. 28, 31, Feb. 2, 1906.

47 Des Moines *Register*, Feb. 2, 1906.

48 *Ibid.*, Feb. 10, 1906; Stephenson, *Aldrich*, 291.

49 Des Moines *Register*, Feb. 15, 1906; JPD to Bicknell, Oct. 2, 1906, *Dolliver Papers*. For a discussion of the Hepburn Bill, see: Ripley, *Railroads*, 499-521; JPD, "Railroad Rate Legislation," *The Independent*, 60:835-8 (April 12, 1906); Briggs, *Hepburn*, 264-75; Sage, *Allison*, 299-305; John M. Blum, "Theodore Roosevelt and the Hepburn Act: Toward an Orderly System of Control," in Elting E. Morison (ed.), *The Letters of Theodore Roosevelt* (8 vols., Cambridge, 1952), 6:1558-71. Cf. Ray Stannard Baker, "Railroads on Trial," *McClure's Magazine*, 31:318-29 (January, 1906), for a discussion of the private car.

50 Des Moines *Register*, Feb. 14, 15, 23, 1906.

51 *Ibid.*, Feb. 24, 1906. Cullom, *Fifty Years of Public Service*, 331; *The Independent*, 60:473-4 (Mar. 1, 1906). Stephenson's view that this was a victory for Aldrich is a part of his ill-founded notion that Aldrich rather than Roosevelt and Dolliver won the fight over the Hepburn Bill. On this particular committee vote, at least, Stephenson's con-

clusion is incredible. Cf. Stephenson, *Aldrich*, 295. John Blum, in "Roosevelt and the Hepburn Act," and in *The Republican Roosevelt*, seems to follow Stephenson astray on this matter. The Aldrich amendment to Dolliver's motion was a petty effort to lead the public to believe that the Old Guard was still in control of the committee. Vice President Alben W. Barkley, one of the greatest authorities on the procedures of the Senate, stated that "no rule of the Senate or of a committee binds a Senator to support a bill from a Committee of which he is a member just as it is reported. . . . Even the Chairman has the right to offer amendments to it . . . and it is not regarded as necessary that the committee adopt a resolution, motion or declaration authorizing such action on the part of individual Senators." Alben W. Barkley to T. R. Ross, March 29, 1956.

[52] Des Moines *Register*, Feb. 24, 27, 1906; Washington *Post*, Feb. 24, 25, 1906; Stephenson, *Aldrich*, 295; Sullivan, *Our Times*, 3:227-34.

[53] Des Moines *Register*, Feb. 26, 1906. A telegram typical of the Midwestern jubilation at Dolliver's triumph came from J. B. Weaver: "Hold her nozzle against the bank till the last galoot's ashore! Congratulations!" Weaver to JPD, Feb. 25, 1906, *Dolliver Papers*.

[54] Stephenson, *Aldrich*, 296. On Feb. 28, Dolliver wrote Cullom: "Brother Aldrich and the fellows with him have claimed that the bill was not worth a cuss for any purpose." *Dolliver Papers*.

[55] Des Moines *Register*, Feb. 27, 1906, quoting interviews in the Philadelphia *Press* and the New York *Times*.

[56] Des Moines *Register*, Feb. 23, 24, 25, 1906; Roosevelt (Feb. 19), and Henry Wallace (Feb. 24), 1906, to JPD, *Dolliver Papers*. The *Register* stated: "It is Senator Dolliver who has been the stumbling block in the way of the allied forces of the opposition. If Senator Dolliver had weakened at any point it is safe to say that the original Hepburn bill would never have been heard of again in the Senate debate." Editorial, Feb. 25, 1906. Henry Wallace wrote: "I am delighted with the stand which you have taken with reference to the rate bill, and the more so because from reports we receive here the President has been disposed to weaken."

[57] Stephenson, *Aldrich*, 285ff., 293, 467n.; Des Moines *Register*, Feb. 10-25, 1906; Roosevelt to JPD, Feb. 19, 1906, *Dolliver Papers*; Clarkson to Leigh Hunt, Mar. 1, 1906, *Clarkson Papers* (Des Moines).

[58] Dolliver said on March 5: "In point of fact I might have proposed amendments . . . in the Committee on Interstate Commerce had I not been afraid that by so doing those of us who were supporting the House bill would have weakened somewhat our strategic advantage. Our chief aim was to get the bill out of the Committee, and into the open Senate. We felt that with that much accomplished we would have victory in sight, for when legislation like this is enacted in broad daylight there is small chance for its enemies to make much headway." Interview, Washington *Post*, Mar. 5, 1906.

[59] Ripley, *Railroads*, 499-521; Stephenson, *Aldrich*, 296-318; Pringle, *Roosevelt*, 421-5; Blum, "Roosevelt and the Hepburn Act," 1558-71; Briggs, *Hepburn*, 269-75; Sullivan, *Our Times*, 3:234-75; Isidor Rayner, "The Railroad Rate Debate in the Senate," *The Independent*, 60:1408-1411 (June 14, 1906); JPD, "The Battle Over the Railway Rate Bill," *ibid.*, 61:65-7 (July 12, 1906).

[60] Theodore Roosevelt, *Autobiography* (New York, 1913), 427; F. B. Simkins, *Pitchfork Ben Tillman, South Carolinian* (Baton Rouge, La., 1944), 426; Sullivan, *Our Times*, 3:233; *The Independent*, 60:474 (Mar. 1, 1906).

[61] *Cong. Record*, 59 Cong., 1 sess. (Feb. 28, 1906), 3102-20.

62 *Ibid.* (Mar. 1, 1906), 3192-3204.

63 Des Moines *Register*, Mar. 2, 1906; Briggs, *Hepburn*, 270.

64 *Cong. Record*, 59 Cong., 1 sess. (May 12, 1906), 6778; JPD, "Railway Rate Legislation," 836-8; Sullivan, *Our Times*, 3:247-9; cf. *Cong. Record*, 59 Cong., 1 sess. (Mar. 14, 1906), 3775-99, for remarks of Senators Rayner, Warren, Foraker, Knox, Aldrich, Lodge, Tillman, and Dolliver.

65 *Cong. Record*, 59 Cong., 1 sess. (Mar. 14, 1906), 3778.

66 *Ibid.*, 3784; cf. *ibid.*, 3797-8.

67 Stephenson, *Aldrich*, 288.

68 *Ibid.*, 288, 297-8, 300; *Cong. Record*, 59 Cong., 1 sess. (Mar. 28, 1906), 4376-84.

69 Des Moines *Register*, Mar. 30, 1906.

70 *Ibid.*, Apr. 3, 4, 1906; *Cong. Record*, 59 Cong., 1 sess. (Apr. 2, 1906), 4570; (Apr. 3, 1906), 4636-49. Cf. Elkins' speech on Apr. 6, *ibid.*, 4832-46. Cf. *ibid.* (Apr. 5, 1906), 4777-82, for Dolliver's speech on the Long amendment. Cf. Oscar D. Lambert, *Stephen Benton Elkins* (Pittsburgh, 1955), 274-5.

71 *Cong. Record*, 59 Cong., 1 sess. (Apr. 5, 1906), 4777; Des Moines *Register*, Apr. 5, 1906.

72 For the details of the Roosevelt-Tillman debacle, see: Sullivan, *Our Times*, 3:250-56; Pringle, *Roosevelt*, 423-4; Stephenson, *Aldrich*, 301-309; JPD, "Railroad Rate Legislation," 835-8; *Cong. Record*, 59 Cong., 1 sess. (May 12, 1906), 6775ff.; (May 15, 1906), 6885-7 — especially Roosevelt's letter to Allison, on p. 6886; Des Moines *Register*, Apr. 18, 21, 1906.

73 Des Moines *Register*, May 5, 1906; Blum, *Republican Roosevelt*, 101-102; Stephenson, *Aldrich*, 266-309; Bowers, *Beveridge*, 226; Sage, *Allison*, 302-305. Bowers records that Aldrich was furious at Beveridge for supporting Dolliver and Roosevelt and that Aldrich told Beveridge: "We'll get you for this." Cf. Sullivan, *Our Times*, 3:274, for Elkins' desertion of Aldrich, and Elkins' explanation that "when the team is running away, I prefer to be on the seat with my hands on the lines rather than in front of the runaway."

74 *Cong. Record*, 59 Cong., 1 sess. (May 8, 1906), 6501; (May 12, 1906), 6778-9; Blum, *Republican Roosevelt*, 102-103. Cf. JPD, "Battle Over the Railway Rate Bill," 67. Dolliver wrote: "The so-called Allison amendment was introduced, not for the purpose of enlarging the jurisdiction of the court, but for the purpose of clearly recognizing it, and whoever has obtained the opinion that the Supreme Court of the United States is likely, under this law, to spend its time weighing consideration of an administrative detail with a view of revising the discretion which the law confides to the Interstate Commerce Commission will be rudely awakened from such a dream when that great tribunal takes up its first interstate commerce case under the new law." Dolliver's view was correct. The Supreme Court expressly recognized that *only* questions bearing upon the authority of the Commission and upon the constitutional rights of carrier or shipper should be reviewed in cases appealed — in effect, therefore, the Court took the position of Roosevelt and Dolliver — a triumph for "narrow review." Ripley, *Railroads*, 540-43; Alfred H. Kelly and Winfred A. Harbison, *The American Constitution: Its Origin and Development* (New York, 1948), 603-604.

75 Des Moines *Register*, May 5, 10, 15, 16, 19, 1906; *Cong. Record*, 59 Cong., 1 sess. (May 12, 1906), 6778-9, 6787. Cf. Stephenson, *Aldrich*, 309-313, 470n-472n, for the theory that Aldrich wrote the Allison amendment and won a victory for "broad review."

[76] *Cong. Record*, 59 Cong., 1 sess. (May 18, 1906), 7088. Aldrich left word that he would have voted yea, had he been present. He found it convenient, however, not to be. Cf. Lambert, *Elkins*, 278-81, for the view that the Hepburn Act included more of Elkins' ideas "than those of any other person."

[77] Ripley, *Railroads*, 499; Blum, *Republican Roosevelt*, 104. Cf. JPD, "Battle Over the Railway Rate Bill," 66. Dolliver wrote that most important was "the simple provision of the new law making the Interstate Commerce Commission the judge of the reasonableness of railway rates which are subject to complaint, with a definite jurisdiction to determine what will be a just and reasonable rate to be observed for the future. . . . The truth is that the President has surrendered nothing which is essential to the operation of the law."

[78] Roosevelt to S. J. Bennett, July 7, 1906, in Fort Dodge *Messenger*, July 9, 1906. Dolliver received letters of congratulations from many parts of the country. Many of these, as well as several newspapers, suggested that Dolliver should be Roosevelt's successor as President. Letters, telegrams, and clippings in *Dolliver Papers*.

[79] Roosevelt, *Autobiography*, 426.

CHAPTER XVII — CHAOS IN IOWA POLITICS

[1] Numerous letters and telegrams, Feb. to June, 1906, commending his stand on these issues are in the *Dolliver Papers*. Cf. Des Moines *Register*, Dec. 4, 1906; La Follette, *Autobiography*, 426.

[2] JPD to H. W. Macomber (Mar. 13, 1906), to Fred W. Bartell (July 2, 1906), to Dr. W. E. Davidson (May 17, 1905), to Meservey (June 8, 1905), to Allison (June 28, 1903), to K. M. White (Jan. 9, Feb. 17, 1904; Apr. 7, 1907), to Beveridge (Sept. 14, 1909); and Alex Allen to M. L. Eidiness, June 14, 1905, *Dolliver Papers*.

[3] English-Ross interview, Oct. 26, 1955.

[4] One can not delve into the *Dolliver Papers* without wondering how a man found time to read, write, say, and do all that Dolliver did. The charge of "indolence" has most recently been circulated by Kenneth W. Hechler, *Insurgency* (New York, 1940), 89-90, who cites no evidence for his statement. Dolliver wrote a friend in 1906: "Since I have been in the Senate I have been compelled to work like a dog, during vacations and even the Christmas Holidays, to prevent the wasting away of the little property I have accumulated in paying the expenses of a rather unsatisfactory style of living." JPD to F. M. Molesberry, May 3, 1906, *Dolliver Papers*.

[5] JPD to Frank Farrell, May 8, 1906, *Dolliver Papers*.

[6] Dolliver usually scheduled his lecture tours through the Redpath and the Central Lyceum bureaus. These schedules and correspondence concerning financial arrangements are in *ibid*. Dolliver turned the management of his finances over to his wife, a careful business woman, soon after their marriage. They had purchased Governor Carpenter's farm, as well as other land in Webster County. Cf. Dolliver's letters to his wife, 1900-1909; and his correspondence with R. H. Dolliver, *ibid*.; Miss Frances P. Dolliver interview, Oct. 27, 1955.

[7] A. B. Funk to JPD, Jan. 18, 1904, *Dolliver Papers*.

[8] Harrington, "Political Ideas of . . . Cummins," 339, 386; Cole, *Iowa Through the Years*, 435-6; Bowers, *Beveridge*, 330.

[9] This conclusion is based upon innumerable specific statements found in the correspondence of these politicians in the *Dolliver* and *Cummins Papers*, 1906-1908, as well as in the more acute newspaper analyses of the political scene. Des Moines *Register*,

Jan. 2, Feb. 22, Mar. 7, 10, July 4, 10, Sept. 15, Nov. 28, Dec. 10, 21, 1906; Jan. 13, 1907; Nevada *Representative*, Dec. 3, 1906.

[10] JPD to Meservey, Apr. 1, 10, 1905, *Dolliver Papers*.

[11] Cummins to Wm. E. Hamilton (July 28, 1905), to A. W. Maxwell (Aug. 8, 1905), to S. F. Prouty (Nov. 28, 1905), to A. M. Case (Jan. 23, 1906), *Cummins Papers*; Des Moines *Register*, Nov. 5, Dec. 8, 9, 1905.

[12] Funk to Perkins, June 12, 1905, *Perkins Papers*. Other pro-Cummins editors and politicians led Perkins to believe in 1905 that they were for him. Cf. Phil A. Boland (Nov. 5), E. D. Chassell (July 11), 1905, to Perkins, *ibid*. Des Moines *Register*, Nov. 20, Dec. 4, 1905.

[13] JPD to Meservey (Feb. 11, 1905), to F. M. Molesberry (May 3, 1906), and to D. W. Norris (Apr. 23, 1906); Meservey to JPD, Feb. 4, 1906, *Dolliver Papers*. Cf. Allison (Nov. 12), and Meservey (Dec. 1), 1905, to Perkins, *Perkins Papers*. Cf. Cole, *Iowa Through the Years*, 425; Des Moines *Register*, Dec. 4, 1905.

[14] Des Moines *Register*, Dec. 8, 9, 18, 1905; Jan. 14, 1906; Cummins to E. C. Roach, Feb. 5, 1906, *Cummins Papers*.

[15] Des Moines *Register*, May 24, 1904. The Standpatters were thinking at that time of running Congressman John F. Lacey for Governor.

[16] Cummins to Wm. E. Hamilton (July 28), and to A. W. Maxwell (Aug. 8), 1905, *Cummins Papers*; Des Moines *Register*, Dec. 8, 9, 17, 1905; A. C. Smith (Dec. 28), and Meservey (Dec. 23), 1905, to JPD; W. S. Kenyon to Meservey, Dec. 19, 1905, *Dolliver Papers*.

[17] Cummins to S. F. Prouty (Nov. 28, 1905), to Wm. E. Hamilton (Nov. 25, 1905), to La Follette (Jan. 20, Mar. 24, 1906), to G. W. Cowden (Apr. 24, 1908), to E. C. Roach (Feb. 5, 1906), *Cummins Papers*. A. C. Smith (Dec. 28, 1905), and Roberts (Mar. 10, 1906), to JPD, *Dolliver Papers*. Des Moines *Register*, Jan. 29, 1906; English-Ross interview, Oct. 25, 26, 1955.

[18] Des Moines *Register*, Jan. 23, 29, Feb. 8, 1906.

[19] Cummins, address at Fort Dodge, in Des Moines *Register*, Feb. 22, 1906; Fort Dodge *Messenger*, Feb. 22, 1906.

[20] Thomas J. Wilcox (Feb. 16), and Thomas D. Healy (Feb. 16), 1906, to Cummins; Cummins to G. M. Curtis, Dec. 24, 1906, *Cummins Papers*. A. C. Smith (Dec. 28, 1905), Meservey (Feb. 20, Mar. 4), A. C. Heath (Feb. 24), Charles I. Reigard (Mar. 27), 1906, to JPD, *Dolliver Papers*.

[21] Cedar Rapids *Republican*, Mar. 7, 1906; Fort Dodge *Messenger*, Mar. 7, 1906. Cf JPD to H. W. Macomber, Mar. 13, 1906, *Dolliver Papers*. Macomber was an attorney and long-time friend, who was for Cummins for Governor and Dolliver for Senator. Dolliver wrote: "I have always felt kindly disposed toward the Governor. . . . I had no idea it was his intention to become a candidate for Governor again, and being led to suppose that he desired the nomination of some one who had taken an active part in the moderate view in respect to the tariff and other matters which you and I have shared in common, it was my opinion, being guided by public expression made by Mr. Funk and . . . [other Cummins leaders] that the nomination of Mr. Perkins would, on the whole, tend to unite the party throughout the State. I was one of those who urged upon him the propriety of becoming a candidate. I did this because he has long cherished that ambition and in my judgment is altogether worthy of the office."

[22] Roberts to JPD, Mar. 10, 1906, *Dolliver Papers*. The pro-Cummins Des Moines *Register*, Mar. 10, 12, 1906, quoted editorials from forty papers commending Dolliver.

The Perkins supporters believed that Dolliver's statement had helped Perkins a great deal. Cf. A. F. Call to Allison, Mar. 9, 1906, *Allison Papers;* Elmer E. Johnston (Mar. 7), and J. B. Hungerford (Mar. 7), 1906, to Perkins, *Perkins Papers.*

[23] Cummins to A. Hillingsworth (Apr. 3), and to G. M. Curtis (Dec. 24), 1906, *Cummins Papers.*

[24] W. S. Kenyon (Mar. 8), and Cyrenus Cole (Mar. 7), 1906, to JPD, *Dolliver Papers.*

[25] Des Moines *Register*, Sept. 12, 1906.

[26] JPD to H. W. Macomber, Mar. 13, 1906, *Dolliver Papers.*

[27] Cummins wrote: "There is no conflict between my candidacy and that of Captain Hull. We have an arrangement by which we are to agree on delegates . . . in Polk County, with the understanding that he is to have the Congressional delegation and I am to have the state delegation." Cummins to Dale Heek, Apr. 19, 1906, *Cummins Papers.* Cf. Harrington, "Political Ideas of . . . Cummins," 349-50.

[28] Cummins to W. H. Torbert, Apr. 19, 1906, *Cummins Papers.*

[29] Haynes, *Third Party Movements,* 462; Cole, *Iowa Through the Years,* 435; Harrington, "Political Ideas of . . . Cummins," 350; Des Moines *Register*, June-July, 1906, *passim,* especially June 28, July 5, 28, 1906; Perkins to Cummins, June 28, 1906; Cummins to Perkins, July 3, 28, 1906, *Cummins Papers.*

[30] Roberts to JPD, July 26, 1906; JPD to Leigh Hunt, July 27, 1906, *Dolliver Papers.*

[31] Des Moines *Register*, July 31, Aug. 1, 2, 1906.

[32] Clarkson (Aug. 7), and A. J. Barkley (Sept. 3), 1906, to JPD, *Dolliver Papers.* Barkley wrote: "I admire the course you took at the convention in the interests of *honesty* and fair play regardless of consequences." Des Moines *Register*, Aug. 3, 5, Sept. 12, 1906.

[33] Des Moines *Register*, Sept.-Oct., 1906, *passim,* especially Oct. 28, 30, 31, Nov. 2; James Wilson to Frank P. Woods, Sept. 14, 1906, in Des Moines *Register*, Sept. 14, 1905. Cf. Dolliver's speech at Hart's Grove, *ibid.,* and JPD to Ben Parks, Oct. 24, 1906, *Dolliver Papers.*

[34] Harrington, "Political Ideas of . . . Cummins," 351, 351n.; Des Moines *Register*, Feb. 3, 1907.

[35] Leigh Hunt to Clarkson, Apr. 15, 1906, *Clarkson Papers* (Des Moines). Dolliver had earlier written Hunt of the situation in Iowa and had told him: "I can not with proper self respect become Cummins' man or Blythe's man. I must be my own man — or retire. For this privilege I must fight and I have already begun to cover the field with plans for the contest next year." He agreed to accept Hunt's offer of financial aid, if needed, because "I believe you are the only man of all my acquaintance, who being in a position to help me financially, would be willing to do it without sending me along an endless road of suspicious and questionable obligations. . . . The fact that you believe in me and stand ready to back me against all comers, is in itself an inspiration and a promise. I may never get even with you — I know I never can — but the thing about your offer of help that touches me most deeply, is that you have never even thought of that aspect of the case. . . . I have no machine, but I have the advantage of having the public with me, and I must not lose simply from the want of organization and energy." JPD to Hunt, June 2, 1905, *Dolliver Papers.*

[36] Des Moines *Register*, Nov. 28, Dec. 29, 1906; Nevada *Representative*, Dec. 3, 1906; Judge S. F. Prouty, speech in Des Moines, Des Moines *Register*, Jan. 24, 1908; Cummins

to G. W. Cowden, Apr. 24, 1908, *Cummins Papers*: "I had an opportunity, as everybody acquainted with the situation here knows, to be elected Senator a year ago last winter."

[37] Clarkson to JPD, Dec. 6, 1906, *Dolliver Papers*. Clarkson also said he had heard of an effort to combine the Standpat and Democratic votes in the General Assembly to elect Shaw Senator in return for the election of a Democratic Speaker of the Iowa House, but thought this unlikely. Cf. *Des Moines Register*, Dec. 4, 1906; Jan. 20, 1907.

[38] Shaw to JPD, Jan. 3, 1906, *Dolliver Papers*.

[39] *Des Moines Register*, Dec. 20, 1906; Jan. 4, 1907.

[40] Cummins to G. M. Curtis, Dec. 24, 1906, *Cummins Papers*.

[41] *Des Moines Register*, Jan. 13, 1907.

[42] John F. Lacey to JPD, Dec. 18, 1907, *Dolliver Papers*.

[43] *Des Moines Register*, Jan. 23, 1907; Clark, *Senatorial Elections*, 248.

[44] Mrs. JPD to JPD, Jan. 27, 1907, *Dolliver Papers*.

[45] Cummins to E. E. Lewis (May 2), and to James A. Smith (May 28), 1907, *Cummins Papers*; English, "Evolution of Iowa Voting Practices," 249-89; Frank E. Horack, *Primary Elections in Iowa* (Iowa City, 1912), 23.

[46] Cummins, campaign speech at Churdan, Sept. 5, 1906, in *Des Moines Register*, Sept. 6, 1906.

[47] Cummins to JPD, Sept. 12, 1907; JPD to Cummins, Sept. 19, 1907, *Dolliver Papers*; JPD to Allison, June 19, 1907, *Allison Papers*; Cummins to Cyrenus Cole, Nov. 23, 1920, *Cole Papers*.

[48] Cummins admitted to Dolliver in 1907 that he had repeatedly assured Dolliver that "I would not be a candidate" against Allison. Cummins to JPD, Sept. 12, 1907, *Dolliver Papers*. In 1920 Cummins wrote Cole: "I stated to Senator Dolliver that if Senator Allison intended to be a candidate for renomination as Senator I would not be a candidate, and somewhere along about that time I wrote Torbert to substantially the same effect." Cummins to Cole, Nov. 23, 1920, *Cole Papers*.

[49] JPD to Kenyon, Dec. 20, 1907, *Dolliver Papers*; JPD to Allison, June 19, 1907, *Allison Papers*.

[50] *Des Moines Register*, Aug. 27, 1907.

[51] Clarkson to Allison, Aug. 31, 1907, *Allison Papers*; W. H. Taft to Perkins, July 31, 1907, *Perkins Papers*; Clarkson to Theodore Roosevelt, Sept. 27, 1907, *Clarkson Papers* (Des Moines).

[52] Cummins to JPD, Sept. 12, 1907; JPD to Cummins, Sept. 19, 1907, *Cummins Papers*.

[53] JPD, "Senator William B. Allison: His Life and Public Services," address at Council Bluffs, Nov. 25, 1907. Printed copy in *Dolliver Papers*. Allison arranged for Dolliver to be invited to make this address. Cf. Allison to JPD, Oct. 8, 1907, *Dolliver Papers*; JPD to Allison, Oct. 10, 1907, *Allison Papers*; Sage, *Allison*, 315, 318-21.

[54] Charles M. Harl to Allison, Nov. 26, 1907, *Allison Papers*.

[55] JPD to Lacey, Dec. 10, 1907, *Lacey Papers*; JPD to Perkins, Dec. 17, 1907, *Perkins Papers*. Dolliver, at first, had thought of quoting the Torbert letter in the Council Bluffs speech, but Allison advised him not to, as Torbert himself wanted to make it public at the proper time. Allison to JPD, Nov. 8, 1907, *Dolliver Papers*.

[56] Des Moines *Register*, Dec. 14, 1907. Torbert wrote Dolliver on December 11, 1907: "For many years I have been an admirer and warm supporter of Governor Cummins in all his campaigns. On October 11, 1905, he was in Dubuque, and his candidacy for re-nomination and re-election as governor became the subject of conversation between us. Suggestions had been frequent that he was an aspirant for Senator Allison's place in the Senate and that his renomination and re-election as governor would only strengthen him for the contest with Senator Allison. These intimations were not only a hindrance in my work for the Governor, but I felt I could not properly do anything injurious to Senator Allison and so on that occasion I mentioned to him that these suggestions were being made and he told me positively that so long as Senator Allison desired to be Senator from Iowa, he, Cummins, would be his (Allison's) friend and supporter." Cf. Torbert's campaign speech for Allison, Feb. 21, 1908, Des Moines *Register*, Feb. 22, 1908; and JPD to Kenyon, Dec. 20, 1907, *Dolliver Papers*.

[57] Cummins to G. I. Miller, Jan. 11, 1908, and numerous others, *Cummins Papers*; Des Moines *Register*, Dec. 15, 1907-June 1, 1908, *passim*, especially Dec. 15, 1907, Feb. 22, 1908; Clark, *Senatorial Elections*, 250ff.

[58] Kenyon to JPD, Jan. 6, 1908, *Dolliver Papers*. Cf. E. F. Cook (Jan. 7), and John T. Adams (Apr. 4, 22), 1908, to JPD, *ibid*. Hepburn to Allison, Oct. 26, 1907, *Allison Papers*; J. W. Blythe to Lacey, Oct. 19, Nov. 7, 17, 1907, *Lacey Papers*; John T. Adams' correspondence in the *Dolliver* and *Allison Papers*, Jan.-June, 1908. Cf. Briggs, *Hepburn*, 296-9.

[59] John T. Adams to JPD, Apr. 4, 1908, *Dolliver Papers*.

[60] Des Moines *Capital*, Apr. 28, 1908.

[61] Des Moines *Register*, Apr. 29, 1908.

[62] *Ibid.*, June 3, 4, 1908; Clark, *Senatorial Elections*, 250ff. The total vote cast was below normal. One authority explains the light vote as being due to the fact that many people resented having to make public announcement and record of their party affiliation. Cf. Horack, *Primary Elections*, 26. It seems more likely that many Iowa farmers did not wish to leave their fields to vote and that many Republicans were thoroughly disgusted with both Cummins and Allison. In the northwest, where Cummins was usually strong, his vote was less than expected. In that section, of course, Dolliver's strength was greatest, and it is probable that many pro-Cummins men preferred not to vote at all rather than vote against Dolliver's old friend. Cummins' failure to carry his strongholds by the usual majorities probably cost him the election. Numerous letters in the *Dolliver Papers* indicate that before the election many former Cummins men were "ready to abandon him now as they have lost confidence in his word." On the other hand, as another wrote, the younger voters did not know Allison and "have never had anything from Allison first hand" and many thought that the old Senator "can not get 1/4 of the votes . . . & that he doesn't deserve that many," despite the fact that they are not for Cummins. Cf. especially E. F. Cook (Jan. 31), and S. J. Robertson (Feb. 5), 1908, to JPD, *Dolliver Papers*.

[63] Clarkson to JPD, June 8, 1908, *Dolliver Papers*.

[64] Des Moines *Register*, 1906-1908, *passim*; Fort Dodge *Messenger*, 1906-1908, *passim*; numerous clippings and letters in the *Dolliver Papers*. On Dec. 11, 1907, Kenyon, then general attorney for the Illinois Central Railroad in Chicago, wrote Dolliver: "I have been meditating a good deal lately and also have talked with Still [Meservey] about my old boom for you for President. No one in the field seems to be entirely satisfactory and there is no enthusiasm for anybody. . . . Now, you know who the new man ought to be, but modesty would forbid you stating his name. There is going to be a casting around in the convention for somebody to beat Bryan . . . and you are the man to do it." Kenyon proposed that he, Roberts, and Meservey get Iowa organized behind Dolliver

as a favorite son. Dolliver replied: "Our state . . . is in a bad condition politically. We have had two brethren out there, each of whom imagined he was the whole push, and our politics have been largely discolored by the hatred of one governor for another [Shaw and Cummins]. I have done the best I could to keep clear of their quarrels, but I . . . do not feel that I ought seriously to encourage a movement which promises little results looking toward getting the support of the state in the national convention. Under these circumstances . . . the suggestion of my name for the Presidency would only weaken me in the fight I have undertaken in behalf of Senator Allison and the good name of Iowa." JPD to Kenyon, Dec. 20, 1907, *Dolliver Papers.*

65 Des Moines *Register,* May 8, 1908; Washington *Post,* May 9, 1908.

66 James Wilson to JPD, June 4, 1908, *Dolliver Papers.*

67 Washington *Post,* June 4, 1908. On June 5, the Kansas City *Star* began a vigorous editorial campaign booming Dolliver: "With Jonathan Prentiss Dolliver as Vice President there would be no more 'Aldrich tricks' accomplished in the Senate for at least four years."

68 New York *Times,* June 2, 9, 1908; Walter Wellman, "Taft and Dolliver Slated as Ticket," Chicago *Record-Herald,* June 14, 1908; Kansas City *Star,* June 3, 1908; Henry F. Pringle, *The Life and Times of William Howard Taft* (2 vols., New York, 1939), 1:354.

69 Des Moines *Register,* June 10, 11, 1908; New York *Times,* June 9, 1908.

70 New York *Times,* June 5, 1908.

71 Grenville M. Dodge to Perkins, June 6, 1908, *Perkins Papers;* Des Moines *Register,* June 5-16, 1908; Washington *Star,* June 11, 1908; Chicago *Record-Herald,* June 11, 1908. George Perkins' Sioux City *Journal* observed that "if the conservative element is to be represented Senator Dolliver is not the logical candidate." Cf. Des Moines *Register,* June 12, 13, 1908.

72 Allison (June 8), Roberts (June 12), and O'Connell (June 12), 1908, to JPD, *Dolliver Papers.*

73 Clarkson to JPD, June 8, 1908, *ibid.*

74 Des Moines *Register,* June 12, 13, 14, 1908.

75 JPD to Perkins, June 11, 1908; E. E. Hart to Perkins, note written during the convention, Chicago, n. d., 1908, *Perkins Papers;* JPD to Lafayette Young, June 11, 1908, published in Chicago *Tribune,* June 14, 1908.

76 W. H. Taft to JPD, May 28, 1908, *Dolliver Papers;* Des Moines *Register,* June 16-20, 1908; New York *Times,* June 15, 16, 17, 1908; Pringle, *Taft,* 1:354; Bowers, *Beveridge,* 288; A. B. Cummins to B. F. Cummins, June 23, 1908, *Cummins Papers.*

77 JPD, campaign speech, 1908, *Dolliver Papers.*

78 McDowell (comp.), *Platforms,* 143; Pringle, *Taft,* 1:421-4.

79 Clark, *Senatorial Elections,* 256ff.; Des Moines *Register,* Aug. 5, 10-31, Sept., Oct., Nov., 1908; Jan., 1909, *passim.* Stephenson's statement, *Aldrich,* 343, that Dolliver "instantaneously stretched forth his hand to Cummins" and "assisted in Cummins' election as senator" is without foundation in fact. Dolliver specifically refused to help either Cummins or Lacey, but Dolliver was so thoroughly disgusted with Cummins that Roberts

and Hunt feared he might help Lacey and used all their influence to bring about a reconciliation between Dolliver and Cummins. Cf. Roberts to JPD, Aug. 21, 1908; Leigh Hunt to Roberts, Aug. 18, 1908; W. S. Lewis to JPD, Aug. 10, 1908, *Dolliver Papers;* JPD to Lacey, n. d., *Lacey Papers;* Cummins to Leigh Hunt, Aug. 28, 1908, *Cummins Papers.*

CHAPTER XVIII — THE LEADER OF INSURGENCY

[1] Sullivan, *Our Times,* 4:357.

[2] H. W. Macomber in Carroll *Herald,* July 13, 1910; J. B. Weaver, Fort Dodge *Messenger and Chronicle,* June 29, 1925.

[3] Medical Examiner's Report, Royal Union Mutual Life Insurance Co., Nov. 28, 1892, *Dolliver Papers.* J. W. McCulloch, president of the Green River Distillery Co., Owensboro, Ky., frequently sent Dolliver "a case of the smoothest Old Green River that ever percolated down a human throat." See McCulloch to JPD, Aug. 2, 1904, Nov. 12, Dec. 22, 1904, Dec. 20, 1905, etc.; JPD to McCulloch, Dec. 28, 1904, *ibid.* Emory English, in interview, Oct. 25, 1955, stated that Dolliver used liquor but never intemperately.

[4] JPD to wife, Nov. 19, 1909, *Dolliver Papers.*

[5] Senator William Alden Smith, interview in Grand Rapids (Mich.) *Herald,* Oct. 21, 1910.

[6] JPD to Kenyon, Dec. 20, 1907, *Dolliver Papers.* It is interesting to note that in this letter Dolliver urged Kenyon to return to Iowa to practice law and engage in politics. Kenyon took Dolliver's advice, and in less than four years he was elected to the Senate to complete Dolliver's term.

[7] Sullivan, *Our Times,* 4:353n. Cf. JPD to R. H. Dolliver, Feb. 24, 1907, *Dolliver Papers.*

[8] Pringle, *Taft,* 1:395, 433.

[9] *Cong. Record,* 61 Cong., 2 sess. (June 13, 1910), 7909; Bowers, *Beveridge,* 337.

[10] Archie Butt, *Taft and Roosevelt: The Intimate Letters of Archie Butt . . .* (2 vols., Garden City, 1930), 1:27; Pringle, *Roosevelt,* 497-503; Bowers, *Beveridge,* 301.

[11] Hechler, *Insurgency,* 13.

[12] Bowers, *Beveridge,* 334; Pringle, *Taft,* 1:421, 422, 426.

[13] Taussig, *Tariff Hist. of U. S.,* 372; for details of the preparation of the Payne bill, see Tarbell, *Tariff in Our Times,* 297-307; Hechler, *Insurgency,* 94-6.

[14] Pringle, *Taft,* 1:428, 429; Hechler, *Insurgency,* 96-9; La Follette, *Autobiography,* 440; Butt, *Letters,* 1:40.

[15] Bowers, *Beveridge,* 335-6; Hechler, *Insurgency,* 99-103; Taussig, *Tariff Hist. of U. S.,* 375-6.

[16] Judson C. Welliver, "Dolliver, The Leader of Insurgency," *Munsey's Magazine* (Sept., 1912), 875.

[17] Sullivan, *Our Times,* 4:358-61.

[18] *Idem;* Welliver, "Dolliver, The Leader of Insurgency," 875; New York *Times,* May, 1909-Oct., 1910, *passim;* Des Moines *Register,* May, 1909-Oct., 1910, *passim;* Stephenson, *Aldrich,* 344; Bowers, *Beveridge,* 328.

19 Mowry, *Roosevelt*, 50; Arthur W. Dunn, *From Harrison to Harding* (2 vols., New York, 1922), 2:106-107; Matthew Josephson, *The President Makers* (New York, 1940), 294-5; Hechler, *Insurgency*, 89-90; Nye, *Midwestern Progressive Politics*, 226-73; Stephenson, *Aldrich*, 344-6; Sullivan, *Our Times*, 4:359-60, 364; and Cyrenus Cole, in *Iowa Through the Years, Hist. of the People of Iowa*, and *I Remember*, are among those who have popularized this view. Cf. Champ Clark, *My Quarter Century of American Politics* (2 vols., New York, 1920), 2:314; Bowers, *Beveridge*, 329, 338; Pringle, *Taft*, 1:414; and La Follette, *Autobiography*, 431-5, for modifications of it which still overemphasize the committee assignment factor.

20 JPD to Aldrich, undated, *Dolliver Papers*. Cf. La Follette, *Autobiography*, 432.

21 JPD to Aldrich, Mar. 16, 1909, *Dolliver Papers*; Stephenson, *Aldrich*, 479n.; cf. La Follette, *Autobiography*, 431-2; Sullivan, *Our Times*, 4:358-60; James E. Watson, *As I Knew Them* (Indianapolis, 1936), 139-40.

22 Stephenson, *Aldrich*, 345, 479n.; La Follette, *Autobiography*, 432; Meservey to JPD, Mar. 24, 1909, *Dolliver Papers*.

23 La Follette, *Autobiography*, 431-4.

24 Bowers, *Beveridge*, 329. Similar statements abound in letters, articles, obituary notices, and memorial addresses.

25 George Roberts to Frances P. Dolliver, Aug. 5, 1946, wrote that Dolliver did not change his "political opinions because he failed to be named as the successor to Senator Allison upon the Finance Committee. . . . The views he expressed in the debate, he had held for a number of years, and he had used his influence so far as seemed practicable for tariff modification."

26 Hechler, *Insurgency*, 12. W. R. Boyd, "Senator Dolliver, Orator, Statesman, Loyal Friend," *Sioux City Journal*, Mar. 27, 1942, and Harvey Ingham, *Des Moines Register*, Mar. 26, 1936, both held that Dolliver did not fight Aldrich because of anger but because he honestly wanted tariff reform.

27 Welliver, "Dolliver, The Leader of Insurgency," 874-7; Hechler, *Insurgency*, 13.

28 Samuel L. Clemens [Mark Twain, pseud.], *A Connecticut Yankee in King Arthur's Court* (New York, 1889), 107.

29 *Washington Times*, Apr. 4, 1909; Hechler, *Insurgency*, 101.

30 Oscar King Davis, *Released for Publication* (Boston, 1923), 168.

31 La Follette, *Autobiography*, 440.

32 Bowers, *Beveridge*, 337; Hechler, *Insurgency*, 102; Roberts to JPD, July 19, 1909, *Dolliver Papers*.

33 Butt, *Letters*, 1:40, 41.

34 Roberts to Frances P. Dolliver, Aug. 5, 1946; La Follette, *Autobiography*, 434. Cf. Hechler, *Insurgency*, 100-101, 128; Tarbell, *Tariff in Our Times*, 308-309.

35 *Cong. Record*, 61 Cong., 1 sess., 1431ff.; La Follette, *Autobiography*, 441-2; Bowers, *Beveridge*, 336.

36 Hechler, *Insurgency*, 105.

37 *Ibid.*, 105, 106; Stephenson, *Aldrich*, 347-8; *Cong. Record*, 61 Cong., 1 sess., 1846.

[38] Tarbell, *Tariff in Our Times*, 309; Hechler, *Insurgency*, 110-112, 117; Josephson, *President Makers*, 300; La Follette, *Autobiography*, 442-4.

[39] *Cong. Record*, 61 Cong., 1 sess. (Apr. 22, 1909), 1450ff.; 1460-64 (Dolliver's speech), 1499.

[40] Correspondence file, Apr. 23-30, 1909, *Dolliver Papers*; Washington *Times*, Apr. 23, 1909; New York *Times*, Apr. 23, 1909; Hechler, *Insurgency*, 104; Mowry, *Roosevelt*, 52; Sullivan, *Our Times*, 4:365.

[41] Frank B. Kellogg to JPD, May 5, 1909, *Dolliver Papers*.

[42] *Cong. Record*, 61 Cong., 1 sess. (Apr. 22, 1909), 1461; (Apr. 22, May 8, 9), 1499, 1911, 2275; (June 8, 1909), 2950 for remarks by the Senators mentioned. It is difficult to agree with Garraty, *Lodge*, 268, in his kindly view of Lodge's position in this tariff fight. It is not "the context of Lodge's protectionist philosophy" that matters, but that he allowed the people to believe until the election was over that revision meant downward revision, and then told New Englanders that the cotton rates *were* increased in the new bill while supporting Aldrich's demonstrable falsehood in Washington that they *were not* increased. Cf. *Cong. Record*, 61 Cong., 1 sess. (May 5, 1909), 1735-7.

[43] Sullivan, *Our Times*, 4:365; Davis, *Released for Publication*, 170-71; Sam H. Acheson, *Joe Bailey, The Last Democrat* (New York, 1932), 256-75.

[44] Albert J. Beveridge, in "Dolliver — A Tribune of the People," *Review of Reviews*, 42:682 (December, 1910).

[45] Tarbell, *Tariff in Our Times*, 310-14; Hechler, *Insurgency*, 107, quoting New York *World*, Apr. 29, May 2, 1909. There are several letters to and from Tichenor and many pages of his statistics and explanations in the period April, 1909-July, 1910, in the *Dolliver Papers*. Cf. *Cong. Record*, 61 Cong., 1 sess. (May 4, 1909), 713.

[46] Hechler, *Insurgency*, 107; *Cong. Record*, 61 Cong., 1 sess. (May 4, 5, 1909), 1706-1723, 1734-42.

[47] *Cong. Record*, 61 Cong., 1 sess. (May 4, 1909), 1706. Subsequent quotations from this speech of May 4-5, are from *ibid.*, 1707-1723, 1734-42.

[48] Chicago *Tribune*, May 6, 1909.

[49] Cedar Rapids *Republican*, May 5, 1909.

[50] Cincinnati *Times-Star*, May 8, 1909.

[51] *Ibid.*, May 10, 1909.

[52] *Cong. Record*, 61 Cong., 1 sess., 1907-1908.

[53] Hechler, *Insurgency*, 113, 114-15; Stephenson, *Aldrich*, 343; *Cong. Record*, 61 Cong., 1 sess., 2328-9. Dolliver voted against putting lumber on the free list.

[54] Bowers, *Beveridge*, 343; Hechler, *Insurgency*, 115, 117, quoting a letter from Joseph L. Bristow to Harold Chase, May 27, 1909.

[55] Bowers, *Beveridge*, 344, 345.

[56] *Cong. Record*, 61 Cong., 1 sess. (June 5, 1909), 2844-59.

[57] Tarbell, *Tariff in Our Times*, 320; Bowers, *Beveridge*, 344.

[58] *Cong. Record*, 61 Cong., 1 sess. (June 7, 1909), 2887, 2897.

[59] *Ibid.*, 2901.

⁶⁰ Hechler, *Insurgency*, 124.

⁶¹ Tarbell, *Tariff in Our Times*, 311.

⁶² Sullivan, *Our Times*, 4:366; Des Moines *Register*, June 9, 1909.

⁶³ *Cong. Record*, 61 Cong., 1 sess. (June 24, 1909), 3728-43.

⁶⁴ Mowry, *Roosevelt*, 58-60; Hechler, *Insurgency*, 146-53, 208-210; Stephenson, *Aldrich*, 354-6, 480n.; Acheson, *Bailey*, 264-73; Butt, *Letters*, 1:62, 124-5, 131; Pringle, *Taft*, 1: 433-6. E. R. A. Seligman, *The Income Tax* (New York, 1911), 592ff.; H. D. Tichenor to JPD, July 8, 1909, *Dolliver Papers*. Tichenor wrote that Marion DeVries, a Democrat and member of the Board of Appraisers, who aided Aldrich as a tariff expert, had been a "close friend of Bailey for some years." Tichenor added that the Democrats were aiding Aldrich on many amendment votes, and that DeVries was putting jokers in the bill increasing the tariff in order that later the Democrats could attack the bill as a violation of campaign promises and win the 1910 election with the tariff issue. Cf. Davis, *Released for Publication*, 170-72: "I am satisfied but that for some very effective Democratic assistance rendered the Old Guard, the Insurgent fight would have been successful."

⁶⁵ Hechler, *Insurgency*, 152; *Cong. Record*, 61 Cong., 1 sess. (July 2, 1909), 4066; Roberts (June 27), and Alson Secor (June 28, 1909), to JPD, *Dolliver Papers*. Secor, associate editor of *Successful Farming*, wrote: "We look to such men as you to do all you can to revise the tariff downward and to secure an income tax instead of a corporation tax."

⁶⁶ Tichenor to JPD, July 8, 1909, *Dolliver Papers*. Cf. Hechler, *Insurgency*, 135; Bowers, *Beveridge*, 362-3.

⁶⁷ *Cong. Record*, 61 Cong., 1 sess. (July 8, 1909), 4314, 4316.

⁶⁸ Hechler, *Insurgency*, 136, 141; Bowers, *Beveridge*, 363; *Cong. Record*, 61 Cong., 1 sess., 4755.

⁶⁹ Pringle, *Taft*, 1:425-41, 448; Butt, *Letters*, 1:40-51, 56, 58, 60, 127, 131, 141-4, 149; Bowers, *Beveridge*, 337-44, 349-51, 363; Hechler, *Insurgency*, 138-40; Sullivan, *Our Times*, 4:367.

⁷⁰ La Follette, *Autobiography*, 451.

⁷¹ William H. Taft to Charles P. Taft, Aug. 1, 1909, quoted in Hechler, *Insurgency*, 141.

⁷² Butt, *Letters*, 1:167.

⁷³ Hechler, *Insurgency*, 143.

⁷⁴ JPD to wife, Aug. 2, 1909; Mrs. JPD to JPD, Aug. 5, 1909, *Dolliver Papers*.

⁷⁵ Tichenor (Aug. 1), Roberts (July 19), Meservey (July 24, Aug. 3), 1909, to JPD, *ibid*. Meservey quoted Kenyon and Roberts.

⁷⁶ *Cong. Record*, 61 Cong., 1 sess. (Aug. 5, 1909), 4925, 4929-32.

⁷⁷ Hechler, *Insurgency*, 144.

⁷⁸ Sullivan, *Our Times*, 4:371.

⁷⁹ Roberts to JPD, July 19, 1909, *Dolliver Papers*.

CHAPTER XIX — BROKEN PARTY, BROKEN HEART

[1] Des Moines *Register*, Aug. 11, 1909.

[2] Hechler, *Insurgency*, 122; Fort Dodge *Messenger*, Oct. 17, 1910.

[3] JPD to Beveridge, Sept. 14, 1909, *Dolliver Papers.*

[4] Taussig, *Tariff Hist. of U. S.*, 378-80, 407; Meservey to JPD, Aug. 3, 1909, *Dolliver Papers.*

[5] Tichenor to JPD, Sept. 24, 1909, *Dolliver Papers.*

[6] Bowers, *Beveridge*, 367, 368-73; Des Moines *Register*, Aug.-Oct., 1909, *passim*, expressed not only Iowa's view but reprinted editorials from numerous newspapers. Cf. Wilfred E. Binkley, *American Political Parties* (New York, 1951), 340-41; Sullivan, *Our Times*, 4:371-2; Mowry, *Roosevelt*, 61, 65, 66.

[7] Clarkson to Grenville M. Dodge, Sept. 17, 1909, *Grenville M. Dodge Collection* (Iowa State Dept. of Hist. and Archives, Des Moines). Hereafter cited as *Dodge Papers.*

[8] Pringle, *Taft*, 1:452-5, 457; Butt, *Letters*, 1:199-201; Bowers, *Beveridge*, 368.

[9] Tichenor to JPD, Sept. 24, 1909, *Dolliver Papers.*

[10] Chicago *Tribune*, Sept. 20, 1909.

[11] Beveridge to JPD, Sept. 25, 1909, *Dolliver Papers*; Des Moines *Register*, Sept. 23, 24, 1909.

[12] Des Moines *Register*, Sept. 21, 1909; Kansas City *Star*, Sept. 21, 22, 1909.

[13] Butt, *Letters*, 1:204; Mowry, *Roosevelt*, 67-8, 71; Des Moines *Register*, Aug. 6, Oct. 22, Nov. 26, Dec. 1, 1909.

[14] Des Moines *Register*, Dec. 7, 8, 1909; Bowers, *Beveridge*, 373-4.

[15] New York *Press*, Nov. 24, Dec. 5, 1909; New York *Times*, Nov. 25, 1909; J. S. Clarkson (Dec. 5), and Grosvenor Clarkson (Dec. 5), 1909, to JPD, *Dolliver Papers.*

[16] Des Moines *Register*, Dec. 9, 11, 15, 17, 1909; Jan. 5, 10, 1910; Pringle, *Taft*, 1:531; Butt, *Letters*, 1:230.

[17] Butt, *Letters*, 1:246. Cf. Mowry, *Roosevelt*, 89-90.

[18] Cf. Rose M. Stahl, *The Ballinger-Pinchot Controversy* (Northampton, Mass., 1926), *passim*; Pringle, *Taft*, 1:470-515; Sullivan, *Our Times*, 4:383-96; Mowry, *Roosevelt*, 66-87.

[19] Des Moines *Register*, Aug.-Dec., 1909, *passim*; Louis R. Glavis, "Whitewashing of Ballinger," *Collier's Weekly*, 14:13ff. (Nov. 13, 1909); Hechler, *Insurgency*, 156; Mowry, *Roosevelt*, 77-9; Pringle, *Taft*, 1:481-506.

[20] Des Moines *Register*, Dec. 22, 23, 1909.

[21] *Ibid.*, Jan. 8, 9, Mar. 2, 1910; Mowry, *Roosevelt*, 79-80. Dolliver said he requested Pinchot to write the letter.

[22] Gifford Pinchot to JPD, Jan. 5, 1910, *Dolliver Papers*; *Cong. Record*, 61 Cong., 2 sess., 368; Des Moines *Register*, Jan. 7, 8, 9, 1910.

[23] Taft to Pinchot, Jan. 7, 1910, in Des Moines *Register*, Jan. 8, 1910.

[24] Des Moines *Register*, Jan. 7, 8, 9, 10, 15, Mar. 2, 3, 5, 1910; Butt, *Letters*, 1:235-6; Mowry, *Roosevelt*, 80; Bowers, *Beveridge*, 374-5; Pringle, *Taft*, 1:508-509.

25 Butt, *Letters,* 1:254, 260-61.

26 Henry Wallace to JPD, Jan. 10, 1910, *Dolliver Papers;* Mowry, *Roosevelt,* 80. Des Moines *Register,* Kansas City *Star, Outlook,* and *Collier's Weekly* were among numerous powerful organs which backed Pinchot.

27 Des Moines *Register,* Jan. 14, 1910.

28 Mowry, *Roosevelt,* 80, 81-7; Butt, *Letters,* 1:245, 251, 261; Lodge (ed.), *Correspondence of Theodore Roosevelt and Henry Cabot Lodge,* 2:356; Alpheus T. Mason, *Bureaucracy Convicts Itself* (Princeton, 1941), 157-77.

29 JPD to Pinchot, Mar. 25, 1910, *Dolliver Papers.*

30 Bowers, *Beveridge,* 375-6; Mowry, *Roosevelt,* 125-6; Pringle, *Roosevelt,* 525-7.

31 Busbey, *Uncle Joe Cannon,* 243-69; Hechler, *Insurgency,* 27-82; Mowry, *Roosevelt,* 88-93.

32 Des Moines *Register,* Sept. 21, 1909.

33 Mowry, *Roosevelt,* 94-6; Bowers, *Beveridge,* 381; Hechler, *Insurgency,* 163-5; JPD to Pinchot, Mar. 25, 1910, *Dolliver Papers;* JPD and Cummins to the Republican voters of Iowa, Apr. 7, 1910, *Cummins Scrapbook* (State Hist. Society of Iowa, Iowa City).

34 Bowers, *Beveridge,* 381; Lambert, *Elkins,* 314-21.

35 Mowry, *Roosevelt,* 97; Des Moines *Register,* Mar. 4, 5, 1910; *Cong. Record,* 61 Cong., 2 sess. (Apr. 25, 1910), 5322-33.

36 Bowers, *Beveridge,* 381-3; Hechler, *Insurgency,* 165-71; *Cong. Record,* 61 Cong., 2 sess. (Mar. to June, 1910), *passim.*

37 Mowry, *Roosevelt,* 100, quoting Wickersham.

38 Bowers, *Beveridge,* 376-7, quoting Beveridge, Apr. 11, 1910.

39 *Cong. Record,* 61 Cong., 2 sess. (Apr. 12, 1910), 4549-64; Hechler, *Insurgency,* 168.

40 *Cong. Record,* 61 Cong., 2 sess. (Apr. 25, 1910), 5322, 5325, 5328.

41 Hechler, *Insurgency,* 171-2; Des Moines *Register,* May 3, 1910.

42 *Cong. Record,* 61 Cong., 2 sess. ((May 13, 1910), 6205-6207, 6213; Des Moines *Register,* May 14, 1910; Stephenson, *Aldrich,* 371-2.

43 Hechler, *Insurgency,* 176-7; Mowry, *Roosevelt,* 102; Lambert, *Elkins,* 320-21; *Cong. Record,* 61 Cong., 2 sess. (May 18, 1910), 6444.

44 JPD and Cummins to the Republican voters in Iowa, Apr. 7, 1910, *Cummins Scrapbook;* JPD to Pinchot (Mar. 25), and to L. E. Stevens (Mar. 12), 1910, *Dolliver Papers.*

45 Des Moines *Register,* Jan. 26, 28, Feb. 15, 23, Mar. 4, 1910; Stephenson, *Aldrich,* 369; Philip C. Jessup, *Elihu Root* (2 vols., New York, 1938), 2:233.

46 *Cong. Record,* 61 Cong., 2 sess., 2761, 2780; Des Moines *Register,* Mar. 6, 1910; Hechler, *Insurgency,* 161; Stephenson, *Aldrich,* 369.

47 Des Moines *Register,* June 24, 1910; Hechler, *Insurgency,* 161.

48 *Cong. Record,* 61 Cong., 2 sess. (June 13, 1910), 7908-20. All quotations from this speech are from these pages.

49 Sullivan, *Our Times,* 4:366.

[50] *Cong. Record*, 61 Cong., 2 sess. (June 13, 1910), 7920.

[51] Washington *Herald*, June 14, 1910; Des Moines *Register*, June 14, 1910; Mowry, *Roosevelt*, 106.

[52] Mowry, *Roosevelt*, 106; Des Moines *Register*, June 17, 1910.

[53] Henry Wallace to JPD, June 20, 1910, *Dolliver Papers*.

[54] Butt, *Letters*, 1:414.

[55] Des Moines *Register*, Jan. 5, 1910.

[56] Hepburn (Feb. 9, 16, 21, Mar. 2), and Taft (Feb. 16), 1910, to Perkins, *Perkins Papers*.

[57] Hepburn (Mar. 9), Frank D. Jackson (Mar. 12), 1910, to Perkins, *ibid.*; M. J. Tobin to JPD, Mar. 10, Apr. 2, 1910, *Dolliver Papers*; Butt, *Letters*, 1:300-301; Des Moines *Register*, Mar. 6, 7, 8, 1910.

[58] Clarkson to Dodge, Sept. 17, 1909; Mar. 16, Apr. 11, 1910, *Dodge Papers*; Clarkson to Roberts (July 28, 1909), and to JPD (July 16, 30, 1909; Aug. 21, 1910), *Dolliver Papers*.

[59] Henry Wallace to JPD, Mar. 11, 1910, *Dolliver Papers*. Cf. Des Moines *Register*, Mar. 10, 11, 12, 1910; Mowry, *Roosevelt*, 113.

[60] Cannon to Perkins, Mar. 22, 1910, *Perkins Papers*; Des Moines *Register*, Mar. 13, Apr. 16, 1910.

[61] Bert F. Keltz (Mar. 14), Frank A. Nimmocks (Apr. 11), 1910, to JPD, *Dolliver Papers*; Des Moines *Register*, Apr. 6, 8, 10, 1910.

[62] Des Moines *Register*, May 12, 1910.

[63] J. H. Macomber to JPD, May 16, 1910, *Dolliver Papers*.

[64] Des Moines *Register*, May 12, 1910.

[65] Henry Wallace (June 13), Emory H. English (June 9), Meservey (June 13), 1910, to JPD, *Dolliver Papers*; Des Moines *Register*, June 8, 9, 10, 1910.

[66] Des Moines *Register*, July 15, Aug. 4, 1910; *Iowa Official Register, 1910*, 345-7.

[67] Des Moines *Register*, Aug. 4, 1910.

[68] Joseph T. Bristow to JPD, Aug. 18, 1910, *Dolliver Papers*.

[69] Des Moines *Register*, Aug. 22, Sept. 1, 2, 1910.

[70] Roosevelt to JPD, July 1, 1910, *Dolliver Papers*.

[71] Clarkson to JPD, Aug. 21, 1910, *ibid.* "It might have been" is, perhaps, worth brief notice in a footnote. In the 1912 Republican convention, when the party was split between Taft and Roosevelt, efforts were made to get both to withdraw in favor of some third person. Taft was said to be willing; Roosevelt refused. (Mowry, *Roosevelt*, 240, 250-52.) It was said that had Dolliver been alive he would have been the one man upon whom both could have united — that, in fact, had he been alive, Roosevelt would not have been a candidate at all. Judson Welliver recorded hearing a politician tell Mrs. Dolliver, who attended the convention because she believed her husband would have been nominated had he lived, that had the Senator survived "He would have been nominated today and elected in November without uncertainty. . . . Colonel Roosevelt said almost exactly that to me." Mrs. Dolliver replied: "Everybody has been telling me

that." (Welliver, "Dolliver, The Leader of Insurgency," 874.) William Allen White shared this view. He wrote in 1935 that Dolliver's loss was a great blow. "He left us just when we needed him most. He had . . . what we lacked in 1912 — perspective, the long view." (White to Frances P. Dolliver, May 7, 1935.) Cf. J. B. Bishop, *Theodore Roosevelt and His Time* (2 vols., New York, 1920), 2:307-309, 312-19. Bishop thought Roosevelt did not want to be a candidate had there been any chance of defeating Taft with anyone else whom Roosevelt trusted. Pringle, *Roosevelt*, 548ff., suggested that Roosevelt did not altogether trust La Follette, otherwise he could have helped him win the nomination. Roosevelt, and many others who did not trust La Follette, did trust Dolliver, but whether the Rough Rider really did not want to run is an unresolved question. Pringle, *Roosevelt*, 564, thought the Colonel would have tolerated no nomination but his own. Certainly the premature death of the real leader of the Insurgents had a great bearing on the events leading up to 1912. Since many Rooseveltians did not trust either La Follette or Cummins, and since Beveridge was defeated in 1910, the demand for Roosevelt's personal leadership was irresistible — at least for Roosevelt.

[72] Des Moines *Register*, Sept. 2, 3, 4, 1910.

[73] *Ibid.*, Sept. 6, 14, 16, 18, Oct. 2, 1910; *Outlook*, 96:137-8 (Sept. 24, 1910).

[74] JPD to Beveridge, Oct. 7, 1910, *Dolliver Papers*.

[75] Fort Dodge *Messenger*, Oct. 17, 1910.

[76] *Ibid.*, Oct. 17, 18, 19, 1910.

[77] Des Moines *Register*, Oct. 17, 1910, quoting George H. Woodson. Cf. Theodore Roosevelt, "Senator Dolliver," *Outlook*, 96:483-4 (Oct. 29, 1910). Roosevelt stressed Dolliver's vision, his broad nationalism, his concern for good government and for justice to all persons and classes; "all the people of the United States have lost one of the ablest, most efficient, and most sincerely patriotic public servants that we have seen in recent years in public life."

[78] Fort Dodge *Messenger*, Oct. 17, 1910. La Follette, seriously ill in a Rochester, Minn., hospital, refused to credit news stories of Dolliver's death and telegraphed a personal friend in Fort Dodge: "Heart-breaking rumor here regarding Dolliver unbelievable. Am praying all is well with him. Must know the truth. Wire immediately."

[79] *Idem*; Bowers, *Beveridge*, 399; Beveridge to Mrs. Dolliver, Nov. 16, 1910. Quoted through the courtesy of Miss Frances P. Dolliver.

[80] Fort Dodge *Messenger*, Oct. 21, 1910.

[81] Sullivan, *Our Times*, 4:357.

Index

Index

Adams, Charles Francis, Jr., 54

Adams, Henry, 57-8, 134

Adams, John T., and Allison 1908 campaign, 229

Aldrich, Nelson W., 172, 173, 179, 185, 239, 279, 284; and Mills bill, 75; JPD meets, 82; for repeal of Silver Purchase Act, 106; and Dingley Tariff, 137-8, 182; and sugar trust, 137-8; opposes reciprocity, 181; as one of "Big Four," 183; praises JPD, 188; opposes Hepburn Act, 199-213 passim; fight for Payne-Aldrich Tariff, 240-64 passim; refuses to put JPD on Finance Committee, 242-3; tariff debate with JPD, 247-60 passim; end of leadership, 266; Taft and, 267, 269; supports Mann-Elkins bill, 274, 275; and Postal Savings bill, 278; aids Iowa Standpatters, 282

Alger, Russell A., 77

Algona, 1886 congressional convention at, 69-71

Alliance, Farmers'. See National Farmers' Alliance; Iowa Farmers' Alliance

Allison, William Boyd, 29, 53, 90, 159, 162, 167, 172, 223, 247, 252; supports J. F. Wilson, 46; meets JPD, 50; Carpenter and, 50; and 1883 legislative election of, 52; on JPD's 1886 candidacy, 69; Clarkson and, 75-8, 101, 226; 1888 candidate for presidential nomination, 75-8; and Mills bill, 75; Henderson and, 77, 78; Hepburn nominates, 78; and Harrison's Cabinet, 84; 1890 election of, 91; advises JPD to specialize, 94-5; favors Silver Act repeal, 106, 107, 108; and 1894 senatorial election, 110; 1896 presidential bid, 123-5; 1896

senatorial election, 124; Blythe supports, 124; on silver, 128; and McKinley Cabinet, 138-9; 1900 senatorial contest and, 156, 157; favors JPD for Vice President, 158; refuses McKinley's offer of vice-presidency, 160; and Gear succession, 162-3; JPD to, 165-6; 1902 election to Senate, 170; JPD tribute to, 170; as one of "Big Four," 183; Iowa 1903 platform and, 184, 185, 186; 1904 delegate-at-large, 189; Mrs. Dolliver hostess for, 192; and Hepburn Act, 196, 200, 201, 210, 211, 212, 213; Cummins and, 216-17; "Torbert Letter" and, 221; Cummins 1908 effort to defeat, 224-31; Blythe aids, 229; 1908 primary election of, 231; opposes JPD 1908 vice-presidential boom, 234, 235; death of, 236; and JPD's Insurgency, 243

"Allison Amendment," to Hepburn Act, 212

Antislavery, J. J. Dolliver and, 5

Arthur, Chester A., 42, 53, 59

Bailey, Joseph, 260

Ballinger, Richard A., vs. Pinchot, 270-73

Barkley, A. J., JPD and, 79, 167

Beaver College, 30

Beecher, Henry Ward, 58

Bennett, S. J., 213; advises JPD on silver, 105

Benton, Thomas Hart, 122

Berry, Jennie, 115

Beveridge, Albert J., 18, 235, 267; on JPD's 1884 speech, 56; JPD and, 192; Hepburn Act and, 211; opinion of Taft, 239; and Payne-Aldrich debate, 241-64 passim; describes work on Payne-Aldrich

353

DATE DUE

NOV 15'61			
GAYLORD			PRINTED IN U.S.A.